Law and Empire

Rulers & Elites

Comparative Studies in Governance

VOLUME 3

The titles published in this series are listed at brill.com/rule

Law and Empire

Ideas, Practices, Actors

Edited by

Jeroen Duindam, Jill Harries,
Caroline Humfress, and Nimrod Hurvitz

BRILL

LEIDEN • BOSTON
2013

Cover illustration: F.3r The King Administering Justice, from 'Justiniani in Fortiatum' (vellum), French School, (14th century) / Biblioteca Monasterio del Escorial, Madrid, Spain / The Bridgeman Art Library XIR 159140.

Library of Congress Cataloging-in-Publication Data

Law and empire: ideas, practices, actors / edited by Jeroen Duindam, Jill Harries, Caroline Humfress, and Nimrod Hurvitz.
pages cm. — (Rulers & elites; volume 3)
"This volume brings together a selection of papers presented at a conference held at the History Institute of Utrecht University in November 2008" — Acknowledgements.
Includes bibliographical references and index.
ISBN 978-90-04-24529-7 (hardback : alk. paper) — ISBN 978-90-04-24951-6 (e-book)
1. Law—History—Congresses. 2. Law, Ancient—Congresses. 3. Law, Medieval—Congresses. 4. Imperialism—Congresses. I. Duindam, Jeroen Frans Jozef, 1962– editor of compilation. II. Harries, Jill, editor of compilation. III. Humfress, Caroline, editor of compilation. IV. Hurvitz, Nimrod, 1958– editor of compilation.

K555.L389 2013
349'.112—dc23

2013021985

This publication has been typeset in the multilingual "Brill" typeface. With over 5,100 characters covering Latin, IPA, Greek, and Cyrillic, this typeface is especially suitable for use in the humanities. For more information, please see www.brill.com/brill-typeface.

ISSN 2211-4610
ISBN 978-90-04-24529-7 (hardback)
ISBN 978-90-04-24951-6 (e-book)

CONTENTS

NOTES ON EDITORS AND CONTRIBUTORS

The Editors

JEROEN DUINDAM, professor of early modern European history at the University of Leiden, focuses on the comparative study of courts and dynasties in Europe and Asia. He is the author of *Vienna and Versailles. The Courts of Europe's Dynastic Rivals* (Cambridge, 2003; Italian and Spanish translations) and *Myths of Power. Norbert Elias and the Early Modern European Court* (Amsterdam, 1995) and co-edited a volume on *Royal Courts in Dynastic States and Empires: a Global Perspective* (Leiden, Boston 2011).

JILL HARRIES is Professor of Ancient History at the University of St Andrews, Scotland. She is the author of books on *Law and Empire in Late Antiquity* (Cambridge, 1999), *Cicero and the Jurists* (London, 2006), *Law and Crime in the Roman World* (Cambridge, 2007) and *Imperial Rome AD 284–363. The New Empire* (Edinburgh, 2012), and articles on late antiquity and Roman legal culture.

CAROLINE HUMFRESS is Reader in History in the Department of History, Classics, and Archaeology at Birkbeck College, University of London. She is the author of *Orthodoxy and the Courts in Late Antiquity* (Oxford, 2007), as well as various essays and articles on legal history and religion. She is currently co-editor (with David Ibbetson and Patrick Olivelle) of the *Cambridge Comparative History of Ancient Law* (Cambridge, forthcoming).

NIMROD HURVITZ teaches at Ben Gurion University, Department of Middle East Studies. His main areas of interest are the interaction between law, society and the state. He has published several studies about the social dimension of Islamic schools of law, such as "From Scholarly Circles to Mass Movements: The Formation of Legal Communities in Islamic Societies," *The American Historical Review*, and public law "Competing Texts, The Relationship Between al-Mawardi's and Abu Ya'la's *Al-Ahkam al-Sultaniyya*," Islamic Legal Studies Program, Harvard Law School.

The Contributors

ANTONIS ANASTASOPOULOS is Assistant Professor of Ottoman History at the Department of History and Archaeology of the University of Crete, and a research fellow of the Institute for Mediterranean Studies/FORTH. His research interests include Ottoman institutions, Ottoman provincial society and centre-periphery relations, and Ottoman tombstones. He has edited or co-edited five volumes, among which *Political initiatives 'from the bottom up' in the Ottoman Empire* (Rethymno, 2012).

ENGIN DENIZ AKARLI, Professor of History at Istanbul Şehir University and Joukowsky Family Professor Emeritus of History at Brown University, received his PhD (1976) from Princeton University. He taught at Princeton, Boğaziçi and Yarmouk (Jordan) Universities and Washington University in St. Louis. He received fellowships from *Wissenschaftskolleg* zu Berlin, Institute for Advanced Study, Islamic Legal Studies Program at Harvard, and Fulbright. His publications include *The Long Peace: Ottoman Lebanon, 1861–1920* (London, 1993); *Political Participation in Turkey* (Istanbul, 1974), and articles on nineteenth-century Ottoman history and Ottoman legal history. He serves on the Board of Advisors of *Islamic Law and Society* and *Journal of Turkish Legal History*.

R. KENT GUY is Professor of History and East Asian Studies at the University of Washington, where he has served as chair of the Chinese Studies Program, and Chair of the History Department. He holds a BA degree in History from Yale, and an MA in Regional Studies-East Asia, with a PhD in History and East Asian Languages from Harvard. He is the author of two books on the history of the Qing Dynasty (1644–1911), *The Emperor's Four Treasuries: Scholars and the State in Late Imperial China* (Cambridge, 1987), and *Qing Governors and their Provinces* (Seattle, 2010), and is editor of a volume of essays entitled *Limits of the Rule of Law in China* (Seattle, 2000). He has taught at the Chinese University of Hong Kong, held research fellowships in Kyoto, Beijing and Taipei, and lectured at Renmin (Peoples') University in China, Academica Sinica in Taipei and the National University of Singapore, among other places. He has also organized and led many groups, including undergraduate groups, in tours of China, and has won several awards at the University of Washington for undergraduate teaching.

BAREND J. TER HAAR is the Run Run Shaw Professor of Chinese at Oxford University. He studied in Leiden, Shenyang (China) and Fukuoka (Japan) and worked at the Universities of Leiden and Heidelberg. He has published widely on the labelling and persecution of new religions in China, the ritual and mythology of Triads, oral traditions, minorities, violence and other topics. In 2009 he completed a survey history of China in Dutch. He recently completed a book entitled *The History of a Reading Experience: a lay-Buddhist Chan-movement in late imperial China* and is presently completing a book-length study of the cult for the Chinese deity Guan Yu.

Karl Härter is research group leader at the Max-Planck-Institute for European Legal History, Frankfurt/M. He also teaches Early Modern and Modern History at the University of Darmstadt and is also a member of the teaching faculty of the International Max Planck Research School on Retaliation, Mediation and Punishment. His major research interests concern the constitutional and legal history of the Holy Roman Empire of the German Nation and the history of police, criminal justice, penal law and crime, notably the history of political crime and the formation of transnational criminal law regimes. He has published monographs on the Imperial Diet in the age of the French revolution and on police, crime and criminal justice in the electorate of Mainz, as well as several edited volumes (*Repräsentationen von Kriminalität und öffentlicher Sicherheit* (Frankfurt am Main, 2010); *Grazia e giustizia* (Il Mulino, Bologna, 2011); *Vom Majestätsverbrechen zum Terrorismus* (Frankfurt am Main, 2012)).

Peter Hoppenbrouwers read History and Italian at Leiden University (The Netherlands). He was Head of the Dutch Institute for Agronomical History (NAHI) at Groningen University (1984–1994), Senior Lecturer in Medieval History at Leiden University (1994–2000), and Professor of Medieval History at the University of Amsterdam (2001–2007). Since 2008 he holds the Chair of Medieval History at Leiden University. He has published extensively on the rural history of the medieval Low Countries. He is the co-author, with Wim Blockmans, of *Introduction to Medieval Europe, 300–1550* (London, New York, 2007).

Natalia Królikowska is Assistant Professor at the University of Warsaw. Her research focuses on the Crimean, Ottoman and Caucasian history in the Early Modern Period. Her publications include 'Muslim Women in the Local Social Life of the Ottoman Empire in the 16th–18th century', *Acta Poloniae Historica* 96 (2006) and 'Crimean Crime Stories. Cases of Homicide and Bodily Harm during the Reign of Murad Giray (1678–1683)' published in the volume *The Crimean Khanate between East and West (15th–18th Century)*, edited by Denise Klein (Wiesbaden, 2012).

Polly Low is Senior Lecturer in Ancient History at the University of Manchester, and has particular interests in the interstate politics of the Classical Greek world. She is the author of *Interstate Relations in Classical Greece: Morality and Power* (Cambridge, 2007) and editor of *The Athenian Empire* (Edinburgh, 2007).

Neil Murphy is lecturer in early modern history at the University of Northumbria, and has published articles on a range of topics in the history of fifteenth- and sixteenth-century France. He completed a PhD at the University of Glasgow in 2009 on ceremonial entries in France (c.1350–c.1570), which he is currently transforming into a book.

Carine van Rhijn is lecturer of medieval history at Utrecht University. She studied medieval history at Utrecht University and King's College London. Her research is in the field of early medieval European history, and focusses on cultural, intellectual and religious aspects of the Carolingian world.

Karen Gottschang Turner is Professor of History and Distinguished Professor of the Humanities at the College of the Holy Cross and a Senior Research Fellow in the East Asian Legal Studies Program at Harvard Law School. Her work focuses on law in early China and comparative legal history. She is completing a book, *Love and Law in China's Early Empires*, that explores how tensions between the demands of the state and duties to kin play out in law in the Qin and Han periods. For the last decade, she has worked on projects involving women and war in Vietnam and has published several articles and a book and directed a film on Northern Vietnamese women soldiers.

ACKNOWLEDGEMENTS

This volume brings together a selection of papers presented at a conference held at the History Institute of Utrecht University in November 2008. Several other specialists stepped in at our request to provide chapters covering themes we thought necessary for the coherence of the volume as a whole. Our thanks go to the conference participants who contributed actively to the discussion even if their papers do not form part of this volume, and to the authors whose patience we have seriously tested.

This initiative would not have been possible without the support of several funding institutions. The Utrecht conference was part of a programme funded by the COST organization (European Cooperation in Science and Technology). Utrecht University, notably its Onderzoeksinstituut voor Geschiedenis en Cultuur (OGC) offered hospitality and contributed in many ways to the success of our initiative. We have also enjoyed financial support from the Trustees of the Philip Leverhulme Prize.

In addition, the support of several persons has been indispensable. Kate Delaney provided invaluable editorial expertise and assistance at several stages. Among our contacts at Brill, we would like to thank Marti Huetink, Arjan van Dijk, Rosanna Woensdregt, and Ivo Romein for their efficient and dynamic support. David Claszen carefully corrected the entire text, and compiled the index.

The articles relating to Chinese history consistently use the common *pinyin* transcription. For articles pertaining to Muslim societies we chose the widely used Arabic system of transliteration for most of the terms. However, terms that are in widespread use through non-Arab usage (such as *kanun*) remain in their original form of transliteration. Titles of articles and books are left in their original form.

The editors

INTRODUCTION

Jeroen Duindam, Jill Harries, Caroline Humfress, and Nimrod Hurvitz

> The manner you must have in the taking of possession of the lands and parts which you will have discovered is to be that, being in the land or part that you shall have discovered, you shall make before a notary public and the greatest possible number of witnesses, and the best known ones, an act of possession in our name, cutting trees and boughs, and digging or making, if there be an opportunity, some small building... and you shall make a gallows there, and have somebody bring a complaint before you, and as our captain and judge you shall pronounce upon and determine it, so that, in all, you shall take the said possession...[1]

In 1514 a formal procedure for 'the taking of possession of [overseas] lands and parts' was laid out in a royal instruction, addressed to a certain Juan Días de Solís: a Portuguese 'explorer' in the service of the Crown of Castile. Whilst the European conquest of the Americas was '... often accomplished by military means or by occupation, its authority—that is, the right to rule—was established by language and ceremony'.[2] Much of the language and ceremony that accompanied early modern European empire-building, in the Americas and beyond, was specifically *legal*. The 1514 Spanish royal instruction, for example, orders that the intention to possess 'discovered' lands must be formally recorded, on arrival, before a Spanish public notary and Spanish witnesses of social standing. The 'legality' of Spanish sovereignty was then to be established by inviting any [native] inhabitants to demonstrate their prior claim to the land. This prior claim was to take the form of a complaint against Spanish possession, to be made before Juan Días de Solís himself—who is described at this point in the text as the king's 'captain and judge'. There is no record of any existing inhabitant lodging a complaint as part of this kind of procedure.[3]

---

[1] 'Instrucción que dió el Rey á Juan Diaz de Solís para el viage expresado. 24 de Nov., 1514', quoted (in translation) from Stephen Greenblatt, *Marvelous Possessions: The Wonder of the New World* (Chicago, 1991), 56. See also Peter Fitzpatrick, *Modernism and the Grounds of Law* (Cambridge, 2001), 163 and more generally, Patricia Seed, *Ceremonies of Possession in Europe's Conquest of the New World* (Cambridge, 1995).

[2] Patricia Seed, 'Taking Possession and Reading Texts: Establishing the Authority of Overseas Empires', *William and Mary Quarterly* 49, (1992), 183–209, 187. See also John H. Elliott's comparative approach in 'Occupying American space' in his: *Empires of the Atlantic World: Britain and Spain in America, 1492–1830* (New Haven and London, 2006), 26–56.

[3] Bernhard Waldenfels, *The Question of the Other* (Hong Kong, 2007), 107. See also Greenblatt, *Marvelous Possessions,* 59–60.

The 'legitimacy' of early modern Spanish conquest and settlement was thus established, to the satisfaction of the Spanish king and his jurists at least, by a formal legal procedure. A formal legal procedure, moreover, whose own 'legitimacy' was assured by legal texts dating back to the empire of the Romans.[4] Our 1514 text, however, also points towards law as a technique for *maintaining* empire: '... and you shall make a gallows there and have somebody bring a complaint before you ...'. Recent scholarship on modern and early modern colonial and postcolonial legal regimes has clearly demonstrated that law's 'imperializing effects' were not limited to justifying the moment or 'act' of conquest; law was also 'a key mechanism of imperial rule'.[5] Peter Fitzpatrick has argued that: 'the violence of imperialism was legitimated in its being exercised through law'.[6] In exploring the ongoing relationship between law and empire both the historian and the lawyer need to be constantly aware of the imperialism of law itself.[7]

Can we expect to identify any kind of shared dynamic in the relationship between historical empires and law? Comparative lawyers and legal historians are perhaps more used to thinking in terms of 'family resemblances' between different legal systems or legal traditions (for example civilian, common law or 'mixed' jurisdictions) as opposed to conceptualising different legal systems according to distinct types of 'state' structures. There are no chapters on 'law and empire', or indeed 'Imperial law', in comparative law handbooks.[8] In fact, thinking in terms of legal systems and legal traditions constantly necessitates moving across—and

---

[4] Greenblatt, *Marvelous Possessions*, 53–54.

[5] Russell Smandych, 'The Cultural Imperialism of Law', in Bernd Hamm and Russell Smandych, *Cultural Imperialism. Essays on the Political Economy of Cultural Domination* (Peterborough, Canada, 2005), 267–289: 267–8.

[6] Fitzpatrick, *Modernism and the Grounds of Law*, 179 and Peter Fitzpatrick, 'Magnified Features: The Underdevelopment of Law and Legitimation', *Journal of South Pacific Law* 4 (2000), 3, www.paclii.org/journals/fJSPL/vol04/5.shtml# (accessed 3 June, 2011).

[7] Jeannine Purdy, 'Postcolonialism: The Emperor's New Clothes?', in Eve Darian-Smith and Peter Fitzpatrick, eds., *Laws of the Postcolonial* (Ann Arbor, 1999), 203–232 offers a forceful critique of what, exactly, is 'post' about 'postcolonial' legal regimes; see further discussion in Ruth Buchanan and Sundhya Pahuja, 'Legal Imperialism: Empire's Invisible Hand?', in Paul Passavant and Jodi Dean, *Empire's New Clothes: Reading Hardt and Negri* (New York and London, 2004), 73–120; and from a different perspective, Turan Kayaoğlu, *Legal Imperialism. Sovereignty and Extraterritoriality in Japan, the Ottoman Empire and China* (Cambridge, 2010).

[8] Mathias Reimann and Reinhard Zimmermann, eds., *The Oxford Handbook of Comparative Law*, 2nd edition (Oxford, 2008); Esin Örücü and David Nelken, eds., *Comparative Law: A Handbook* (Portland, OR, 2007); H. Patrick Glenn, *Legal Traditions of the World: Sustainable Diversity in Law*, 3rd Edition (Oxford, 2007); and Pierre Legrand and Roderick

beyond—the boundaries of states and state-type institutions. A legal historian might, for example, opt to group legal traditions according to their respective writing systems: 'Greek law', written in ancient Greek; 'Chinese law', in Chinese ideographs; 'Hindu law', in Devanagari alphabets.[9]

Alternatively, studying comparative law from a 'global', 'cosmopolitan' perspective may involve comparisons between different 'model jurisdictions' (such as France; Central and Eastern Europe; the United States; East Asia) or comparisons across different subject areas of law (such as contract law; family law; constitutional law).[10] Some legal traditions, including what (Western) scholars refer to as 'Islamic law', 'Hindu law', 'Canon law', 'Jewish law', or 'Traditional / Indigenous law' are not necessarily linked to political state structures at all. For example, William Twining explains that Islamic law is '... also "institutionalized" trans-nationally in respect of literature, juristic traditions, recognized figures (e.g., muftis, ayatollahs) etc., yet may exist and be observed as a social practice in a place where there is no mosque or Islamic school or imam'.[11] Even the most cursory analysis thus highlights the fact that the study of law and legal history extends far beyond the boundaries of historical empires. What, then, can we gain by looking at the relationship between law and empire in specific historical contexts?

According to Jane Burbank and Frederick Cooper 'ideal type' empires differ from nation-states as political entities because:

> Empires are large political units, expansionist or with a memory of power extended over space, polities that maintain distinction and hierarchy as they incorporate new people. The nation-state, in contrast, is based on the idea of a single people in a single territory constituting itself as a unique political community. The nation-state proclaims the commonality of its people—even if the reality is more complicated—while the empire-state declares the non-equivalence of multiple populations. Both kinds of state are incorporative—they insist that people be ruled by their institutions—but

---

Mundy, eds., *Comparative Legal Studies: Traditions and Transitions* (Cambridge, 2003), but including chapters on 'The Colonialist Heritage' and 'The Nationalist Heritage'.

[9] As well as 'Pali Buddhist law', in Pallava grantha alphabets; 'Jewish law', in Hebrew; 'Slav law', in Cyrilic; 'Islamic law', in Arabic etc., see Andrew Huxley, 'Buddhist Law, Asian Law, Eurasian Law', in Nicholas Foster ed., 'A Fresh Start for Comparative Legal Studies? A Collective Review of Patrick Glenn's *Legal Traditions of the World*, 2nd Edition', *Journal of Comparative Law* 1, no. 1 (2006), 158–164: 163.

[10] Reimann and Zimmermann, *Oxford Handbook of Comparative Law*.

[11] William Twining, 'A Post-Westphalian Conception of Law. Review Essay: Brian Tamanaha, *A General Jurisprudence of Law and Society* (New York, 2001)', *Law and Society Review* 37, no. 1 (2003), 199–258: 216 at fn. 77.

> the nation-state tends to homogenize those inside its borders and exclude those who do not belong, while the empire reaches outward and draws, usually coercively, peoples whose difference is made explicit under its rule.[12]

In other words, as Burbank and Cooper conclude: 'The concept of empire presumes that different peoples within the polity will be governed differently'.[13] Exploring the relationships between 'law and empire' thus invites us to consider how multiplicities of law and legal orderings, interlegalities and conflicts can exist within ('single') universalist, expansionist frameworks.[14]

The very fact that empires differ structurally from nation-states—even though some nineteenth- and twentieth-century 'nation-states' were also empire-builders—can help us to break out from what William Twining has termed 'the Country and Western Tradition' of legal scholarship; a tradition that has, until recently, dominated mainstream Western comparative law.[15] According to Twining, 'the Country and Western Tradition' focuses almost exclusively on 'the positive laws and "official" legal systems of nation states' and more specifically on 'legal doctrine' in European and American Western capitalist societies.[16] Yet, as Twining states: 'Things can look very different from local points of view, whether these are members of a political elite, their opponents, minority groups, or individual citizens confronted in daily life with a variety of regulatory orders'.[17] An interest in law from the 'local' point of view is by no means confined to scholarship on 'law and empire'. Nonetheless, 'law and empire' scholarship has been crucial in opening up this kind of approach. Some of the most important advances in understanding how different legal and regulatory orders function, in dialectic with unequal power relations 'on the ground', have come from recent studies of colonial and postcolonial legal regimes.[18]

---

[12] Jane Burbank and Frederick Cooper, *Empires in World History: Power and Politics of Difference* (Princeton, NJ, 2010), 8; see also the perceptive discussion of the Qing empire and its successor-states in China, Pamela Crossley, 'Nationality and Difference in China: The Post-Imperial Dilemma', in *The Teleology of the Modern Nation-State Japan and China* (Philadelphia 2005).

[13] Burbank and Cooper, *Empires in World History*, 8.

[14] See especially the essays by Królikowska and Hoppenbrouwers in this volume.

[15] William Twining, 'Comparative law and legal theory: the country and western tradition', in Ian Edge, ed., *Comparative Law in Global Perspective* (Ardsley NY, 2000), 21–76.

[16] Twining, 'Comparative law and legal theory', 25. See also Andrew Huxley, 'Introduction', in Andrew Huxley, ed., *Religion, Law and Tradition. Comparative Studies in Religious Law* (London and New York, 2002), 6–7.

[17] William Twining, 'Diffusion of Law: A Global Perspective', *Journal of Legal Pluralism and Unofficial Law* 49 (2004), 1–45, 25.

[18] For example, Jeannine Purdy, *Common Law and Colonised Peoples: Studies in Trinidad and Western Australia* (Aldershot, Eng. and Brookfield, VT, 1997); Sally Merry, *Colonizing Hawai'i: The Cultural Power of Law* (Princeton, NJ, 2000); Diane Kirkby and Catharine

Modern colonial situations clearly invoke multiple legal orders and orderings.[19] Studies associated with what has been termed 'classical legal pluralism' are '... typically concerned with describing and explaining how new (usually European) legal systems and laws brought by colonizers were superimposed on Indigenous customary laws and pre-existing methods of dispute settlement and social control'.[20] Plural legal regimes and pluralities of law are understood as an integral part of modern imperial states. For example, in her studies of colonial legal regimes between 1400 and 1900 Lauren Benton has argued for a fundamental shift in what she terms 'the history of variegated legal spaces in empire'—a shift that occurred between the colonial regimes of the early modern world and the nineteenth-century era of 'high colonialism'.[21] Early modern (European) empires, according to Benton, drew a certain institutional continuity from self-consciously maintaining multi-centric legal orders.[22] By the mid-nineteenth century, however, 'state-centered legal pluralism was being promoted as a model of governance by European administrators'.[23] New technologies of government (including statistical analysis and other 'post-enlightenment' sciences of knowledge), Benton suggests, assisted '... the articulation and acceptance (at least among European administrators) of a more state-centered view of law in the nineteenth century [which] was an inherent and indispensable part of the "success" of European colonialism—and, indeed, part of European nation-state building itself'.[24]

Coleborne, *Law, History, Colonialism: The Reach of Empire* (Manchester, 2001); Lauren Benton, *Law and Colonial Cultures. Legal Regimes in World History 1400–1900* (Cambridge, 2002); Lauren Benton, *A Search for Sovereignty. Law and Geography in European Empires 1400–1900* (Cambridge, 2010); and Lisa Ford, *Settler Sovereignty: Jurisdiction and Indigenous People in America and Australia 1788–1836* (Cambridge, MA, 2010).

[19] Masaji Chiba, *Asian Indigenous Law: In Interaction with Received Law* (London and New York, 1986), 6. For further discussion of legal pluralism in the context of (post)colonial studies see Prakash Shah, *Legal Pluralism in Conflict: Coping with Cultural Diversity in Law* (London and New York, 2005) and Werner Menski, *Comparative Law in a Global Context: The Legal Systems of Asia and Africa* (Cambridge, 2006).

[20] Smandych, 'The Cultural Imperialism of Law', 268, summarizing the key article by Sally Merry, 'Legal Pluralism', *Law and Society Review* 22, (1988), 869–896.

[21] Benton, *Law and Colonial Cultures*; Lauren Benton, 'Empires of Exception: History, Law, and the Problem of Imperial Sovereignty', *Quaderni di Relazioni Internazionali* (2007), 54–67; and Benton, *A Search for Sovereignty*.

[22] Benton, *Law and Colonial Cultures*, 7–12 and 31–126.

[23] Benton, *Law and Colonial Cultures*, 6 and also 127–252. See also Benton, *A Search for Sovereignty*, 5–9.

[24] Smandych, 'The Cultural Imperialism of Law', 281. Benton's argument that there was a global drive by nineteenth-century colonial states to control plural regimes of law in Latin America, North America, Asia, Australia and Africa, and that this led to a 'loss

The 1514 Spanish royal instruction opening this introduction indicates that law involves a variety of agents and perspectives: in this case the distant king, his captain, a legal specialist, witnesses, and complainants. The pattern of dominion and subjection seems entirely clear-cut here. However, law, even if devised as an instrument for top-down domination, tends to develop a dynamic of its own that makes room for initiatives by agents as well as subjects. While rulers and their captains could be limited by the dictates of law, legal specialists could further their own cultural and social status on the basis of their arcane knowledge. Finally, surprisingly large groups among the populace could learn to flexibly use the institutions and language of law to pursue their own purposes—a perspective elaborated in the last section of this volume.

The historiography of European state-building has called into question in various ways the easy association of positive laws and the rise of powerful rulers and states. The 'legal absolutism' of Louis XIV, long a model of the centralising power of the ruler, has been revised to leave more room for elite corporations so important for the regional fabric of France, the courts of law or *parlements* notable among them.[25] The centre, clearly, had to make room for local groupings and local varieties of law even in relatively unified monarchical states. Before 1789, European states were almost by definition characterized by legal pluralism, with specific rights—or privileges—for regions, corporations, and social groups. In addition, the stress on official legal doctrine and top-down procedures has been complemented by a more extensive appreciation of law in the everyday life of wider social groups. Litigation was very much present in the daily life of ordinary French people in the *grand siècle*. With or without the help of literate associates, even peasants brought their grievances to one of the

of plurality' in the modern legal world, has been challenged from a number of different perspectives, see Lisa Ford, *Settler Sovereignty*, 4. See also Christopher Tomlins, *Freedom Bound: Law, Labor, and Civic Identity in Colonizing English America, 1580–1865* (Cambridge, 2010) and in a different context, Peter Fitzpatrick, 'The Immanence of Empire', in Passavant and Dean, *Empire's New Clothes*, 31–72.

[25] On Louis XIV and law see e.g. Albert N. Hamscher, *The Conseil Privé and the Parlements in the Age of Louis XIV: A Study in French Absolutism* (Philadelphia, 1987); David Parker, 'Sovereignty, Absolutism and the Function of the Law in Seventeenth-Century France', *Past & Present* 122, (1989), 36–74; for a more recent statement critical of the revisionist stance of these authors see John J. Hurt, *Louis XIV and the Parlements: the Assertion of Royal Authority* (Man-chester, 2002).

two courts of appeal in the Holy Roman Empire.[26] In these respects the impulses generated by postcolonial studies and early modern European studies point in the same direction, exchanging a monolithic, top-down and doctrinal model of law for a more differentiated view stressing social practices and initiatives at various levels.

All pre-modern empires and states were subject to major infrastructural limitations and therefore necessarily accommodated variety—grudgingly or willingly. This holds true for the colonial enterprises, for the land-based empires of Eurasia, for the territorially more modest composite monarchies of early modern Europe, and even for city-states with mixed populations. Empires are frequently created through the rise of one power to dominance over others, via military, political or economic action. Relationships between ruler and ruled might be determined by conquest or annexation; by force or consent; by assertion of control over economic resources; through the levy of tribute or taxation; or by treaties and other legal agreements. Some empires, especially perhaps those whose supremacy depended largely on military force and coercion, were short-lived. Long-lasting empires, the essays in this volume suggest, developed techniques of accommodation and assimilation that incorporated subject populations. Law was necessary for all rulers who wanted to be seen as legitimate, and a measure of legitimacy is necessary for the long-term success of any form of political power. Law inevitably forms part of the endeavour to integrate peoples into overarching political structures, although this process can take many shapes. 'Empire' in the title of this volume, hence, can be read as 'rule over a diversity of peoples', and legal pluralism will be a recurring theme.[27] The European seaborne empires of the early modern world do not form part of this collection, however, nor do the colonial empires emerging in the late-nineteenth-century phase of global competition. While omitting this arguably most conspicuous category of empire, we draw attention to forms of rule that are not usually defined as empires.

[26] See e.g. on France, Julie Hardwick, *Family Business: litigation and the political economies of daily life in seventeenth-century France* (Oxford, 2009) and recently Rafe Blaufarb, 'Conflict and Compromise: Communauté and Seigneurie in Early Modern Provence', *The Journal of Modern History*, 82, no 3. (2010), 519–545; on the Holy Roman Empire, see Karl Härter in this volume, and e.g. Peter Blickle, 'Paysan et état dans le Saint Empire Romain Germanique', *Francia* 8 (1980), 191–211; Sabine Ullmann, *Geschichte auf der langen Bank: Die Kommissionen des Reichshofrats unter Kaiser Maximilian II. (1564–1576)*. Veröffentlichungen des Instituts für Europäische Geschichte Mainz (Mainz, 2006).

[27] Burbank and Cooper, *Empires in World History*, 11.

This volume brings together a selection of ten contributions originally presented at a conference held at Utrecht University in November 2008, with four additional papers commissioned to strengthen the scope and coherence of this collection. The conference formed part of a European COST-ESF-funded research initiative on tributary empires. This project, initially concentrating on the Roman, Ottoman, and Mughal empires, soon abandoned this restrictive focus, accepting a wider comparison of empires and states as a necessary precondition for more specific definitions and typologies. Our initiative considered three levels: the imperial centre, the experience of empire in the provinces, and the historical sociology of empire. Conferences focused on specific themes such as dynastic courts, universalism and frontiers, or warfare, combining perspectives from centre and periphery. Several volumes emerging from this initiative have already been published.[28]

The essays collected in this volume illustrate the many complexities of analysing 'law and empire' and 'law in empire' in concrete historical contexts. Our contributors, specialists in their own fields rather than comparatists, together cover a long phase of pre-modern history, in what may seem a relatively haphazard geographical selection. Our aim was to combine at least East Asian, West Asian, and European perspectives on law. Studying law in these different domains over a long period allows us to come to some more general reflections. The essays do not deal directly with comparisons. No single study isolates a topic and compares its characteristics across different empires. A first section on 'Legal Authority and Imperial Frameworks' traces general characteristics of law as part of the traditions of religion, morality and governance in Europe, West Asia and East Asia. The second section on 'Institutionalising Empire: Practices of Law Making and Adjudication', still largely concentrating on the top-down-imperial framework of law, offers more specific and detailed examples of law making from rulers to legal specialists. The third and last section on 'Legal pluralism in Empires: Encounters and Responses' focuses squarely on legal pluralism and the initiatives of subordinate or subjected groups, as well as imperial elites.

---

[28] Björn Forsén, Giovanni Salmeri, ed., *The Province Strikes Back: Imperial Dynamics in the Eastern Mediterranean. Papers and Monographs of the Finnish Institute at Athens, 13* (Helsinki, 2008); Jeroen Duindam, Tülay Artan and Metin Kunt, ed., *Royal Courts in Dynastic States and Empires. A Global Perspective* (Leiden, 2011); Peter Fibiger Bang and Chris Bayly, ed., *Tributary Empires in Global History* (Basingstoke, 2011); Peter Fibiger Bang and Dariusz Kolodziejczyk, ed., *Universal Empire. A Comparative Approach to Imperial Culture and Representation in Eurasian History* (Cambridge, 2012).

This tripartite division allows readers to understand law as a moral-political notion, as a practice of government, and as a social process in very different settings. Rather than offering summaries of papers that can speak for themselves, this introduction will highlight thematically some of the contrasts and parallels, providing a framework through which the reader can begin to compare and contrast. Thereby, we hope to encourage further comparative reflection on the relationships between law and empire with reference to the multitude of historical contexts that we have not been able to address here.

Legal Authority and Imperial Frameworks

The imperial encounter assumes domination, yet it frequently also entails a universal mission. According to Aelius Aristides, writing in praise of Rome in the second century CE, the imperial subjugation of weaker to stronger was part of a much broader process of civilised man seeking mastery over the natural world:

> What was said by Homer, 'The earth was common to you all', you have made a reality, by surveying the whole inhabited world (*oikoumenê*), by bridging the rivers in various ways, by cutting carriage roads through the mountains, by filling desert places with post stations, and by civilizing everything with your way of life and good order... And now, indeed, there is no need to write a description of the world, nor to enumerate the laws of each people, but you have become universal geographers for all... by opening up all the gates of the inhabited world (*oikoumenê*)... and by organising the whole inhabited world like a single household (*oikos*).[29]

The idea of the Romans as the 'universal geographers of all' also had its concrete and material expressions: for example, a vast technical and juridical apparatus had to be developed in order to measure, quantify and assess provincial land for taxation purposes.

Aspirations to 'universalism' came in many different forms.[30] Each of these forms, moreover, changed over time, even while cherishing age-old principles. The status of law in the moral economy of the territories

[29] Aelius Aristides, *Oration* 26, 101–2, in *The Complete Works. Vol. II, Orations XVII–LIII*, ed. and trans. Charles Behr (Leiden, 1981), 78.

[30] On local aspirations to Islamic 'universalism' see Judith Scheele, 'A Taste for Law: Rule-Making in Kabylia (Algeria)', *Comparative Studies in Society and History* 50, no. 4 (2008), 895–919. Donald Davis, *The Spirit of Hindu Law* (Cambridge, 2010) makes a similar argument with respect to Indic history and legal traditions.

discussed here differed, but law itself universally served as a high-minded principle, as a tool of governance and as an instrument of oppression: empires both spread and impose law. Roman law, the principal influence in European legal tradition, emerged in the context of a 'small face-to-face agricultural community', where parochial and familial concerns predominated. Jill Harries' essay shows how Roman law retained a strong focus on the city and the citizen, even while it adapted successfully to a large-scale empire governed by an emperor.

The monopoly that later Roman emperors (fourth-sixth centuries CE) exercised over law making marks the final progression of ancient Rome from a city-state republic with an empire to a world-empire governed by 'autocratic' rulers. Other ancient Mediterranean city-states also expanded into 'empire-type' structures: Sparta, Athens, Syracuse and Carthage all established and settled 'colonies' within an imperial framework. It is only in the case of Rome, however, that we find the transition from city-state to ancient empire marked by emperors who legislate. This shift from a 'city-state republic with an empire' to a 'universal empire with a law-making emperor' was by no means inevitable, as a comparative study of the rise of the city of Venice from Republic to 'Republican empire' might demonstrate. So what difference did a 'universal' legislating emperor make?

Under the later Roman empire, emperors promulgated various types of legal enactments—some addressed to all their imperial subjects and others targeted more narrowly at specific individuals and groups—thus creating what scholars now refer to as a distinct body of 'Imperial law'.[31] Two late Roman emperors, Theodosius II and Justinian I, went further in ordering authoritative collections (*codices:* 'codes') of previous Roman law to be made and promulgating them under their own names.[32] It is this *late* Roman image, the universal emperor as both the legislator of future law and the ultimate guarantor of all past legal tradition, which seems to underpin many Western ideas of the relationship between law and empire.[33]

In the Athenian empire, Polly Low argues, Athens dictated its norms to a series of subject cities, while never systematically transplanting its

---

[31] On the concept of 'Imperial law' as a distinct type of Roman law see J.-P. Coriat, *Le prince législateur. La technique législative des Sévères et les méthodes de création du droit impérial à la fin du Principat* (Rome, Paris, 1997).

[32] On the late Roman 'law codes' of Theodosius II and Justinian I see the paper by Humfress in this volume.

[33] Including the 'universal empire' imagined in Dante Alighieri's early fourteenth-century work of political theory, *De Monarchia*.

political structures to these cities, usually leaving room for local urban political arrangements. In contrast to the Roman and Athenian examples, Chinese law appears to lack this notably urban-civic character. Relying on archaeological evidence, Karen Turner corrects the classic view which downplays the importance of law in China; Turner underlines the relative strength of legal norms and practices in Early-Imperial China, suggesting the implementation of codes and procedures even at the regional level. The consistent application of law could become a bone of contention between the emperor and his bureaucratic servants; Turner stresses the recurring role of imperial women in this struggle.

Engin Akarlı, locating Ottoman rulership and law making in the Islamic legal tradition, differentiates between various practices of law. In addition to the co-existence of *shari'a* and sultanic *kanun*, Akarlı points to the different positions of social and functional groups vis à vis the law. While the customs of guilds and other social collectivities were on the whole accepted and could be adopted into formal law, the sultan showed himself less accommodating towards his own military-administrative elite. Representing sultanic power they held sway over subjects while remaining highly vulnerable to the sultan's punishment. This martial custom, the harsher side of Janus-faced sultanic power, Akarlı argues, influenced the nineteenth-century phase of reforms. Karl Härter highlights the immense importance of law and litigation in that most atypical of imperial constellations: the Holy Roman Empire of the German Nation. The intricate balances among the imperial estates (*Reichsstände*) and the multiple legal institutions of the *Reich* suggest that the *processes* of law making and litigation were as important as their outcomes, offering an ongoing medium of communication and accommodation—an interpretation that can also be applied to the Imperial Diet.

Adaptation and flexibility seem to be as characteristic for law as respect for antiquity and established practice. Harries stresses the *rescriptive* character of many imperial decrees, responding to appeals rather than initiating law making. Even the high-handed power of the sultan, Akarlı shows, would on the whole leave room to the *shari'a* and social practices. Both the Chinese and the Ottoman cases highlight the potential tension between rulers and high-level bureaucrats. Benevolent despots, clearly, were not always keen on the consistent application of law codes. On the other hand, they could lend their ear to popular appeals, accusing their bureaucrats of corruption or the abuse of power. Such tactics could strengthen their legitimacy as well as curb the pretensions of their highest servants.

Institutionalising Empire: Practices of Law Making and Adjudication

Different types of empires established different kinds of relationships between imperial centres and peripheries, and relied on different views of legitimacy and rule. The provinces of the ancient Roman and Chinese empires, for example, '...were not managed as colonies and retained in a division of labour controlled by the metropolitan regions, such as in the European Atlantic system'.[34] Relationships of rule between centre and periphery also changed over time, for example as the latter developed from conquered territories into integrated regions, linked to the centre by constant economic, political and social exchange—as well as by imperial ideology and physical infrastructure. We should also, however, be wary of assuming that the 'centre' of any given empire was necessarily a stable and fixed entity.

How provincial elites were co-opted into imperial power structures, as well as how relations between imperial centres and provincial elites could break down, is explored by Nimrod Hurvitz and R. Kent Guy. Nimrod Hurvitz's paper on early Islamic rulers picks up some of the themes mentioned by Akarlı and Turner. Public or administrative law was left out of the historical discourse of Islamic law; rulers checked abuse of power by state servants through separate legal channels. Hurvitz focuses on the *mazalim* tribunals, a form of popular appeal to the ruler that allowed the disclosure and punishment of bureaucratic malpractice. This 'Abbasid mechanism to suppress elite corruption continued into the Mamluk period. Guy, carefully analysing a corruption case in Qing China, shows how examining and prosecuting elite malpractice was complicated by family connections and personal standing with the emperor. The Qianlong emperor (r. 1736–1795) requested the advice of numerous top administrators, who almost unanimously pleaded in favour of execution. In the end the emperor brushed aside their advice and even restored the culprit to his original rank. Corruption had to be condemned, but the corrupt person could be pardoned—particularly when he could still serve the state. Family, community and social standing were integral to the framing and judging of criminal law cases. Guy's case-study again demonstrates how '...in China, justice was due to communities as well as to individuals'.[35]

---

[34] Peter Fibiger Bang, 'Commanding and Consuming the World: Empire, Tribute, and Trade in Roman and Chinese History', in Walter Scheidel, ed., *Rome and China. Comparative Perspectives on Ancient World Empires* (Oxford, 2009), 110–120: 116.

[35] Kent Guy, paper in this volume.

'Universalism' in modern European empires was reflected in the activities of Christian missionaries just as much as, or even more than, in the activities of either central or local imperial bureaucrats. Carine van Rhijn's paper conveys the strength of a universal moral-religious perspective in Charlemagne's empire and shows how the clerical hierarchy from bishop to local priest played a vital role in the communication and implementation of law from the centre to the provinces. We need to remember that neither the will nor the ability of imperial centres to impose uniform legal ideas and structures can simply be assumed. Geography was perhaps the most obvious difficulty that pre-modern empires faced, and it left a profound mark on their politics and shaped their legal environments. In the words of Peter Brown, the imperial regime was 'involved in a perpetual battle with distance'.[36] The hardships and time involved in travel and communication placed a serious obstacle in the way of any 'centralised' regime and made the sustaining of relationships with regionally based armies and local elites, the implementation of policy, and the enforcement of law in the localities formidable tasks.[37]

The practice of law making is a practice of 'powermaking'—yet the power to make laws also presupposes the authority to do so. In the specific context of *imperial* powermaking, exploring how (state) law is made enables us to approach political elites and pressure groups from a unique angle. In some cases elite lawmakers are the most powerful political authorities in an empire. In other cases legislative authority is not accompanied by (extensive) political influence. Law can function as an arena in which social tensions are negotiated; in other cases it can be used by ruling elites in attempts to buttress their power and prevent social change. Conversely, some of the most politically powerful figures and groups, such as generals, royal entourage and administrators, may not be involved in the law-making process at all. Looking at empires and their inner workings through the process of law making thus helps to expose the relative power structures of elites and pressure groups within numerous different spheres of political action.

---

[36] Peter Brown, *Power and Persuasion in Late Antiquity: Towards a Christian Empire* (Madison, WI, 1992), 10.

[37] For a comparative perspective in terms of early modern 'mercantile' empires see John Law, 'On the methods of long-distance control: vessels, navigation and the Portuguese route to India', in John Law, ed., *Power, Action and Belief: A New Sociology of Knowledge?* (London, 1986), 234–63.

The legislative authority of any given ruler of empire was, in practice, dependent on relations with political, military, economic and cultural elites. Relations with an intellectual elite—including, where relevant, experts in legal knowledge—were also of fundamental importance. Within some imperial frameworks, the law-making capacities of legal experts, where present, were subordinate to the rulers: for example, under the later Roman empire a more 'bureaucratised' class of legal experts—*iurisperiti*, 'jurists'—seems to have been shaped by the needs of empire. In other cases, the formation of a 'professional' class of legal experts was dependent on other factors: the rise of the early modern English legal profession, for example, was determined by 'a slow but steady' growth in internal market complexity and concepts of property ownership. In fact, divisions of labour between 'men of power 'and 'men of learning' are not peculiar to imperial structures of power—as Clifford Geertz, writing with reference to Southeast Asia, notes:

> The sorts of tribunals found throughout the Indic world before colonial regimes attempted, with mixed success, to standardize them were as diverse and multitudinous as the rules they sought to apply, the groups that sought to apply them to, and the justifications they sought to give for them. But the principle that men of learning did the justifying and men of power did the applying seems to have been pervasive.[38]

In early Islamic empires scholars with expertise in the sciences of Islamic law played a dominant role, whilst the rulers played relatively minor roles in law making. This was due to Islamic legal culture, whose fundamental prerequisite for participation in law making was mastering the Islamic holy texts, their interpretations and the massive body of legal opinions that had accrued over time. Since individuals usually studied twenty or thirty years in order to achieve the required level of proficiency, the rulers and most of their administrators could not participate in such learned traditions of legal discourse. As a consequence we have at our disposal numerous, multi-volume works of law, all written by jurists, which barely refer to the rulers.

The fuller picture of early Islamic legal development is, of course, more complex. Caliphs and government officials certainly forged principles of governance, established institutions, appointed judges (*qadhis*) to both

[38] Clifford Geertz, 'Local knowledge: Fact and Law in Comparative Perspective', in Clifford Geertz, *Local Knowledge* (London, 1983), 167–234: 204.

regular and administrative tribunals and put forward administrative regulations; nonetheless, the Muslim public in general and the jurists in particular did not recognize administrative and public law as part of their 'legal' corpus. Nor did Classical Muslim jurists tend to think of administrative and public law as, strictly speaking, a branch of *fiqh*.[39] The idea that a caliph might collect the opinions of Muslim jurists and even decide between them was not, however, entirely alien to the early Islamic period. In the eighth century CE, the (Persian) Arabic scholar Ibn al-Muqaffaʿ (d. 756CE) suggested to the ʿAbbasid caliph al-Mansur that '...he could strengthen his legitimacy and his government by preparing a codification of laws and legal decrees and by uniting under his authority the different opinions of the jurists'.[40] As Maribel Fierro explains:

> The promotion of a legal codification implied the notion of caliphal authority over ideology and doctrine and this notion was an attack against traditional 'ulama'. In spite of the existence of standard texts and manuals, law was 'jurists' law' in the sense that it was not codified but rather derived from jurists and not from texts legislated by the state.[41]

The caliphs of early and Classical Islam did not claim that the principles of governance they established were a body of legal doctrine—nor did their Muslim subjects, in general, consider caliphs to be 'lawmakers'.[42] Most modern historians of Islamic law consider this to be an expression of the rulers' weakness in their competition with the scholars.[43] It is perhaps clear why most Islamic jurists embraced this division of labour which gave them a virtual monopoly over law making, especially in the sphere of private legal relations. Yet why did most Islamic rulers enable and espouse this division of authority?[44]

There were, of course, significant shifts in the historical relationship between jurists' law and Sultanic law making under the Ottoman legal system.[45] From at least the fifteenth century Ottoman sultans consolidated their own legislative and juridical authority, whilst still maintaining a

---

39 On the definition of *fiqh* see the essay by Akarlı in this volume.

40 Maribel Fierro, 'The Legal Policies of the Almohad Caliphs and Ibn Rushd's Bidayat Al-Mujtahid', *Journal of Islamic Studies* 10, no. 3 (1999), 226–248: 246.

41 Fierro, 'The Legal Policies of the Almohad Caliphs', 246–7.

42 Geertz, 'Local knowledge', 204.

43 For a survey of this historiography see the essay by Hurvitz in this volume.

44 See the essay by Hurvitz in this volume.

45 See the essay by Akarlı in this volume.

traditional 'Islamic' division of legal labour between judges and jurists. Mehmet II (r. 1444–1446, 1451–1481), for example, issued code-like collections of his own decrees. It was only in the late nineteenth century, however, that an Ottoman sultan promulgated 'codified' *shariʿa*, in the 'civil' Islamic code generally known as the *Mecelle*. Put in force by successive decrees of the Sultan between 1870 CE and 1876 CE, the *Mecelle-i Ahkâm-ı Adliyye* was the first attempt by any Islamic state to codify part of the *shariʿa*.[46] The decision to draft the *Mecelle* was apparently taken as the result of a dispute over whether the Ottoman empire should incorporate the French civil code within its territorial boundaries; according to Vaughn Findley it should thus be understood as '... a case of successful resistance, unique in the late Ottoman Empire and Turkish Republic, to the tendency to adopt European law.'[47] As Akarlı shows in his essay in this volume, however, Ottoman resistance to nineteenth-century 'European law' also needs to be understood within the context of over five hundred years of Ottoman legal history—a legal history that has only recently begun to attract scholarly attention.

Different traditions of law and governance mingled continuously, particularly along the frontiers of great empires. Natalia Królikowska singles out a specific case for discussion: the Crimean Khanate in the early modern period. The Crimean Khans cherished their descent from Chingis Khan; yet this successor state of the Golden Horde now increasingly operated under the imperial umbrella of the Ottomans. The Crimean Khans were autonomous and to some extent sovereign rulers, but clearly needed to adapt themselves to their bigger neighbour's requirements. Królikowska carefully shows how the khans combined Islamic and Mongol examples while at the same time adopting Ottoman practice in law, taxation and governance. The Ottomans wrapped their recurring interventions in the Crimean Khanate in terms of respect for Crimean traditions and practices. A basically pragmatic outlook seems to have mingled naturally with the tendency to seek support and legitimacy among previous examples.

---

[46] Carter Vaughn Findley, 'Mecelle', in *The Oxford Encyclopedia of the Islamic World. Oxford Islamic Studies Online*, www.oxfordislamicstudies.com/article/opr/t236/e0523 (accessed 01-Jun-2011).

[47] Findley, 'Mecelle' (accessed 01-Jun-2011).

Legal Pluralism in Empires: Encounters and Responses

Not all law within empires is imposed by top-down command. As the cases of Islamic *shariʿa* and the Romanist *ius commune* of medieval Europe show, individuals and communities regularly seek out formal law for themselves, frequently as a mark of their status or to demonstrate their inclusion in a wider moral and/or socio-religious order.[48] Barend ter Haar's study of punishment through popular religious cults in late Qing China, moreover, shows that control of deviant behaviour could also originate among the populace itself. This perspective entails thinking about mutual legal ordering, what Paul Dresch has termed 'sideways law', in the context of imperial structures. In ancient and medieval China, for example, what we might identify as 'civil' law—the law that governed relations between individuals—was largely to be found outside imperial statutory law—with socio-legal norms and customs influenced by Confucian ideas and doctrines.[49] Archival research by Bettine Birge has revealed, however, that individuals in tenth- to fourteenth-century China still, nonetheless, resorted to imperial courts in disputes over family matters, in particular concerning marriage contracts agreed according to customary norms.[50] Andrew Huxley has suggested a similar type of situation with reference to the sixteenth-century Burmese Toungoo Empire, exploring how the compilations of legal and ethical material known as the *Dhammathats* came to be pleaded in cases tried before royal officials.[51] The provision of courtroom-type venues and the institutionalising of specific law-persons, law-places and law-procedures/ceremonies, could all contribute towards creating an institutional framework that served to concretise imperial power. Often, however, that framework was facilitative as well as, in some cases, coercive. The recognition that some spheres of law can work 'sideways'—as well as top-down—thus also affects how we frame questions of imperial enforcement and imposition of law.

---

48 I owe this point to Paul Dresch (personal communication). See also Scheele, 'A Taste for Law'.

49 Karen Turner, 'Law and Punishment in the Formation of Empire', in Walter Scheidel, ed., *Rome and China. Comparative Perspectives on Ancient World Empires* (Oxford, 2009), 52–82.

50 See Bettine Birge, 'Rock, Paper, Scissors: The Nature of Local Sources and Understanding Regional History in Imperial China', *Journal of the Economic and Social History of the Orient* 52, no. 1 (2009), 4–13 and her forthcoming monograph, *Marriage and the Law in the Age of Khubilai Khan.*

51 Andrew Huxley, 'The Importance of the Dhammathats in Burmese Law and Culture', *Journal of Burma Studies* 1 (1997) 1–17.

The papers included within this volume all share—in one form or another—what has been termed a 'classical' legal pluralist perspective: they are each concerned with how multiple legal orders operated within, or were suppressed by, a hegemonic law of empire(s). The papers collected in Part III of this volume, however, also seek to explore some of the wide-ranging approaches that have been variously associated with what socio-legal scholars and legal anthropologists term 'new legal pluralism'. As the name suggests, 'new legal pluralism' is also interested in multiple legal orderings and plural systems of law, but it expands the approaches of 'classical' legal pluralism in two main ways: first, through an acknowledgment that law can exist outside government, through 'unofficial' forms of legal ordering; and second, through a focus on explaining how 'official' and 'unofficial' forms of legal ordering interact with each other, as well as with various other types of non-legal, 'social' norms of behaviour.[52] To borrow Smandych's succinct definition, studies associated with new legal pluralism are typically interested in: '... the different ways in which state and non-state forms of legal ordering and social control [interact] to produce social order'.[53] Academic lawyers and scholars of analytical jurisprudence, in particular, have offered sophisticated critiques of 'new legal pluralism' as a coherent theoretical perspective.[54] Nonetheless, the work of legal historians and legal anthropologists within this broad area offers numerous insights into the role of law in political domination, as well as the 'constitutive' role that formal systems of law can play in local contexts.

According to Lauren Benton, writing with specific reference to colonial empires between 1400 and 1900:

> Wherever a group imposed law on newly acquired territories and subordinate peoples, strategic decisions were made about the extent and nature of legal control. The strategies of rule included aggressive attempts to impose

[52] The secondary scholarship is now vast, but for a sample—chosen from different disciplinary backgrounds—see John Griffiths, 'What is Legal Pluralism?', *Journal of Legal Pluralism and Unofficial Law* 24 (1986), 1–55; Merry, 'Legal Pluralism'; Franz Benda-Beckmann, 'Who's Afraid of Legal Pluralism?', *Journal of Legal Pluralism and unofficial law* 47 (2002), 37–82; Shah, *Legal Pluralism in Conflict*; and Brian Tamanaha, 'Understanding Legal Pluralism, Past to Present, Local to Global', *Sydney Law Review* 30 (2008), 375–411.

[53] Smandych, 'Cultural Imperialism of Law', 268.

[54] Important critiques include Chris Fuller, 'Legal Anthropology, Legal Pluralism and Legal Thought', *Anthropology Today* 10, no. 3 (1994), 9–12; Simon Roberts, 'After Government? On Representing Law Without the State', *The Modern Law Review* 68, no. 1 (1995), 1–24; and Brian Tamanaha, 'A Holistic Vision of the Socio-legal Terrain', *Law and Contemporary Problems* 71 (2008), 89–97. See also Merry, 'Colonial Law and its Uncertainties'.

> legal systems intact. More common, though, were conscious efforts to retain elements of existing institutions and limit legal change as a way of sustaining social order. Conquered and colonized groups sought, in turn, to respond to the imposition of law in ways that included accommodation, advocacy within the system, subtle delegitimation, and outright rebellion.[55]

It is this idea of a local strategic response, within the context of specific conditions, which is one hallmark of scholarship associated with 'new legal pluralism'. For example, the papers by Humfress and Anastasopoulos in this section both explore the phenomenon of 'forum shopping': where certain individuals attempt to move tactically between judicial venues and negotiate their way through formal legal procedures in their own interest. As the essay by Anastasopoulos on the Ottoman Empire shows, moreover, this kind of strategising might involve negotiating between different 'religious' systems of law and/or jurisdictions, as well as across different kinds of socio-religious boundaries.

A focus on forum shopping thus uncovers how some subjects attempted to make imperial legal systems work for them. At the same time the phenomenon raises a number of questions, not least of which is who, under different imperial frameworks, had the right and the opportunity to 'shop', and under what circumstances did the occasion to do so present itself.[56] Peter Hoppenbrouwers highlights the role of various co-existing ethnically defined conceptions and practices of law in Charlemagne's empire: the provenance of litigants could define the composition and the procedure of a court of law. Hoppenbrouwers' discussion, however, also shows that legal pluralism could be a conscious instrument, protecting a mobile layer of *franci* or other agents of imperial power against local laws, and creating inequality among the various groups in the empire. The royal right of pardon or grace, effected during royal entries in France, Neil Murphy shows, triggered a response among the population at large. Convicts and refugees flocked to the king's mobile court, to receive his grace and escape from legal retribution. This intriguing ritual meeting of urban and royal forms of law exemplifies the multiplicity of legal-political structures in late-medieval and early modern Europe.

---

[55] Benton, *Law and Colonial Cultures*, 2.

[56] Further discussion in Uriel Simonsohn, *A Common Justice: The Legal Allegiances of Christians and Jews Under Early Islam* (Philadelphia, 2011); Najwa al-Qattan, 'Dhimmis in the Muslim Court: Legal Autonomy and Religious Discrimination', *International Journal of Middle East Studies* 31, no. 3 (1999), 429–44; and Elizabeth Kolsky, 'Maneuvering the Personal Law System in Colonial India: Introduction', *Law and History Review* 28, no. 4 (2010), 973–78.

We have already seen how power relations were structured in very particular ways within different imperial frameworks. It is also worth stressing here, however, the perhaps rather obvious point that not all legal subjects who interacted with law did so 'strategically'. Individuals, communities and groups could all be affected by law 'without resorting to it': including those accused of (public) 'crimes', illegal immigrants, and the dispossessed.[57] Outright resistance and rebellions are also a feature of empires, across space and time. Although as Peter Garnsey and Dick Whittaker have explained with particular reference to Roman imperialism:

> Resistance within the empire was not to be expected, and did not come, from the évolué, who despite his provincialism was committed to the values of the empire, and was prepared, even anxious, to participate in the exercise of power and the economic exploitation of the mass of provincials... the spirit of rebellion was by and large the preserve of the poor and the fringe members of Roman provincial society. Their resistance was the least likely to be effective.[58]

However, the authority of the state was not invariably an issue. Barend ter Haar shows that throughout society religious cults could punish deviant behaviour without recourse to formal law, invoking divine retribution while on the whole adhering to accepted Confucianist moral canons. There thus appears to be no simple formula to capture the multiple movements of law between rulers, the populace, and intermediary groups, as well as among many contesting corporations at each of these levels.

Conclusion

Empires and states in East Asia, West Asia, and Europe adhered to distinct and different moral and religious codes. These codes affected the ideals and practices of rulership, as well as the position of the ruler in law making and justice. Yet, despite such major differences, the same questions can be asked in each of the concrete historical contexts brought together in this volume. These regions, moreover, were far from static. Sanctified moral traditions of law and governance were constantly—unobtrusively or conspicuously, consciously or unknowingly—adapted to fit changing social and political realities. Within the geographical horizons of East

---

57 Twining, 'A Post-Westphalian Conception of Law', 212.

58 Peter Garnsey and Dick Whittaker, 'Introduction' in Peter Garnsey and Dick Whittaker, *Imperialism in the Ancient World* (Cambridge, 1978), 1–6: 6.

Asia, West Asia and Europe, a permanent process of example and imitation took place, whereas contacts among the major regions of the Eurasian continent exerted influence more incidentally. Królikowska's study of 'Mongol' law and Ottoman influences in the Crimean Khanate highlights one of these zones of contact.

Rulers and legal specialists had a marked role in the adaptation of legal traditions. The position of each of these groups and their changing relationships form an important part of our comparative effort. The convergence of religious and legal roles in Europe and the Islamicate world gave the agents of law a sanctified power that could serve as a bulwark against the ruler. The agents and specialists of law in these regions, moreover, never entirely overlapped with the rulers' administration. In China, where the remarkably developed though thinly spread Confucian bureaucracy was itself responsible for justice, the learned scholar-officials conventionally maintained a level of independence, and the household (or inner court) never absorbed the state (or outer court). The Confucian moral code, moreover, stressing harmony and deference, sometimes frowned upon a strictly 'legalist' stance. On the whole, however, Chinese emperors at least in theory seemed to have enjoyed a greater power over their agents than most of their West Asian or European compeers.

The development of separate regional and corporate forms of law as opposed to central law has been hotly debated: was this a particular European development or a more-or-less universal phenomenon? Our volume, circumventing this potentially ideological *cul-de-sac*, instead stresses forms of participation and initiative in law in each of the regions studied. Neither at the level of moral-religious ideals, nor at the level of implementation, it seems, could law ever comfortably be monopolized by the ruler. Even in arguably the most asymmetric of power relations, the colonial context, more mixed practices emerged.

Law can be—has been and will continue to be—studied as 'placeless principle', *pace* Clifford Geertz. Thinking about 'new legal pluralism' in the context of historical empires, however, means thinking seriously about the 'local' *and* the 'central' in relation to the legal. Movement from the centre to the (provincial or colonial) periphery changes law itself; movement in time—from the Roman republic to the Empire, or indeed to the reception of Roman law in medieval Europe—again reflects change and reinterpretation. Models of legal diffusion and reception invite us to think about law as 'local knowledge', wherever we find it practiced. They also highlight the fact that law does not necessarily lie at the heart of any system of social order, 'imperial' or otherwise.

The discourse and practice of law took shape in several interacting processes, some rigidly hierarchical and top-down, others arising in competition among contesting groups within a plural legal establishment, or originating in local initiatives. Our volume stresses the permanent tension between the potentially universal, doctrinal aspect of law and its endless practical ramifications and variants; between law as an aspect of a moral-religious ideal and as an instrument in the hands of rulers; between this instrument of domination and the strategic responses it generated among both elite and subordinate echelons in society, who used law for their own purposes. This perspective is borne out in detail in the contributions to this volume. It questions the legal dimensions of the notion of 'oriental despotism'; for the student of legal systems and for the historian of rulership and empire, it raises numerous questions that need to be answered by comparative research.

PART ONE

LEGAL AUTHORITY AND IMPERIAL FRAMEWORKS

LAW, AUTHORITY AND LEGITIMACY IN THE ATHENIAN EMPIRE*

Polly Low

The existence of a connection between law and empire (both broadly defined) in fifth-century BCE Athens has long been recognised: it is a subject for comment in contemporary sources and has also been repeatedly studied in modern analyses of the Athenian Empire (and, to a lesser extent, of Athenian Law).[1] Commentators, both ancient and modern, have been interested in two aspects of legal behaviour: questions of jurisdiction (to what extent did the Athenians assert control over the subject states' legal processes and, in particular, over issues of trial and punishment) and questions of legislation (how and why did the Athenians create laws for their empire and for individual states within the empire). In practice, these two aspects can be hard to disentangle, particularly since the former type of legal intervention is often (although not always) dependent on the latter, and the following discussion will deal with both.

---

* My thanks to Caroline Humfress for the invitation to contribute to this volume, to Peter Liddel and Robert Pitt for sharing with me their expertise on fifth-century Attic (and non-Attic) epigraphy, and to Stephen Todd for advice on homicide. (Any errors and misunderstandings are, of course, my own responsibility.) The following abbreviations are used: *FGH*: F. Jacoby, *Die Fragmente der griechischen Historiker* (Berlin and Leiden, 1923–58). *IG* I³: D. Lewis, with L. Jeffery and E. Erxleben, *Inscriptiones Graecae*, vol. 1, 3rd ed: *Inscriptiones Atticae Euclidis anno anteriores* (Berlin, 1981–8). *IK Erythrai*: H. Engelmann and R. Merkelbach, *Die Inschriften von Erythrai und Klazomenai* (Bonn, 1972–3). RO: P.J. Rhodes and R.G. Osborne, *Greek Historical Inscriptions, 404–323 BC* (Oxford, 2003).

[1] Ancient comments: note in particular [Xenophon] (= the 'Old Oligarch') *Constitution of the Athenians* 1.16–18; Thucydides 1.77; Aristophanes *Birds* 1021–57; Isocrates 12.63–6. Significant modern studies: R.J. Hopper, 'Interstate juridical agreements in the Athenian Empire', *Journal of Hellenic Studies* 63 (1943), 35–51; G.E.M. de Ste Croix, 'Notes on jurisdiction in the Athenian Empire, I', *Classical Quarterly* 11 (1961), 94–112; *id.* 'Notes on jurisdiction in the Athenian Empire, II', *Classical Quarterly* 11 (1961), 268–80; R. Meiggs, *The Athenian Empire* (Oxford, 1972), ch. 12; C. Koch, *Volksbeschlüsse in Seebundangelegenheiten: das Verfahrensrecht Athens im ersten attischen Seebund* (Frankfurt am Main, 1991) [*non vidi*]. From a legal perspective: S.C. Todd, *The Shape of Athenian Law* (Oxford, 1995), 329–32; D.M. MacDowell, *The Law in Classical Athens* (London, 1978), 224–8.

This essay also seeks to ask the same basic question about both of these fields of activity: how did the Athenians legitimise their legal intervention in the affairs of their allies? Accounts of the processes of legislation and jurisdiction within Greek cities (especially Athens) place considerable emphasis on the importance of citizen participation in the creation and, particularly, enforcement of laws: a well-known Demosthenic soundbite claims that the laws themselves have no power; only the willing co-operation of the Athenian citizens ensures that wrongdoing is punished:

> And what is the strength of the laws? If one of you is wronged and cries aloud, will the laws run up and be at his side to assist him? No; they are only written texts and incapable of such action. Wherein then resides their power? In yourselves, if only you support them and make them all-powerful to help him who needs them. So the laws are strong through you and you through the laws (Demosthenes 21.224–5, tr. Vince).[2]

What I aim to explore here is whether that view of legal authority has any place in an imperial context, particularly in an empire which (on many accounts) relied extensively on brute force to impose its political and military authority on the subject states.[3] I will suggest that we can see the Athenians employing two quite different, though not necessarily incompatible, strategies. One approach is to effectively sidestep the problem of creating specifically imperial legal authority by treating imperial jurisdiction and legislation as, in essence, an integrated part of Athenian domestic law. But it is also possible to see traces of a rather more inclusive policy, in which Athenian legal activity is more closely integrated with the structures, procedures and personnel of the subject states.

Before beginning this investigation, some brief comments on terminology and evidence might be useful. Two features of the evidence for Athenian relations with their subject allies should be highlighted. First, the material is predominantly epigraphic, it is far from complete (that is: we have only a tiny proportion of the records which originally existed; and many of those records are themselves very fragmentary), and it is often of disputed date. This last characteristic is particularly frustrating: both

---

[2] See V. Hunter, *Policing Athens: Social Control in the Attic Lawsuits, 420–320 BC* (Princeton, N.J., 1994), ch. 5.

[3] A picture of the empire which is ultimately traceable back to Thucydides' *History of the Peloponnesian War*. For an attempt to argue against the Thucydidean view, see G.E.M. de Ste Croix, 'The character of the Athenian Empire', *Historia* 3 (1954/5), 1–41; in support of Thucydides (and against de Ste Croix), D.W. Bradeen, 'The popularity of the Athenian empire', *Historia* 9 (1960), 257–69; J. de Romilly, 'Thucydides and the cities of the Athenian empire', *Bulletin of the Institute of Classical Studies* 13 (1966), 1–12.

common sense and other historical evidence suggest that the Athenian Empire will have changed considerably over its roughly seventy-year history (not least because, certainly in its very early years and perhaps for rather longer, it presented itself as a military alliance rather than a fully-fledged empire), but chronological uncertainty, coupled with the lacunose nature of the record, makes it very hard to chart developments with any confidence.[4] Second, the material is almost exclusively created by Athens: this is itself a historically significant point whose implications will be touched on below, but it has the unfortunate consequence that any attempt to explore allied perceptions of Athenian rule will often be somewhat speculative.

Turning to terminology, a point worth emphasising is that there is considerable vagueness about what exactly counts as a 'law' in this period. In fifth-century Athens, the process for creating laws (*nomoi*) was formally identical to the process for creating short-term decrees or regulations, and the choice of which label to use is often more or less subjective. Modern scholarship tends to talk in terms of 'regulations' rather than 'law' when discussing Athenian attempts to control their empire, but it is not at all clear that the Athenians, or their subject allies, would have thought in the same categories.[5] To confuse matters further, treaties and other interstate agreements were also created by this same process (that is, they were passed as decrees of the Athenian assembly) and, in formal terms, cannot be distinguished from either domestic laws or interstate regulations. Some of the practical and symbolic implications of these procedural features of law-making will be discussed further below; for now, it should be noted that the account which follows will take a deliberately broad approach to deciding what counts as a 'law', on the grounds that anything which was passed as a decree in the fifth-century BCE might (to fifth-century eyes) have qualified for that label.

---

[4] Two very useful recent studies survey the current state of play in the chronology (particularly the epigraphic chronology) of the Athenian Empire: P.J. Rhodes, 'After the three-bar sigma controversy: the history of Athenian imperialism reassessed', *Classical Quarterly* 58 (2008), 500–6; N. Papazarkadas, 'Epigraphy and the Athenian empire: re-shuffling the chronological cards', in J. Ma, N. Papazarkadas, and R. Parker, eds., *Interpreting the Athenian Empire* (London, 2009) 67–88. In what follows (except where stated otherwise), I accept Rhodes' proposed datings for the inscriptions discussed.

[5] See, e.g, Aristophanes *Birds* 1035ff (discussed below, p. 35), in which the seller of decrees (*psephismata*) attempts to impose laws (*nomoi*) on a subject state. For further discussion, see M.H. Hansen, '*Nomos* and *psephisma* in fourth-century Athens', in *The Athenian Eccelesia: a Collection of Articles*, vol. 1 (Copenhagen, 1983), 161–77 (at 162–3).

Centralisation: Enslaving the Allies?

The most well-known contemporary summary of Athenian imperial legal policy is that of the so-called 'Old Oligarch', a critic both of democracy and of empire, who probably wrote some time between 430 and 413 BCE.[6] This author describes an Athenian policy of widespread, systematic meddling in the legal affairs of its subject states; his account is worth quoting in full:

> Also in another point the Athenian people are thought to act ill-advisedly: they force the allies to sail to Athens for judicial proceedings. But they reason in reply that the Athenian people benefit from this. First, from the deposits at law they receive their dicastic pay through the year. Then, sitting at home without going out in ships, they manage the affairs of the allied cities; in the courts they protect the democrats and ruin their opponents. If the allies were each to hold trials locally, they would, in view of their annoyance with the Athenians, ruin those of their citizens who were the leading friends of the Athenian people. In addition, the people at Athens profit in the following ways when trials involving allies are held in Athens: first, the one per-cent tax in the Peiraeus brings in more for the city; secondly, if anyone has lodgings to rent, he does better, and so does anyone who lets out on hire a team of animals or a slave; further, the heralds of the assembly do better when the allies are in town. In addition, were the allies not to go away for judicial proceedings, they would honour only those of the Athenians who sail out from the city, namely generals, trierarchs, and ambassadors. As it is now, each one of the allies is compelled to flatter the Athenian populace from the realization that judicial action for anyone who comes to Athens is in the hands of none other than the populace (this indeed is the law at Athens); in the courts he is obliged to entreat whoever comes in and to grasp him by the hand. In this way the allies have become instead the slaves of the Athenian people (*Constitution of the Athenians* 1.16–18, tr. Marchant).

There are good reasons to be sceptical about the reliability of this text (in general as well as in this particular passage). As his (nick-)name suggests, the writer is highly partisan, and his eagerness to tell a damning story has certainly led to exaggeration and misrepresentation: it is extremely unlikely, for example, that jury pay was entirely funded from legal fees paid by litigants from subject states.[7] Moreover, his account, while sweeping

---

[6] For the date, see (briefly) R.G. Osborne, *The Old Oligarch: Pseudo-Xenophon's Constitution of the Athenians* (London, 2004), 4–10, who also summarises other possible views.

[7] 'An absurd exaggeration', according to J.L. Marr and P.J. Rhodes, *The 'Old Oligarch'* (Oxford, 2008), 91. The best argument against a necessary connection with imperial revenues is that jury pay far outlives the Athenian Empire (M.H. Hansen, *The Athenian*

in its condemnation, is also surprisingly narrow in its focus. Legal intervention, for the Old Oligarch, can be equated with centralisation and more specifically with *physical* centralisation: the Athenians assert their control over the legal processes of the subject states by transferring all (it is implied) legal activity from the periphery to the centre of the Empire.

But although this version is exaggerated, it is not a complete fabrication. Other evidence shows that the Athenians did require certain legal procedures to take place in Athens, even if the motivation for centralisation might sometimes be less straightforwardly exploitative or coercive than the Old Oligarch suggests. There is good evidence that Athens acted unilaterally to insist that certain types of case were transferred from allied states to Athens: these could be categorised by type of crime (murder—particularly murder of Athenian citizens or those friendly to Athens)[8] or by the penalty which they carried (death, exile, loss of citizen rights).[9] It is easy to see why Athenians would be eager to intervene in such cases: their concern (as the Old Oligarch must be right to point out) would be not only to ensure that those who were hostile to Athens were properly punished but also, and perhaps more importantly, that their supporters were not subject to malicious or excessive prosecutions. The use of the law courts as a venue for the covert (or even quite blatant) continuation of political or personal feuding is very well attested within Athens itself,[10] and the Athenians were almost certainly right to worry that their subject allies would engage in similar behaviour if given the chance. The opening

Democracy in the Age of Demosthenes (Oxford, 1991), 188–9). Nevertheless, the assertion of a connection between jury pay and imperial revenue does appear elsewhere (e.g. Aristophanes *Wasps* 520–1); on this perception, see L. Kallet-Marx, 'Money talks: rhetor, demos, and the resources of the Athenian Empire', in R.G. Osborne and S. Hornblower, eds., *Ritual, Finance, Politics: Athenian Democratic Accounts Presented to David Lewis* (Oxford, 1994), 227–51.

[8] Murder of those friendly to Athens: this is a protection offered in a number Athenian decrees of proxeny (a status, roughly equivalent to the modern role of honorary consul, offered to Athenian supporters in subject cities). For examples, see A.S. Henry, *Honours and Privileges in Athenian Decrees: the Principal Formulae of Athenian Honorary Decrees* (New York, 1983), 168–71; for the connection with penalties for murder of Athenian citizens, de Ste Croix, 'Notes on jurisdiction, II', 274–5; Meiggs, *Empire*, 227–8.

[9] The clearest example can be found in the regulations for Chalkis, *IG* I^3 40, lines 70–6, discussed in detail by J.M. Balcer, *The Athenian Regulations for Chalkis: Studies in Imperial Law* (Wiesbaden, 1978), 102–18 (although his suggestion that the Chalkis decree implies the existence of an empire-wide regulation transferring such cases to Athens is not persuasive). Further (more fragmentary) cases are discussed in de Ste Croix, 'Notes on jurisdiction II', 270–2.

[10] See, e.g, D.J. Cohen, *Law, Violence, and Community in Classical Athens* (Cambridge, 1995), esp. ch. 5.

stages of the violent civil war (and anti-Athenian insurrection) in Corcyra, for example, were played out in the law courts: the pro-Athenian Peithias was put on trial 'on a charge of enslaving Corcyra to Athens' (Thucydides 3.70); on acquittal, he brought a counter-charge of sacrilege against his accusers; in order to avoid punishment for these (alleged) offences, his opponents assassinated Peithias and his supporters; from there, events deteriorated into full-scale *stasis*.

Closing off this potentially disruptive forum for political unrest, and political victimisation, makes impeccable sense from a perspective of imperial control. However, it seems that the Athenians never applied this policy universally or even systematically. Our evidence is incomplete, but enough survives to suggest an approach which was, for the most part, both reactive and inconsistent: Athenian actions seem to have been prompted by specific events and tailored to the circumstances of specific cities or individuals. Athenian supporters in allied cities might be rewarded (and, presumably, their loyalty reinforced) with offers of special legal protection: the honours for a certain Apollonophanes of Colophon, for example, stipulate that it is not permissible for him to be punished 'without [*sc.* the approval of] the Athenian *demos*'.[11] Cities whose loyalty to Athens was questionable might be penalised by losing the right to control certain types of case or punishment. The regulations for the city of Chalkis, almost certainly imposed in the wake of an unsuccessful rebellion in 446/5, include a clause ruling that penalties of exile, loss of citizen rights, or death had to be referred to the courts in Athens.[12] Conversely, a more favourable decree for the loyal city of Samos seems to have taken care to make it explicit that Samian courts could retain control over a (similar,

---

[11] *IG* I³ 65, lines 20–2, discussed by Henry, *Honours and Privileges*, 164 (who notes only one other extant example of this clause: *IG* I³ 70); see also de Ste Croix, 'Notes on jurisdiction, II', 272–5.

[12] *IG* I³ 40, lines 70–4. The details of the process are not entirely clear: interpretation hinges on the translation of the term 'ephesis', which might imply immediate transfer to Athens of the relevant cases, or (more plausibly, in my view) might better be translated as 'appeal' (that is: an initial hearing would be held in Chalkis, but either party could appeal an unfavourable result to Athens). For this reading, see de Ste Croix, 'Notes on jurisdiction, II', 271–2; Balcer, *Regulations for Chalkis*, 108–9, makes the case for the alternative interpretation. The regulations for Miletus (*IG* I³ 21) also included clauses outlining the circumstances in which certain cases would be referred to Athens: for an (optimistic) attempt to reconstruct the relevant parts of the decree, see D.W. Bradeen and M.F. McGregor, *Studies in Fifth-Century Attic Epigraphy* (Norman, 1973), 42–8.

but not identical) range of high-profile penalties: in this case, death, exile and confiscation of property.[13]

The Athenians did, of course, pass some regulations which they intended to be binding across the whole empire, and it is in the context of those regulations that the rare examples of wholesale centralisation of certain categories of legal action can be found.[14] The notorious decree imposing a single system of coins, weights and measures on the subject cities (the so-called 'Standards Decree') stipulated that violations of the regulation were to be tried before the Heliaia (the main law court) of Athens.[15] A decree regulating the collection of the tribute similarly specified that cases of alleged embezzlement of the tribute funds should be heard in Athens: first by the Council and then by one of the Athenian courts.[16] In the case of the tribute regulations there must be an element of pragmatism in this choice of location: it would be at Athens that the funds were collected and counted, and therefore at Athens where wrongdoing was most likely to be uncovered; holding the trial in the place of the crime's discovery is not unreasonable. But that argument is harder to make for the regulations on coins and measures: while it is, theoretically, conceivable that an allied citizen might recklessly have flaunted local currency in the Athenian market place, violations against this regulation were surely much more likely to take place out in the cities of the empire. It seems preferable, therefore, to assume that the Athenian decision to try these cases in their own city was motivated by factors similar to those which prompted the removal of trials for other high-profile crimes from the subject states: these regulations were deemed to be so important (or perhaps so liable to be transgressed) that their policing and enforcement needed to be kept under close control; holding trials at Athens was a straightforward way of ensuring that level of control.

But the Athenian location of these trials has a wider significance too. As the Old Oligarch points out, a consequence of centralisation was that jurisdiction of these specific cases and general regulations fell under the control of Athenian courts. The author interprets this as a simple piece

---

[13] *IG* I³ 96, lines 6–7. Lines 7–9 of this decree seem also to have allowed Athenian intervention in some legal activities, but the text is too fragmentary to allow any certainty on what sort of actions were allowed (or under what circumstances). For brief discussion, see de Ste Croix, 'Notes on jurisdiction, II', 272 and n. 4.

[14] De Ste Croix, 'Notes on jurisdiction, II', 268–70.

[15] *IG* I³ 1453, §2–4.

[16] *IG* I³ 34, lines 31–5.

of vindictiveness: not content with depriving the allies of their legal independence, the Athenians then added insult to injury by handing control to the unruly mob that was the Athenian popular jury. There is a degree of truth in this accusation: the Athenian law court was undoubtedly an important symbol of the radical democracy, and its use in imperial jurisdiction introduced an element of explicitly democratic control of the empire that would be absent were enforcement delegated to individual Athenian officials or handed over to (possibly elite-dominated?) law courts in the subject states.[17]

There is something less narrowly ideological happening here too. By bringing these cases into this sphere, the Athenians start to dissolve the difference between domestic and foreign behaviour, and between Athenian citizens and allied subjects. The elision of the gap between Athenian citizen and subject ally could, on occasion, be almost complete. Cleinias' regulation on tribute makes it explicit that the penalties for transgression of the decree will apply equally to Athenians and to allies; both Athenians and allies are entitled to bring prosecutions against those violating the rules; and all cases will be heard before the same magistrates, and according to the same procedure, regardless of the identity of the accused or the prosecutor.[18] This example is unusual in the extent to which it aligns Athenian and ally, but it does highlight something which must have applied more widely: once cases were brought into Athenian courts, the boundary between Athens and the empire inevitably became less rigid. This need not, of course, have been a positive development, not least from the perspective of the subject state: this was not a merger on equal terms but a hostile takeover. It does, however, provide an answer to the problem of legitimisation: if we were to apply Demosthenes' question ('what is the strength of the laws?') to this field of imperial jurisdiction, then the answer would be the same as the one he provides for the domestic laws of

---

[17] On Athenian juries as symbols (and manifestations) of radical democracy, see A.J.L. Blanshard, 'What counts as the demos? Some notes on the relationship between the jury and "the People" in Classical Athens', *Phoenix* 58 (2004), 28–48. Note that in the regulations for Chalkis, the people of Chalkis are required to swear an oath of loyalty to the Athenian *demos* (*IG* I^3 40, line 21); the corresponding Athenian oath is sworn not by the assembly but by the jury (line 4). For discussion of the wider significance of this point, see M. Ostwald, 'Athens and Chalkis: a study in imperial control', *Journal of Hellenic Studies* 122 (2002), 134–43 (at 137–9). The suggestion (not implausible) that the law courts of subject states would be dominated by local anti-Athenian elites is made by de Ste Croix, 'Notes on jurisdiction, II', 272, n. 1.

[18] *IG* I^3 34, lines 31–5.

Athens: the strength of the laws rests in the power of the Athenian people to patrol and enforce them.

A similar process could be identified in the sphere of imperial legislation. An obvious, but vitally important, point is that Athenian regulations for the empire were passed in exactly the same way as Athenian regulations governing their own internal affairs: they were decrees of the Athenian *demos*, proposed and debated only by Athenians and authorised only by the Athenian assembly. Even regulations which might be relatively favourable to the allies are presented as unilaterally Athenian decisions. It is worth emphasising that the fifth-century Athenian approach was not inevitable. Athenian behaviour in the fourth century reveals the possibility of a quite different solution to the problem of imperial legislation—or in fact, two quite different solutions. One alternative employed by fourth-century Athens was to create a council (*synedrion*) of allied states and to give this body a role both in creating laws and regulations, and in enforcing regulations already passed.[19] (The fifth-century empire had a joint assembly [*koine sunodos*] of allied states, but there is no evidence of it ever being used as an authorising body for any imperial regulations or of it functioning as a law court.)[20] The other fourth-century method was to persuade (or require) allied legislative bodies to pass regulations which suited Athens' wishes, an approach best illustrated in a set of decrees passed by the cities of Ceos and regulating those cities' trade in *miltos* (ruddle).[21] The substance of this regulation is dominated by the interests of Athens, and it seems clear that the Athenians have, in effect, dictated the terms of the agreement to the states involved (the decrees open with a reference to 'the things which the Athenians say…').[22] But the

[19] Enforcement of regulations: violations of certain terms of the 'Prospectus' of the League are to be heard by the *synedrion* (RO 22, lines 41–6); creation of regulations: see RO 29 (League and Athenian regulations for Paros), though note that even here the role of the *synedrion* seems to be subordinate to that of Athens (for further discussion, see P.A. Low, *Interstate Relations in Classical Greece: Morality and Power* (Cambridge, 2007), 92–3).

[20] For the existence of the *sunodos*, see Thucydides 1.97, Diodorus Siculus 11.70.4. J.A.O. Larsen, 'The constitution and original purpose of the Delian League', *Harvard Studies in Classical Philology* 51 (1940), 175–213 (at 196) speculates that the common council must have acted as a law court for cases involving enforcement of imperial regulations; if this happened, it left no trace in our sources.

[21] RO 40: the inscription (which was set up in Athens) is a dossier of decrees passed in the Cean cities of Cartheia, Coresius and Iulis. The oppressive nature of the substance and structure of these regulations is argued for by R.G. Osborne, 'Religion, imperial politics, and the offering of freedom to slaves', in V. Hunter and J. Edmondson, eds., *Law and Social Status in Classical Athens* (Oxford, 2000), 75–92 (at 86–9).

[22] RO 40, lines 9–10 (decree of Coresus), 25–6 (decree of Iulis).

immediate authority for the regulation derives not from Athens but from the governing bodies of the various states. This must have been a deliberate decision, and it seems reasonable to assume that the Athenians hoped that it would assist both the introduction and the enforcement of this (presumably unpopular) piece of legislation. It is also an approach which fits well with fourth-century Athens' persistent, albeit never entirely convincing, attempts to deny that they still harboured any aggressive imperial ambitions.[23] Conversely, the apparent absence of this approach from the fifth-century empire also seems to fit well with the general image of the fifth-century empire as an entirely domineering force, untroubled by being perceived as a 'tyrant', rejoicing in Athens' own unfettered power.[24] If, as the Old Oligarch suggests, the transfer of cases to Athens provided one venue in which the Athenian *demos* could enslave their subjects, the creation of regulations allowed that same *demos* (sitting in the assembly rather than the law court) an equivalent level of unmitigated control over the allies. But here too, as in the use of Athenian law courts, it is possible to see a wider significance: by asserting that a decree of the Athenian people had authority over all the cities of the empire, the Athenians implicitly subsume those *poleis* into their own legislative sphere of influence.

Imperial Outreach: Coercion or Collaboration?

The validity of such an approach is, however, based on a large, and so far unsubstantiated, assumption: how (if at all) is that inwardly-focussed Athenian assertion of power—made in Athens, by Athenians, to a primarily Athenian audience—projected outwards into the empire? The Athenians may have been perfectly able to create and enforce imperial legislation within the confines of their own city, but such activity would be futile if no Greek outside the boundaries of Attica was paying attention to events in the Athenian courts or the assembly-place. How, then, did the Athenians attempt to ensure that their regulations were obeyed in the subject cities, and how did they see to it that decisions made in their law courts—particularly those which needed to be implemented back in

23 Denial of imperialism: see above all the 'Prospectus' of the Second Athenian League (RO 22); for contemporary scepticism about Athens' sincerity, see, e.g., Theopompus (*FGH* 115), F98.

24 For Athens as imperial tyrant, see above all the speeches of Thucydides' *History*: e.g. Pericles at 2.63, Cleon at 3.37.

the subject cities (confiscations of property, for example, or sentences of exile) were actually put into effect?[25]

One answer to that question—and probably the dominant one in our literary sources—is that control was created above all through coercion, and that this coercion was exercised by Athenian officials, sent out in order to enforce Athenian laws. This is the opposite process, in spatial terms, to the one described by the Old Oligarch, but it is based on a similar underlying principle: only Athenians can be trusted to ensure that the allies follow the rules. This approach is famously caricatured in Aristophanes' *Birds*, in a scene in which the play's heroes find their newly-created city of Cloudcuckooland suddenly visited by meddlesome Athenian officials: an *episkopos* (inspector), dispatched by an Athenian decree (1024–5), followed closely (1037) by a 'decree-seller' (also from Athens). The latter is portrayed as 'bringing new laws (*nomoi*)' from Athens to the new settlement, one of which parodies the Standards Decree: 'the people of Cloudcuckooland are to use the same weights and measures and decrees as the people of Olophyxos...' (1040).[26] Attempts to resist this decree are met with a further barrage of attempts at coercive control: the *episkopos* tries to summon the Cloudcuckoolanders to Athens for trial; the decree-seller produces further regulations banning attacks on Athenian officials (1046–53).

The implication of this scene is that the task of enforcing Athenian regulations overseas rested with visiting officials, and that these officials received their authority from the Athenian *demos*. And while the 'decree-seller' is a piece of Aristophanic fantasy, the position of *episkopos* did in fact exist and even seems to have fulfilled a role which is broadly similar to that of Aristophanes' official: visiting allied states and ensuring that regulations passed in Athens were enforced out in the empire.[27] The clearest example of this comes in the Athenian regulations for Erythrae

[25] Note that the scope of regulations might extend beyond the primary 'target' city: the regulations for Erythrae, for example, specify that a murderer, if sentenced to exile, will be banished from all cities in the alliance (*IG* I[3] 14, line 31).

[26] A connection originally hypothesised (before the discovery of the epigraphic material) by U. von Wilamowitz-Moellendorff, 'Von des attischen Reiches Herrlichkeit', in A. Kiessling and U. von Wilamowitz-Moellendorff, eds., *Aus Kydathen* (Berlin, 1880), 1–96 (at 30). The connection between the Aristophanic passage and the Standards Decree is further discussed by D.M. Lewis, 'The Athenian coinage decree', in *Selected Papers in Greek and Near-Eastern History*, P.J. Rhodes, ed. (Cambridge, 2002), 116–30.

[27] Evidence for Athenian officials in the subject cities is collected by J.M. Balcer, 'Imperial magistrates in the Athenian Empire', *Historia* 25 (1976), 257–87.

(probably of the 450s), which (among other things) establish a new constitution for the city: Athenian *episkopoi*, in conjunction with the (Athenian) garrison-commander, are instructed to ensure that the part of the regulation which establishes the city's new governing Council is properly put in place.[28] *Episkopoi* also appear in Cleinias' regulations for the payment of tribute (a text probably to be dated to the 420s) where they are given a role in checking that tribute is properly collected and transferred to Athens; again, the responsibility is shared with other Athenian officials, in this case the Council in Athens, and Athenian officials (*archontes*: an unhelpfully vague term) in the allied cities.[29]

These officials seem to have an almost symbiotic relationship with the decrees which they were charged with enforcing. On the one hand, they are responsible for upholding Athenian regulations in the subject cities; on the other, their authority to do so derives, at least in part, from those same regulations. The Athenians have created a house of judicial cards: not, perhaps, a terribly elaborate one but nevertheless a rather fragile structure. And it is here that the authority of the decrees themselves—and in particular, the monuments on which the decrees were inscribed—has been seen as playing a crucial stabilising role. Decrees, though passed in and deriving their legitimacy from Athens, included provision for their promulgation and commemoration far beyond the centre of the empire. This was in part a process of oral communication (a series of heralds are dispatched to announce the Standards Decree in the cities, for example)[30] but, more importantly, also involved the creation of a permanent inscribed monument. Again, the Standards Decree illustrates this neatly: the decree includes a clause stating that it should be inscribed on stone and set up in the market place; if the subject states fail to do this for themselves then the Athenians will do it for them.[31] Other regulations similarly specify that copies should be set up in the territory of the state to which they apply:

---

[28] *IG* I³ 14, lines 13–14. *Episkopoi* are also mentioned in another Athenian decree for Erythrae (*IG* I³ 15, line 19), but the context is not preserved.

[29] *IG* I³ 34, lines 5–11.

[30] *IG* I³ 1453, §9. For further examples and discussion, see P.P. Liddel, 'Epigraphy, legislation and power within the Athenian Empire', *Bulletin of the Institute of Classical Studies* 53 (2010), 99–128 (at 100–1).

[31] *IG* I³ 1453, §10. The findspots of the fragments of the decree demonstrate that this clause was put into effect: no fragments have been found in Athens (although a copy of the decree should have been erected there); single fragments have been found in Cos, Siphnos, Smyrna, Odessa (the last two have possibly been moved from their original location); two fragments in Syme and Aphytis; a fragment from Hamaxitos (*IG* I³ 1454 *ter*) should possibly also be associated with this decree.

a copy of the regulations for Chalkis was to be erected in that city's sanctuary of Zeus Olympios, for example.[32] The placing of the decree in sacred space should be seen as a further means of bolstering the authority of the text, partly by providing it with the religious protection associated with the location and also by providing another, implicit, indication of the reach of Athenian power: even the city's sanctuaries—typically the most tightly controlled of spaces—were not immune from Athenian intervention.[33] The Athenian general Nicias is claimed to have said that he set up an inscription to act as a 'guard' over a religious dedication which he had made on the island of Delos,[34] and it is tempting to think that a similar sentiment underpinned Athenian epigraphic activity in the subject states: the inscribed monuments stood as permanent symbols of the reach of Athenian power, as reminders of Athens' commitment to asserting that power, and as warnings of the consequences of disobedience.[35]

It need not follow that the allies were always willing to accept the monuments in that spirit: Aristophanes' Cloudcuckoolanders (infamously) reminisce about 'that night when you crapped on the column where the [sc. Athenian] decrees were posted' (*Birds* 1054), and vandalism of local copies of Athenian inscribed decrees, while not directly attested in the fifth century, is surely very likely to have occurred.[36] We might wonder, too, whether occasional visits from Athenian inspectors would have been a sufficient deterrent against defection from (or simple ignoring of) imperial regulations, although lack of evidence makes it hard to reach any firm conclusions on this question. While numerous full-scale revolts from the

---

[32] *IG* I^3 40, lines 61–3.

[33] The more diplomatic procedure would be for a state to request permission to set up a copy of its decrees in the territory of another state: this seems to have happened in the Athenian settlement with Colophon (*IG* I^3 37, lines 40–3) but is otherwise uncommon in fifth-century imperial decrees. See further, G. Lalonde, 'The publication and transmission of Greek diplomatic documents', PhD University of Washington (1971), 159–69.

[34] Plutarch *Nicias* 3.6.

[35] On inscriptions as symbols of Athenian imperial power, see R. Thomas, 'Literacy and the city-state in archaic and classical Greece', in A. Bowman and G. Woolf, eds., *Literacy and Power in the Ancient World* (Cambridge, 1994), 33–50 (at 45); C. Pébarthe, *Cité, démocratie et écriture: histoire de l'alphabétisation d'Athènes à l'époque classique* (Paris, 2006), 307–10; Liddel, 'Epigraphy, legislation and power', 100–5.

[36] The regulations for Miletus might have included a clause specifically barring destruction of the inscribed decree: '[And the Milesians] will neither destroy nor deface for false intent [the inscribed stele?]' (*IG* I^3 21, lines 47–8; tr. (adapted) from Balcer, 'Imperial magistrates', 265). The best example of anti-Athenian epigraphic destruction comes in the fourth-century Athenian decree RO 39, lines 27–45: punishments are imposed on rebels from the Cean city of Iulis, who (among other crimes) have destroyed Athenian stelae carrying regulations for their city.

empire are well attested,[37] acts of day-to-day resistance or subversion are harder to trace, although it is tempting to infer their existence from scattered pieces of circumstantial evidence (the creation of repeated sets of Athenian regulations on the same or similar subjects;[38] the lack of any clear sign in the numismatic record that the Standards Decree had any effect on the coins used in the fifth-century Aegean;[39] the fact that Aristophanes could make jokes about the ineffectiveness of Athens' meddling officials).[40] Promulgation of decrees from the centre of the empire was certainly a method which the Athenians hoped would carry sufficient authority to enforce compliance, but it is possible that this approach might have been based more on optimism (or over-confidence) than reality.

However, not all attempts at imperial legislation were effected at arm's length. Some Athenian regulations attempted not only to control the behaviour of the subject states, but also to establish new political or judicial structures within the allied cities. Athens' fondness for establishing democratic governments in the allied cities has been much discussed (though it was probably a less comprehensive or systematic policy than has sometimes been assumed);[41] evidence for any such wholesale restructuring of allied judicial systems is more elusive, although occasional examples do appear. One text which does stand out is the decree which sets out Athenian relations with the Euboean city of Hestiaea. Here, it seems that the Athenians did try to establish permanent judicial structures for the city and to specify quite closely the ways in which those structures would function. The text is too incomplete to allow for certainty about all the details, but it seems that there is to be a panel of judges (*dikastai*) who will operate both

---

[37] For a brief catalogue, see de Ste Croix, 'The character of the Athenian empire', 4–10.

[38] E.g. Tribute: *IG* I^3 34, followed shortly after by *IG* I^3 71. Standards: *IG* I^3 1453, §12 contains a reference to a 'previous decree', presumably on the same subject; the epigraphic fragments of the decree (detailed in n. 31 above) certainly preserve different versions of the text, and might possibly derive from different decrees (for discussion of the possibilities, see M. Hatzopoulos, 'Νέο ἀπότμημα ἀπὸ τὴν Ἄφυτι τοῦ ἀττικοῦ ψηφίσματος περὶ νομίσματος, σταθμῶν καὶ μέτρων', *Horos* 14–16 (2000–3), 31–43 (at 35–7); A.P. Matthaiou, *The Athenian Empire on Stone Revisited* (Athens, 2010), 10–11). Erythrae: *IG* I^3 14, 15 (probably both to be dated around the late 450s, although the precise chronology is unclear).

[39] Lewis, 'Coinage decree', 128–30; J. Kroll, 'What about coinage?', in J. Ma, N. Papazarkadas and R. Parker, eds., *Interpreting the Athenian Empire* (London, 2009), 195–209 (at 201–3).

[40] See above, p. 35.

[41] See now R. Brock, 'Did the Athenian Empire promote democracy?', in J. Ma, N. Papazarkadas and R. Parker, eds., *Interpreting the Athenian Empire* (London, 2009), 149–66.

in Hestiaea and in the neighbouring settlements of Dium and Ellopia.[42] But Hestiaea is perhaps a special case. These regulations should almost certainly be connected with the city's revolt of 446/5, in response to which the Athenians expelled the entire native population and replaced them with Athenian settlers.[43] The formal status of these settlers is uncertain (it is not clear whether they retained their Athenian citizenship or whether they were constituted as an independent colony), but the fact that the Athenians had, essentially, established a new political community in Hestiaea might explain the unusually close level of legal and judicial interference in this instance.[44]

Even in this decree, however, the level of Athenian control does not seem to have been absolute: lines 104–6 of the decree are restored as saying that the Hestiaean officials will initially be appointed from Athens but that subsequent boards of magistrates will be selected by the Hestiaeans themselves. While the accuracy of the restoration cannot be established with absolute certainty, it does fit with other indications in the document that responsibility for various activities will be split between Athens (and Athenian officials) and Hestiaea (and local officials). And this approach is in line with Athenian behaviour elsewhere. In Erythrae, for example (as already noted) Athenian *episkopoi* are dispatched to ensure that the first Council of the new (Athenian-imposed) democracy is properly enrolled; 'for the future', however, this task will revert to the Erythraean Council (in collaboration with, or under the surveillance of, the Athenian

[42] On the legal arrangements for these (probably dependent) *poleis*, see R.J. Hopper, 'Interstate juridical agreements in the Athenian Empire', *Journal of Hellenic Studies* 63 (1943), 35–51 (at 48–9); on the decree's legal provisions as a whole, M.F. McGregor, 'Athens and Hestiaia', in *Studies in Attic Epigraphy, History and Topography. Presented to Eugene Vanderpool* (Princeton, 1988), 101–11.

[43] The revolt and its consequences are described in Thucydides 1.114. H.B. Mattingly, 'Two notes on Athenian financial documents', in *The Athenian Empire Restored* (Ann Arbor, 1996), 205–314 (at 246–8) suggests that this decree should be disassociated from that revolt and placed instead in the 420s, but this argument has not received much support (see, briefly, Rhodes, 'After the three-barred sigma controversy, 504–5); even if Mattingly is correct, the decree must post-date the dispatch of the Athenian settlers.

[44] The regulations for Miletus (*IG* I[3] 21) also included some quite detailed regulations for the conduct of legal processes in that city, which are to be implemented by a board of five Athenian officials. But it is unclear whether these are (as at Hestiaea) intended to be long-term arrangements or whether the Athenians are simply concerned with the short-term measures required to restore order. The fact that the appointment of the five officials seems to be a one-off process and that they are not permitted to refuse the appointment (lines 4–6), might suggest that the latter alternative is more likely, but the state of the text makes certainty impossible.

garrison-commander).[45] The Erythrae decree goes on to set out various regulations on legal process and punishment, but the *episkopoi* have no role—or no explicit role—in enforcing these aspects of the decree. It seems reasonable to infer that, here too, responsibility for this task would have passed to local officials, a hypothesis which might receive some support from another decree, this time passed by the Erythraeans themselves.[46] This Erythraean decree includes various regulations concerning procedures for prosecution (probably of magistrates) and scrutiny of citizens. The date of the decree is unknown, and it is not clear whether it precedes or postdates the Athenian intervention, but a reference to a jury drawn from the Council and consisting of at least sixty-one members might imply that the Athenian-imposed Council of 120 was now in place: on this model, at least half of the Council would be required to serve on the jury.[47] If this reconstruction of the chronology is correct, then it seems that the Erythraeans, although functioning in the overall context of an Athenian-imposed political system, retained the flexibility to create their own judicial processes and structures within that system. This Erythraean decree would therefore provide good evidence for the persistence of a high level of local legal autonomy, even after a major act of Athenian intervention, as well as for the fact that the success of such interventions relied on the co-operation of local officials. It is important to remember, too, that the level of Athenian intervention visible at Erythrae is probably atypical. There must have been some—probably even a majority—of states in the Athenian Empire which never became the target of such focussed interference. There were certainly states with no permanent Athenian official presence at all: the possibility of such a situation is demonstrated in, of all places, the highly interventionist Standards Decree, which stipulates that 'if there are no Athenian governors, the chief magistrates (i.e.: local magistrates) [of each city shall perform all that is in the] decree'.[48]

These hints of collaboration and co-operation between Athenians and subject allies are worth pursuing a bit further. A recent study of Athenian imperial regulation has persuasively argued that, while the Athenian

---

[45] *IG* I^3 14, line 14–15.

[46] *IK Erythrai* 2.

[47] *IK Erythrai* 2, A, lines 24–5. The connection with the size of the Council is made by the text's editors (*ad loc.*), although they prefer to place this decree before the Athenian intervention (in which case, it might follow that the influence works the other way: the Athenian decision on the appropriate size of the Council is informed by existing Erythraean structures).

[48] *IG* I^3 1454, §4.

decrees for the empire may well have seemed alien in some respects (particularly in their length and complexity), they also contained elements which might have been quite familiar to their target audience. The Erythrae decree, for example, uses a term for prosecution (*dioxis*) which is rare in Athenian epigraphic texts but which is attested in legal regulations from Erythrae and from the nearby city of Teos; the Athenians were perhaps, therefore, employing local Ionian legal terminology in their regulations for the Erythraeans.[49] The use of oaths as a way of ensuring loyalty to a set of regulations also seems to have been a fairly widespread habit and one which would have been familiar to the allies before the appearance in their cities of Athenian decrees which insisted on similar oath-taking routines.[50]

This familiarity could affect both allied and Athenian attitudes. It might have made (at least some) allies more willing to accept the legitimacy of Athenian legislation since the regulations were couched in terms which were not completely alien to their own customs. From an Athenian perspective, the fact that there was not necessarily a massive gulf between local and Athenian practice might have made their policy of delegation to local officials seem more workable (or, to put it another way, made it seem less essential to exercise detailed, hands-on control over every aspect of jurisdiction in the subject cities). Concessions to local customs might even have extended to more substantive matters. The regulations for Erythrae include clauses which specify the penalties to be imposed in cases where a citizen of Erythrae kills another citizen: either the death penalty or exile.[51] These punishments are similar to those which would apply were such a crime committed in Athens, but they are not identical: the Erythraeans have a more restricted range of options (there is no provision for judging something to be accidental homicide, for example), and the process by which the choice between death or exile is made seems much more open-ended than is the case in Athens (although the text is, admittedly, both elliptical and damaged at this point).[52] It is hard to know

---

49 Liddel, 'Epigraphy, legislation and power', 118–22.

50 Loyalty oaths in Athenian imperial regulations: *IG* I^3 14 (Erythrae), 37 (Colophon), 39 (Eretria), 40 (Chalkis), 48 (Samos); further examples in Meiggs, *Athenian Empire*, Appendix 16. In non-Athenian contexts: Liddel, 'Epigraphy, legislation and power', 120.

51 *IG* I^3 14, lines 29–32. The interpretation is suggested by L. Highby, *The Erythrae Decree: Contributions to the Early History of the Delian League and the Peloponnesian Confederacy* (Leipzig, 1936), 26.

52 Athenian penalties for homicide are discussed by D.M. MacDowell, *Athenian Homicide Law in the Age of the Orators* (Manchester, 1963), 110–29; Todd, *Shape of Athenian Law*, 271–6.

exactly how this gap between Erythraean and Athenian practice should be interpreted: a negative reading would be that the Athenians were in some sense short-changing the people of Erythrae by offering them a stripped-down (or dumbed-down) version of the Athenian system of punishment. But a more positive reading might be that these punishments were used because they were the ones with which the Erythraeans were already familiar, and that in this clause the Athenians are not imposing a new or alien set of penalties, but simply confirming the Erythraeans' right to continue to treat these offences as they previously had done.[53] The latter approach would be broadly consistent with the one adopted in regulations for Chalkis: some trials are transferred to Athens, but it is explicitly ruled that those cases which remain in Chalkis are to be tried in accordance with local laws.[54]

More generally, these pieces of overlapping practice should be set in the wider context of a legal world in which judicial co-operation and collaboration between cities was not unknown. The practice of establishing bilateral inter-polis agreements (*symbolai*), which set out procedures for dealing with legal cases involving citizens of different states, was very probably in existence before the development of the Athenian Empire and certainly continued to operate during (and after) this period; it was not restricted to Athens, nor was it a feature only of imperial legal relationships.[55] Although the rhetoric of *autonomia* (legal and political independence) was a powerful part of the ideology of the Greek city-state, in practice many Greek *poleis* would be quite familiar with the legal procedures of other Greek states and also familiar with the possibility that their own citizens might be subject to another state's laws. Athenian imperial intervention is, of course, qualitatively quite different from the sort of arrangement seen in *symbola* agreements, above all in the unilateral

---

[53] Lack of evidence for the nature of early homicide laws outside Athens makes it impossible to reach a firm conclusion on this question. (The exiguous evidence is discussed by M. Gagarin, *Early Greek Law* (Berkeley, 1986), 89, n. 23).

[54] *IG* I[3] 40, lines 71–3. The qualification that local laws will be used at Chalkis 'just as for an Athenian at Athens' seems best understood not to mean that the Athenians have imposed their own laws on Chalkis, but rather that, just as an Athenian would expect to be tried by his own laws, so too a citizen of Chalkis will be judged by the laws of Chalkis. (On the lack of intervention in internal Chalkidian affairs which characterises this decree, see Ostwald, 'Athens and Chalkis'.)

[55] Generally on these agreements, see P. Gauthier, *Symbola: les étrangers et la justice dans les cités grecques* (Nancy, 1972); S. Cataldi, *Symbolai e relazioni tra le città greche nel V secolo a.C* (Pisa, 1983). For their use during the Athenian Empire, see de Ste Croix, 'Notes on jurisdiction, I'.

method by which it was created, but it is important to remember that it took place in a world in which interstate legal intervention itself was not entirely unheard of.[56]

Conclusion

This brief study has not come close to providing a comprehensive survey of the legislative and judicial activities of the Athenian Empire, but it has (I hope) done enough to show that Athenian attitudes to this question are very far from being consistent or coherent. There is certainly a strong centralising urge, which at times might even suggest that the Athenians were starting to conceptualise their empire as a single *polis*. On this model, the authority of the Athenian *demos*—whether exercised in the assembly or in the law courts—extended throughout the empire; the absence of separate legislative or judicial arrangements for the cities over which the Athenians asserted their power could be seen as a sign of the strength of Athenian imperial control rather than an indication of weakness.[57] But things look rather different when the focus shifts from the centre of the empire to its periphery: a corollary of Athens' centralising focus is that the city's power in the empire itself can, at times, seem surprisingly elusive. This is not to deny that the Athenians had the capacity to impose their will on the subject cities (and to do so extremely brutally) when they wished to do so; but I would suggest that the sort of extreme interventionism visible at (for example) Hestiaea should be thought of as an exception rather than a general rule.

This rather low-impact approach to imperial legislation and jurisdiction is in keeping with other aspects of Athenian activity in this period: there is very little Athenian imperial building outside Athens, for example, and (as noted above) probably no systematic attempt to impose Athenian political structures on the states of the empire. It is also an approach which brings various practical advantages: the Athenians did just enough to establish

[56] Note, for example, *IG* I³ 10: the Athenians impose a legal settlement on the people of Phaselis (a favourable settlement but one in which they had no explicit say); this settlement reveals (at lines 11–14) the existence, and continuing validity, of a *symbola* agreement between the two states (which would, presumably, have been established on more egalitarian, or at least bilateral, terms).

[57] For the Athenian Empire as an example of state-formation rather than imperialism, see I. Morris, 'The greater Athenian state', in I. Morris and W. Scheidel, eds., *The Dynamics of Ancient Empires: State Power from Assyria to Byzantium* (Oxford, 2009), 99–177.

their authority over the cities of the empire and to make plausible their assertions of their right to legislate for those cities and to intervene in their judicial affairs. But they then rather neatly sidestepped at least some of the problems of actually exercising that authority, by allowing many of those powers to revert back to the subject cities.[58] This is a pragmatic approach rather than a glamorous one, and it is probably not coincidental that it is much easier to find boasting assertions of the extent of Athenian *kratos* in our fifth-century (Athenian) sources than it is to find accounts of co-operation with the subject states.[59] But it might not be a coincidence, either, that Athens' revived attempts at imperialism in the fourth century place much greater emphasis on not just the practice but also the rhetoric of legislative and judicial co-operation. In imperial contexts, as in domestic, the 'strength of the laws' rested on the co-operation—willing or coerced—of those whom the laws sought to control.

[58] On a policy of 'surrender-and-grant' as a central (and recurring) tool of Greek imperialism, see J. Ma, 'Empire, statuses and realities', in J. Ma, N. Papazarkadas and R. Parker, eds., *Interpreting the Athenian Empire* (London, 2009), 125–48 (at 127–9).

[59] H. B. Mattingly, 'The language of Athenian imperialism', in *The Athenian Empire Restored* (Ann Arbor, 1996), 361–85.

ROMAN LAW FROM CITY STATE TO WORLD EMPIRE

Jill Harries

Law and the Citizen

Let us begin with an imaginary Roman citizen, resident in Rome, a small settlement on the Tiber early in the latter half of the fifth century BCE. He stands before a display of twelve bronze tablets on which, for the first time, were inscribed for all to see the laws which applied to him as a citizen. They describe his rights to seek legal redress, the means of asserting those rights and the consequences should those rights be infringed. If, like nine tenths of the population, he could not read and required explanation from others, he could still respond to the symbolic value of the display of the citizens' law in material and—it was hoped—permanent form.

The citizen is at the heart of the rules laid out in the Twelve Tables. Its opening clauses explain how a citizen with a grievance may summon a defendant 'to law' and the measures he may take if the defendant 'drags his feet' or claims to be too old or ill to attend. The two were expected to arrive in the Forum or Comitium at Rome and there present their case, although, if the magistrate were delayed or occupied by other cases, they had till sunset to lodge their pleas. What might these disputes be about? The concerns of the Twelve Tables are those of a small, face-to-face agricultural community: debt, theft, personal injury and assault; the household, guardians and funerals; roads, boundaries and overhanging trees, rainwater damage and damage to crops through the chanting of magical incantations.[1]

The Twelve Tables would be the reference point for future Roman law down to the sixth century CE, surviving Rome's transition from small state to world-empire and republic to autocracy. Wisely, the Romans never offered a formal definition of what they meant by 'law'. In the first century BCE Cicero offered a list of what advocates might discuss when dealing with the topic: these included *inter alia* statutes passed by the people, resolutions of the Senate, edicts of magistrates, court decisions and the

[1] For law in the Twelve Tables, see Alan Watson, *Rome of the Twelve Tables: Persons and Property* (Princeton, 1976).

unwritten dimensions to law of custom and equity.[2] More philosophically, the third-century Roman legal thinker, Ulpian, claimed that legal interpreters were, in some sense, the priests of law as a true religion, the purpose of which was moral education—to make men good:

> Of that art (sc. the 'good and the fair') we (the jurists) are rightly described as the priests. For we cultivate the virtue of justice (*iustitia*, justice, derived from *ius*) and assert our understanding of the good and the fair, differentiating between what is fair and what is not, and separating the lawful from the unlawful, aiming to make men good.[3]

Ulpian's *ius* means 'legal right', a concept at the heart of how Romans viewed the purpose of law. The Roman citizen who launched a lawsuit 'went to right' (*in ius ire*) or 'sought right' (*ius petere*) and the purpose of Roman legal procedure was to enable the citizen to assert his legal rights in the proper manner and before the right adjudicator. While the state (*res publica*, an entity notionally 'owned' by the People)[4] had a duty to enforce the outcome of disputes referred to the adjudication of its magistrates, neither enforcement nor policing were central to Roman concepts of how law worked or what it was for. Magistrates did have policing powers relevant to their own jurisdictions, but there was no public 'police' or 'detective' service as such. Even where offences against the community were involved, such as treason, murder, public violence, forgery and suchlike, the initiative for bringing prosecutions on behalf of the community lay primarily with the individual citizen (or, in the exceptional case of treason, any concerned individual). This focus on individual responsibility for seeking legal redress extended to a broader legal condoning of self-help justice, legitimising killing done in self-defence or, under controlled circumstances, in defence of family honour.[5]

The free citizen (as opposed to the slave, resident alien, prisoner of war or other legally disadvantaged category of person), his legal rights to property and personal security, and his obligations stood at the heart of

---

[2] Cicero, *Topica* 28 (44 BCE, addressed to a Roman jurist, Trebatius Testa).

[3] Justinian, Digest 1.1.1.1 = Ulpian, *Institutes*, 1.1. Cicero, *On the Laws* 1.19 (late 50s BCE) concedes the 'popular usage' of 'law' (*lex*) as 'that which sets out in writing what it wishes to command or forbid'.

[4] Cicero *de Republica*, 1.39.

[5] Augustus' law *On Adulteries* (18 BCE) limited the contexts in which an outraged father or husband could kill an erring daughter or wife with her lover on grounds of adultery. This modified previous exercise of family justice by the *pater familias*, or head of household. On this see T.A.J. McGinn, *Prostitution, Sexuality and the Law in Ancient Rome* (Oxford 1998), 140–247.

Roman law. Romans therefore called their law, the *ius civile*, the law of the citizen. However, in the ancient Mediterranean world, law and citizenship in general went together. As the jurist Gaius stated in the mid-second century CE, the *ius civile* was the law which appertained solely to its own *civitas*:

> What each people establishes for itself as law (*ius*) is unique to that citizen body and is called the citizens' law, because it is the law unique to that citizen community (*civitas*).[6]

This was contrasted with the *ius gentium*, or law of all peoples in general, which could be equated with natural or, on occasion, international law. Those who lost their rights as a citizen through disenfranchisement still retained their rights under universal law.

Before the rise of Rome, the Mediterranean world was a mosaic of many cities and citizenships, all with their own laws. Even after the Roman conquest of her eastern provinces from the second century BCE, many cities were classified as 'free' and retained their previous laws and distinctive civic identities, although these were gradually eroded over time. Political life in the cities of the Greek East remained vigorous and competitive, posing problems for conscientious governors like Pliny the Younger (Bithynia, 110–112 CE), who had to deal with the fallout of the resultant extravagance and corruption.[7] But where Rome differed was that its empire came to outclass the competition; by 212 CE, almost all the inhabitants of the Roman Empire were Roman citizens.[8] So the *ius civile*, written and unwritten, was the law of the Roman *civitas*, the Roman citizen body and that citizen community was now coextensive with the population of an empire extending from Hadrian's Wall to the Sahara and the Euphrates.

Well into the imperial period, Roman legal writers prided themselves on the separateness of 'their' *ius civile*. In his explanation of the Roman *ius civile*, Gaius was at pains to point out that certain revered institutions and legal practices were unique to the Romans. These included *patria*

---

[6] Gaius, *Institutes* 1.1. A book entitled *Institutes* (cf. Ulpian's *Institutes* cited above) was a teaching book, explaining the basic principles of its subject. Gaius' *Institutes*, one of the few legal works to survive in almost complete form from Roman antiquity, is still an excellent introduction to the subject for modern students of Roman law.

[7] Pliny, *Letters* 10, 15 onwards.

[8] See A.N. Sherwin White, *The Roman Citizenship* (Second edition, Oxford 1972), 380–394 for the *Constitutio Antoniniana*, the emperor Caracalla's grant of universal citizenship, and those few excluded from it.

potestas, which gave power to the head of household over all descendants through lawful wedlock and dependants, including slaves and freedmen;[9] *manus*, the legal control of a husband married in a certain form, over his wife;[10] and certain forms of purchase and sale.[11] Unlike many jurists, Gaius was aware that others did things differently. In an aside, he acknowledges that the Galatians also operated some form of *patria potestas*[12] and later notes restrictions among the Bithynians on the legal capacity of women to enter into contracts.[13] More generally, he observes that, among non-citizens (*peregrini*), the Roman distinction between absolute ownership (*dominium*) and possession (*possessio*), which in practice was equivalent to full ownership, was simply not observed—and therefore, we may presume, not much understood either.

The diverse and far-flung character of this new empire-wide Roman citizen community was very different from that of the small republic by the Tiber, where the concepts and procedures of the Roman *ius civile* had first been formulated. Some procedural adjustments were relatively straightforward, as the legal responsibilities of the provincial governor were brought into line with that of the principal judges in Rome, the praetors (who were usually expected to proceed to a governorship after their year of office at Rome). But the process of adaptation had to take account of processes explicitly limited to the city of Rome itself—such as the residence requirements for elite (but not senatorial) jurors on the extortion court in the second century BCE[14]—and other technicalities, such as those relating to landownership.

In many areas, the Roman solution to the exercise of their citizen law in the context of imperial expansion was deceptively simple. Relevant sections of the statutes and other legal texts were adapted to the requirements of provincial and other jurisdictions; the rest was ignored. The Romans accepted that processes changed to suit their contexts; no formal legislation was required. On extortion, and other serious crimes perpetrated (allegedly) by senators or other rich Romans, the convention grew

---

9 Gaius, *Inst.* 1.55; 189.

10 Gaius, *Inst.* 1.108.

11 *mancipatio*, *in iure cessio*, usucapion, Gaius, *Inst.* 2.65.

12 Gaius, *Inst.* 1.55.

13 Gaius, *Inst.* 1.193

14 'The praetor (*peregrinus*) ... is to see that he choose 450 men, provided that he does not choose any of those who (sc. have held various offices at Rome or been members of the Senate), or who [may not have his domicile] in the city of Rome or nearer the city than one mile'. (*Lex Repetundarum*, lines 12–15, Michael Crawford and others, *Roman Statutes* (London, 1996), vol. I.86).

up under the Early Empire that governors accused of administrative malpractice and members of the elite denounced for other public crimes were tried by the Senate at Rome; for some limited purposes, therefore, even at Rome the Republican courts simply fell into disuse or were bypassed by a political class capable of modifying procedure to suit itself.[15] Similarly, homicide was legislated for by the dictator Sulla (81–80 BCE), who established a homicide court based at Rome,[16] but provincial murderers were hauled before the governor, who acted as supreme judge in capital cases. Any doubts the provincial judge may have had, for example about whether being struck by a saucepan demonstrated intent to kill,[17] had either to be solved by reference to a jurist, passed on to the emperors, or dealt with by the judge himself through creative use of argument by analogy:

> [Statutes or senatorial resolutions cannot deal with every specific point] but whenever in any case, the sense is clear, the president of the tribunal should proceed by reasoning based on analogy and proclaim the law (or legal verdict) accordingly.[18]

Two other recognised modes of adaptation of the *ius civile* to world empire were also at work. One was the creation of parallel institutions in the provinces to mirror those at Rome. For example, manumission of slaves under 30 would be justified at Rome before a formal advisory committee (*consilium*) of five senators and five *equites* (rich non-senators), while in the provinces, the same function would be carried out by a committee of 20 *recuperatores*, of Roman citizen status:

> The *consilium* is composed in the city of Rome of five senators and five *equites*; in the provinces of 20 Roman citizen *recuperatores* and it takes place on the last day of the (governor's) assizes; at Rome manumissions take place before a *consilium* on fixed days.[19]

15 On the Senate as court, see Richard Talbert, *The Senate of Imperial Rome* (Princeton, 1984), 460–87.

16 Under the Severans in the early third century, juristic commentary reported and commented on the limited application of Sulla's Lex Cornelia on knife crime and poisoners (c. 80 BCE) to the city of Rome and up to a mile from it (Ulpian, *On the Duties of the Proconsul* VII = *Collatio of Roman and Mosaic Law* 1.3).

17 Justinian, Digest, 48.8.1.3.

18 Justinian, Digest, 1.3.12 = Salvius Julianus, *Digest*, Book 15. This is important evidence for how precedents may be created by the court decisions of governors, independently of imperial rulings.

19 Gaius, *Inst.* 1.20.

A second was the practice of treating provincial situations 'as if' they were, in law, fully Roman. Thus, for example, although technically provincial land could not be declared 'religious', because it was 'owned' by the Roman People or the emperor, relevant land could be regarded 'as if' religious:

> In the provinces however, the general opinion is that land does not become *religiosum*, because the ownership of provincial land belongs to the Roman people or to the emperor, and individuals have only possession and enjoyment of it. Still, even if it be not *religiosum*, it is treated as such. (7a) Also, a thing consecrated in the provinces and not by the authority of the Roman people is not *sacrum* in the strict sense, but it is treated as if *sacrum*.[20]

But the *ius civile* was not only about procedures but also about the legal rights of the individual citizen and his access to justice. As the Roman Empire underwent its protracted transition from a collective system of government by the 'Senate and People of Rome' (SPQR) under the Republic, to the rule of one man (albeit one who represented himself as a 'citizen-emperor'), strains were inevitable.[21] The *ius civile* had adapted to the new conditions of empire in the first two centuries CE, and by 212, almost all residents were also Roman citizens. But in Late Antiquity from the late third century CE onwards, the imperial government became one of overt autocracy. In such a situation, would the basic character of the *ius civile* and the concept of 'legal right' on which it rested also be eroded?

Jurists and Empire

From the late first century BCE, the emperor Augustus and his successors took for themselves all constitutional power to make law. However, they were bound by two constraints. One was that their citizen 'image', and the public support it was designed to win, depended on the appearance of respect for law and the avoidance of arbitrary or 'tyrannical' behaviour. Respect for law meant also respect for the rights of the citizen and those who ruled in an arbitrary or despotic fashion did not last long. Secondly,

---

[20] Gaius, *Inst.* 2.7–7a. A different line on this was taken by Trajan to his governor, Pliny, which may explain Gaius' aside about the 'general' opinion, implying that there were exceptions. Pliny, *Letters* 10, 50, allows the removal of a temple, 'as the soil of an alien country is not capable of being consecrated according to our laws'.

[21] See Andrew Wallace-Hadrill, 'Civilis Princeps: Between Citizen and King', *Journal of Roman Studies* 72 (1982), 32–48.

not all emperors were lawyers. They therefore relied on expert advice as to what the law was and, to be credible, the legal and intellectual content of such advice had to be independent of political pressure (although the advisers themselves might well be politicians). The result of these two requirements was the emergence and perpetuation of a group of what might be termed legal intermediaries, who were crucial to the process of adaptation from city-state to empire—the Roman jurists.[22]

These eminent and authoritative legal interpreters were not formal legislators, though they were often drawn from the legislating classes, nor were they necessarily directly involved in the power politics of the Roman Republic and Empire, although, again, many were also eminent senators and, later, imperial administrators. Their documented work begins in the late Republic, in the second century BCE (although interpretative activity had begun much earlier), and was to culminate in the issuance of the *Corpus Iuris Civilis* of the emperor Justinian in the 530s CE.[23] But by the time of Justinian, a significant religious dimension had been largely obscured, a dimension, which links the origins of the Roman jurist with interpreters of religious law in other cultures. The roots of Roman jurisprudence lie in the role of the College of Pontiffs (*Pontifices*) and its head, the Pontifex Maximus, as interpreters of religious law under the Roman Republic, in particular as it related to the religious identity of the *familia*, or household. The Pontifex Maximus was concerned with the proper perpetuation of the sacred identity (*sacra*) of the household, as an integral part of the community as a whole, and his remit therefore extended to certain forms of adoption, which could entail the termination of a *familia* (see below); guardianship (the safeguarding of the interests of a head of household who was still a minor); funerals; and, by extension, succession, as the people responsible for funerals were also those likely to be the main heirs of the deceased and thus the perpetuators of the *familia*. In the late second and early first centuries BCE, pontifical jurisprudence began to acquire a more secular character (as we would understand the word 'secular'), under the guidance of two holders of the chief pontificate, Publius Mucius Scaevola

[22] For Republican background, see Bruce Frier, *The Rise of the Roman Jurist* (Princeton, 1985), and note 24 below.

[23] Justinian's *Corpus* consisted of the *Codex Justinianus*, edited imperial laws from the time of Hadrian to that of Justinian; the Digest, in 50 books, an edited collection of extracts from the jurists down to the early fourth century CE and designed for use in the official law schools, and the law courts; and Justinian's *Institutes*, based mainly on Gaius, but with additions from Ulpian and others.

(consul in 133 BCE) and his son, Quintus (consul, 95 BCE, died 82 BCE). The latter was the author of an eighteen-book guide to the *ius civile*, the purpose of which was probably to educate the new Roman citizens from Italy created in the aftermath of the Social War (90–88 BCE).[24] Thereafter, jurisprudence moved out of the pontifical domain, through the work of Servius Sulpicius Rufus (consul 51 BCE, died 43 BCE) and his pupils.

The work of the Roman jurists down to the third century CE played a crucial, but not always entirely helpful, role in managing the transition of the *ius civile* from the law of a small state to an empire-wide construct. Juristic discussion was both helped and hindered by the traditionalist nature of their discipline. As will be argued more fully below, excessive respect for the Rome-centred nature of much of the early legal documentation, which formed their main points of reference, underlay what jurists in the second century CE came to refer to as the 'order' (*ordo*). In order to accommodate legal change, the jurists, referred to certain kinds of innovation as 'going outside the order', an awkward device, which allowed the jurists to accommodate radical change within a traditional, and Rome-centred framework. In other words, the 'order', as used by jurists, is a technical concept, essential for purposes of specialist juristic discourse but of limited relevance to the real world of emperors, judges and litigants. Its use therefore also expresses the downside of excessive adherence to tradition, allowing continued reference to a device, which both enabled, in a formal sense, and also inhibited processes of change and adaptation. But the positive role played by jurists was of greater significance. Although in practice the rights of citizens were not (and never were) equal under the Roman system,[25] and were further eroded under the Later Empire,[26] respect for a legal tradition focussed on the individual citizen could still act as a bulwark against arbitrariness and the whims of late Roman autocracy. Though not formally constituted as such, the jurists were arguably the guardians of the *ius civile*, preservers of its traditions in the face of ignorance, prejudice, and conflicting imperial priorities.

---

[24] On Scaevola, see Jill Harries, *Cicero and the Jurists. From Citizens' Law to the Lawful State* (London, 2006), 17–26.

[25] See Peter Garnsey, *Social Status and Legal Privilege in the Roman Empire* (Oxford, 1970).

[26] For increased criminalisation of unlawful behaviours in Late Antiquity, see Ramsey MacMullen, 'Judicial Savagery in the Roman Empire', *Chiron* 16 (1986), 147–66.

'Outside the Order': Jurists as Prisoners of the Roman Past

There are thus two aspects of law as Rome progressed from Republic to Empire, which could have proved problematic. The first is the focus on the individual citizen and his rights: how far could these be honoured under an autocracy, and how far did the character of the *ius civile* itself affect the operation of autocracy, especially in Late Antiquity? Second, how was the transition from a legal system based on the city of Rome to universal application over a world-empire to be managed? Both the geographical and the political dimensions were to be addressed through the emperor as lawgiver, the governor as judge, and the cumulative impact of court decisions on the breaking down of the Rome-centred 'order'. We can trace this through the jurists, while conceding that they often appear to be more part of the problem, than of the solution.

To understand the conservatism of the Roman jurists of the Early Empire, we must appreciate their context. Although, by the second century CE, there were legal modernizers at Rome, both Pomponius and Gaius, who were academic jurists, not imperial advisers, looked back to, and commented on, the Twelve Tables and the by now outdated treatise on the civil law by Q. Mucius Scaevola. Their attachment to the minutiae of the Roman past had authority in the practice of at least part of the juristic tradition under the Empire, going back to the time of Augustus and the late first century BCE. One jurist, Masurius Sabinus, regarded erroneously by Pomponius as the founder of the more conservative of the two Roman law schools active in the second century, could easily be mistaken for an antiquarian. If we had only the scientifically minded elder Pliny (died 79 CE) on Masurius Sabinus, we would take it that 'Masurius' was an antiquarian of distinction. Pliny drew on a treatise in eleven books on *Memorialia*, in which Sabinus discussed the origins of ritual, perhaps in the context of sacral law, which was still a legitimate area for the jurist. Sabinus knows about the ritual uses of certain trees and plants, such as the myrtle wreath of the *triumphator*[27] and the use of laurel for purposes of purification[28] and the historical reasons why that was so. From the second-century miscellanist Aulus Gellius we also learn of Sabinus' notes on the ancient ceremony of the *ovatio*[29] and his recording of the 'recent'

[27] Pliny, *Natural History* (*NH*) 15.38.126.

[28] Pliny, *NH* 15.40.135. See also *NH* 7.43.135 on the Roman triumph.

[29] *Attic Nights* 5.6.27.

innovation that the Flamen Dialis was no longer required to wear his sacred hat indoors.[30]

The habit of antiquarian study was not confined to litterateurs and lawyers. The city of Rome in the second century proved exceptionally tenacious of its ancient institutions, and archaic survivals from the dawn of Roman history continued to operate. Take the rules on adoption, for example. The oldest of all the Roman public assemblies was the Comitia Curiata, the assembly of the curiae, which no longer met as an assembly of the people as such, but nonetheless still held notional meetings, which represented the *populus* and could be summoned for specific duties. One of these duties, attested by Gaius as still operative in the mid-second century CE, was the approval of a special form of adoption, known as adrogation. This was the process, conducted by the Pontifical College and *per populum*, before the Roman People, by which a man who was legally independent and thus a head of household was adopted by another head of household, thus forfeiting his legal independence and that of his descendants. It thus affected the public interest because it entailed the termination of a household. As the *populus Romanus* could meet only at Rome, this form of adoption could happen only at Rome:

> (98) Adoption happens in two ways, either by authority of the People (*populus*), or by the *imperium* of a magistrate, such as the praetor. (99) By the authority of the People, we adopt those who are legally independent (*sui iuris*). This category of adoption is called adrogation, because both the man who adopts is asked (*rogatur*) or rather cross-questioned, whether he wishes that the man he is about to adopt should be his lawful son, and he who is to be adopted is asked whether he consents to this adoption taking place, and the People is asked whether it commands that this should happen. [Adoption by *imperium* of a magistrate]. (100) And the former adoption, which takes place through the People, happens nowhere except at Rome; but the latter is customarily carried out in the provinces too through the provincial governors.[31]

---

[30] *Attic Nights* 10.15.7. For a story about periods of gestation probably told by Sabinus and derived by Gellius from Pliny, see *Attic Nights* 3.16.23 citing Pliny *NH* 7.5.40. For antiquarianism in Rome in Gellius' day, see A.J. Stevenson, 'The Roman Antiquarian Tradition', in L. Holford-Strevens and A. Vardi, eds., *The World of Aulus Gellius* (Oxford, 2004), 118–55.

[31] Gaius, *Inst.* 1.98–100, extracts. See also Aulus Gellius, *Attic Nights* 5.19 on the two categories of adoption, the one before the praetor and the other before the 'people' (adrogation). For the case of the adrogation of the future tribune P. Clodius by a 'father' younger than himself into a plebeian family (because as a patrician he was debarred from standing), see Cicero, *On His House* 37 (57 BCE); Jill Harries, *Cicero and the Jurists. From Citizens' Law to the Lawful State* (London, 2006), 153–6.

Nor was it, as one might suspect, a useless, albeit colourful, relic of the ancient past. The College of Pontiffs, as Gaius reported, still had questions to ask the emperor about its operation: was a head of house, who was still short of puberty, eligible for adrogation?

> (102) Also, adoption of a minor before the People has been forbidden at one time and permitted at another. But now, on the authority of a letter of our excellent emperor Antoninus (Pius), which he wrote to the Pontifices, if a just cause for the adoption (= adrogation) can be demonstrated, subject to certain conditions, it is allowed.[32]

By contrast with this quaint Roman survival, adoption, in the usual sense, was routinely carried out before anyone with the *imperium* of a magistrate at Rome and in the provinces. Women, too, who were not eligible for adrogation because they could not be heads of households, had no problems with adoption elsewhere:

> Further, women cannot be adopted by authority of the People, for that legal opinion has prevailed, but before a praetor or, in the provinces, before the proconsul or legate, women too are often adopted.[33]

Such was the traditionalist environment at Rome within which the juristic concept of the 'order', and its use as a point of reference to identify change, evolved. So what was the 'order'? The phrase '*cognitio extra ordinem*', a legal hearing held outside the 'order', much favoured by modern scholars but for which there is very limited ancient authority, begs the question of what the 'order' was.[34] In my view, the 'order' was not in general usage at all but was a part of technical juristic vocabulary, to be interpreted in legal, rather than general or popular terms. This is why historians should be careful about using it in the first place. For the 'order', as I see it, was juristic shorthand for two authoritative Rome-based legal quasi-codifications, one on praetorian law, the law based on the Praetor's Edict (*ius honorarium*), and the second on the courts and criminal law, which together helped to define the judicial system and how it should operate.

Both were initially focussed on the situation at Rome. The first master-text was the Praetorian Edict, issued annually by the Roman praetors and codified under Hadrian in the 130s CE. Writing a generation later, Gaius

---

32 Gaius, *Inst.* 1.102.

33 Gaius, *Inst.* 1.101.

34 See, for example, I. Buti, 'La cognitio extra ordinem da Augusto a Diocleziano', *ANRW* II.14 (1982), 29–59.

explained that in the provinces the governors did what the praetor (and aediles) did at Rome:

> A very large amount of law is contained in the edicts of the two praetors, urban and peregrine (at Rome), whose jurisdiction is exercised in the provinces by the provincial governors.[35]

Moreover, the duties of the aedile (in charge of city administration at Rome) were, in the senatorial provinces, carried out by quaestors. In other words, provincial administration was modelled on the administration of the City of Rome as far as possible.

The Praetor's Edict consisted in part of a list of legal actions, which could lawfully be brought before the praetor and the situations to which they could apply. Praetors were chosen annually and could modify their predecessors' edict if they chose. However, after the Hadrianic codification, such modifications by anyone other than the emperor were no longer possible. Thus, if a suit was brought before a governor, which appeared not to fall under the terms of the Edict, the judge had to decide whether to refer the case to the emperor, to ascertain whether he could hear it or not, or hear the case *extra ordinem*, probably on grounds of arguments from analogy. Such examples as survive in the juristic writings are, as one might expect, drawn from referrals to emperors, and show a reasonable willingness to be flexible in interpreting how the Edict should be applied.

The second element in the 'Order' was the statute passed by Augustus on the Public Courts, or *iudicia publica*, in c. 17 BCE. This marked the end in a process of development of a set of public courts or *quaestiones*, established by statute at Rome to try those accused of public offences, such as treason, murder, forgery and so on, beginning with a statute against extortion, the Lex Calpurnia, passed in 149 BCE.[36] By the second century CE, Augustus' law on the public courts and the dossiers of late Republican and Augustan statutes on the criminal courts had created a sort of canon of criminal offences. Jurists under the Republic had shown no interest in commentating on the criminal law, partly because it was public,[37] and partly because it was concerned mostly with questions of fact. But, from the second century CE onwards, some jurists began to take an interest

[35] Gaius, *Inst.* 1.6.

[36] On this see John Richardson, 'The Purpose of the Lex Calpurnia *de Repetundis*', *Journal of Roman Studies* 77 (1987), 1–12.

[37] For the jurists' general lack of interest in public law, see David Johnston, 'The Jurists', in C. Rowe and M. Schofield, eds., *The Cambridge History of Greek and Roman Political Thought* (Cambridge, 2005), 625–7.

in commentating both on the public criminal law, and on administrative law. Treatises duly appeared on taxation and on the job descriptions of various administrative officials. Early in the third century, there was a small flurry of treatises on Augustus' law on adultery, passed two hundred years before, and commentary on the now recognised canon of criminal statutes became more prominent in general guides to the *ius civile*. There is therefore some evidence for a shift of legal attention towards administrative and criminal law, in parallel with the evolution of the empire's government itself towards a more bureaucratic and autocratic system.

Because of the focus of the ancient sources and modern historians on the person of the emperor and his central administration, it is often assumed that the rise in Late Antiquity of 'judicial savagery', to use Ramsay MacMullen's phrase, and the expansion of offences classified as 'criminal' was due to imperial policy, backed by the inhumanity of faceless bureaucrats. But a central point to understand about Roman imperial rule, throughout the period of the Empire, is that imperial legislation was largely, though not exclusively, issued in response to issues raised, and proposals made, by administrators and judges. If the Late Antique judicial system was harsher, and the salutary terror wielded by the autocratic regime more overtly expressed, this was not due solely to a change in the administrative ethos at the centre. Changes were driven in part by problems confronting provincial governors acting as judges of 'criminal' offences and the solutions to which they chose in practice to resort. Thus, for example, the extension up the social scale of the use of torture, initially confined to slaves, was driven by the need of the judges to ascertain the 'truth'.[38]

Moreover, the expansion of the number of criminal charges can be traced also to the initiatives taken by litigants seeking 'revenge', who tested the 'order' by submitting accusations (duly signed) and hoping for the best. What happened, for example, if a financial penalty was imposed on someone who was unable to pay?

> It is generally agreed that in terms of the statutes which deal with criminal proceedings and with private charges, prefects or governors conducting hearings *extra ordinem* should impose punishment *extra ordinem* on those who escape a monetary penalty by their lack of means.[39]

---

[38] See Jill Harries, 'Contextualising Torture: Rules and Conventions in the Roman Digest', in A.F. Lang, A.F. and A. Beattie, eds., *War, Torture and Terrorism. Rethinking the Rules of International Security* (London, 2009), 39–53.

[39] Justinian, Digest 48.19.1.3 = Ulpian, *Disputations* 8.

The *ordo*, as envisaged by the jurists, was flexible and adherence to it preferred. Wrongdoing that appeared to fall outside the provisions of any of the public statutes might be assimilated to an existing 'crime'; penalties, such as interdiction from fire and water within a hundred miles from Rome, were superseded over time by those operated by courts throughout the provinces, which ranged from deportation to capital punishment. So when jurists referred to the 'penalty of the Lex Cornelia', they did not mean by that the penalty specified in 80 BCE by the statute passed by the dictator (Cornelius) Sulla, but the penalty operative 'now' for those convicted under the statute. The statute had specified 'interdiction from fire and water', a quasi-religious penalty meaning, in effect, exile from Rome and its environs. Ulpian explained that this was later modified to deportation, meaning exile to an island[40] and became the 'penalty of the lex Cornelia', even though the original text had specified something different. Ulpian's reference to deportation was, however, already out of date. By his day, in the third century it had undergone a further modification:

> The penalty of the Lex Cornelia on knife crime and poisoners is deportation to an island and the forfeiture of all property. However, nowadays, capital punishment is customary.[41]

Moreover, where the offence under discussion was itself not part of the 'order', because it was not covered by the existing statutes and their accretions, the judge had considerable discretion in sentencing:

> Nowadays [a judge] who is hearing a criminal case *extra ordinem* may lawfully pass what sentence he pleases, whether heavier or lighter, provided only that he does not exceed what is reasonable in either direction.[42]

There was nothing contrary to the spirit of Roman law in this; both custom and the acceptance of desuetude, by which laws ceased to matter if they were no longer operative, were accepted parts of the working of the system.[43] So too was the concession to judges, which allowed them to operate, in theory, without reference to the emperor, on the basis of analogy;[44] this allowed them to accept hearings on new legal question on grounds of comparability with existing topics already accepted as part of the system. In practice, governors probably paid far more attention to the

40 Justinian, Digest 48.19.2.1 = Ulpian, *On the Edict* 48.
41 Justinian, Digest 48.8.3.5 = Marcian, *Institutes* 14.
42 Justinian, Digest 48.19.2.13 = Ulpian, *On Appeals* 1.
43 On desuetude, Salvius Julianus at Digest 1.3.32.1 (= Julianus, *Digest* 84).
44 Justinian, Digest 1.3.12 = Julianus, *Digest* 18.

exigencies of their job as judges than they did to the juristic 'order'. But it could matter in practice, because the 'order' could inhibit acceptance of a case before a judge, if the complaint made or remedy sought could be shown to be incompatible with the traditional categories.

Juristic discourse, therefore, could have blocked avenues of legal redress because the Rome-centred nature of the *ordo* and jurists' professional concern with what was or was not contained in the Edict or the criminal statutes had the potential to inhibit legal change in the courts of the provinces of the empire. And there was no practical advantage to be had in clinging to an outworn tradition; types of legal hearing or changes in penal law, labelled as being 'outside the order' or 'extraordinary', were in fact neither, except in a very limited, technical juristic sense. But if the jurists created this problem for themselves, they also solved it, by moving 'outside the order' to accommodate innovation and change. They thus contributed, even in this unpromising area, to the adaptation of the *ius civile* to an empire, in which the capital city would become a sideshow, by legitimising the processes of change in terms of the Roman legal tradition.

Law and Empire

How do these apparent technicalities affect the questions we should ask about the relationship of citizens' law to the Roman Empire? An obvious, but seldom stated, feature of the *ius civile* is that the concept does not depend for its effectiveness on the existence of any system of government or constitution. As was the case with the ancient idea of 'Law' in general, it stands apart from the daily vicissitudes of politics and power games. But what is remarkable about the Romans' *ius civile* is its tenacity over a very long period, which saw the rise and partial fall of an Empire, the incorporation of numerous diverse legal systems and customs into the Roman order, and the replacement of a republic by a sole ruler, who, by the time of Justinian, was a theocratic autocrat.

A number of reasons for this resilience may be suggested. First, the monarchy, which was founded by Augustus in the late first century BCE, exploited the constitutional forms and ideology of Republican rule. The emperor himself was simply the 'first citizen' and his immediate successors, with a few unfortunate exceptions, projected themselves as 'citizen-emperors'. This meant that they had an obligation to behave like citizens, and that meant being accessible to petitioners and observing also the citizens' law. This ideology continued to operate, even in Late Antiquity. Emperors in the fourth century CE referred to the empire-wide community as the *res publica*, and one even wrote to the senate at Constantinople, prefacing his letter with the traditional formulaic greeting of a Republican army general to the senate at Rome. They also claimed, not always with complete conviction, that they toiled without rest for their people's good; one fifth-century emperor even invented an oil lamp, which refuelled itself, so that he could work through the night without interruption.[45]

In line with this 'citizen' ideology, emperors, though not formally constrained by the laws, were obliged to advertise their adherence to them. As supreme legislators, they also had the power to change the law, and often did so. But the fact that most of these changes occurred as a result of consultations on a particular issue or question and that they were issued in the form of replies to proposals or petitions, taking the form of letters or edicts or rescripts, meant that legal change was cumulative, rather than sudden or radical. The defining characteristic of the laws of Roman emperors was that they were responsive to representations from the proposers or petitioners; they were part of a conversation between emperors and citizen-subjects. Moreover, the language of Late Antique imperial legislation often, though not invariably, makes a point of situating the new decision in the contexts of the juristic tradition or 'the ancient laws' and previous emperors' decisions on the same or similar point. Where changes were authorised, they required justification.

But the men who ensured that Late Antique autocratic emperors respected the legal traditions of the *ius civile*, are the largely nameless and faceless legal experts who worked in the legal bureaux of the autocrats. Under the Early Empire, we know the names of the jurists, often high-profile senators and consuls, who lent their legal expertise to the emperors' advisory council and sat behind him when he acted as a judge. The eminent juristic administrators, Papinian, Paulus and Ulpian, had glittering careers, of which something is known and between them created a golden age of jurisprudence under the Severan dynasty in the late second and early third centuries.[46] We know too the names and perhaps the literary styles of many 'imperial quaestors' who drafted and formulated imperial laws in Late Antiquity. But by the fourth century, the legal expert had

45 Sozomen, *Church History*, preface.

46 See especially Tony Honoré, *Emperors and Lawyers* (Oxford, 1994), and *Ulpian, Pioneer of Human Rights* (Oxford, 2000).

been absorbed into the bureaucratic machine, or he had taken up a teaching position in one of the great law schools at Rome, Constantinople or Beirut. The jurists who lent their learning to the legal codifications of Theodosius II in the 430s and of Justinian a century later are named and honoured by those emperors, but they were not to survive as independent authors in their own right. Jurisprudence had not died, but, apart from its exercise in the schools, it was dependent on the imperial will.

That is not, quite, the whole story. The late imperial jurists not only had access to emperors; they used it. Late Antique emperors were in general soldiers, not lawyers; while complaining bitterly of juristic obscurities, unhelpful petty disputes and 'ambiguities', they relied on the experts to get things right. Imperial legislation and the great codifications of Late Antiquity, especially the *Corpus Iuris Civilis* of Justinian, through which the *ius civile* was preserved, were the work of the legal bureaucrats. The faceless administrators are usually the villains of history—unaccountable, incompetent, perhaps corrupt, all adjectives used by the emperors themselves regarding their unlucky servants. But the *ius civile*, in all its complexity and subtlety, owed its survival to those very bureaucrats and their knowledge of the legal tradition; to the continued public expectation of emperors that they would act in a lawful way; and to the responsive nature of imperial lawmaking, which enabled a continuing dialogue between citizens and emperor.

Above all, Roman law in the context of empire owed its resilience to the centrality of the citizen, not the emperor, or any other ruler, to the concept of what law was. The relationship of law in action to freedom or to the empowerment of the individual may be debated; much of Roman law was drafted by, and in the interests of, members of the moneyed elite, and the lower orders had limited access to its benefits. But the idea of law itself could not have existed at Rome, or indeed in the ancient Mediterranean world in general, without the citizen, the member of a citizen community, big or small, with a civic identity, obligations, and rights. In the twenty-first century, an era of transnational institutions, which, in the view of some, could make the 'citizen' redundant, along with the autonomous nation state, it becomes even more important that we recollect the essential connection in Western thought between citizenship and the rule of law.

LAWS, BUREAUCRATS, AND IMPERIAL WOMEN IN CHINA'S EARLY EMPIRES

Karen Gottschang Turner

> Do not bend the statutes and laws out of affection for your people. The laws are more important than the people (*Guanzi*, composed around 300 BCE).[1]

Writers and statesmen who witnessed the development of the centralized state in China from the fourth through the second centuries BCE faced a dilemma. On the one hand, they believed that centralized control of "All under Heaven" under the aegis of a single ruler promised the best hope for stability and order. On the other, they understood very well the dangers inherent in ceding to one man and his clan the right to make life-and-death decisions. But the trade-off had to be worth the risk. The period that followed the demise of the Zhou Dynasty after 771 BCE was marked by ever more costly wars and a political culture almost devoid of constraints against the arbitrary use of violence, even—or especially—among elites. During the period aptly named the Warring States (481–221 BCE) a multi-state system emerged in which autocratic kings competed for mastery of "All under Heaven". Massive armies composed of tax paying peasants replaced aristocratic warriors. The successes of these competing kingdoms hinged on the diplomatic and strategic talents of "new men", who gained influence by dint of merit rather than noble birth, and who linked their fate with that of the state they served. Some of them left records of the theories they developed to strengthen states, and others observed from a distance to appraise and in some cases resist the demands of territorial kings and their officials. Well before the Qin Dynasty announced that it had unified the warring kingdoms in 221 BCE, ruling elites had experienced for themselves the demands of the state and were thus prepared to assess the costs of a much larger imperial apparatus.

Warring States writers were preoccupied with defining roles for rulers and ministers during this era, and a variety of models of proper kingship emerged.[2] Some thinkers toyed with the idea of a divine kingship, but

---

[1] The *Guanzi* is an eclectic text which contains a wealth of information about theories of law and punishment. For an analysis and translation in English, see W. Alllyn Rickett, *Guanzi: Political, Economic, and Philosophical Essays from Early China* (Princeton, 1985), 261.

[2] For a discussion of conceptions of monarchy and government, see Yuri Pines, *Envisioning Eternal Empire: Chinese Political Thought of the Warring States Era* (Honolulu,

most of the major writers supported conditional monarchy and some tacitly rationalized the right to rebel against a ruler who failed in his duties to serve the general welfare. Some writers and texts celebrated passive kings who allowed their officials to bear the burden of ruling while others advocated for more active managerial monarchs. No writer, however, dared to legitimate a monarch who would ignore his officials, for the well-being of the literati rested on their ability to advise the man who held ultimate power. Discussions about the proper role of law permeate the texts, and by the late fourth century many writers linked effective governance with clear laws and consistent punishments, to be overseen by rulers in tandem with incorruptible bureaucrats.[3]

The historical and excavated materials reveal that by the time that the Qin (221–202 BCE) and Western Han (206 BCE–25 CE) empires took shape, emperors were expected to uphold these values. Their power to override or ignore the laws was challenged by a few high-ranking officials, who were willing to defend the state from the whims of rulers, often at the cost of their lives. True, no institutional checks could thwart the will of an angry emperor, but emperors knew all too well that they did not possess the resources to operate by force alone. Moreover, the fate of the empire in the end rested on the stability of the ruling dynasty. Emperors not only had to oversee the bureaucratic apparatus, but were bound to attend to their duties to the imperial clan. Inevitably their role as head of the clan as well as head of state entangled them in complex networks in which claims of kinship, unclear succession practices, and personal affection called for flexibility and partiality. As much as possible, emperors tried to avoid confrontations with relatives by delegating to high-ranking officials or imperial women the authority to preside over sensitive cases. When emperors themselves were at fault, Empress Dowagers most often decided how to treat their errant kin. Indeed, according to the historical records, high-ranking women exerted a great deal of influence in court affairs, and served as an important check on the power of emperors to impose their

2009). While I do not agree with all of his points, the author does convey the variety of ideas about monarchy that emerged in this era.

[3] A great deal of controversy surrounds the dating of these texts for some were composed later than the times they represented and some were composed by multiple authors. Nonetheless, the major texts I use here are most likely products of the Warring States and Western Han eras. For a comprehensive and new view of the dating of Warring States texts, see E. Bruce Brooks and A. Taeko Brooks, *The Emergence of China: From Confucius to the Empire* (Amherst, Massachusetts, 2011).

will in legal matters. This interplay between different measures for legitimating legal decisions, and between emperors and the forces, both formal and informal, that thwarted their power to act as supreme lawmakers and judges, is the subject of this paper.

Sources and Frameworks

Our knowledge about the workings of the early empires in China was confined to two histories until excavations in China beginning in the late 1970s brought to light materials that were not part of the transmitted tradition and so were not figured into early sinological evaluations of law in the late Warring States and early imperial periods.[4] Armed now with fragments of codes, documents for reporting legal decisions, and casebooks for deciding difficult cases, historians can begin to piece together a tentative scenario about how law worked on the ground. But the materials we have to date are fragmentary and confined for the most part to an area in the Warring States kingdom of Chu, a large, culturally distinct territory in South Central China.[5] As archaeological work continues in China, new materials from excavated sites can challenge or support our current understandings of law in theory and practice. At this stage, anyone who proposes a grand theory of law in the formation of empire would be foolhardy indeed. What we can do, however, is to check the historical accounts against new data and perhaps revise the standard view of law that prevailed before the 1980s, which, on the one hand, celebrated China for its commitment to disdain formal law in favour of more benign mechanisms to maintain order and, on the other, denigrated Chinese political culture for allowing emperors to impose harsh punishments at whim. Such simplistic visions no longer make sense now that so much evidence shows that even at the lowest levels of imperial society, bureaucrats worked with legal guidelines that offered little room for arbitrary decisions. And at the top, emperors and their high-ranking legal officials paid a great deal of attention to monitoring and reforming the laws to maintain consistency and clarity.

---

4 For an outline of some of these new sources, see Michael Loewe, *Early Chinese Texts: A Bibliographic Guide* (Berkeley, 1993). I have used the pin-yin system of Romanization for this paper but keep the old Wade Giles system when it is used in a title of a published work. Thus in the old system, the first empire is 'Ch'in' and in pin-yin 'Qin'.

5 For discussions of the unique features of Chu culture, see Constance Cook and John Major, eds., *Defining Chu: Image and Reality in Ancient China* (Honolulu, 1999).

Of course, the stability of the system depended on the quality of the ruling elite in power at any given time, but powerful forces did operate to quell flagrant abuses of laws and punishments. As I noted above, and will expand upon later, even the most competent emperors negotiated with their bureaucrats, and their mothers and grandmothers, when cases of consequence had to be decided.

New materials on law have attracted a great deal of attention from scholars of early China, but the histories remain the most useful repositories of information about events, personalities, and policies over time and place in the early empires. China's first historian, Sima Qian (145–86 BCE), experienced first-hand the abuse of imperial power when Han Wudi (r. 141–87 BCE) ordered him castrated and imprisoned for questioning the Emperor's decision to punish an upright military man.[6] Sima Qian decided not to commit an honourable suicide, but to live in shame with his mutilated body, in order to complete *The Records of the Historian* [*Shiji*], a history of China from the earliest times. His memoirs and biographies of officials and emperors are carefully constructed to warn the Emperor he reluctantly served of the dangers of imposing unjust, harsh punishments. Ban Gu (32–92) composed his *History of the Han Dynasty* [*Hanshu*] after a crisis that almost destroyed the Liu dynasty's hold on power.[7] The attitude toward harsh punishments seems to have become sterner in his time, despite rhetoric from Confucian officials about the importance of educating rather than punishing the people. Emperors and officials whose views on punishments were surveyed in Ban Gu's chapter on the history of the Han penal system display a relatively tolerant stance toward harsh punishments compared to earlier Han writers. Of law and the common people, for example, Emperor Jingdi (157–141 BCE), after arguing about the precise number of strokes that should be used to punish criminals, concluded that, "The bastinado is the way to teach them: Therefore regulate the size of the stick".[8] Ban Gu also included many examples of Han emperors

[6] Most sinologists agree that his father, Sima Tan, wrote some of the early sections of the history but do not agree about which parts can be attributed to the father and which to the son. For a discussion of the context in which this work was written, see Stephen W. Durant, *The Cloudy Mirror: Tension and Conflict in the Writings of Sima Qian* (Albany, 1995). The most accessible English translations are those by Burton Watson, *Records of the Grand Historian* (New York, 1961–93). Citations are taken from the revised editions, 1993.

[7] Citations from the *Hanshu* are keyed to the Sibu beiyao edition. For a partial translation see *History of the Former Han Dynasty*, trans. Homer H. Dubs (Leiden, 1937).

[8] This passage is found in Ban Gu's survey of Han penal practices, *Hanshu*, ch. 23:1103. For a translation of this treatise, see A.F.P. Hulsewe, *Remnants of Han Law* (Leiden, 1955).

ordering that the statutes be cleansed of ambiguities and contradictions, an ambition consistent with other imperial governments as reflected for example in the interest in supervising the codes taken by Roman emperors in the fifth and sixth centuries CE.[9] In the Chinese case, the belief that emperors must not offend the natural order of things dictated that they needed to ensure that capital punishments be carried out in the proper season and after careful consideration. In sum, judging from the attention that China's early historians devote to law, they must have believed that a dynasty's legitimacy rested in part on the ability of its emperors to manage the legal system.

These Chinese materials are so interesting for students of tributary empires in general because they preserve deliberations about the most effective mechanisms for extending and maintaining control over vast territories most often gained initially by sheer force. When the founder of the Han Dynasty complained that he was tired of being reminded of his duties by references to models of the past in the most revered texts, he reminded his retainers that he had gained power on horseback rather than by reading the old books. One of his most loyal and honourable statesman, Lu Jia, famously replied, "You might have gained the empire by force, but you cannot rule it on horseback".[10] Some early Han writers also warned emperors and bureaucrats to learn the customs of the common people before allowing magistrates to impose standardized punishments. The significance of transferring to the state and its officers the right to inflict punishment is described eloquently in Danielle Allen's work on punishments in ancient Greece. As she points out, informal bodies, such as clans and guilds, do not have to rationalize their decisions to harm the bodies of their members: 'By contrast, legitimate punishments based on state authority must be justified at large within the political community. Punishments that make use of state power... must be defensible according to definitions of fairness and justice that prevail throughout the polity and that arise from the rules and principles giving legitimacy to the political authority under which the citizens are unified into a society'.[11]

---

[9] See Jill Harries, *Law and Empire in Late Antiquity* (Cambridge, England, 1999).

[10] *Shiji*, 97:2699. Citations are keyed to the Zhonghua Shuju edition and cited by chapter and page numbers. For a translation of this chapter, see Burton Watson, *Records*, Vol. 1, 219–33.

[11] Danielle Allen, *The World of Prometheus: The Politics of Punishing in Democratic Athens* (Princeton, 1999), 4. See the introduction to this study for a very useful summary of the issues around the use of state-sponsored violence.

All traditional empire builders faced the problem of legitimating their authority to override local customs and kinship practices on a much larger scale than elites in a small city state. As S.N. Eisenstadt points out in his comparative work on bureaucratic empires, these fragile polities survived only if able to satisfy the demands of 'new men', unfettered by kinship obligations and dependent on the state for their positions in the bureaucracy as well as the more conservative expectations of powerful families whose livelihood and status hinged on control of land and resources.[12] In general in China, landed elites and imperial relatives appealed to tradition when the law was invoked while career bureaucrats supported reforms to maintain uniformity and clarity in the laws. This bureaucratic commitment to standardization is not surprising, for as Max Weber observed, the technical requirements necessary to control any large, complex territory demanded uniform codes and procedures to guide and control bureaucrats sent out to extend the state's directives far beyond the metropole.[13]

Emperors and Bureaucrats

Before I proceed, I want to introduce readers to the rich quality of the Chinese materials with a few telling anecdotes about emperors and laws from the early years of the Han Dynasty. Tales that betray how much influence imperial women could wield, how ministers manipulated imperial succession, and how courageous and cruel officials asserted their authority, percolate through the histories. After the death of the founding emperor, Gaodi (202–195 BCE), his wife, Empress Lü (r. 188–180 BCE), took advantage of weak Liu heirs to place her own relatives in high positions.[14] The histories portray her as a cruel and manipulative woman who ignored her promise to the dying Emperor that she would support only blood relatives of his own family. But the histories also include enough information to demonstrate that she capably managed state affairs during this critical time for the new regime: one of her public acts was to take the role of the

---

[12] S.N. Eisenstadt, *The Political Systems of Empires* (New York, 1963). Much of his data on the Chinese empires are outdated, but the framework for comparisons remains useful.

[13] Weber's theories of rationality have been questioned, but in the Chinese case, his understanding that a vast territory could be governed by bureaucrats armed with uniform, written, consistent, written laws makes sense. See Max Weber, *Economy and Society*, Vol. 2, edited by Roth and Wittich (Berkeley, 1978).

[14] I refer to the founder of the Han Dynasty as Liu Bang before he became emperor, by his title Gaodi after his accession.

beneficent ruler to eliminate the harshest punishments. Moreover, she inadvertently perhaps, established a precedent for empresses and dowager empresses to manage the empire when no male kin seemed suited to the task.[15] Only after her death could the high officials who were loyal to the Liu Dynasty temper the power of the Lu clan and appoint an appropriate successor. They deemed the natural heir unfit to govern and agreed to select the King of Dai from among the 'throne-worthy' candidates. In their view he was the best man for the job at that time: he had a reputation for docility and his mother was not a known troublemaker. After appropriate gestures of humility, the King of Dai took the throne and was given the posthumous name, Xiao Wendi (r. 180–157 BCE), the filial, refined, civilian emperor. The histories portray Wendi and his officials as unusually preoccupied with defining the role of the emperor in the penal system.[16]

Early in his reign, Wendi convened two court debates with his high-ranking ministers and advisers to examine the harshest punishments: mutilating the criminal body and exterminating the relatives of sentenced criminals. In this arena the Emperor demonstrated his benign care for his people but also signalled his authority to make life and death decisions. To the Emperor's pleas for lenience, some of the officials replied that the practice of mutilation and the principle of mutual responsibility for crimes were not only ancient, but necessary: 'People cannot govern themselves.'[17] Wendi turned the debate against his opponents by pointing out that it was not ignorant commoners but incompetent and corrupt officials who needed to be monitored if the laws were to be applied fairly. Despite his orders to abolish the extreme punishments, they continued to be assigned—in one case by Wendi himself—especially in cases of treason.

The Emperor on more than one occasion ordered unduly severe punishments when his person or the symbols of the dynasty were threatened. In one famous incident, Zhang Shizhi, Commandant of Justice, and highest law officer in the bureaucracy, disobeyed Wendi's order to punish severely a commoner who had endangered the Emperor by startling his horses.[18] Wendi made the tactical error of ordering Commandant Zhang to mete

---

[15] For a concise and clear account of the founding of the dynasty, see Grant Hardy and Anne Behnke Kinney, *The Establishment of the Han Empire and Imperial China* (Westport, CT, 2005).

[16] *Shiji* 10. See the account of his reign in English in Watson, *Records*, Vol. I, 285–310.

[17] These exchanges are recorded in *Shiji* 10. See Watson, *Records*, 340–66.

[18] For a discussion of the history of the office of Commandant of Justice (tingwei), see A.F.P. Hulsewe, 'The Functions of the Commandant of Justice during the Han Period',

out a harsher punishment than the crime warranted. Famously, the official replied: 'The Commandant of Justice is charged with keeping the empire in balance. To allow even one deviation in the laws would cause them to not be taken seriously. And then how would the people behave?'.[19] Here Zhang asserted the authority of the laws over the whims of the Emperor. More than the issue of proper sentences was at stake. Zhang Shizhi at this juncture defined the role of the emperor in the legal system: 'The law is what the Son of Heaven shares with his people. If it were made harsher in this case, the people would no longer trust it'. The angry Emperor then reminded the bureaucrat that he could have had the man executed on the spot. But Zhang Shizhi countered that once a case entered the domain of legal officials, correct standards had to be followed.

Han Wendi has been memorialized in the histories as an exceptionally benign ruler, and Zhang Shizhi appears as an unusually upright official—in another case he took upon himself the task of sentencing a member of the imperial clan. Most of Zhang's successors did not display his courage or commitment to fairness, but by virtue of their position as head of the legal bureaucracy, they could not avoid direct involvement in high profile cases. The office was inherited from the Qin bureaucratic structure, and the Han founder added to its portfolio by extending its authority to supervise local cases.[20] Sima Qian's biographies of the high officials offer clues about the workings of the office and the dangers faced by its incumbents. Zhang Tang, for example, took his cues from the tough-minded Emperor Wu and added the crime of 'disapproval of the heart' to the list of capital crimes, a treason law in effect. With the Emperor's support, he removed ambiguities from the existing statutes and brought in experts on the ancient texts who could help him rationalize judgments about hard cases. He was forced to commit suicide when jealous officials turned the Emperor against him by charging that he had too often violated the old laws.[21] In fact, most of the officials who tampered with the laws met a violent end—especially if they interfered with the privileges of imperial relatives and other landed nobles.

Charles Le Blanc and Susan Blader, eds., *Chinese Ideas about Nature and Society* (Hong Kong, 1987), 249–64.

[19] See the biography of this remarkable official in *Shiji* 102; Watson, *Records*, Vol. 1, 467–72.

[20] Newly discovered Han texts confirm that Gaodi did enlarge the scope of the office. See Michael Nylan, 'Notes on a Case of Illicit Sex from Zhangjiashan: A Translation and Commentary', *Early China* 30 (2005–2006), 25–45.

[21] *Shiji* 122 contains the biographies of officials categorized as 'harsh', which included officials who had dealings with the laws. In English, see Watson, *Records*, Vol. II, 419–51.

Patterns from the Past

Change, necessary even if dangerous, was often cloaked under what Henry Maine called the 'legal fiction'.[22] Emperors often appealed to the laws of the former kings, or the laws of the founder, even while they sponsored legal reform. Chengdi (r.33–7 BCE), after ordering the legal officers to clarify the statutes governing the death penalty, declared: 'We must strive to conform with the laws of antiquity'.[23] The historian, Ban Gu, ended his survey of Han penal practices with his vision of the grand picture: 'I will present what has happened since the Han arose to show how the laws and regulations have been fixed to conform with antiquity, even though changed to suit the present age'.[24] The tradition by Han times consisted of a bricolage of mixed messages that could provide fodder for both sides of an argument about good government. Revered texts, such as *The Book of Songs*, a collection of folktales critical of government interference in the lives of the common people, or *The Book of History*, a record of the activities of the ancient sage kings, were called upon at times to support decisions about governing. For example, Han Wendi appealed to *The Book of History* to legitimate his proposal to pass over his son and search the realm for a competent successor in the manner of the revered sage kings. His startled advisers reminded him that the welfare of the Liu dynasty should take priority over his foolish desire. By the Han period, father-son succession was the preferred method, but models from the past did afford justification for rejecting an unsuitable heir.[25] Indeed, one of the strongest messages from Warring States thinkers was that the person of the ruler was less important than the people, the dynasty, or the laws.

---

[22] Henry Maine, *Ancient Law* (New York, 1983).

[23] This reluctance to admit that new laws must be created to meet the times is in part due to reverence for the past, especially important in the Han as officials were attempting to legitimate decisions. See Michael Puett, *The Ambivalence of Creation: Debates Concerning Innovation and Artifice in Early China* (Stanford, 2001) for an interesting discussion about fear of innovation.

[24] See Ban Gu's survey of penal practices in *Hanshu* 23: 1103, Hulsewe, *Remnants of Han law*, 340.

[25] For a survey of debates about succession practices and ideal monarchy, see Yuri Pines, *Envisioning Eternal Empire: Chinese Political Thought of the Warring States Era* (Honolulu, 2009). I disagree with the author's contention that by the imperial period father-son succession was the norm, but his survey is useful for understanding how many models of good rulership emerged from classical Chinese writers.

Mencius (379–304 BCE), following Confucius (d. 479 BCE), placed the welfare of the people above the needs of the state, and justified rebellion against kings who abused the population to suit their own preferences.[26] The earliest prominent legalist, Shang Yang (d. 338 BCE), argued that the personalities and passions of rulers and magistrates must be tempered to protect the interests of the state. Institutions would not survive even the best of rulers: 'Sages cannot transfer to others the personality and nature that is inherent in them. Only through law can this be accomplished.'[27] Moreover, the ruler was bound to follow the laws himself as he warned: 'The enlightened ruler must be careful with the laws and regulations ... and never carry out state activities that are not centered in law'.[28] Later, Han Fei (d. 233 BCE) developed a more coherent political theory that emphasized harsh but consistent punishments backed by clear, published laws as the basic tools for running a state. The Legalist writers have been accused by later generations of acting as the original sponsors of despotic government, but in fact they separated the state from its rulers and attempted to impose measures to eliminate lawlessness at all levels of society.[29] The 'law' in its broadest sense offered a neutral mechanism for balancing crime with the proper punishment, but the ruling elite made sure that their ranks within the bureaucratic structure offered some protection from state-imposed physical violence or public humiliation. Perhaps their greatest fear was that impartial laws imposed by strangers, which was fair for the common people, might extend to the detriment of the ruling class. A great deal of propaganda was put forth to mask this double standard.

One of the most eloquent statements about a workable compromise between human discretion and formal laws was put forth by Xunzi, (c. 310–230 BCE), a teacher and administrator who lived at a time when force ruled the day and sage kings were all too rare. He recognized that a centralized state imposed great burdens on the common people but also that it offered the best chance for peace and order. He pointed out that

---

26 See Pines, *Eternal Empire* for an account of how these writers contributed to models of monarchy and governance.

27 *Shangjunshu* 4.9. For an English translation of the text, see J.L.L. Duyvendak, *The Book of Lord Shang* (Chicago, 1963).

28 Duyvendak, *The Book of Lord Shang*, Chapter 1, contains an interesting description of the debates about reforming the old laws in the Qin state.

29 For an example of a contemporary Chinese critique, see Liang Zhiping, 'Explicating 'Law': A Comparative Perspective of Chinese and Western Legal Culture', *Journal of Chinese Law* 81 (1989), 55–91. For a counterargument see Karen Turner, 'Rule of Law Ideals in Early China?', *Journal of Chinese Law* 6 (1992), 1–44.

a state would survive only when its managers balanced human wisdom with institutional stability:

> Laws cannot stand alone... for when they are implemented by the right person, they survive, but if neglected they disappear... Law is the basis of good government but the superior man is the foundation of law. So when there is a superior man, the law, even if sparse, will cover any situation. If there is no superior man, even if the laws are all embracing, they will neither apply to all situations, nor be flexible enough to respond to change.[30]

Xunzi's vision rested on placing educated men like himself above the laws, but he did acknowledge that laws served as a necessary framework for making decisions about public affairs, from implementing correct punishments to waging a just war. By the fourth century some writers went a step beyond Xunzi to place their faith in clear laws and consistent punishments that left no room for arbitrary actions.[31] Perhaps the most eloquent statements are found in *Guanzi, a* text associated with a powerful Warring States minister but redacted during the Han. In one passage, the text argues in favour of following standards that did not rely on historical models or human discretion as a superior means to secure popular support:

> Statutes, regulations and measures must be modeled on the *dao*. Commands and ordinances must be clear and open, rewards and punishments trusted and definite. These are the constant standards for bringing a just order to the people. When an enlightened ruler is on the throne, laws modeled on the *dao* will be implemented throughout the realm and people will give up what they desire and instead do what is [ordinarily] abhorrent to them.[32]

The *dao*, or path, here refers to a principle as consistent as the unchanging order of the seasons, a standard for governing that remained immune from human manipulation. Any change could bring about unforeseen consequences and had to be carefully considered.

The anonymous author of *Jingfa*, one of the texts unearthed in China in the late 1970s, portrays the sage ruler as one who acts only in the public interest: 'The world is not the world of one man.' The anonymous author of this treatise assigns great weight to the virtue of impartiality: 'Laws and regulations are of the utmost importance in governing... if you are public

---

30 *Xunzi* 8.1. For a translation of this text see John Knobloch, trans., *Xunzi: A Translation and Study of the Complete* Works, *Vol. 1 and 2* (Stanford, 1988).

31 See Karen Turner, 'War, Punishment, and the Law of Nature in Early Chinese concepts of the State', *Harvard Journal of Asiatic Studies* 53 (1993), 285–324, for an interpretation of the meaning of this turn toward nature as a guide for governing.

32 *Guanzi* 6: 4b–5a. See Rickett, trans., *Guanzi*, 256–257.

spirited and without private bias, your rewards and punishments will be trusted'.[33] Envisioned here is a utopian world in which rulers repaid their people for contributing their labour and taxes to the state by maintaining clearly defined and published criminal laws. But this conception of law did not allow for ordinary people to judge whether or not laws merit obedience: only a sage king, imbued with special powers, could interpret the messages contained in the workings of nature and apply them to the legal system.[34] Other models that rely less on human intervention are embedded in texts that accepted the principle that law was a more necessary component of a viable state than the ruler. The *Huainanzi*, a Han text assembled by a rebellious imperial relative, focused mainly on the art of ruling, but recognized the vital importance of law: 'A state on the brink of disaster is not one without a ruler, but one without laws'.[35]

No writer disagreed with the Confucian contention that women had no place in public affairs or that a civilized society rested on maintaining a strict separation of the sexes. But patterns from the past that demonstrated that kingship was not necessarily the privilege of blood relatives and that a state could not survive without a capable manager did open up the possibility that a woman could run the government in the absence of a strong male leader. By the Qin and Han periods the prevailing cosmological scheme assumed that the male, *yang* figure, associated with the sun, summer, and the stern patriarch, must be balanced by the female, *yin* figure, associated with the moon, autumn, and the benevolent matriarch. Eventually Dong Zhongshu, an influential Han Confucian, presented a model that rendered the female force, identified with punishment, subordinate to the male force, identified with education. But while his scheme rationalized female subordination as a natural state, he could not deny that the female force was a necessary component to keep the human and

[33] This text has been divided by the editors into treatises, which I cite by title. The text I use is *Mawangdui Hanmu boshu* [Books on silk from the Han tomb at Mawangdui] (Beijing, 1980).

[34] In the 'Junjing' section. For a discussion of the text see Karen Turner, 'The Theory of Law in the Ching-fa.', *Early China* 14 (1989), 55–76. R.P. Peerenboom argues that these texts represent the thought of a particular time in the early Han. See *Law and Morality in Ancient China: The Silk Manuscripts of Huang-Lao*. (SUNY, 1993.) I argue that many of the ideas in the text are reflected in other Han and Warring States writings. See Turner, 'War, Punishment and the Law of Nature'.

[35] *Huainanzi*, 9.14. For a complete recent translations, see John Major et al., editor and translator, *The Huainanzi: A Guide to the Theory of Practice and Government in Early Han China* (New York, 2009), 321.

natural worlds ordered. In this system, Heaven, Earth, and all living creatures were connected so that when one element became out of balance the consequences would resonate throughout the cosmos.[36] The emperor was believed to serve as the pivotal figure between the heavenly powers that granted his mandate to rule and the earthly realm that governed the welfare of his people. Ensuring that punishments be neither too harsh nor too lenient was one of the emperor's most serious tasks for only a suitable punishment would cancel out the disorder caused by deviance. As a prominent Han official wrote, 'When punishments fit the crime, villainy and evil will stop. When rewards are appropriate for excellence, then the people will be encouraged [to obey]'.[37] And other texts include passages that directly place blame for mismanagement: 'Inappropriate punishments will bring calamity upon the ruler himself'.[38]

Emperors allowed the death penalty to be misapplied at their own peril and so attempted to keep watch over procedures in capital cases. Jia Yi (201–169 BCE), one of the most influential early Han statesmen and a critic of the Qin regime, articulated a sentiment that was unusual in a legal culture that automatically assumed guilt before innocence: 'If punishments are warranted by the crimes [in question], you can punish many people without being at fault. If punishments are not correct and you kill one person [unjustly], your crime will be reported to the heavenly power'.[39]

How 'Heaven' (*Tian*) was envisioned is a subject of debate, for the term could refer to a vengeful deity, a supreme ancestor, or a non-human cosmic space. But clearly in this context, it was conceived as a force that acted as a supreme judge, superior to and capable of punishing any ruler. The signs of divine displeasure would be manifested as natural disasters or anomalies: eclipses, earthquakes, draught, locusts, or floods, and these could be interpreted by anyone, not simply courtiers, as signs of misrule. It was the duty of the reigning emperor to correct the imbalances that brought harm to his people. *The History of the Han Dynasty* contains accounts of emperors publicly accepting responsibility for these unnatural events. In one interesting incident, when Han Wendi was informed that flooding was caused by an excess of the yin power associated with the female and rain, he responded by sending a number of women out of

[36] For a comprehensive study of Han cosmology and politics, see Aihe Wang, *Cosmology and Political Culture in Early China* (Cambridge, England, 2000).

[37] From *Hanshu*, 48.3a.

[38] *Jing fa*, 'Guoci' section. See Turner, 'The Theory of Law in the *Ching-fa*.'

[39] *Xinshu*, 7.4b. This text has not yet been translated into English.

his court.[40] Wilful or inept emperors could ignore or neglect their responsibilities to keep the world in order, but they were literate men who were well aware that dissenters could call on a powerful vocabulary to justify their positions.

Law and Empire: The Qin Dynasty (221–207 BCE)

Warring States writers were not bystanders who shied away from politics—they wrote from observation and experience. Confucius served as a local judge. Shang Yang and Han Fei, a student of Xunzi, actively involved themselves in reforming the laws in the state of Qin: so dangerous were their challenges to entrenched interests that they were executed when they lost the support of the kings they served. By the middle of the third century it became clear that the king of the far Western state of Qin harboured the ambition to eliminate his six rival kings, and that he was backed by abundant resources and a well-organized army. Xunzi travelled to Qin around 244 BCE to see for himself how the government worked and reported that the kingdom was stable and its subjects law abiding.[41] Xunzi's teachings had influence on patterns of history. Han Fei was his student and Li Si, the true architect of empire, had also studied with him. As Imperial Chancellor at the time that the Qin Shihuangdi took the title of emperor in 221 BCE, Li Si changed the course of Chinese history when he mapped out a blueprint for the new centralized state. He advised the Emperor to standardize the laws, burn the time-honoured books that justified regicide and rebellion, and reject the customary practice of enfeoffing imperial relatives to administer newly conquered territories.[42] Instead he outlined a grid in which territory was divided into units of organization created to secure centralized control, administered by a trinity composed of a military commander, civil governor, and imperial inspector who reported directly to the emperor. Administrators could not pass on their offices to family members, and so the central government maintained the authority to appoint personnel that would support its goals. Local control was delegated to magistrates salaried and appointed by the state. This policy replaced a system organized by kinship ties with a bureaucracy run

---

[40] See *Shiji* 10, *Hanshu* 4.13b, Dubs, *History of the Former Han Dynasty*, Vol. I, 252.

[41] For an account of Xunzi's influence and travels, see Knoblock, *Xunzi*, ch. 2.

[42] For an account of his life see Derk Bodde, *China's First Unifier: A Study of the Ch'in Dynasty as Seen in the Life of Li Ssu* (Hong Kong, 1938).

by servants of the state. Although large, landed families did at times exert influence on politics, the bureaucracy reconstituted itself with each new dynasty and provided continuity when new dynasties established their regimes.

Despite advice that he should break with the past, the First Emperor of Qin called upon time-honoured models to legitimate his conquest. As he progressed through newly conquered territories to display his power and beneficence, Qin Shihuangdi ordered that inscriptions on stone steles record his promise to keep the laws clear and consistent in order to honour the model rulers of the long-distant past.[43] The historians portray the First Emperor as a workaholic who intruded in all aspects of government, but we cannot assess with available materials to what degree he influenced the statutes and procedures for determining punishments. We do have independent evidence, however, about the goals of the legal experts who formulated the laws and procedures for administering punishments in local areas far from the Qin capital. The most important cache of bamboo slips, dated from around 217 BCE, was found in 1975 in the grave of a low-level Qin official charged with supervising convict labour and trying criminal cases in one of the areas that had been most resistant to the Qin impositions.[44] Among the treasures included in this tomb were samples for reporting crimes to higher authorities, manuals with questions and answers about interpreting the statutes, and strict guidelines for measuring and extracting human and material resources.

The worth of individual labourers, in this case conscripts, was determined by regulations to measure their labour potential and the exact amount of food necessary to keep them working—officials who overfed the labourers under their supervision would be fined, or punished if they couldn't reimburse the state for wasted resources. Strict procedures for tracking and reporting decisions about punishments and the quality and quantity of the labour pool to higher authorities allowed no room for discretionary judgments. James Scott's description of the 'politics of measurement' that informed the early modern European state's drive to create a legible blueprint for extracting resources aptly characterizes the

[43] See *Shiji* 6 and Martin Kern, *The Stele Inscriptions of Ch'in Shi-huang: Text and Ritual in Early Chinese Representation* (Honolulu, 2000) for a study of the First Emperor's attempt to legitimate his rule.

[44] For a full translation of this important text, see A.F.P. Hulsewe, *Remnants of Ch'in Law* (Leiden, 1985). For a discussion of the important information in these materials see Robin D.S. Yates, 'Social Status in the Ch'in: Evidence from the Yun-meng Legal Documents, Part One', *Harvard Journal of Asiatic Studies* 47 (1987).

strategies employed by the Qin state.[45] But unlike early modern reformers in Europe, the Qin lawmakers displayed no interest in implanting new norms in the minds of their subjects. Control of labouring bodies was their single-minded goal. It is clear that the anonymous architects of this legal system placed a high premium on correct procedures, not in the interest of protecting officials and their local charges from abuse but in order to curb corruption and mismanagement. From laws designed to punish resistance or manipulation, we can infer that the lawmakers worried about a backlash when laws were imposed. This strict system did provide some protection from arbitrary punishments, for everyone supposedly knew the rules, and the rules were ideally consistently applied. But such benefits were accidental offshoots of a system that placed the needs of the state above the welfare of its subjects.

Law and Legitimacy: The Western Han Dynasty (202 BCE–23 CE)

The disintegration of the Qin union after the First Emperor's death in 210 BCE was interpreted by early Han officials as a popular response to Qin's draconian laws and punishments. Whatever the reality might have been, Han writers and officials had to make sense of the precipitous fall of the First Empire if they hoped to create a solid foundation for their own ruling house, which had resorted to strategy and military force to eliminate the Qin dynasty. Sima Qian described the founder of Han, Liu Bang, as a rude commoner who had once worked as a lowly official in the service of the Qin. When leading a group of corvée labourers to work on the emperor's tomb, he was delayed by a storm. Knowing that he and his men would be punished for a late arrival, with nothing to lose, he raised a rebellion against the Qin. After learning the ways of a warrior, Liu Bang began to display signs that he might turn out to be a capable administrator by reforming the laws of Qin. After the last Qin heir surrendered, Liu Bang prepared the way for his dangerous foray into the old Qin heartland by issuing amnesties and tax reliefs and promising the people that he would

[45] See James Scott, *Seeing Like a State* (New Haven, 1998). Foucault's conception of 'bio-power' offers insight relevant to assessing the Qin state's preoccupation with harvesting human resources, without the technological apparatus that characterized Foucault's early modern European State. See especially *Discipline and Punish: The Birth of the Prison* (New York, 1990). See Karen Turner for a discussion of the link between the criminal body and the state: 'The Criminal Body and the Body Politic: Punishments in Early Imperial China', *Cultural Dynamics* 11 (1999) 237–54.

simplify the laws. Once installed as emperor, he ordered that doubtful cases from lower-level officials be sent through the official hierarchy and finally, if necessary, to the Commandant of Justice or in capital cases to the emperor himself for a decision: 'Those cases that the Commandant of Justice cannot decide must be sent to the emperor, with a carefully prepared memorial and the appropriate precedents, statutes and edicts'.[46] We know now that this was not an empty promise. Materials excavated in 1983 from a grave at Jiangjiashan include a manual to guide local officials when deciding hard cases, at times with the Commandant of Justice in attendance, and strict guidelines for reporting up the chain of authority, even to the emperor himself in sensitive cases.[47] One case involved finding a proper sentence for a wife who was reported to the authorities for fornicating with another man behind the chamber that held her husband's coffin and his grieving mother.[48] According to the record, after a great deal of deliberation, the officials decided that she should not be punished for her disrespectful behaviour because her husband was already dead at the time of the offense.

Records from the histories and texts composed by high officials who served the Han dynasty show that they made good use of the fall of Qin to warn their own rulers of the price of abusing the laws. In the words of one Han official, the Qin dynasty lost the empire because the laws proliferated and became confusing, thus allowing the magistrates, 'to take advantage of the numerous, ambiguous laws to bolster their authority ... and to make life and death decisions according to their own wanton lights'.[49] The most famous Han Confucian, Dong Zhongshu (ca. 179–104 BCE), opined that the rulers of Qin 'failed to convince the good that they would be safe from violence and the evil that they would face certain punishment'.[50] Despite this rhetoric, in fact the laws of Qin became the basis for the Han legal codes. Before ordering the Qin capital burned, Liu Bang sent one of his most trusted counsellors to save copies of the laws and regulations stored

[46] For an account in English of these events, see Hardy and Kinney, *The Establishment of the Han Empire*.

[47] Li Xueqin and Xing Wen outline the dating and contents of this corpus in 'New Light on the Early Han Code: Reappraisal of the Zhangjiashan Bamboo-slip Legal Texts', *Asia Major* 14 (2001). Ulrich Lau provides more information in 'The Scope of Private Jurisdiction in Early Imperial China', *Asiatische Studien/Etudes Asiatiques* 49 (2005).

[48] Michael Nylan offers an interesting summary and interpretation of this event in 'Notes on a Case of Illicit Sex from Zhangjiashan', 25–45.

[49] *Hanshu* 49:2296.

[50] *Hanshu* 56.

there. With new evidence for comparing the Qin and Han codes, we know that, despite Liu Bang's declaration that he would simplify the laws, in fact he adopted the Qin laws wholesale and his successors added statutes.[51] According to Ban Gu, the laws became more cumbersome and confusing as time went on, and emperors continued to assume responsibility for clarifying the laws, supervising the officials, and determining the timing and severity of capital punishments. Han emperors took care to present themselves as the guardians of the laws that would protect innocent subjects from abuse.[52] Han Xuandi, (r. 74–49 BCE) for example, had been raised among the common people and was thought to understand their problems from first-hand experience. When a clerk in the Commandant of Justice's office complained to the Emperor that the Han had not succeeded in simplifying the laws of Qin, which placed a strain on his office, the Emperor ordered the staff enlarged so that 'lawsuits would be carried out according to the emperor's wishes'.[53] This supposedly benign ruler is in fact declaring that the will of the ruler rather than the statutes should serve as the ultimate authority in law cases.

Family troubles cropped up as soon as Liu Bang became emperor. First, his attempt to secure peace and consolidate power by allotting his lands to his trusted warriors instead of his relatives backfired as they rebelled one by one, in some cases simply because they did not believe that he deserved to act as an emperor any more than his companions. He had no choice but to grant kingdoms to his own sons and grandsons, but they too could not be trusted and posed a constant threat to the dynasty. Second, he did not inherit his position and his father was still alive. His advisers worried that 'the world will not be at peace if two emperors coexist' and warned him that he would have to discontinue his filial visits to his father and sort out the relationship to show that his father assumed the role of subject rather than head of the imperial clan. When he next visited, as the story goes, his father greeted him with symbols of subservience and declared that he would not want his son to show him favouritism or violate the laws of the empire on his account.[54]

Later emperors never resolved the problem of punishing members of their family according to the values of consistency and impartiality that

---

[51] See Li Xueqin, 'New Light on the Early Han Code'.
[52] *Hanshu* 23. See Hulsewe, *Remnants of Han Law.*
[53] *Hanshu* 23: 1102, Hulsewe, *Remnants of Han Law*, 338.
[54] In *Shiji* 8; See Watson, *Records*, Vol. 1, 77.

ideally applied to everyone else. In charged cases dealing with the imperial family, emperors ceded the nasty job to the Commandant of Justice or to their mothers and grandmothers—when it suited them. It was one matter to order officials to punish the common people according to strict guidelines but quite another to harm relatives even when they threatened the dynasty and its symbols of authority. Treason laws were necessary to protect the emperor from violence in Han China and to guard the symbols of the dynasty from irreverent acts.[55] When a commoner stole a jade ring from the founder's tomb, Wendi ordered the elimination of the criminal and his family—despite having earlier ordered that the practice of punishing the innocent families of criminals be eliminated. When Zhang Shizhi pointed out that according to the statutes the criminal alone should be executed, Wendi discussed the matter with his mother and backed down. But when Zhang reported that the heir apparent and his brother had violated imperial privileges when they failed to halt their horses at the palace gates, Wendi apologized to his mother for failing to raise his sons properly and obeyed the Dowager's order to pardon the boys.

In the reign of the autocratic Wudi, only a fool would risk his life to interfere in matters involving the imperial clan. The famous *fangshi* (court jester) at Han Wudi's court, Dongfang Shuo, cloaked his cynicism about the emperor's favouritism in nonsense riddles.[56] But in some situations, he was very clear and direct. In one case, the Emperor's son-in-law, the only son of an imperial princess, was so unruly that his mother before she died paid for a commutation of the death sentence should her obviously delinquent son commit a capital offense that she would not be around to fix. He did commit murder and the Commandant of Justice referred the case to the Emperor. Despite pleas from various parties on the murderer's behalf, 'weeping and sighing', the Emperor approved the death sentence. He justified his decision to get rid of an obviously dangerous relative by appealing to his duty to respect the laws of the former emperors and the founder of the Han and to keep faith with the common

---

55 Gary Arbuckle argues that loyalty to the dynasty and its symbols was more important than loyalty to the reigning emperor, and in the cosmological scheme that prevailed in Han times symbols could be manipulated to serve ambitious contenders. The hold of the Liu clan on the office of emperor was fragile indeed. See 'Inevitable Treason: Dong Zhongshu's Theory of Historical Cycles and Early Attempts to Invalidate the Han Mandate', *Journal of the American Oriental Society* 115 (1985), 585–97.

56 These incidents are recorded in *Hanshu* 65; See Burton Watson, *Courtier and Commoner in Ancient China* (New York, 1974), 78–106.

people. As Wudi carried on with grief, Dongfang Shuo stepped up to toast him for emulating the sage kings, 'who did not spare their own flesh and blood when punishing a criminal act'. After suffering the Emperor's anger, the court jester reminded him that he was drinking to him to honour his refusal to bow to favouritism, adding, besides, 'nothing is better than wine to chase away grief'.[57]

At times a profound ambivalence about harming a kinsman, even one that threatened the dynasty, surfaces in the Chinese texts. During Han Wendi's reign, his brother, one of the territorial kings, openly expressed his intent to raise a rebellion. But despite the entreaties of court officials, the emperor could not bear to punish him. Finally after his brother had been formally charged by officials at court for so disrespecting the laws of the dynasty that he was not fit to rule his kingdom, Wendi agreed to send him into exile, but he died along the way. Sima Qian's response to this incident is interesting. Even though the historian had every reason to rail against favouritism in legal decisions, and even though he was implicitly critical of Wendi for his passive stance in the face of rebellious relatives, he ended his account by repeating a ditty that supposedly indicated widespread disapproval of Wendi's decision: '...What of two brothers, older and younger, who could not spare a bit of land for each other?'[58] We know from the Jiangjiashan materials that by this time regulations for governing the behaviour of the Liu kings were on the books. But historical accounts of cases involving the emperor's kin reveal that the statutes were rarely invoked to justify a decision to sanction a member of the imperial family. Instead far more malleable guidelines were called upon—the practices of the ancient sage kings, or the founder of the dynasty, or simply the revered laws of old.

Despite Wudi's reputation as a tyrant, when two of the dynasty's most loyal servants, both at the rank of marquis and relatives of the imperial clan, were involved in a dispute, Wudi sent the matter to his court for a decision. His mother berated him for allowing the case to be tried outside the clan, whereupon he replied that if the men were not relatives he would have turned to matter over to any legal official but instead gave them the benefit of a hearing that might be tempered by men with ties to the imperial family. The conflict between the laws and family ties is

---

[57] Watson, *Courtier and Commoner*, 88; *Hanshu*, 65:2853.

[58] The account of Wendi's debates with his officials about punishing Liu Chang is recorded in *Shiji* 118; See Watson, *Records*, Vol. 11, 357–387.

illustrated clearly in a case in which Han Jingdi (r. 157–141 BCE) discovered that his brother, the King of Liang, was plotting rebellion. He was advised not to punish the king on these grounds: 'If the affair is brought to light, your brother will have to be punished and the laws of the dynasty will be violated. If he is ordered to suffer the most extreme punishment according to the law, then your mother, the Empress Dowager, will be so distressed that she will not eat or sleep and that will cause your majesty great worry.' The Emperor backed down and rewarded his advisor with a high position.[59] The power of the dowagers was vividly demonstrated when bureaucrats argued that imperial women should not be allowed to petition the emperor or interfere with state business. Some of these brave officials were simply ignored, while others were imprisoned, and in one case driven to suicide.

The dual identity of the Han emperor as a manager in affairs of state and head of the imperial clan informed succession rituals. The title, *Tianzi*, Heaven's Son, was bestowed as soon as the new emperor was chosen—so that the machinery of government could continue without interruption—and once invested with the title, he could begin to carry out public acts such as issuing edicts and amnesties. But only after he had demonstrated his capacity to honour his dynastic ancestors by demonstrating proper behaviour during the funeral rites for his predecessor was he allowed to sacrifice in the temple of the founder and then assigned the title of *Huangdi*, August Sage. Nishijima Sadao observed that *Tianzi* was a rank, the highest in the official hierarchy, while *Huangdi* marked a new ruler as the ritual head of the imperial clan.[60] In one famous incident, an heir who flagrantly violated the rules of appropriate behaviour was dethroned after ruling as Son of Heaven for only twenty-seven days. One of the officers at the court justified this unusual intervention:

> The ancestral temples are of greater importance than the ruler. The present emperor has not yet received the mandate to rule in the temple of the founder. He is not fit to carry on the succession as defined by the Heavenly spirits…or to watch over the ten thousand clans like a father. He should be deposed.[61]

---

59 *Shiji* 104, see Watson, *Records* Vol. 1, 356–61.

60 Nishijima Sadao, *Chugoku kodai teikoku no keisei to kozo* (Tokyo, 1961).

61 *Hanshu* 68.

The Dowager Empress, fifteen years old at the time, presided over the hearing, dressed in a splendid garment sewn for the occasion, made up of pearls—potent symbols of water, fertility and female power.

Conclusion

The Han Dynasty finally collapsed in 220 CE when the balance of power shifted from bureaucrats to eunuchs and their allies among the relatives of empresses who directed state affairs in the name of weak or very young heirs. Powerful local families sapped resources from the central government and the legal system suffered in the bargain, according to Ban Gu's accounts. In the absence of rulers capable of managing the bureaucracy and career bureaucrats willing to advise and censure them, the laws proliferated and became unclear and punishments more arbitrary and unfairly harsh. As we have seen, power shifted among ruling elites, and sometimes emperors would side with their career officials or submit hard cases to their mothers, when it suited their purposes. But with each new dynasty, the bureaucratic structure was reconstituted, and now and again a few brave men, who sided with the fate of the empire, stepped forward to challenge emperors and their relatives when their actions endangered the state—and the integrity of the bureaucratic structure that legitimated their official positions.

The Qin and early Han era, when the empire and a workable legal system to manage it were in the process of creation, represents an unusual moment in the long span of Chinese history. With the promulgation of China's first systematic code during the Tang Dynasty (619–906), relationships that were once open to negotiation became much more hierarchical and rigid. Some emperors personally supervised the legal system, while others took a more laissez-faire approach. The first emperor to deliberately use law as a means to promote his stern vision of morality was the founder of the Ming Dynasty (1368–1644). But the belief that the emperor assumed personal responsibility for the taking of life remained constant. Even non-Chinese rulers, such as the Manchu Kangxi of the Qing Dynasty (1644–1911), continued to supervise the sentencing and administration of punishments for capital crimes.

Strong-willed imperial women wielded power throughout the imperial period. Empress Lü of Han stepped in to manage public affairs in the absence of a strong heir, but the only woman to rule in her own name was Empress Wu (ca. 623–705) of the Tang Dynasty. She cleverly manipulated symbols of legitimacy in order to bolster female power and codified into law some of the rituals that honoured women. In some views, the imperial system itself was fatally weakened in the early twentieth century by the machinations of a Dowager Empress, Cixi (1868–1913), who so feared the prospect of a constitutional monarchy that she tried to halt reforms that might have saved a system that had endured for over a thousand years. The Chinese empire endured as long as it did, however, because the bureaucratic and legal traditions offered continuity as each new dynasty consolidated power. And the conception of monarchy that allowed the most suitable member of the 'throne-worthy' clan, even a woman, to actually guide affairs of state provided flexibility for dealing with changing times.

THE RULER AND LAW MAKING IN THE OTTOMAN EMPIRE*

Engin Deniz Akarlı

Empires of the early modern era were composite formations. They incorporated societies with different cultural and political traditions through various arrangements and levels of submission or accommodation. Changing conditions led to intermittent renegotiation and adjustment of these arrangements—particularly in the case of empires that endured several centuries.[1]

Law (in the sense of legal institutions and practices as well as rulings and regulations) played a crucial role in perpetuating an imperial order and sustaining the fluid social and political networks it comprised. A major challenge in this regard was to maintain law's claim to universality (hence consistency) along with its ability to accommodate differences in space and changes over time. All major legal traditions, including the modern ones, face this challenge, but pre-modern empires had to respond to it without the benefit of modern technological and organizational means of coordination and control. How did law work or failed to work as a force that helped generate a sense of order, continuity and legitimacy in the diverse social environments of pre-modern empires? Ottoman history provides some clues.

The Ottoman State

The Ottoman state emerged in a culturally heterogeneous frontier zone between the Saljuk and Byzantine territories in northwestern Anatolia around 1300. It was one of the smallest of the many principalities vying for dominance in the region upon the collapse of the Saljuks and the

* A National Endowment for Humanities fellowship at the Institute for Advanced Study in Princeton, an Islamic Legal Studies Program fellowship at Harvard Law School, and the support of Brown University made possible the research behind this article. I am grateful to these institutions.

[1] Karen Barkey, *Empire of Difference: The Ottomans in Comparative Perspective* (Cambridge, 2008) and Frederick Cooper, *Colonialism in Question: Theory, Knowledge, History* (Berkeley, 2005), 152–203, discuss the Ottoman Empire in a comparative perspective.

weakening of the Byzantine state. The Ottomans[2] prevailed and built an enduring empire that spanned southeastern Europe, western Asia, and North Africa. This was a gradual development that enabled the formation of adaptable institutions and sustainable networks. The Ottomans crossed the Dardanelles in the 1330s and slowly expanded their control in both the Balkans and Anatolia. Only in 1453 did they finally capture Istanbul and inherit from the Byzantine emperors the glory and advantages of having a major world metropolis as their capital city as well as the patronage of the Ecumenical Church of Constantinople. The conquest of the major cities of the Arab Middle East early in the sixteenth century brought the Ottomans the added prestige of the custodianship of the sacred pilgrimage sites of all three Abrahamic religions in addition to access to rich manuscript collections of Islamic scholarship. The empire did not begin to contract irretrievably until the last quarter of the eighteenth century and even then it maintained its cultural pluralism well into the nineteenth century.

Failures of the Ottoman state in the modern era and of the ethnic and religious wars that marked its final decades should not diminish a historian's curiosity about the arrangements, institutions and cultural traditions that sustained the Ottoman regime over a vast and culturally diverse area as long as it did. One would logically expect law to be an important dimension of this curiosity, for no state can last long without a working legal system and commitment to reasonably practicable notions of justice. Yet only recently have the rich sources of Ottoman legal history begun to attract attention.[3] We now have a fairly good idea about the formation and development of Ottoman legal institutions and practice. However, making sense of Ottoman legal history on its own terms remains a challenge, partly because modern conceptions of religion in general and Islam in particular as a sectarian force make it difficult to imagine how the imperial nature and the Islamic basis of Ottoman legal culture could have meshed. A long-dominant consequence of this predicament has been to pit the 'secular' sultanic laws of the state against its 'religious' laws. This position is problematic not only because it projects modern presuppositions and sensibilities backward into history. It also rests on an undifferentiated, unreflective and communitarian concept of religion that kills in

[2] By 'Ottomans' I mean not only the sultans but also the ruling elite or the leadership of the state in general—after Norman Itzkowitz, *The Ottoman Empire and the Imperial Tradition* (New York, 1972).

[3] *Türk Hukuk Tarihi*, special issue of *Türkiye Araştırmaları Literatür Dergisi* 3/5 (2005), offers a valuable survey of the current state of research on different aspects of Ottoman legal history.

the bud any curiosity about the possible effects of universalist connotations of the notion of God on the formation of broadly relevant norms of good governance and justice.[4]

This article attempts to make sense of the Ottoman legal system on its own terms, with due attention to contemporaneous ideals and concerns that influenced its formation and operation. The Ottomans relied on Ottoman Islamic legal norms to build a distinctive legal system in which the ruler's legislative powers played a crucial role. However, it is not so much the ruler's abstract power and prerogatives that account for the Ottoman difference, as it is the legislative processes through which they were exercised. These processes aimed at balancing interests while maintaining adherence to certain broad legal norms and procedures. The legal system began to change radically in the early nineteenth century, partly because of its failures in the face of new challenges and partly because the Ottoman leaders who were determined to respond to these challenges autocratically gained the upper hand. This turn culminated in the reification of the state that the ruler symbolized. Law became a tool to shape society rather than a means of balancing interests and maintaining regime legitimacy. This article will point to the origins of this new turn but otherwise focus on the early modern period, for the clues to the longevity of the Ottoman regime lie there.

Islamic Legal Tradition

The Ottoman state was an Islamic state in the sense that its ruling class upheld and felt bound by high ideals of Islam and its '*shari'a*.' *Shari'a*[5] in this pre-modern context must be understood as a moral abstraction, literally and figuratively meaning the straight path leading a believer to the eye of the spring of fulfilment in this life and the hereafter.[6] By the time the Ottoman state emerged as a political entity in the northwestern frontiers of Islamdom in the early fourteenth century, the efforts to understand

[4] For a thoughtful discussion of some of these issues, see Talal Asad, *Formations of the Secular: Christianity, Islam, Modernity* (Stanford, 2003).

[5] I transliterate legal terms according to their original forms in the Arabic script (without the diachronic marks except for *'ayn*) but write Ottoman-Turkish words according to modern Turkish orthography. I indicate both forms where the spelling of shared words diverges significantly.

[6] For an elaboration on *shari'a* as a moral concept see Khaled Abou El Fadl, *Speaking in God's Name: Islamic Law, Authority and Women* (Oxford, 2001), 76 and *Rebellion and Violence in Islamic Law* (Cambridge, 2001), passim. Also, see Hanna Mikhail, *Politics and Revelation: Mawardi and After* (Edinburgh, 1995), 79–80 n. 231.

the implications of *shariʿa* for legal relations among human beings had developed into a prestigious field of specialized knowledge called *fiqh* (literally, discernment). *Fiqh* focused mainly on understanding God's will as a guide to establishing and maintaining peaceful relations among human beings in this world without forgetting the hereafter. The explicit ideal objective of this endeavour was to protect not God, who could not possibly have needed protection by definition, but God's servants, individuals, especially the weak and the vulnerable among them, against oppression and injustice.[7]

Fiqh discussed the fundamentals or roots (*usul*) of law as well as their practical implications (*furuʿ*, literally, 'fruit' or 'branches'). The fundamentals, which can be construed as the jurisprudence and/or hermeneutics of 'Islamic' law, dealt with the sources, methods and principles of legal reasoning as well as techniques of reaching a legal opinion or judgment. This field of legal knowledge had become highly structured by the fourteenth century. Scholars with extensive knowledge of legal classics and other relevant literature continued to make incremental contributions to the field but were in general reluctant to tamper with its established structure.

Branches of *fiqh* developed practicable rules and injunctions pertaining to certain specific categories of human relations.[8] The category that preoccupied the courts most was 'transactions' (*muʿamalat*), which included family relations (*munakahat*) (issues of marriage, divorce, inheritance and the like), commercial relations (such as sales, leases, employment, and contracts), and matters pertaining to charitable endowments (*waqf*s). Stipulations regarding transactions came fairly close to what one can call 'positive law' but with reservations. Islamic legal tradition encouraged seeking consensual solutions to legal issues through disciplined debate but also allowed significant differences of opinion so long as these opinions were deduced according to established hermeneutical principles

---

[7] Wael B. Hallaq, *A History of Islamic Legal Theories: An Introduction to Sunni usul al-fiqh* (Cambridge, 1997) and Baber Johansen, *Contingency in a Sacred Law: Legal and Ethical Norms in the Muslim* Fiqh (Leiden, Boston and Cologne, 1999), esp. 1–72.

[8] Formal rituals (*ʿibadat*) of Islamic faith constituted one of the main branches of *fiqh*. Rituals were taught as an integral part of *fiqh* studies, and jurists relied on them for analogy and were expected to answer questions related to rituals competently. Otherwise rituals, as faith, were considered matters of conscience, of the inner world (*batin*) and hence between the believer and God. Judging by the Ottoman example, these issues came before the courts when their negligence was perceived as a threat to social order and prompted an executive order. However, unrepentant and public defiance of religion and religious symbols was subject to prosecution and punishment under penal law.

and methods. Thus there had emerged not only different schools of law (*madhhabs*) but also divergent opinions within each school, which provided a degree of flexibility and adaptability to the doctrine but also undermined its consistency.

Other branches of law were less structured. Legal scholars had laid down the general framework and the basic principles of a criminal law but recognized the prerogative of rulers to pass supplementary regulations on penal matters. The legal tradition allowed the ruler an even greater leeway in managing the military, administrative and financial affairs of his realm although, again, in keeping with certain broad principles and constitutional norms intended to guide rulers seeking legitimization in Islamic terms. Most significantly, an Islamic government was expected not to transgress its competence in ways that disturbed the sphere of private legal relations and the fundamental objectives of the law that it was supposed to guard.[9]

Rulers appointed judges (*qadis*), normally from among people who studied *fiqh*, to hear and settle legal disputes in the so-called *shariʿa* courts. Judges were responsible to the ruler but were also the representatives of a legal tradition that was held to be universalistic and therefore above a specific ruler or realm. 'Jurists' were there to remind judges of this legacy of the profession. Jurists were legal experts who gave their opinion (*fatwa*) on specific legal questions directed to them by individuals. Reputable jurists were also accomplished scholars and taught law in colleges (*madrasas*). Financed by endowments, colleges provided an institutional basis for the desired autonomy of scholarship. Although a jurist's opinion was legally nonbinding, it carried moral weight. Judges felt obliged to consult reputable jurists on complicated matters and to heed legal opinions obtained by litigants. Likewise, conscientious rulers and government officials consulted jurists to maintain their image of legitimacy if not actually to do their job properly—with due respect to law as ideally expected of them.[10]

---

[9] Baber Johansen, 'Secular and Religious Elements in Hanafite Law' in his *Contingency in a Sacred Law*, 189–218.

[10] For a succinct history of Islamic legal courts, see the editors' introduction in M. Khalid Masud, Rudolph Peters, and David S. Powers, ed., *Dispensing Justice in Islam: Qadis and their Judgments* (Leiden and Boston, 2006), 1–32, and for jurists see the editors' introduction and other articles in M. Khalid Masud, Brinkley Messick and David S. Powers, ed., *Islamic Legal Interpretation: Muftis and their fatwas* (Cambridge, Mass., 1996), 1–149.

Nevertheless, institutional frameworks within which political expediency and legal ideals could be balanced remained weak. The rulers exercised their regulatory prerogatives in penal and other public matters in a way that blurred functional distinctions between executive and judicial authority. The administrative tribunals set up by the rulers or governors tended to be unpredictable and harsh. They paid little heed to the procedures and evidentiary norms that applied in regular courts on grounds that they unduly encumbered the prosecution of crimes. Bridging the growing gap between the criminal procedures that applied in regular and administrative tribunals emerged as a major concern. Several prominent fourteenth-century legal scholars addressed these problems and the felt need for the systematization of court practices. They developed ideas from which the Ottomans benefited in their efforts to build a coherent legal system. At the time, however, the practical implications of these ideas remained uncertain.[11]

The Ottoman Legal System

This was the state of Islamic law in general when the Ottomans turned to it from the very beginning to assert their commitment to lawfulness.[12] Finding adequately trained legal experts was a challenge for a fledgling state on the fringes of Islamdom. The Ottomans endowed schools (*madrasas*) to address the problem first in Iznik in 1331 and then virtually in every major town they conquered.[13] The early Ottoman *madrasas* were modest institutions with a few teachers, who encouraged their talented students to seek advanced training in established centres of learning in Egypt, other Arab lands, Iran, and Inner Asia. Some of the best-known jurists of early Ottoman history came from the ranks of these students. The state's growing prestige and resources attracted scholars from around the Muslim world as well. The diverse background of the legal experts who

---

[11] For a summary of these developments, see Frank E. Vogel, *Islamic Law and Legal System* (Leiden and Boston, 2000), 178–205 and 313–318 and Nimrod Hurvitz's contribution to this volume.

[12] One of the first acts of Osman, the eponym of the state, was to appoint a judge. For a thoughtful history of the formative years of the Ottoman state, see Cemal Kafadar, *Between two Worlds: the Construction of the Ottoman State* (Berkeley, 1995).

[13] İsmail Hakkı Uzunçarşılı, *Osmanlı Devleti'nin İlmiye Teşkilatı* (Ankara, 1965), 19–31; Hasan Akgündüz, *Klasik Dönem Osmanlı Medrese Sistemi: Amaç, Yapı, İşleyiş* (Istanbul, 1997), 247–69; Cahid Baltacı, *Onbeşinci ve Onaltıncı Asırlar Osmanlı Medreseleri: teşkilat, tarih* (Istanbul, 1976), 7–14, and Mustafa Bilge, *İlk Osmanlı Medreseleri* (Istanbul, 1984).

worked as judges, teachers and bureaucrats[14] in Ottoman lands provided a broad range of ideas and practical legal experience on which the Ottomans could count. This range served the state well in its formative stages. A legal system and culture that was unmistakably Islamic but also had certain distinctive features gradually formed.

Most notably, the Ottoman legal system became more bureaucratically organized than its counterparts in other Muslim dominated countries in the pre-modern era. Efforts to standardize legal training, procedure and rulings accompanied bureaucratization. Custom acquired a distinctly important place as a source of right and basis of regulation in legal practice. In general, the Ottomans relied on the ruler's regulatory prerogatives to validate these practices but in keeping with routinized legal procedures and an institutional framework that set limits to the ruler's authority. These features of the Ottoman legal system merit attention.

Bureaucratization

The "*shariʿa* courts" constituted the backbone of the Ottoman legal system as in other pre-modern states dominated by Muslims but were organized relatively hierarchically and subject to closer bureaucratic supervision. Furthermore, they implemented sultanic laws and regulations along with the strictly *fiqh*-based laws. Each major district (*qada'*) had a court headed by a judge or *qadi*. Judgeships were ranked by their importance and by a corresponding level of remuneration decided by the laws of the state. Deputy judges (*naib*s) assisted judges or served in the sub-districts. The judges came from Istanbul, were normally graduates of the imperial colleges in Istanbul, and served for a short tenure in each position. The deputy judges and other provincial court officials, however, were normally appointed locally from among the qualified residents of each place.[15] This

---

[14] The majority of the viziers were lawyers by training in the formative stages of the state, when the sultans were directly involved in running the government and military campaigns. Viziers were in charge of the fledgling bureaucracy. See the short biography of viziers provided in İsmail Hami Danişmend, *Osmanlı Devlet Erkanı* (Istanbul, 1971), 7–12.

[15] For Ottoman courts and judges, see Uzunçarşılı, *İlmiye Teşkilatı*, 83–143; Ronald C. Jennings' articles in his *Studies in Ottoman Social History in the Sixteenth and Seventeenth Centuries* (Istanbul, 1999); Mehmet Aydın, *Türk Hukuk Tarihi* 3rd ed. (Istanbul, 1999), 78–86; Halil İnalcık, 'Mahkama, 2(i)', in *The Encyclopaedia of Islam*, new ed. (1991); Haim Gerber, *State, Society and Law in Islam: Ottoman Law in Comparative Perspective* (Albany, NY, 1994); Mehmet İpşirli, 'The Ottoman State Organization,' in *History of the Ottoman State Society and Civilization*, 2 volumes, edited by E. İhsanoğlu, vol. 1 (Istanbul, 2001), 135–285, esp. 251–285.

practice kept the courts under imperial supervision while leaving them in touch with local conditions.

The chief judges (*qadi al-qudat*)[16] of the European and the Anatolian provinces held the first and the second highest positions, respectively, in Ottoman judicial hierarchy. In addition to supervising the judgeships within their respective jurisdiction, the chief judges served on the Imperial Council (*Divan-ı Humayun*) to assist it in legal matters. The council was the highest decision-making organ of the state and also had the duties of a high court. Appeals against judges and executive officials, requests for revision of a government regulation, conflicts resulting from equally valid legal claims that called for interpretation of norms with a view to maintaining social peace, and similar cases that in theory had implications for "public good" (*maslaha*) came before the council. The chief judge of the European provinces heard these cases. His colleague on the council as well as other senior judges assisted him depending on the volume and nature of the work at hand.

These judges adhered to the same legal procedure that applied in the regular (*shari'a*) courts. However, they formulated their decision as a recommendation to the ruler, normally through the grand vizier, his deputy and chief executive official who headed the Imperial Council (after the 1450s). The ruler's ratification was necessary for the implementation of these decisions because they pertained to "public good" as indicated above. Once ratified, the decisions carried the force of law or regulation binding the courts. The judges relied on the authority delegated to them by the ruler in handling these matters, but it was the judges' advanced knowledge of the law and due process that substantiated the legitimacy of the consequent edict.[17] Likewise, the appointment, promotion and dismissal of judges were the ruler's prerogative. He exercised this power in consultation with the grand vizier but based on the evaluations and recommendations of the chief judges. The chief jurist became the main

[16] It should be clear that each chief judge, other judges, and the chief jurist discussed below had assistants and scribes working under them in numbers commensurate with the duties of their office.

[17] On the *divan* and its judicial functions, see Ahmet Mumcu, *Divan-ı Hümayun*, 2nd ed. (Ankara, 1986), M. Akif Aydın, 'The Ottoman Legal System', in *History of the Ottoman State, Society and Civilization*, 2 volumes, edited by E. İhsanoğlu (Istanbul, 2001), vol. 1, 456–458, and Akarlı, 'Law in the Marketplace: Istanbul, 1730–1840', in Masud, Peters, and Powers, ed., *Dispensing Justice in Islam* (Leiden, 2006), 245–270. On chief judges, also see Mustafa Şentop, *Osmanlı Yargı Sistemi ve Kazaskerlik* (Istanbul: Klasik, 2005), Mehmet İpşirli, 'Osmanlı Devleti'nde Kazaskerlik', in *Belleten* 61 (1997), 597–699, and Uzunçarşılı, *İlmiye Teşkilatı*, 151–160.

evaluator and recommender of all high-ranking judges, including the chief judges, after the 1560s.

The Ottomans maintained the division of juridical labour between a judge and a jurist (*mufti*) observed in other Islamic countries. Quite uniquely, however, the Ottomans created a bureau of government-paid jurists as a component of the legal system. Long tradition encouraged rulers to consult prominent scholars in Islamic countries. Sometimes this relationship became routine and formal. Otherwise, jurists normally remained off government payroll–unless they accepted a judgeship or some bureaucratic position within the government organization. As indicated above, jurists represented the autonomy of *fiqh* and the idea that Islamic legal tradition transcended temporal realms. Early Ottoman rulers regularly conferred with prominent jurists. This relationship acquired a more formal nature with the designation of an official jurist in 1425. In the sixteenth century, the appointment of official *mufti*s to provincial centres became routine. A hierarchy of official jurists formed, parallel to the judiciary but with many fewer posts. The Jurist of Istanbul, also called the Chief Jurist (*shaykh al-Islam*), was their head. His responsibilities and stature steadily increased. By the 1560s, his office became the highest position that a lawyer in government service could aspire to.

Official jurists, like their non-official counterparts, issued nonbinding advisory responses (*fatwas*) to questions addressed to them by individuals, judges or administrative officials regarding legal issues. Often, they also taught law at a level corresponding to their experience and scholarly reputation. The chief jurist himself served as the rector of the imperial colleges, in addition to his other responsibilities of issuing *fatwa*s, supervising official jurists, and professional evaluation of candidates for senior judgeships. Chief jurists were qualified to evaluate judges because virtually every chief jurist came from the ranks of senior judges by government regulations, just as most of the other high-ranking official jurists had experience as judges. Indeed, jurists and judges belonged to two sub-branches of the same bureaucratic career line; crossovers between the two sub-branches were frequent and necessary to rise to top positions in both of them.[18] Thus senior jurists had first-hand court experience, while judges had opportunities to strengthen their qualifications as legal scholars.

[18] Richard C. Repp, *The Müfti of Istanbul: A Study in the Development of the Ottoman Learned Hierarchy* (London, 1986); Colin Imber, *Ebu's Su'ud: The Islamic Legal Tradition* (Stanford, 1997) along with my review in *Islamic Law and Society* 6, no. 2 (June 1999), 284–287, and Haim Gerber, *Islamic Law and Culture, 1600–1840* (Leiden, 1999) along with

To be sure, official jurists constituted only a fraction of the individuals who were qualified to issue *fatwas* in Ottoman lands at any given time. In other words, the Ottomans did not (and could not) attempt to establish an official monopoly over the interpretation of the law. Furthermore, official jurists did not have a place on the Imperial Council, the councils of provincial governors, or any other executive organ. Technically, their duty was to provide their 'independent' legal opinion to questions directed at them. Nevertheless, their incorporation into government bureaucracy compromised the idea of the autonomy of the legal tradition, as it had been understood in pre-Ottoman days. At the same time, however, this development enabled lawyers knowledgeable about the legal tradition as well as the practical conditions prevailing in different parts of the empire to influence the legal system directly–in an official capacity and not merely based on moral authority. These lawyers played a crucial role in shaping the legal system, the routinization of the legal process and the relative standardization of legal norms.

Standardization of Legal Norms and Training

From the beginning the Ottomans preferred the Hanafi doctrine of *fiqh* in general, after the Saljuks and arguably because the Hanafi doctrine was relatively less equivocal and allowed the ruler more room to control the judiciary compared to other doctrines. The Ottomans turned their preference into an official policy by the early-sixteenth century as part of their efforts to streamline legal norms and procedures. Royal appointment diplomas of judges now routinely enjoined them to adjudicate according to the Hanafi doctrine. Where significant segments of the population adhered to other doctrines, as in Arab provinces, the centrally appointed Hanafi judge continued to work with deputies belonging to the locally prominent schools of law. However, the Ottoman-Hanafi norms remained definitive in fundamental procedural matters, such as the litigants' choice of forum. Thus the Ottomans continued to honour established schools of law in deference to legal tradition while relying on state authority to establish the hegemony of the Hanafi doctrine over others.[19]

---

my review in *Islamic Law and Society* 7, no. 3 (October 2000), 403–407. For brief biographies of chief jurists, see *İlmiyye Salnamesi* (modern Turkish transcription of the original 1916 edition) (Istanbul, 1998), 281–532.

[19] Rudolph Peters, 'What does it mean to be an official *madhhab*: Hanafism and the Ottoman Empire', in P. Bearman, R. Peters, and F. Vogel, ed., *The Islamic School of Law: Evolution, Devolution and Progress* (Cambridge, Mass., 2005), 147–158; Hayrettin Karaman,

Nevertheless, significant differences of opinion existed on various major and minor issues within the Hanafi doctrine as well. A relatively uniform implementation of the Hanafi law in courts regarding such issues required the delimitation of the choices available to judges. This was a task referred to senior members of the legal bureaucracy. In general, they favoured views that were long recognized as being the most authoritative in the doctrine based on the consensus of the great jurists of the past. However, they favoured alternative positions on a significant number of points on grounds that the realities of the times and the land made them preferable. These decisions emerged from the deliberations of legal experts and were articulated in compliance with hermeneutic principles of *fiqh*. The chief jurist played a crucial role in these discussions and was in a position to influence them. He submitted to the ruler a detailed legal opinion summarizing the highlights of the issue with a specific proposal at the end. The ruler then issued a decree instructing judges to act accordingly. The ruler could not decide a *fiqh*-related issue on his own because he lacked the requisite competence. A chief jurist, in turn, would be cautious not to impose an opinion on the ruler until it won sufficient consensus among his colleagues, who were in a position to attract the attention of the ruler and other dignitaries of the state.

Reaching that consensus proved difficult sometimes. A famous case in point is the controversy about permitting cash investments as a source of revenue for charitable foundations (*waqf*s). This practice was widespread in the Anatolian and European provinces but contravened the basic legal norms that governed charitable foundations according to one group of jurists. Another group, however, considered it justifiable based on a minority position in the Hanafi doctrine and on the ground that it was a widespread practice beneficial to the public as well as to the foundations. The latter group eventually prevailed and reversed a decree prohibiting the so-called cash endowments.[20]

'The Sectarian Preference in Ottoman Jurisprudence', in *Ottoman Turkish Civilization*, vol. 3, 646–75, and Aydın, *Türk Hukuk Tarihi*, 89–94.

20 For the debate on cash endowments see, for instance, Murat Çizakça, *A History of Philanthropic Foundations* (Istanbul, 2000), 27–65; Ahmet Akgündüz, *İslam Hukukunda ve Osmanlı Tatbikatında Vakıf Müessesesi* (Ankara, 1998), 151–167; Richard Repp, 'Qanun and Shari'a in the Ottoman Context', in *Islamic Law: Social and Historical Contexts*, edited by Aziz Al-Azmeh (London and New York, 1988), 124–145, and Tahsin Özcan, *Osmanlı Para Vakıfları: Kanuni Dönemi Üsküdar Örneği* (Ankara, 2003).

Legal scholars in Arab provinces did not find the legal opinion favouring the cash *waqf*s agreeable despite the imperial decree that empowered the courts to act on it. Similarly, a royal decree that required the registration of all marriages by the courts in all urban centres

The common educational background of legal experts and their bureaucratic station arguably kept the differences of opinion among them at a manageable level in general. Virtually all lawyers who rose to a high position in the judiciary establishment were graduates of—and/or had taught at—the richly endowed network of colleges in Istanbul. These colleges—the most prestigious of which was the complex built by Süleyman I (r. 1520–66)—offered a relatively standardized curriculum of legal studies. Students read a regular set of Hanafi law manuals at different levels of their training. (Advanced students studied the more detailed Hanafi works and the classics of Islamic law in general with scholars specializing in these texts.) Furthermore, young graduates who embarked on a judiciary career relied on standard handbooks that included samples of typical legal contracts and court decisions. Judges and jurists read compilations of the selected opinions (*fatwas*) of prominent chief jurists (*shaykhs al-Islam*) and other distinguished contemporary jurists. Arranged according to the typical format of a law manual, these compilations reflected the cumulative wisdom of Ottoman legal experience and served as authoritative legal texts.[21]

This shared educational background contributed to the formation of a like-minded corps of legal experts. Being part of a distinct and distinguished branch of the government provided them with an esprit de corps that bound them closer together—despite their intellectual differences, professional rivalries and jealousies. Compared to other government officials, legal experts (whether judges, jurists or teachers) enjoyed certain privileges in deference to the traditional esteem in which their profession was held and the autonomy associated with it. Nevertheless, their career shaped them as loyal bureaucrats committed to the causes of the state. They influenced Ottoman elite culture and were also influenced by it. They had much in common especially with the accountants and secretaries who formed the 'scribal' branch ('*kalemiye*') of the government. Many of these bureaucrats had received some form of legal training

based on the legal opinion of the chief *mufti* did not apply in Arab provinces. Certain aspects of the Ottoman land-tenure laws, however, became more broadly accepted and implemented although they too were based on scholastically controversial interpretations of the law.

[21] For the major legal texts used in legal training and practice, see Aydın, *Türk Hukuk Tarihi*, 96–101 and Hasan Akgündüz, 373–407. For more detailed information, see Recep Cici, 'Osmanlı Klasik Dönemi Fıkıh Kitapları'; Şükrü Özen, 'Osmanlı Dönemi Fetva Literatürü', and Süleyman Kaya, 'Mahkeme Kayıtlarının Kılavuzu: Sakk Mecmuaları' in the *Türk Hukuk Tarihi* issue of *Türkiye Araştırmaları Literatür Dergisi* 3, no. 5 (2005), 215–416.

in the same colleges and frequented the same Sufi and literary circles attended by judges and jurists. The most distinguished Ottoman men of letters, including poets, historians and authors of treatises on political ethics, came from the ranks of the scribal branch.[22] Furthermore, the senior bureaucrats authored the imperial laws and regulations, with due input from judges and jurists.

Penal Laws and the Regulation of Land-Tenure Relations

Imperial 'laws' came in various forms, ranging from statutes (*kanunnames*) and regulations (*nizamnames*) to decrees (*fermans*, *hatt-ı humayuns*) of a regulatory nature on specific-issues, and they served different purposes. As indicated above, one of these purposes was to provide a degree of consistency to the implementation of *fiqh* norms. Penal laws can be considered partly in the same category. Islamic legal tradition had developed certain norms and injunctions that set the general framework of criminal justice. However, it allowed the ruler a greater leeway in the regulation of penal maters than of transactions. From 1480 (if not earlier) to 1700, the Ottomans set down code-like compilations of regulations and statutes regarding criminal offenses left uncovered or only broadly covered in Islamic-Hanafi criminal law literature. Each compilation (and various supplementary decrees on specific penal issues) improved on previous provisions technically while adapting concepts conforming more closely to Islamic legal terminology. A distinctly Ottoman but also Hanafi penal law gradually formed and was absorbed into Ottoman-Hanafi legal texts and court practice.[23]

Imperial laws governing land tenure relations and agrarian taxes in most of the Ottoman provinces represent an even more novel combination of *fiqh*-based and practical legal points of reference. These laws were deliberately based on established practices and relevant customs in each province or sub-province. Along with the formal incorporation of a particular region into the empire, special committees headed by judges surveyed the customary local taxes, land-use patterns, and revenue sources in

---

22 For the careers and cultural world of this group, see Cornell Fleischer, *Bureaucrat and Intellectual in the Ottoman Empire: The Historian Mustafa Âli (1541–1600)* (Princeton, 1986).

23 Uriel Heyd, *Studies in Old Ottoman Criminal Law*, V.L. Ménage, ed. (Oxford, 1973); Mehmet Akman, *Osmanlı Devleti'nde Ceza Yargılaması* (Istanbul, 2004), and Rudolph Peters, *Crime and Punishment in Islamic Law: Theory and Practice from the Sixteenth to the Twenty-first Century* (Cambridge and New York, 2005), 69–102.

that region. The results of these surveys were then reviewed in Istanbul to maintain conformity to certain basic standards and practical guidelines. The laws thus prepared and duly ratified by the ruler defined the administration of specific provinces and sub-provinces with a special emphasis on land-tenure relations and revenue-collection arrangements. Subsequent surveys led to periodic adjustments.[24]

The basic premise of almost all[25] of these laws was that the bare ownership (*raqaba*) of agricultural lands in general belonged to the public and was therefore a perpetual trust (similar to a *waqf*) to be administered by the public treasury (*bayt al-mal*). Since the ruler was the custodian of the public treasury, he (or the Ottoman leadership acting in his name) could regulate the inheritable use rights on these lands, the rent and fees the users owed the public treasury, and the collection of these fiscal obligations along with the strictly *fiqh*-based taxes. The authoritative legal (*sharʿi*) justification of this premise is an ingenious lawyerly text that illustrates how Ottoman jurists used hermeneutical techniques for pragmatic purposes of the state on issues where *fiqh* left rulers room to manoeuvre.[26] The effort signifies the Ottoman commitment to the idea of law as a universally valid reference point. This commitment constitutes an important but not the only dimension of the processes by which the laws in question were prepared with a view to making them valid, relevant and compelling. In the case of the provincial laws, as in most other cases of imperial regulation, those processes helped balance various interests of relevant government and societal groups. Balancing did not mean equality but it took into consideration local practices and secure access to means of subsistence at the minimum to assure the receptivity of the laws among people to whom they would apply.

The conditions prevailing in the empire and methods of provincial administration and revenue collection changed over time. Nevertheless, the basic presumption of Ottoman regulations governing land-tenure relations and consequently revenue-collection arrangements proved remarkably resilient, where these regulations applied effectively, as in the

---

[24] Halil İnalcık, 'Ottoman Methods of Conquest', *Studia Islamica* 2 (1954), 104–129 (reprinted in his *The Ottoman Empire: Conquest, Organization and Economy: Collected Studies* [London, 1978], 105–138). For the provincial land laws promulgated in 1477–1622, see Ahmed Akgündüz, *Osmanlı Kanunnameleri ve Hukuki Tahlilleri*, 9 volumes (Istanbul, 1990–96).

[25] A different logic applied in areas populated largely by pastoralists.

[26] For analyses of the Ottoman jurists' justification of the land laws, see Baber Johansen, *The Islamic Law on Land Tax and Rent* (London, 1988) and Imber, *Ebu's-s'uud, The Islamic Legal Tradition*, 115–138.

Ottoman Balkans, Anatolia, and parts of geographical Syria. For better or worse, a distinct pattern of land-tenure relations that favoured small-scale production, generated multiple layers of ownership, and facilitated the preservation of the central government's position as the principal distributor of tax collection privileges survived well into the nineteenth century.[27] A proper analysis of the complex history of Ottoman land-tenure relations and taxation methods is beyond the scope of this article. The point here is that laws mattered. They served as reference points not only for the ruling class but also for the main body of agricultural producers, namely peasant households, whose use rights over the means of their subsistence was protected as a measure of public good. Peasants continued to bear the heaviest tax burden as in other agrarian societies, but the bias of Ottoman laws toward small-scale peasant household production provided peasants with a handle to negotiate with the regime. Peasants took their grievances to courts based on these laws. At times they resisted oppressive officials and justified their resistance by appealing to the notions of right and justice promised in the laws.[28]

Custom as Basis of Particular Regulations

The types of imperial legislation reviewed so far—from preference of one *fiqh* view over another to provincial laws regulating land-tenure relations—cite custom as an underlying reason but along with the assertion that custom also served general public interest in these instances.

The Hanafi legal doctrine recognized custom as a limited source of right but downplayed it, lest large-scale recognition of custom open the door to irreconcilable particularistic interests or undermine Islamic legal norms that were held to be universally valid. As a rule, the courts could not act upon claims based on custom if they contravened a well-established *fiqh* norm. The Ottomans tended to recognize widespread custom so as not to cause undue hardships for the people while also trying to bring it in line with basic *fiqh* norms.[29] Custom meshed with the notion of common good

---

[27] For the long-term effect of land laws, see, for instance, Halil Cin, *Osmanlı Toprak Düzeni ve Bu Düzenin Bozulması* (Istanbul, 1985); Fikret Adanır, 'The Ottoman Peasantries, c.1360–c.1860', in *The Peasantries of Europe: from the fourteenth to the eighteenth centuries*, edited by Tom Scott (London and New York, 1998), 269–312, and Martha Mundy and Richard S. Smith, *Governing Property, Making the Modern State* (London and New York, 2007).

[28] Suraiya Faroqhi, 'Political Activity Among Ottoman Taxpayers, 1570–1670', in *Journal of the Economic and Social History of the Orient* 35 (1992), 1–39.

[29] Katib Çelebi (d. 1657) provides an eloquent defence of this position in *The Balance of Truth*, translated with notes by G.L. Lewis (London, 1957), 89–90 and passim. Legal documents, especially the judicial files of the Imperial Council, substantiate the same point.

or public interest in such cases, thereby forming a basis for the ruler's legislative intervention. The Ottomans also recognized the custom of a specific locality or collectivity as a source of right and hence regulation, if with certain restrictions. Evidently, such "particular" customs were considered not a threat to the overall system but a means to accommodate the composite demography and diverse conditions of Ottoman lands.

Thus, the Ottoman legal system allowed a significant degree of autonomy to various social collectivities in handling their internal affairs and differences according to their custom. Religious communities were of this order, including tiny Muslim or Christian sects as well as major non-Muslim communities, whose 'custom' was recognized as their '*shari'a.*' Other collectivities identified with their customs ranged from tribes and villages to residents of the same urban quarters and guilds. So long as they managed their affairs peacefully, their practices did not concern the law directly. However, if any person brought his or her dispute or business to court, then the Ottoman-Hanafi norms and the relevant imperial decrees applied.

Court records related to artisans and traders[30] indicate that the members of a particular collectivity could register their 'custom' by the courts, which also served as notary publics. In this case 'custom' acquired the force of a consensual contract that bound its individual participants jointly and equally, irrespective of their religious or social status.[31] If the group could not handle an internal dispute on its own and the case ended up in court, the judge would refer to the group's registered custom to settle the dispute and to restore the group's pact. Normally the courts would not consent to the registration of a 'custom' that contradicted fundamental legal (*shar'i*) principles (such as unreasonable restriction of entry into a trade, division of estates or formation of endowments not in conformity with *fiqh* norms, or the involvement of a Muslim in the sale of alcoholic beverages).

[30] See Engin Deniz Akarlı, 'Gedik: a bundle of rights and obligations for Istanbul artisans and traders, 1750–1840', in Alain Pottage and Martha Mundy, ed., *Law, Anthropology, and the Constitution of the Social: Making Persons and Things* (Cambridge, 2004), 166–200. For specific cases illustrating the points made below regarding artisans and traders, see Akarlı, 'Law in the Marketplace' and 'Gedik.' Also see, Eunjeong Yi, *Guild Dynamics in Seventeenth Century Istanbul: Fluidity and Leverage* (Leiden and Boston, 2004) and Suraiya Faroqhi, *Artisans of Empire: Crafts and Craftspeople under the Ottomans* (London and New York, 2009).

[31] These contracts were similar to deeds of business transactions and partnerships, which bound the parties equally, irrespective of the differences in their legal status by gender and religion that might apply under certain circumstances according to the Hanafi doctrine.

Consequently, a group that sought the protection of courts paid due attention to the prevailing legal norms in formulating its 'custom' registered by the courts. However, a particular group could appeal—on its own or upon the recommendation of the district judge—to the Imperial Council in order to win approval of its 'custom' if it contained elements not fully concordant with fundamental *fiqh* norms but deemed necessary for the well-being of the group and the society. For instance, a group could request restriction of entry into their trade as a means of controlling standards of quality or public security, the fixing of rents to curb price hikes, and special arrangements for the division of a deceased artisan's tools, license and shop space. If the ruler approved such appeals upon the recommendation of the senior judge who heard them, then the decree issued to that effect would elevate the custom of the group to the level of an imperial charter or regulation (*nizam*) for the group.

If customary relationships within a group or between different groups and parties were disturbed because of conflicting but equally valid claims and the district judge failed to reconcile the parties, these cases as well would frequently come before the Imperial Council (or an experienced judge it authorized to hear the case in the provinces). The judges' primary concern in such cases was to obtain the voluntary commitment of the parties to a sustainable compromise. These settlements aimed at balancing mutual claims and responsibilities—for instance the right of *waqf*s and other landlords to fair rent with the right of the tenant of a shop to an income sufficient to sustain his business and family. The ultimate purpose was the maintenance or restoration of more or less harmonious (although not necessarily equal) relations in society with the participation of the relevant actors. When the ruler ratified the consequent agreements, they acquired the force of a regulation that defined that particular relationship.

Imperial decrees regulating relations and order in urban marketplaces were largely based on agreements reached through the mediation of the courts as indicated above. These regulations originated from custom or customary relationships and were justified on that basis but also on grounds that they served public good (*maslaha*). If conditions necessitated new accords, the regulations changed accordingly through a similar process—if incrementally in keeping with the meaning of custom as a time-honoured way of doing things. In this way, the courts made and remade the laws of the marketplace, in the practical sense of the word as binding provisions, with the participation of those actors to whom the provisions would apply.

Custom as Basis of Administrative Laws

As a distinct collectivity, the Ottoman ruling class had its own customs. A good portion of the Ottoman decrees and statutes of the late fifteenth and sixteenth centuries concerned regulations and protocol governing the government institutions, including the judiciary. 'Imperial custom' (*'urf sultani*) was the term used to designate and justify them. Senior bureaucrats continued to prepare updated compilations of such regulations, sometimes adding their reflections on problems.[32] These reflections bear the influence of advice literature. The Ottoman examples of this genre, written mostly by bureaucrats, reflect a combination of Islamic legal principles, Islamic Peripatetic tradition of political ethics and an Ibn Khaldunian sense of history with a focus on the Ottoman state. They discuss the ideals that should guide the Ottoman ruling class and institutions.[33] The influence of the same ideals is evident also in imperial 'edicts of justice' (*'adaletnames*), which warned officials, including the judiciary, to abide by laws and regulations and to uphold principles of justice and good governance.[34]

Martial Custom

These edicts and other evidence make clear that maintaining discipline throughout the military-administrative branch of the government was the biggest challenge. A special code of military conduct emerged early on primarily to meet this challenge. This mostly unwritten customary code (*'urf*) emphasized discipline and absolute obedience to superiors culminating with the reigning sultan. Breach of conduct entailed summary trials by superiors and harsh punishments, including a special form of capital punishment called 'execution for political reasons' (*siyaset*). Confiscation of the excessive wealth of deceased military governors and viziers was routine practice. The frequent killing of princes under the orders of the ruler

[32] For some of these regulations, see A. Akgündüz, vol. 1: 317–45; vol. 2: 125–36; vol. 3: 133–47; vol. 4: 433–52 and 594–606, and vol. 8: 137–54; Yaşar Yücel, ed., *Osmanlı Devlet Teşkilatına dair Kaynaklar* (Ankara, 1988), and Hazerfan Hüseyin (d. 1676), *Telhisü'l-Beyan fi Kavanin-i Al-i Osman*, Sevim İrgürel, ed. (Ankara, 1998).

[33] Fleischer, *Mustafa Âli.* For samples of this literature in English, see Sarı Mehmed Pasha (d. 1717), *Ottoman Statecraft: the book of counsel for vezirs and governors*, Turkish text, with introduction, translation and notes by Walter L. Wright, Jr. (Westport, Conn. 1971) and Katib Chelebi (d. 1657), *The Balance of Truth*, translated by G.L. Lewis (London, 1957).

[34] For examples of these edicts, see Halil İnalcık, *Osmanlı'da Devlet, Hukuk, Adalet* (Istanbul, 2000), 75–168 and A. Akgündüz, vol. 8: 101–103 and vol. 9: 555–577.

in the first three hundred years of Ottoman history was also based on martial tradition. By extension, martial custom applied to the scribal branch of the government as well, particularly to those in charge of finances.

High-ranking military executive officials (beginning with the grand vizier) authorized to act on behalf of the ruler could resort to harsh punitive measures associated with 'martial custom' against civilians as well under extraordinary circumstances. Thus these executive officials could take matters of justice into their hands in war zones during a military campaign or in actions against armed rebels or bandits. Social unrest perceived as a threat to public order at times of severe political crisis could trigger similar conduct. The officials could thereby summarily punish civilians and execute them for political reasons to set an example to others and to strike fear into hearts in order to deter potential threats to public peace and order.[35]

Resort to brute force to repress unarmed civilian protests was a controversial matter because it verged on abuse of coercive power, the prevention of which was the main justification of martial custom. According to *fiqh* norms, political ethics literature, and the people in general, abuse of power was tyranny and oppression (*zulm*) unequivocally.[36] Oppression was the opposite of justice and equity (*ʿadl*), the very purpose of law, whether *fiqh*-based or sultanic. Edicts of justice and other decrees warned military governors and viziers to shun oppressive behaviour and not to punish any person without a court trial. They also cautioned the judiciary to spurn any cooperation with abusive officials and to report to the centre all complaints against such behaviour. Nevertheless, the two-edged sword of 'rule by [martial] custom' (*ʿidarat al-ʿurfiyya*) remained a part of the Ottoman legal arsenal. It was intended to check wielders of coercive power under normal circumstances but could also empower them to take the law into their hands under unusual circumstances. It was the only area of law where the ruler's power was conceptually absolute and where the concept of public well-being (*maslahat al-ʿamma*)—the ultimate objective

---

35 Ahmet Mumcu, *Osmanlı Devleti'nde Siyaseten Katl* (Ankara, 1973) and Akarlı, 'Law in the Marketplace.' *Siyasa* as described here should not be confused with *siyasa sharʿiyya*, administrative justice. The latter developed as a result of the efforts to bring the criminal procedure that applied in administrative courts in fourteenth-century Mamluk Egypt and Syria closer to *fiqh* norms. The Ottomans incorporated most of these ideas to form a relatively uniform criminal procedure that applied in regular (*shariʿa*) courts as well as the cases brought to the Imperial Council. While cases of *siyasa* involving civilians make references to *fiqh* norms, *siyasa* appears to be a derivative of Inner Asian martial traditions.

36 Ahmet Mumcu, *Osmanlı Hukukunda Zulüm Kavramı*, 2nd ed. (Ankara, 1985).

of the law and the basis of the ruler's legislative authority—tended to morph into *raison d'état* (*nizam al-dawla*). Indeed, the Ottoman legal system began to change fundamentally early in the nineteenth century, when martial custom dominated other components of the complex legal tradition that had developed in Ottoman lands over half a millennium.

On the Verge of the Modern Era

Fiqh, the ruler's legislative prerogatives, and custom were the sources of right (and law) in the Ottoman Empire. Imperial legislation remained closely related to *fiqh*, on the one hand, and custom, on the other. The Ottomans relied on the ruler's legislative authority as a means to bridge the generality and universality attributed to *fiqh* and the particular relationship patterns or consensual concerts of self-regulation that custom represented. The ruler stood at the final phase of the various processes whereby the laws, regulations and decrees were made to accommodate the needs of the state and the population while also maintaining a defendable degree of conformity to *fiqh* norms. These processes often encouraged the parties interested in the outcome to negotiate their mutual claims, expectations and responsibilities—if with unequal weight especially in instances that involved the government as a party to the negotiations. Practical concerns for the efficacy of the regulations in order to cut the cost of their implementation should make this inclusive approach intelligible. Ottoman notions of governance as a balancing act[37] reinforced by the classical Islamic idea of the state as an entity which "serves best when it seeks to regulate reciprocity in ways that do not contravene the scope accorded the individual and the community"[38] must also be taken into consideration.

The courts (including the courts of senior judges affiliated with the Imperial Council) played a crucial role in making the Ottoman legal system work. In addition to their adjudicatory functions, they facilitated business activities, reconciled differences, offered hopes for redressing grievances, and prepared the groundwork for many imperial regulations. They disseminated Ottoman-Islamic norms of justice and served as the major

[37] Barkey, *Empire of Difference*, passim.

[38] Lawrence Rosen, *The Justice of Islam: Comparative Perspectives in Islamic Law and Society* (Oxford and New York, 2000), 156. Rosen's work offers insights that make much sense in the Ottoman context as well.

conduit between the governed and the government. Judges were routinely instructed to inquire into complaints against officials, audit tax accounts, and report misdeeds to the central government. When judges became the object of complaints, which were by no means sparse or inconsequential, inspector judges were dispatched to inquire into them.[39] Fierce rivalries, nepotism, and corruption, partly resulting from short tenures, adversely affected the professional quality of judges and their collective reputation, especially in the seventeenth century. Nevertheless, judges in general commanded respect, for their office if not personally. Even when political power became considerably diffused and decentralized in the eighteenth century, the network of courts continued to expand, became busier than ever, and remained the most visible and accessible manifestation of Ottoman sovereignty.

From the 1770s onward, changing economic conditions and the government's financial problems intensified struggles over the distribution of increasingly scarce resources. Complicated deals and regulations especially about property relations and business contracts strained the capacity of the courts to accommodate differences effectively and enduringly.[40] Overhauling some of the fundamental concepts of Islamic legal tradition that informed the Ottoman legal system might have helped. To the best of our knowledge at this point, Ottoman jurists responded to the challenge mechanically, insisting on hermeneutic techniques that had worked well in the past but now contributed to the complications encumbering the courts and litigants alike.[41]

Meanwhile, a faction determined to strengthen the central government militarily at all costs as a solution to its internal and external problems gained the upper hand under Sultan Mahmud II (r. 1808–39). They encouraged the sultan to rule autocratically on grounds that the very existence of the state was in jeopardy. This move marked the beginnings of fundamental changes. The sultan had been the symbolic embodiment of the state from the beginning but without a public attribution of omnipotence to him or his state. The sultans' potentially absolute authority was basically

39 Ahmet Mumcu, *Osmanlı Devleti'nde Rüşvet* (*Özellikle Adli Rüşvet*) (Ankara, 1969).

40 For examples, see Akarlı, 'Gedik.'

41 Zouhair Ghazzal elaborates on this point in his *The Grammars of Adjudication: The economics of judicial decision making in fin-de-siècle Ottoman Beirut and Damascus* (Beirut, Lebanon, 2007). It is a pertinent point. However, Ghazzal's inability to use legal sources in Ottoman Turkish and his backward projections of impressions based on mostly nineteenth-century data on Damascus and its vicinity undermine the quality of his analysis. (See my review in *Law and History Review* 28, no. 1 (February 2010), 50–52)

confined to the military administrative branch of the government by the logic of martial custom. Mahmud II's autocratic rule, based on administrative fiat to a significant extent and affecting a broad range of state activity as well as civilian life, invited widespread reaction. Urban and rural uprisings, dissent within the ruling class, and civil war turned the empire into a war zone, in a sense justifying his claim to rule by martial custom in a vicious circle.[42]

Mahmud II died as a ruler defeated by internal opposition, but some of the institutional and ideological changes of his era served as the foundation of the reforms that marked the remaining decades of Ottoman history. A discussion of the reasons behind this development and its nature is beyond the scope of this article. It has to be underlined, however, that a reified notion of state as the ultimate good became dominant. Law came to be seen as a tool of the state to control society and to move it toward desired ends defined by a cadre of military and civilian bureaucrats trained in new schools. The interactive legal processes of the past disappeared. Bureaucratic institutions, including the new judiciary, developed into elaborate hierarchical structures but with little input from the population. Even the office of the chief jurist turned into just another state department—responsible for the religious affairs of the state's Muslim subjects in its case. Institutions intended to provide a sense of inclusion to the politically conscious elements of the population remained marginal and mostly ineffective, although they laid the foundations of participatory politics of post-Ottoman days.

Many historians celebrate these developments as positive steps towards modernization and the formation of the modern secularist Republic of Turkey, for good reasons. One should be careful, however, not to overlook the influence of Ottoman martial custom on the same developments or to praise it unreflectively as the force that facilitated a turn in the right direction. Unrestrained by a civic sense of law and responsiveness to the people to whom the laws apply, a martial sense of order would be suitable for a police state or a nation imagining itself as an army camp. Isolation of Ottoman martial custom from the complex legal system and culture of which it was a part would also amply justify the popular representations of the Ottoman state as an Oriental despotism in Western literature. Had

---

[42] See Engin D. Akarlı, 'Provincial Power Magnates in Ottoman Bilad al-Sham and Egypt, 1740–1840', in A. Temimi, ed., *La vie sociale dans les provinces arabes à l'époque ottomane* (Zaghouan, Tunisia, 1988), vol. 3, 41–56.

the Ottomans been that despotic and martial, they would not have had an empire to start with or not have been able to maintain it as long as they did. The rich sources of Ottoman legal history indicate that a working legal system and fairly sensible notions of justice contributed to that longevity. Indeed, the very existence of these sources is evidence of the significance Ottomans attributed to law. Closer attention to them than it has been the case so far would enlarge the universe of our discourses on law and empires.

THE EARLY MODERN HOLY ROMAN EMPIRE OF THE GERMAN NATION (1495–1806): A MULTI-LAYERED LEGAL SYSTEM

Karl Härter

The Composite Reichssystem*: Constitutional Order and Multi-layered Legal System*

After the fall of the Roman Empire in the fifth century CE, the legal history of Europe evolved in the context of the sovereign nation-state, in which legislative and judicial powers were, over time, monopolised and centralised, and homogeneous legal systems were established. However, recent research has drawn quite a different picture of early modern legal history and state-building, framing them in terms of the transnational *ius commune* and supranational empires.[1]

How are these two models to be reconciled? The Holy Roman Empire of the German Nation in its early modern shape (1495–1806) appears as an exemplary case for study:[2] it comprised various members with different languages, religions and cultures (from northern Italy to Denmark, from Burgundy to Bohemia), legally associated through feudal relations and the *Reichsstandschaft* under the universal power of the *Imperium* manifested in the supreme authority of the Emperor—the *Kaiser*.[3] In the early modern period some members, such as the Swiss Confederation or the Dutch Republic, had separated from or remained only loosely bound to the 'imperial federation' (*Reichsverband*). The Imperial Estates (*Reichsstände*)—seven to ten Prince-Electors, far more than two hundred Principalities (most of them 'territorial states') and about fifty Imperial Cities—formed the nucleus of the Empire. They possessed the right to participate through 'seat and vote' in the Imperial Diet (*Reichstag*), the

---

1 Manlio Bellomo, *The common legal past of Europe, 1000–1800* (Washington DC, 1995); Manlio Bellomo, *Europäische Rechtseinheit. Grundlagen und System des Ius Commune* (Munich, 2005); Paolo Grossi, *A history of European law* (Oxford, 2010), 33–35, 43, 99.

2 Lauren Benton, *A search for sovereignty. Law and geography in European Empires, 1400–1900* (Cambridge, 2010), 3–9.

3 For a recent overview see R.J.W. Evans/Michael Schaich/Peter H. Wilson, ed., *The Holy Roman Empire, 1495–1806* (Oxford, 2011); for the new perspective on the history of the Empire cf. Karl Otmar Freiherr von Aretin, *Das Alte Reich 1648–1806*, 4 vols. (Stuttgart, 1993–2000).

pivotal constitutional and political institution of the Empire, as well as to wield independent powers concerning legislation and jurisdiction in their immediate territories—the so-called *Landesherrschaft* (territorial rule).[4]

The composite imperial system (*Reichssystem*) was heterogeneous, polycentric and diverse, in terms of both rights and legal cultures. It was predominantly based on a conglomeration of imperial law, i.e. traditional, customary and feudal law, privileges, treaties and agreements, *leges fundamentales*, imperial legislation as well as conventional legal and constitutional practice, political rituals/proceedings and customs (*Reichsherkommen*), which all together formed a constitutional system—the *Reichsverfassung*.[5] As successor of the Roman Empire the early-modern Empire 'of the German Nation' was also embedded in the Roman law tradition and deeply integrated in the European *ius commune* to which it contributed substantially in the early modern period, notably in the field of public law.[6] Though the roots of the imperial legal culture can be traced back to the Middle Ages, the legal system of the Empire developed in its entirety between the late 15th and the early 16th centuries. This development was marked by such fundamental processes as the reception of Roman law (*Rezeption*),[7] based on the idea (or myth) of the *translatio imperii* and driven by the establishment of law faculties as well as the practice of jurists. The reception gave rise to a burgeoning jurisprudence of the *ius commune*—the learned law (*gelehrtes Recht*). It also led to the formation of professionally trained jurists as a new

---

[4] Barbara Stollberg-Rilinger, *Das Heilige Römische Reich Deutscher Nation. Vom Ende des Mittelalters bis 1806* (Munich, 2006); Peter Claus Hartmann, *Das Heilige Römische Reich deutscher Nation in der Neuzeit 1486–1806* (Ditzingen, 2005); Peter H. Wilson, *The Holy Roman Empire, 1495–1806* (Houndmills, 1999).

[5] Bernd Roeck, *Reichssystem und Reichsherkommen. Die Diskussion über die Staatlichkeit des Reiches in der politischen Publizistik des 17. und 18. Jahrhunderts* (Wiesbaden, 1984); Heinz Duchhardt, *Deutsche Verfassungsgeschichte 1495–1806* (Stuttgart et al., 1991); Karl Härter, 'Das Recht des Alten Reiches: Reichsherkommen, Reichsgesetzgebung und "gute Policey"', in Stephan Wendehorst/Siegrid Westphal, ed., *Lesebuch Altes Reich* (Munich, 2006), 87–94.

[6] Helmuth Coing, ed., *Handbuch der Quellen und Literatur der neueren europäischen Privatrechtsgeschichte. Vol. II: Neuere Zeit. Das Zeitalter des gemeinen Rechts (1500–1800)* (Munich, 1976/77).

[7] Peter Stein, *Roman law in European history* (Cambridge et al., 1999), 88–92. Still of relevance is the extensive research of Helmut Coing; cf. the surveys in English: 'The Roman law as ius commune on the continent', *The law quarterly review* (1973), 505–517; 'Roman law and the national legal systems', in R.R. Bolgar, ed., *Classical influences on Western thought AD 1650–1870* (Cambridge, 1979), 29–37; 'European common law: Historical foundations', in Mauro Cappelletti, ed., *New perspectives for a common law of Europe* (Leyden, 1978), 31–44.

functional elite (*Juristenstand*), acting in imperial, territorial or communal institutions.[8] Imperial law was finally formalised in the comprehensive codes of Imperial Cities (*Stadtrechtsreformationen*), some territories, and the procedural code of the Imperial Chamber Court (*Reichskammergerichtsordnung*), enacted by the Imperial Diet of 1495. The code stated that the *ius commune* should be considered as a legal source or be applied in the courts, and its revised editions, along with the draft code of the Imperial Aulic Council, consolidated the adoption of the *ius commune* as subsidiary imperial law. The procedural codes, the imperial penal code of 1532 (*Constitutio Criminalis Carolina*) and more imperial laws after 1495 were part of the so-called imperial reform (1495–1555), during which the Empire established pivotal legal institutions such as the Imperial Chamber Court and amplified the legislative power of the reformed Imperial Diet, resulting in an increasing amount of imperial legislation (*Reichsgesetzgebung*).[9]

Nearly in parallel, the Imperial Estates (*Reichsstände*) completed the organisation of the government at the level of the territories, which resulted likewise in legislation and legal institutions valid only for these territories, such as manorial courts (*Hofgerichte*) and courts of appeal or privy councils (*Hofrat*), the latter often also administering penal justice. The Reformation strengthened the territorial rule of the Imperial Estates and caused a further differentiation of the legal culture while demolishing the sacred universal quality of the Empire as the incarnation of the Christian world.

The Holy Roman Empire finally transformed into the association of the German 'nations'.[10] The Imperial Estates participated in nearly all matters of imperial politics and obtained various degrees of autonomy, especially with regard to legislative, jurisdictional, penal and military powers, but they did not achieve sovereignty in the modern sense, and their power of ruling—*Landesherrschaft*—remained legally bound to the imperial constitution. The separate constitutional arrangements of the Imperial

---

8 Roman Schnur, ed., *Die Rolle der Juristen bei der Entstehung des modernen Staates* (Berlin, 1986).

9 Heinz Mohnhaupt, 'Gesetzgebung des Reichs und Recht im Reich vom 16. bis 18. Jahrhundert', in Barbara Dölemeyer/Diethelm Klippel, ed., *Gesetz und Gesetzgebung im Europa der Frühen Neuzeit* (Berlin, 1998), 83–108; Karl Härter, 'Reichsgesetzgebung und Reichsrecht', in Josef Pauser/Martin Scheutz/Thomas Winkelbauer, ed., *Quellenkunde der Habsburgmonarchie (16.–18. Jahrhundert). Ein exemplarisches Handbuch* (Wien, 2004), 312–326.

10 Thomas A. Brady Jr., *German histories in the age of Reformations, 1400–1650* (Cambridge et al., 2009).

Estates and the failure to establish a permanent governmental institution at the imperial centre demonstrate that the early modern Empire lacked essential elements of a 'modern' state or a powerful empire: permanent military forces, taxes, colonies, an imperial capital or a powerful central government.[11]

Nevertheless, with regard to law and the judiciary the imperial system shows similarities with other pre-modern empires such as the Ottoman or the Russian. The early modern Holy Roman Empire provided a basic legal order and a central legal framework, which integrated the supranational *ius commune* tradition but devolved partial legal autonomy, regional law and customs to its various members.[12] The composite constitutional nature of the Empire formed a multi-layered legal system with various overlapping legal spaces, comprising Roman law/*ius commune*, imperial law and legislation (*Reichsrecht*), and particular customary law and legislation of the different territorial rulers.[13] The variety of law corresponded to various jurisdictions and courts, ranging from the imperial Supreme Courts and the manorial courts of the Imperial Estates to a variety of lower courts and jurisdictions, not counting the privileged forums of the clergy and the nobles, or the church jurisdiction.

Using an ideal-typical schema we can distinguish the following legal layers:

1. The *ius commune* which incorporated Roman, canon and feudal law was developed further by jurisprudence, which flourished at an increasing number of universities within the Empire. Canon law was especially applicable in the ecclesiastical Imperial Estates, which formed the imperial church (*Reichskirche*) and church jurisdiction. On the whole,

---

[11] For a well-informed survey of the discussion on the 'statehood' of the Empire see Peter Wilson, 'Still a monstrosity? Some reflections on early modern German statehood', in *The Historical Journal* 49 (2006), 565–576; compare furthermore Johannes Burkhardt, 'Europäischer Nachzügler oder institutioneller Vorreiter? Plädoyer für einen neuen Entwicklungsdiskurs zur konstruktiven Doppelstaatlichkeit des frühmodernen Reiches', in Matthias Schnettger, ed., *Imperium Romanum—irregulare corpus—Teutscher Reichs-Staat* (Mainz, 2002), 297–316.

[12] Colin Imber, *The Ottoman Empire, 1300–1650. The structure of power* (Basingstoke et al., 2002), 216.

[13] Heinz Duchhardt, 'Gesetzgebung im alten Reich: Ein Dreischichtenmodell', in Serge Dauchy/Jos Monballyu/Alain Wijffels, ed., *Auctoritates. Xenia r.c. van caenegem oblata. De auteurs van de Rechtsontwikkeling* (Brüssel, 1997), 112–117; Arno Buschmann, 'Kaiser, Reich und Landesherren. Reichsrecht und Landesherrschaft im Heiligen Römischen Reich', in Dietrich Murswiek/Ulrich Storost/Heinrich A. Wolff, ed., *Staat—Souveränität—Verfassung. Festschrift für Helmut Quaritsch zum 70. Geburtstag* (Berlin, 2000), 449–474.

the Empire adopted Roman law in the shape of the *ius commune* as subsidiary imperial law and as a consequence created a symbolic 'great legal tradition', the *translatio imperii*: the legend that Lothar III had decreed in 1135 the use of Roman law. Despite Hermann Conring's debunking of this story as a myth in 1643, Roman law nevertheless obtained an eminent theoretical as well as practical importance on all legal levels in the early modern Empire.[14]

2. The imperial level, formed by the imperial law, the legislation of the Imperial Diet and the Imperial Courts (Imperial Chamber Court and Imperial Aulic Council).[15]
3. The territorial rule (*Landesherrschaft*) of the Imperial Estates, characterised by an increasing amount of particular legislation, mostly enacted as ordinances, edicts, and regulations dealing with matters of the 'good order' (the so-called *Policeygesetzgebung*), but also comprising penal, private, procedural or administrative law(s). The expansion of the legislative powers of the Imperial Estates—finally fixed by the Treaty of Westphalia (1648)—was accompanied by the establishment of central legal and governmental institutions and state-based court systems in which mostly professionally trained jurists acted.[16]
4. Local, traditional, customary and statutory law within the context of territorial rule. This applies in regions or districts (*Landrecht* or *Weistümer*: the law of the land), municipalities (*Stadtrecht* or *Willkür*: municipal/statutory law) and other communities such as the guilds, village communes or judicial associations (*Gerichtsgenossenschaften*). This immense bulk of law corresponded to a variety of different local jurisdictions and lower courts, mostly restricted to private law issues, petty crimes and misdemeanours, non-contentious jurisdiction or administrative matters.[17]

---

[14] Georg Schmidt, *Geschichte des Alten Reiches: Staat und Nation in der Frühen Neuzeit 1495–1806* (Munich, 1999); Hermann Conrad, *Deutsche Rechtsgeschichte, vol. 2: Neuzeit bis 1806* (Karlsruhe, 1966), 339–373; Shmuel Noah Eisenstadt, *The political systems of empires* (New Brunswick, NJ et al., 1993), 137–143.

[15] This will be more detailed in the following.

[16] Cf. Coing, *Handbuch*, vol. II/2; Karl Härter/Michael Stolleis, ed., *Repertorium der Policeyordnungen der Frühen Neuzeit*, vol. 1–10 (Frankfurt/M., 1996–2010; as a case study see Karl Härter, *Policey und Strafjustiz in Kurmainz. Gesetzgebung, Normdurchsetzung und Sozialkontrolle im frühneuzeitlichen Territorialstaat* (Frankfurt/M., 2005).

[17] Cf. as exemplary case study: André Holenstein, *'Gute Policey' und lokale Gesellschaft im Staat des Ancien Régime. Das Fallbeispiel Baden(-Durlach)*, 2 vol. (Tübingen, 2003).

These different levels didn't necessarily form a hierarchical order, but rather a system of legal spaces with complex interactions and interconnections. It was characterised by legal diversity and legal pluralism, a feature of many pre-modern empires[18], but none the less embedded within the imperial legal framework and the imperial constitution as well as bound together by the numerous writings of the *ius commune* jurists, the emerging public law and the public discourse on legal and political issues of the Empire, the so-called *Reichspublizistik*.[19] The complexity of the imperial legal culture resulted in ambiguity, uncertainty and conflicts, but also facilitated options for the Imperial Estates, their subjects (*Untertanen*), or minorities such as the Jews to make use of the imperial legal institutions, for instance to appeal to the Imperial Courts or even to litigate against their ruler.[20] In this regard the Empire facilitated not only 'forum shopping' or *Justiznutzung*, (see also Caroline Humfress's paper in this volume) but produced a specific culture of litigation, inspired innovations in jurisprudence and public law, and stimulated the process of juridification (*Verrechtlichung*): the increase of legal norms, legal procedure, lawsuits and court action, particularly with regard to conflict resolution.[21]

In view of the complexity and variety of the imperial legal culture the following analysis is restricted to the level of the Empire per se, in other words to imperial law and legislation, the Imperial Supreme Courts, and the jurisprudence of public law (including the *Reichspublizistik*), since it is nearly impossible to describe the distinct legal structures of the various Imperial Estates and the underlying, extremely diverse local communities. However, attention will be paid to the interdependences between

---

[18] With regard to (colonial) empires see Lauren Benton, *Law and Colonial Cultures. Legal Regimes in World History, 1400–1900* (Cambridge, 2004), 7–12. Compare furthermore the corresponding approach to early modern state formation: Wim Blockmans/André Holenstein/Jon Mathieu in collab. with Daniel Schläppi, ed., *Empowering Interactions. Political Cultures and the Emergence of the State in Europe 1300–1900* (Farnham et al., 2009); Ronald G. Asch/Dagmar Freist, ed., *Staatsbildung als kultureller Prozess. Strukturwandel und Legitimation von Herrschaft in der Frühen Neuzeit* (Cologne et al., 2005).

[19] Hanns Gross, *Empire and sovereignty. A history of the public law literature in the Holy Roman Empire, 1599–1804* (Chicago et al., 1973); Michael Stolleis, *Geschichte des öffentlichen Rechts in Deutschland, vol. I: Reichspublizistik und Policeywissenschaft 1600–1800* (Munich, 1988).

[20] For recent approaches cf. Jason Philip Coy/Benjamin Marschke/David Warren Sabean, ed., *The Holy Roman Empire, reconsidered* (New York et al., 2010).

[21] Martin Dinges, 'The Uses of Justice As a Form of Social Control in Early Modern Europe', in Herman Roodenburg/Pieter Spierenburg, ed., *Social Control in Europe, vol. 1, 1500–1800* (Columbus, 2004), 159–175; Winfried Schulze, *Einführung in die Neuere Geschichte* (Stuttgart, 1991), 61–65.

the imperial level, the *ius commune*, and the particular legal systems of the Imperial Estates, taking into particular account the options of local communities and subjects to interact with imperial institutions such as the Imperial Courts, which notably influenced the culture of litigation.

Reichsrecht: *Imperial Law and Legislation*

Imperial law was composed of various legal norms, including customs, privileges, treaties, *ius commune*, public law, and imperial legislation. From the end of the 15th century the power of the Emperor to enact laws without the consent of the Imperial Estates was restricted to executive edicts based on imperial law; imperial legislation as well as all other decisions in imperial matters required the consent of the Imperial Diet. From 1663 onwards the Diet held permanent sessions (in Ratisbon), and the Imperial Estates were represented by deputies/envoys (but without a free mandate), some of them learned jurists, who promoted the juridification of the deliberations.[22]

Not only the Emperor himself as 'the source of all law', but every Imperial Estate and moreover, all other members of the Empire and even common people could try to initiate legislative proceedings by submitting or applying to the Diet via decrees, petitions, supplications, requests or complaints. The non-permanent diets of the 16th century constituted special commissions (*Supplikationsausschuss*) dealing solely with the vast number of supplications addressed to the Empire by different estates, social groups, and individual supplicants.[23] Particularly the Imperial Cities initiated

22 Klaus Schlaich, 'Maioritas—protestatio—itio in partes—corpus Evangelicorum: Das Verfahren im Reichstag des Hl. Römischen Reichs Deutscher Nation nach der Reformation', *Zeitschrift der Savigny-Stiftung für Rechtsgeschichte: Kanonistische Abteilung* 94 (1977), 264–299 and 95 (1978), 139–179; Anton Schindling, 'The Development of the Eternal Diet in Regensburg', *Journal of Modern History* 58 (1986), Supplement (Politics and Society in the Holy Roman Empire 1500–1806), 64–75; Karl Härter, *Reichstag und Revolution 1789–1806: Die Auseinandersetzung des Immerwährenden Reichstags zu Regensburg mit den Auswirkungen der Französischen Revolution auf das Alte Reich* (Göttingen, 1992), 58–66; Karl Härter, 'The Permanent Imperial Diet in European Context, 1663–1806', in Evans et al., ed., *Holy Roman Empire*, 115–135.

23 Helmut Neuhaus, *Reichstag und Supplikationsausschuß. Ein Beitrag zur Reichsverfassungsgeschichte der ersten Hälfte des 16. Jahrhunderts* (Berlin, 1977). For a broader view on supplications with regard to legislation and justice see: Peter Blickle, ed., *Gemeinde und Staat im alten Europa* (Munich, 1998); Cecilia Nubola/Andreas Würgler, ed., *Suppliche e "gravamina". Politica, amministrazione, giustizia in Europa (secoli XV–XVIII)* (Bologna, 2002).

imperial legislation concerning commerce, trade, guilds, crafts, and other economic and social issues, which were related in some way to the everyday life of common subjects (the *Gemeine Mann*).[24] However, law-making from below was very limited, and only a few 'private' individuals succeeded in initiating formal procedures (not to mention actual decisions). The subjects of the Imperial Estates could at best try to influence their rulers via supplication or complaint to promote a law or legal issue on the imperial level. But in the majority of cases only serious conflicts and issues of more common interest were brought to the Diet, and formal procedure was initiated only with the consent of the Emperor and the principal Estates.

To pass a new imperial law a complex formal procedure was required, during which the envoys stated the votes of the Imperial Estates in the respective council of the Diet (Electors, Princes and Cities), from which a conclusion was formed from the majority or the dominant opinion. Finally the three council decisions had to be combined into an agreed-upon statement and brought to the attention of the Emperor, who could reject or ratify the Diet's advice (*Reichsgutachten*) via his own statement; the approval of both the council of the Diet and the Emperor were required to create imperial law. Only in religious matters was this ordinary procedure suspended and the Diet split into two religious corpora (*corpus evangelicorum* and *corpus catholicorum*), which had to negotiate a mutual agreement.

All in all the legislative process of the Imperial Diet oscillated between the principles of majority rule and consensus, and was actually based on negotiation and compromise to preserve the fragile balance of the imperial system. Imperial legislation possessed the character of agreements, contracts and treaties, and therefore differs from historical models such as the absolutist *potestas legislatoria*, wielded for instance by the early-modern kings of France.[25] Law-making on the level of the Empire was not a 'top to down' operation from the imperial centre to its members, but rather a matter of imperial politics and a complex process of communication and interaction between different actors: the Emperor and

---

[24] Kristina Winzen, *Handwerk—Städte—Reich: Die städtische Kurie des Immerwährenden Reichstags und die Anfänge der Reichshandwerksordnung* (Stuttgart, 2002); Fritz Blaich, *Die Wirtschaftspolitik des Reichstags im Heiligen Römischen Reich: Ein Beitrag zur Problemgeschichte wirtschaftlichen Gestaltens* (Stuttgart, 1970).

[25] However, recent research has fundamentally questioned this model: Ronald G. Asch/Heinz Duchhardt, ed., *Der Absolutismus—ein Mythos? Strukturwandel monarchischer Herrschaft* (Cologne, 1996).

the Estates, and to some degree their envoys, learned jurists, immediate subjects, and even foreign powers, who acted as guarantors of the imperial constitution (France and Sweden) or maintained delegations at the courts of the Emperor and the major Imperial Estates or at the Diet in Ratisbon.[26]

From the end of the 15th century the Diet passed many imperial laws. Up to 1654 enactments were compiled in more than 50 comprehensive recesses (*Reichsabschiede*), later also enacted as single laws (ordinances, mandates, edicts). Many of them were considered as 'fundamental laws' (*leges fundamentales*): the *Reichskammergerichtsordnung* (procedural code of the Imperial Chamber Court), the *Notariatsordnung* of 1512, the penal code from 1532 (*Carolina*); the three police-ordinances (1530, 1548, 1577), regulating matters of public order, several coinage regulations (*Münzordnungen*), the *Ewige Landfrieden* (permanent peace of the Empire), and the *Reichsexekutionsordnung* regulating matters of external and internal peace, public security, and the military constitution of the Empire. However, the complexity of the legislative process within the Diet and increasing conflicts between the Emperor and the more powerful Estates (especially Prussia) led to fewer laws being passed in the second half of the 18th century. But the Diet still managed to enact several regulations, for example, concerning crafts and guilds (1731 and 1771/72) and prescribing that women and children of infamous people (*Unehrliche*) must not be excluded from crafts; in 1793 the Diet reacted with several anti-revolutionary laws in response to the challenge of the French revolution and the *expansion révolutionnaire*.[27]

The imperial legislation of the Diet formed a vital part of the *Reichsrecht*, which comprised other legal norms and customs such as the 17 electoral

---

[26] Jörg Ulbert, 'Der Reichstag im Spiegel französischer Gesandtenberichte (1715–1723)', in Olaf Asbach/Klaus Malettke/Sven Externbrink, ed., *Altes Reich, Frankreich und Europa: Politische, philosophische und historische Aspekte des französischen Deutschlandbildes im 17. und 18. Jahrhundert* (Berlin, 2001), 145–169; Nikolaus Leiher, *Die rechtliche Stellung der auswärtigen Gesandten beim Immerwährenden Reichstag zu Regensburg: Eine rechtshistorische Untersuchung unter Auswertung der Schriften zum Ius Publicum des Alten Reiches* (Aachen, 2003).

[27] Karl Härter, 'Entwicklung und Funktion der Policeygesetzgebung des Heiligen Römischen Reiches Deutscher Nation im 16. Jahrhundert', in *Ius Commune* 20 (1993), 61–141; Johannes Burkhardt, 'Verfassungsprofil und Leistungsbilanz des immerwährenden Reichstags: Zur Evaluierung einer frühmodernen Institution', in Heinz Duchhardt/Matthias Schnettger, ed., *Reichsständische Libertät und habsburgisches Kaisertum* (Mainz, 1999), 151–183; Karl Härter, 'Reichsrecht und Reichsverfassung in der Auflösungsphase des Heiligen Römischen Reichs deutscher Nation: Funktionsfähigkeit, Desintegration und Transfer', *Zeitschrift für Neuere Rechtsgeschichte* 28 (2006), 316–337.

capitulations (*kaiserliche Wahlkapitulationen*) negotiated between the Emperor and the electors or the Peace of Westphalia (1648) as well as several international peace treaties of the 17th and 18th centuries up to the treaty of Lunéville (1801) and the so-called *Reichsdeputationshauptschluß* (1803), the last fundamental law of the Empire which sealed its fate. These provisions covered not only international issues, but also regulated constitutional, religious and confessional matters of the Empire; they therefore influenced law at the level of the imperial Estates as well as to some degree the life of the common subjects.[28] Beyond the written and published laws, political observance and imperial conventions (*Reichsobservanz und Reichsherkommen*) were also regarded as an integral part of the *Reichsrecht*. In this respect every political action of the Emperor or the Estates within the imperial framework (especially in the Diet or the Supreme Courts) could be considered as an exemplary claim or an original precedent to create a new imperial convention or norm. For that reason ceremonial, symbolic and ritual elements of procedure and imperial politics played an important role in establishing a calculable normative order or in restricting precedents.[29]

The vast corpus of imperial law was collected and published several times (from 1501 onward) in more than forty different semi-official editions, the so-called *Corpus constitutionum imperialium*. In addition some authors of the *Reichspublizistik* published voluminous systematic collections of imperial law—including customs and precedents—with Johann Jacob Moser leading the way and publishing more than a hundred volumes of his *Teutsches Staatsrecht*.[30]

---

[28] Karl Härter, '"Gute Ordnung und Policey" des Alten Reiches in der Region: Zum Einfluß der Reichspoliceygesetzgebung auf die Ordnungsgesetzgebung süddeutscher Reichsstände', in Rolf Kießling/Sabine Ullmann, ed., *Das Reich in der Region während des Spätmittelalters und der Frühen Neuzeit* (Konstanz, 2005), 187–223; Karl Härter, 'Religion, Frieden und Sicherheit als Gegenstand guter Ordnung und Policey: Zu den Aus- und Nachwirkungen des Augsburger Religionsfriedens und des Reichsabschieds von 1555 in der reichsständischen Policeygesetzgebung', in Wolfgang Wüst/Georg Kreuzer/Nicola Schümann, ed., *Der Augsburger Religionsfriede 1555. Ein Epochenereignis und seine regionale Verankerung* (Augsburg, 2005), 143–164.

[29] Barbara Stollberg-Rilinger, 'On the Function of Rituals in the Holy Roman Empire', in Evans et al., ed., *Holy Roman Empire*, 359–373; Barbara Stollberg-Rilinger, *Des Kaisers alte Kleider. Verfassungsgeschichte und Symbolsprache des Alten Reiches* (Munich, 2008); compare also with regard to the Emperor: Jeroen Duindam, *Vienna and Versailles. The courts of Europe's dynastic rivals, 1550–1780* (Cambridge et al., 2003), 181 ff.

[30] Gross, *empire and sovereignty*; Stolleis, *Geschichte*, vol. I; Härter, *Reichsgesetzgebung und Reichsrecht*; Mack Walker, *Johann Jakob Moser and the Holy Roman Empire of the German nation* (Chapel Hill, 1981).

Although private, penal and public law were covered, the focus of imperial law and legislation was predominantly on constitutional and public law. All in all the essence of imperial law was not to regulate everything down to the smallest village, but only to provide a legal framework which left its members legislative and judicial powers. It also established legal options for the Estates and their subjects to make use of the imperial legal provisions and institutions, especially via the Imperial Supreme Courts. This delegation of (legal) authority was a characteristic feature of premodern empires,[31] and it becomes even more apparent in the implementation and enforcement of imperial law. First of all, the imperial laws were not addressed directly to the subjects, but had to be applied and enforced by the imperial institutions and above all by the Imperial Estates themselves. The Empire's only executive institutions consisted of the imperial chancellery (*Reichskanzlei*), which was primarily a small office of the vice-chancellor, who commanded only some secretaries and envoys, and the ten imperial circles (*Reichskreise*). The latter were formed as supraterritorial regional organisations of the Imperial Estates, but were often dominated by their more powerful members. For that reason four circles ceased nearly all activities after 1648, and the more active ones focused on military issues (the levying of imperial troops in case of an imperial war) and transborder problems of order such as coinage, trade control, the prosecution of bandits and other security issues.[32]

In theory the imperial law was binding on every member of the Empire, who had to implement and apply imperial legislation. Because of its agreed-upon character the Imperial Estates often complied and published imperial laws or integrated provisions and regulations within their particular legislation. However, many norms—such as the penal code of 1532—were adopted only implicitly and partially by the territorial governments and courts, which still relied on their particular law and/or applied *ius commune* in its different shapes. This was possible, because some imperial laws granted salvatoric clauses with regard to diverse regional

---

31 Benton, *Search for Sovereignty*, 3.

32 Karl Härter, 'War as Political and Constitutional Discourse: Imperial Warfare and the Military Constitution of the Holy Roman Empire in the Politics of the Permanent Diet (1663–1806)', in Angela De Benedictis, ed., *Teatri di guerra: rappresentazioni e discorsi tra età moderna ed età contemporanea* (Bologna, 2010), 215–237; Winfried Dotzauer, *Die deutschen Reichskreise (1383–1806). Geschichte und Aktenedition* (Stuttgart, 1998); Wolfgang Wüst, ed., *Reichskreis und Territorium, die Herrschaft über die Herrschaft? Supraterritoriale Tendenzen in Politik, Kultur, Wirtschaft und Gesellschaft. Ein Vergleich süddeutscher Reichskreise* (Stuttgart, 2000).

customs, existing customary law and specific local conditions. Moreover, at least since the Treaty of Westphalia the Empire had conceded power to all territorial rulers within the scope of their *Landesherrschaft* to maintain traditional particular law and to enact new laws on the basic prerequisite that these laws fitted somehow into the imperial legal framework and did not impinge upon the imperial laws or privileges of its members. This delegation and division of legislative powers resulted in ambivalent developments. Since the 17th century the amount of legislation issued by the Estates was considerably greater than that issued by the Empire, and fragmentation, collisions, and contradictions between the different levels increased. But the amorphous, partially inconsistent and even confusing nature of the imperial law stimulated, on the other hand, the process of juridification (*Verrechtlichung*), particularly with regard to the 'scientification of law', the 'professionalisation of jurists' and the formation of legal discourses revolving around the *Reichsrecht*—the *Reichspublizistik*.

Public Law and Reichspublizistik

Since the 16th century the peculiar constitutional structure of the early-modern Empire and the diversity of imperial law, as well as the resulting ambivalences and collisions, influenced the development of jurisprudence and juristic discourses. At the end of the 16th century a new discipline emerged at the universities of the Empire: public law (*ius publicum*), focussing at first on imperial law and the constitution of the Empire. This was accompanied by a wider public discourse, since not only members of the law faculties but also other scholars and Imperial Estates or parties published writings on legal issues (or conflicts) of the Empire, which together comprised the *Reichspublizistik*. The learned jurists of the *Reichspublizistik* collected, systematized and commented on the imperial law as well as customs, exemplary cases and court decisions and discussed (often controversially) the constitutional nature of the Empire and its multi-layered legal system, especially with regard to confessional questions, the relationship between Emperor and Estates, the reform of the Empire (*Reichsreform*), and numerous constitutional issues, thus producing a growing body of writings, consisting of a plethora of collections, textbooks, tracts, commentaries, and more than 5,000 dissertations in the field of imperial public law. Moreover, the Emperor, the imperial institutions and the Estates themselves published treatises, documents, papers and pamphlets, which were often distributed at the location of imperial institutions—for instance at the Diet in Ratisbone—or among the members of the Empire.[33]

The burgeoning public law fulfilled a crucial function in the imperial legal system, for it helped to produce consistency and homogeneity in the imperial law and contributed to the university studies and the training of jurists. In this regard it fostered also the professionalisation of jurisprudence and influenced the imperial elites: judges, diplomats, envoys, advisors, administrators or ministers in the services of the Emperor, imperial institutions or Estates often had studied public and imperial law or had been students of famous *Reichspublizisten* such as *Johann Stephan Pütter*. Thus learned jurists and legal experts were integrated into the political, administrative and judicial practice of the imperial legal system, and knowledge of imperial law remained an important qualification for administrative, judicial or political services.[34]

This process of professionalisation and elite formation was enhanced even with regard to the *ius commune*, private and penal law. After the establishment of the Imperial Supreme Courts, the procedure of the Imperial Chamber Court and the obligation of imperial codes such as the *Constitutio Criminalis Carolina* (1532) to seek legal advice from supreme courts and law faculties promoted a new culture of litigation and consultation. On the level of the Imperial Estates the territorial rulers had to adapt to a certain extent to the standards of the Imperial Chamber Court and established a regular court system with supreme or appellate courts, learned judges/jurists and a procedure that converged more or less with the written romano-canonical procedure of the Chamber Court (*Reichskammergerichtsprozeß*). Moreover, the local and communal lay courts on the

---

33 Gross, *Empire and sovereignty*; Stolleis, *Geschichte*, vol. I, 126 ff.; Karl Härter, 'Ius publicum und Reichsrecht in den juristischen Dissertationen mitteleuropäischer Universitäten der Frühen Neuzeit', in Jacques Krynen/Michael Stolleis, ed., *Science politique et droit public dans les facultés de droit européennes (XIIIe–XVIIIe siècles)* (Frankfurt/M., 2008), 485–528.

34 Anette Baumann/Peter Oestmann/Stephan Wendehorst/Siegrid Westphal, ed., *Reichspersonal. Funktionsträger für Kaiser und Reich*, (Cologne et al., 2003); Siegrid Westphal, 'Does the Holy Roman Empire Need a New Institutional History', in Evans et al., *Holy Roman Empire*, 77–94; Filippo Ranieri, 'Juristen aus dem Alten Reich (16.–18. Jahrhundert). Ein Forschungsresümee', in Johannes-Michael Scholz, ed., *El tercer poder. Hacia una comprensión histórica de la justicia contemporánea en España* (Frankfurt/M., 1992), 109–118; see also the rich data on the biographies, dissertations and professional careers of more than 10,000 early modern jurists: Filippo Ranieri/Karl Härter, ed., *Biographisches Repertorium der Juristen im Alten Reich, 16.–18. Jahrhundert, A–E;* Ulrich Dingler/Karl Härter, ed., *Katalog der Sammlung Lehnemann: juristische Schriften des 16.–18. Jahrhunderts*, 1 CD-ROM (Frankfurt/M., 1997).

regional level were increasingly obliged or even forced by the imperial laws to ask for legal advice and to consult learned jurists, law faculties, or supreme courts. As a result the courts had to send their written records to such institutions—the so-called *Aktenversendung*—and had to adapt to a certain professional standard.[35] In this regard the imperial law exerted a considerable indirect influence on the professionalisation of the territorial and local judiciary and integrated to a certain degree the territorial/local levels and court practice into the sphere of the learned jurists and law faculties, while encouraging the elimination of laymen from local and communal courts.[36]

On the whole, the imperial legal system facilitated the development of jurisprudence—notably in the field of public law—stimulated the legal discourses of the *Reichspublizistik* and enabled (or compelled) to a certain degree the legal communications between territorial and local/communal levels and the learned law, thus promoting such processes as professionalisation and *Verrechtlichung*. Though one could not deny that very divergent interpretations of imperial law existed as well as a considerable diversity of law, the resulting collisions and conflicts were mostly dealt with within the imperial legal framework.[37] All members of the Empire as well as the subjects of the Estates could still use imperial law as a resource to manage conflicts, for it guaranteed their rights, privileges and customs and provided legal protection (*Rechtsschutz*) and legal access (*Rechtsweg*) to the Imperial Supreme Courts.

Imperial Jurisdiction and Supreme Courts

At the end of the 15th century the Empire featured a diversity of jurisdictions on every level: a patchwork of imperial, territorial, seigniorial, ecclesiastical, aristocratic, communal, and local jurisdictions, sometimes overlapping and exercised by different 'higher' or 'lower' courts in which lay jurors or 'law-finders' (*Schöffen*) often applied local customary law.

---

[35] Ulrich Falk, *Consilia. Studien zur Praxis der Rechtsgutachten in der frühen Neuzeit* (Frankfurt/M., 2006).

[36] Bernhard Diestelkamp, 'Verwissenschaftlichung, Bürokratisierung, Professionalisierung und Verfahrensintensivierung als Merkmale frühneuzeitlicher Rechtsprechung', in Bernhard Diestelkamp, *Recht und Gericht im Heiligen Römischen Reich* (Frankfurt/M., 1999), 263–281.

[37] Peter Oestmann, *Rechtsvielfalt vor Gericht. Rechtsanwendung und Partikularrecht im Alten Reich* (Frankfurt/M., 2002).

Though this 'patchwork' remained to some extent until the dissolution of the Empire in 1806, the process of juridical institutionalisation on the imperial level strongly influenced the 'lower' jurisdictions with regard to the professionalisation and hierarchization of judiciary and adjudication. First of all the 'reform-diet' of 1495 established a new Imperial Supreme Court: the *Reichskammergericht* (Imperial Chamber Court).[38] This was followed in the first half of the 16th century by the transformation of the Emperor's council into a second Supreme Court, the *Reichshofrat* (Imperial Aulic Council or Court), which exercised the royal jurisdiction of the Emperor, and in addition conducted to a certain extent governmental and administrative tasks.[39] The Emperor formally remained the head of both Supreme Courts, but the Imperial Estates could exercise a strong influence on the Imperial Chamber Court. Via the Imperial Circles they elected the 'judges'/jurors—the so-called *Reichskammergerichtsassessoren*—enacted via the Imperial Diet the procedural law (the *Reichskammergerichtsordnungen* 1495 to 1555), and the court was placed beyond the direct grip of the Emperor in an Imperial City (Frankfurt, Speyer and from 1689 onward Wetzlar).

The Aulic Council and to an even greater degree the Chamber Court were highly professionally organised: different benches and senates with learned and examined councillors (*Hofräte*) or judges (*Reichskammergerichtsassessoren*), presiding judges, and a professional staff (lawyers, advocates, procurators, solicitors, secretaries etc.).[40] The judges adjudicated not only according to imperial law, but applied different legal sources: *ius commune*/Roman law, particular territorial, and communal law as well as customary law. This provided the judges with discretionary power and scope for decision-making, but also gave them the task to 'mediate' to a certain degree between the different legal layers and diverse law of the Empire, and to establish a kind of legal balance or settlement. Despite the problem that the Imperial Courts often could not conclude judicial

---

[38] Bernhard Diestelkamp, ed., *Das Reichskammergericht in der deutschen Geschichte. Stand der Forschung, Forschungsperspektiven* (Cologne et al., 1990); Bernhard Diestelkamp, ed., *Die politische Funktion des Reichskammergerichts* (Cologne et al., 1993).

[39] Leopold Auer, 'The Role of the Imperial Aulic Council in the Constitutional Structure of the Holy Roman Empire', in Evans et al., ed., *Holy Roman Empire*, 63–75; Michael Hughes, *Law and Politics in Eighteenth Century Germany. The Imperial Aulic Council in the Reign of Charles VI* (Woodbridge, Suffolk, 1988).

[40] Sigrid Jahns, *Das Reichskammergericht und seine Richter. Verfassung und Sozialstruktur eines höchsten Gerichts im Alten Reich, vol. 1–2* (Cologne et al., 2003/2011); Anette Baumann: *Advokaten und Prokuratoren—Anwälte am Reichskammergericht (1690–1806)* (Cologne et al., 2006).

proceedings with a final judgement, many conflicts were prevented and absorbed or even settled by an agreement, mediated by the Chamber Court or the Aulic Council.

Both Imperial Courts acted on the basis of *ius commune* procedural law (*Reichskammergerichts- und Hofratsordnungen*) and provided different elaborate modes of litigation, using ordinary as well as extraordinary proceedings: first-instance trial in public matters of the Empire (breach of the peace), appeal proceeding, summons and summary process (*Zitations- und Mandatsverfahren*), impeachment process (especially in case of refused justice or procedural errors)—all of them conducted in written form and therefore producing a tremendous body of court files comprising well over 150,000 cases, most of them still available in several archives.[41] They covered a broad range of social, economic, political and constitutional issues and conflicts, since both courts exercised several jurisdictions and functions: maintaining public peace and security, especially with regard to feuding, revolt and social upheaval; imposing the *Reichsacht* (imperial outlawry) on 'criminal' (rebellious, feuding) members of the Empire or appointing Imperial Commissions; acts of grace and pardon (*Gnadensachen*); feudal conflicts and matters of the 'good order' (*Policeysachen*); religious and confessional conflicts; social and constitutional conflicts within the Imperial Cities as well as between the different members of the Empire and their subjects if their guaranteed rights, privileges and customs were concerned. With regard to civil law they functioned as courts of appeal, albeit restricted by special non-appellation privileges (*privilegium de non appellando*) granted to the more powerful territorial Estates, especially if they had implemented a judiciary according to the standards of the Supreme Courts.[42]

---

41 Bettina Dick, *Die Entwicklung des Kameralprozesses nach den Ordnungen von 1495–1555* (Cologne, 1981); Tilman Seeger, *Die Extrajudizialappellation* (Cologne et al., 1992); Peter Oestmann, ed., *Zwischen Formstrenge und Billigkeit. Forschungen zum vormodernen Zivilprozeß* (Cologne et al., 2009). See also the nearly finished project: Bernd Schildt, 'Erschließung der Reichskammererichtsakten', in Friedrich Battenberg/Bernd Schildt, ed., *Das Reichskammergericht im Spiegel seiner Prozessakten Bilanz und Perspektiven der Forschung* (Cologne et al., 2010).

42 Filippo Ranieri, *Recht und Gesellschaft im Zeitalter der Rezeption. Eine rechts- und sozialgeschichtliche Analyse der Tätigkeit des Reichskammergerichts im 16. Jahrhundert* (Cologne et al., 1985); Anette Baumann, *Die Gesellschaft der frühen Neuzeit im Spiegel der Reichskammergerichtsprozesse. Eine sozialgeschichtliche Untersuchung zum 17. und 18. Jahrhundert* (Cologne et al., 2001).

Hence, the Imperial Courts dealt with numerous conflicts between 'common people' or subjects and rulers, and nearly all social groups—among them women and minorities like the Jews—made use of imperial justice.[43] Subjects could litigate against their territorial rulers if they had enacted a law or carried out administrative measures which had infringed the subjects' traditional privileges, rights or customs guaranteed by the Empire or somehow backed by imperial norms. Such law suits—called *Untertanenprozesse*—ranged from jurisdictional to constitutional conflicts, from business to sanctuary, from the forest to crafts and guilds.[44] After the Peace Treaties of Augsburg (1555) and Westphalia (1648) the Courts gained further importance by dealing with religious/confessional conflicts and protecting religious rights of the subjects: the right to emigrate in confessional matters (1555) and the free practice of religion (after 1648 and restricted to the Christian creeds) as well as the status of the Jews as *kaiserliche Kammerknechte* (servants of the Emperors chambers) and *Reichsbürger* (citizens of the Empire).[45] As a result the Supreme Courts not only guarded the rights of subjects and granted to some extent legal protection[46] but facilitated the process of juridification (*Verrechtlichung*) and a new culture of litigation: burghers, peasants and religious minorities made actively use of imperial justice in conflicts with authorities, utilized different legal options (concerning law and procedure), engaged learned jurists or law faculties and gained legal experience and knowledge. In this

---

43 Siegrid Westphal, ed., *In eigener Sache. Frauen vor den höchsten Gerichten des Alten Reiches* (Cologne, 2005); Friedrich Battenberg, *Das Reichskammergericht und die Juden des Heiligen Römischen Reiches. Herrschaft und korporative Verfassung der Judenschaft in Fürth im Widerspruch* (Wetzlar, 1992); Andreas Gotzmann/Stephan Wendehorst, ed., *Juden im Recht. Neue Zugänge zur Rechtsgeschichte der Juden im Alten Reich* (Berlin, 2007).

44 Compare the case studies: Julia Maurer, *Der 'Lahrer Prozeß' 1773–1806. Ein Untertanenprozeß vor dem Reichskammergericht* (Cologne et al., 1996); Rita Sailer, *Untertanenprozesse vor dem Reichskammergericht. Rechtsschutz gegen die Obrigkeit in der zweiten Hälfte des 18. Jahrhunderts* (Cologne et al., 1999); Stefan von Below/Stefan Breit, *Wald—von der Gottesgabe zum Privateigentum. Gerichtliche Konflikte zwischen Landesherren und Untertanen um den Wald in der frühen Neuzeit* (Stuttgart, 1998); Karl Härter, 'Frühneuzeitliche Asylkonflikte vor dem Reichshofrat und anderen europäischen Höchstgerichten', in Leopold Auer/Werner Ogris/Eva Ortlieb, ed., *Höchstgerichte in Europa. Bausteine frühneuzeitlicher Rechtsordnungen* (Cologne et al., 2007), 139–162.

45 Jürgen Weitzel, 'Das Reichskammergericht und der Schutz von Freiheitsrechten seit der Mitte des 18. Jahrhunderts', in Diestelkamp, *Funktion*, 157–180; Stefan Ehrenpreis, *Kaiserliche Gerichtsbarkeit und Konfessionskonflikt. Der Reichshofrat unter Rudolf II. 1576–1612* (Göttingen, 2006).

46 Michael Hughes, 'The Imperial Aulic Council ('Reichshofrat') as guardian of the rights of mediate estates in the later Holy Roman Empire', in Rudolf Vierhaus, ed., *Herrschaftsverträge, Wahlkapitulationen, Fundamentalgesetze* (Göttingen, 1977), 192–204.

regard the Imperial Supreme Courts enabled to some extent 'legal paths from below', connected and mediated between the different actors and legal levels of the Empire and facilitated 'forum shopping' or *Justiznutzung*, since the jurisdiction of the competing Courts was not clearly separated and actors could bring a case separately to both.

Consequently, the Supreme Courts did not follow 'altruistic' or modern ideas of civil rights and liberties, but tended to control the local, territorial, and communal jurisdictions and courts with respect to their own professional standards and to extend imperial authority over all members of the Empire (some of them already en route to sovereignty). Since all actors could use the legal system, the more powerful—and to an even greater extent the powerless—had to adjust to a certain degree to the practice and procedures of the Imperial Courts and to respect their adjudication. Not even the more powerful territorial states, which often tried to elude imperial justice, could ignore the Supreme Courts entirely because aggrieved parties or their subjects could seek the help of the imperial legal system and use it if for nothing else as a forum for 'public impeachment'. In this regard the imperial legal system prevented to some extent absolutist state-building, but also hindered legal reforms.[47]

Imperial justice, on the other hand, proved to be impaired and limited by its dualistic and competitive structure, its overall aim to maintain the constitutional and social structure of the Empire, and the tendency of the more powerful territorial Estates (including the Emperor as ruler of his principalities) to elude the Supreme Courts (or even obstruct them). Furthermore, in matters of criminal law and public order (the so called *Policeysachen*), appeal was prohibited and imperial jurisdiction was limited to procedural errors and the infringement of traditional rights and privileges. As a consequence, the territorial states could develop their own state-based penal law and criminal justice systems, arguing that the imperial criminal and public law was imperfect and inappropriate, and were granted salvatoric clauses as well as legislative and judicial powers. Moreover, most territorial rulers restricted legal consultation and *Aktenversendung*, which the imperial penal code of 1532 had prescribed, to the courts and universities of their principalities, and therefore intensified the monopolisation and centralisation of discretionary powers as well as

[47] Siegrid Westphal, *Kaiserliche Rechtsprechung und herrschaftliche Stabilisierung. Reichsgerichtsbarkeit in den thüringischen Territorialstaaten 1648–1806* (Cologne et al., 2002).

the elimination of lay people from local and communal courts. Concerning the wide-ranging matters of the 'good order' and criminal justice, in the 18th century the well-ordered territorial police states of many Imperial Estates were characterised by diversity, arbitrariness and diminished legal protection.[48]

Concluding Remarks: Significance and Limits of the Imperial Legal System

The early modern Holy Roman Empire was characterised by an unique multi-layered legal system that provided a legal framework with essential legal norms and institutions—imperial law, *ius commune* and Supreme Courts—but also left legal spaces and various degrees of autonomy for the territorial and local levels. In this regard it may be comparable to other pre-modern Empires like the Ottoman or Russian.[49] However, the peculiar nature of the imperial legal system also produced and maintained legal diversity and pluralism and a constitutional system of 'political-legal' interaction, in which legislation, law and jurisdiction were negotiated, mediated and agreed upon between the different actors, ranging from the Emperor, territorial or communal Estates to intermediary powers and the subjects. In some respect this limited the legislative and judicial powers of the Emperor and it also provided legal protection (*Rechtsschutz*) and options of 'forum-shopping' and *Justiznutzung*, especially for the more powerless members of the Empire and the subjects of the Imperial Estates. The latter had to adapt to a certain extent to the professional standards and model of the imperial legal system especially with regard to the Supreme Courts and the professionalisation of jurisprudence and jurists.

On the one hand, this was based on the reception of romano-canonical law and the *ius commune* system, which provided a 'great legal tradition', legitimacy, continuity, and a permanent stimulus for the burgeoning

---

48 Christian Szidzek, *Das frühneuzeitliche Verbot der Appellation in Strafsachen. Zum Einfluß von Rezeption und Politik auf die Zuständigkeit insbesondere des Reichskammergerichts* (Cologne et al., 2002); Karl Härter, 'Das Reichskammergericht als 'Reichspoliceygericht'', in Friedrich Battenberg/Filippo Ranieri, ed., *Geschichte der Zentraljustiz in Mitteleuropa. Festschrift für Bernhard Diestelkamp zum 65. Geburtstag* (Weimar et al., 1994), 237–252; Harriet Rudolph/Helga Schnabel-Schüle, ed., *Justiz = Justice = Justicia? Rahmenbedingungen von Strafjustiz im frühneuzeitlichen Europa* (Trier, 2003).

49 I refer in particular to Eisenstadt, *Systems of Empires*, 137–140; Imber, *Ottoman Empire*, 216–225; Benton, *Search for Sovereignty*, 3–10.

jurisprudence. The complexity of the composite imperial system and its legal layers, on the other hand, gave rise to public law, the *Reichspublizistik*, and ever-expanding 'political-legal' discourses in the public sphere of the *Reichssystem*. That, in turn, enhanced the juridification (*Verrechtlichung*) of the Empire and its different legal layers, which none the less were characterised by persistent structural collisions and conflicts, resulting in an on-going need to establish and maintain some kind of balance through legal and political means—or resorting to violence, feud, and internal war. Since the Empire provided imperial law, Supreme Courts, legally based constitutional institutions and a public sphere, the legal system was partially successful in solving, mediating, preventing, or absorbing conflicts, and affected in the longer term imperial politics. Neither the Emperor nor the more powerful territorial states—not to mention the numerous weaker members—could utterly ignore imperial law, justice or the *Reichspublizistik*, and had to adjust to a certain degree to legal norms, procedures, rituals, customs, argumentation, and a 'constitutional fashion' (albeit sometimes merely in pretence).

On the whole, the imperial legal system achieved the juridification (*Verrechtlichung*) of imperial politics and religious or social conflicts, which were settled, managed, or absorbed via legal mechanisms, as well as the preservation of rights and privileges of immediate estates and mediate subjects. A multi-layered, polycratic, multiconfessional, and powerless system like the early modern Empire could ensure stability and integration of its diverse members only through law and a constitutional legal system, which hindered or impaired the ability of the territorial states to establish absolutist regimes and full sovereignty. Balance and stability, the maintenance of the status quo and the preservation of the status, rights, and privileges of all members through a constitutional legal system was the best the powerless Empire (in terms of power politics and military power) could achieve. However, this could as well result in stagnation, as is demonstrated by the decline in imperial legislation in the 18th century or the dilatory justice of the Imperial Courts—some lawsuits lasted more than ten years while others fizzled out without a final decisions. Imperial justice and politics could aggravate conflicts, hinder and delay formal proceedings and decisions or finally paralyze the Empire, ending up in incapacity and even territorial losses; and with respect to the more powerful estates the legal system was not able to prevent all violent and armed conflicts. Moreover, the traditional, conservative character of the imperial legal system obstructed reforms and modernisation on the local, territorial and most of all the imperial level itself. In the age of codification and reform the Empire was not able to agree on a modern criminal or civil code and persevered in its traditional *ius commune*/imperial law system. The Empire was trapped in its own 'great legal tradition'. The challenge of the French Revolution made it finally clear that it could not withstand the power of the nation-state, and the Empire was dissolved by revolutionary and Napoleonic France with the compliance of its more potent members (including the Emperor himself), resulting in the establishment of sovereign states exercising a legislative and judicial monopoly. By contrast with the new order, the traditional constitutional legal system of the Empire lacked the capacity to modernise on the basis of a monopoly of power, sovereignty and a homogenous nation-state. Indeed, the example of the early modern Holy Roman Empire seems to confirm that an imperial legal system with diverse levels, legal pluralism, a predominance of law, and *Verrechtlichung* was incompatible with modernisation and the building of the nation-state.

PART TWO

INSTITUTIONALISING EMPIRE: PRACTICES OF LAWMAKING AND ADJUDICATION

THE CONTRIBUTION OF EARLY ISLAMIC RULERS TO ADJUDICATION AND LEGISLATION: THE CASE OF THE *MAZALIM* TRIBUNALS

Nimrod Hurvitz

Islamic Rulers and the Legal System

There is an interesting discrepancy in the early Islamic empires between law making and the perception of law making. Although early Islamic rulers—the Rashidun (the first four caliphs that succeeded Muhammad, known as the Rightly Guided caliphs), the Umayyads and the early 'Abbasids—determined the rules and regulations in several areas of the law, their contributions went unmentioned in legal literature.[1] What is more, the caliphs themselves made no effort to record their contributions to the burgeoning body of Islamic legal doctrine.[2] Furthermore, not only were the caliphs not considered as law makers, the areas of the law that they forged—public and administrative law—were not part of the body of legal literature. In other words during the first five centuries of Islam, its rulers ran huge empires on the basis of principles of governance that barely received any attention from jurists.

The marginality of public law was manifested in two, interrelated ways: The first, rulers were not deemed to be legislators. The second, the regulations and administrative policies that they established were not considered to be a branch of law. The marginal position of the rulers in the legal discourse indicates that legislation was separated from the political

[1] For a comment on the lack of documentation regarding the *mazalim* tribunals see Emile Tyan, *Histoire de L'organisation Judicaire en Pays D'Islam* (Leiden, 1960), 434. On the dearth of legal sources that deal with the *mazalim* see also in Emile Tyan, 'Judicial Organization', in Majid Khadduri, and Herbert J. Liebesny, eds., *Law in the Middle East* (Washington, D.C., 1955), 263.

[2] For an explicit statement on the dearth of caliphal legal documentation see Wael B. Hallaq, *The Origins and Evolution of Islamic Law* (Cambridge, 2005), 178, where he writes: 'No edicts regulating law are known to have come down from caliphs, no constitutions, and certainly no legal codes of any kind.' For a similar remark on the lack of such writings on the part of jurists see Noel J. Coulson, *A History of Islamic Law* (Edinburgh, 1991), 120: '...the jurists had formulated standards of conduct which represented a system of private, and not of public, law...' Coulson continues with a general remark on p. 123: 'Accordingly the early doctrine contained no system of constitutional law, nor... matters which make up the field of public law.'

establishment. This is not to say that every law or institution that the rulers put forth was totally ignored. In some areas their decisions were recorded and integrated into the legal literature. However, when the rulers did determine the law, it was deemed to be an act that was based on their being knowledgeable and pious Muslims and not as emanating from their position as rulers. For example, when the Rashidun forged the fiscal law and institutions of the expanding Islamic empire, it was not perceived as part of the legislative authority of rulers, but rather as deriving from the fact that they were the Prophet's Companions (*Sahaba*). Later, when Umayyad and 'Abbasid caliphs continued to shape the law, their decisions were considered as personal opinions and again, not as part of the caliphs' capacities. In other words, Islamic legal literature does not link political authority and legislative authority.[3]

It was only in the eleventh century CE that two Muslim jurists, Abu al-Hasan 'Ali ibn Muhammad ibn Habib al-Mawardi (d. 1058) and Abu Ya'la Muhammad ibn al-Husayn al-Farra' (d. 1066), composed tracts on public law (*siyasa shar'iyya*).[4] Both of these authors named their composition *Ordinances of Government*, (*al-Ahkam al-Sultaniyya*).[5] Clearly, one of the two works was the original and the other copied approximately seventy percent of the original. However, despite the obvious relationship

---

[3] Frank E. Vogel, *Islamic Law and Legal System Studies of Saudi Arabia* (Leiden, 2000), 196; Hallaq, *The Origins*, 181.

[4] For biographical information about Mawardi, see *Encyclopedia of Islam* (second edition), 'Mawardi', C. Brockelman; On Mawardi's life, works and the reception of the *al-Ahkam al-Sultaniyya* see Hanna Mikhail, *Politics and Revelation* (Edinburgh, 1975), 59–68. Studies of Mawardi's ideas abound. The foundational works were by Hamilton A.R. Gibb, 'Some Considerations on the Sunni Theory of the Caliphate', in Stanford J. Shaw and William R. Polk, eds., *Studies on the Civilization of Islam*, (Boston, 1962), 141–150. Also, ibid., 'al-Mawardi's Theory of the Caliphate', 151–165; A comprehensive study of the historical context in which Mawardi operated is Henri Laoust, 'La Pensee et l'Action Politiques d'Al-Mawardi (364–450/974–1058', *Revue des Etudes Islamiques* 36 (1968), 11–92. For biographical information about Abu Ya'la, see *Encyclopedia of Islam* (second edition), 'Ibn al-Farra' ', H. Laoust. For a study of one of his works see Wadi Z. Haddad, *Kitab al-Mu'tamad fi Usul al-Din* (Beirut, 1974). For an overview of his life and work see 13–28. A full study of his life and work see Muhammad 'Abd al-Qadir Abu Faris, *al-Qadi Abu Ya'la al-Farra' wa-Kitabuhu al-Ahkam al-Sultaniyya* (Beirut, 1400/1980). For a reference to his life in a biographical dictionary see Abu al-Husayn Ibn Abi Ya'la, *Tabaqat al-Hanabila* (Cairo, 1371/1952), vol. 2, 193–230.

[5] Abu al-Hasan 'Ali b. Muhammad al-Mawardi, *al-Ahkam al-Sultaniyya wa-al-Wilayat al-Diniyya* (Beirut, 1985). For an English translation see Wafaa H. Wahba, *The Ordinances of Government* (Reading, 1996). Abu Ya'la Muhammad ibn al-Husayn al-Farra', *al-Ahkam al-Sultaniyya* (Misr, 1966). For a comparison of these two works see Nimrod Hurvitz, *Competing Texts: The Relationship Between al-Mawardi's and Abu Ya'la's al-Ahkam al-Sultaniyya* (Cambridge, Mass., 2007).

between the two works, the remaining parts that differed reflect the contrasting agendas of the two camps that existed within the scholarly elite of eleventh-century Baghdad to which each of these jurists belonged. Modern scholars tend to believe that Mawardi wrote the first of the two treatises and that Abu Yaʿla's version is the second. If that is the case, Abu Yaʿla's tract is a sophisticated rhetorical act which combines large parts of Mawardi's tract and at the same time inserts numerous subversive observations that promote his own legal and political agenda, that of the Hanbali school of law (*madhhab*).

Yet, notwithstanding these differences, the two works make a similar contribution to the development of Islamic public law. Their structure is identical, i.e., both of them address approximately twenty institutions and the officials that headed them and make up the military, economic, administrative and religious elite of the regime. Their underlying motive was to explain, from a legal point of view, how the political system should work and how it should adjust itself to changing political circumstances. Both works share an implicit, underlying premise that the rulers did not engage in legislation. They took into consideration that rulers may set historical precedents, but they also assumed that these rulers did not rework historical patterns of governance into legal principles. They also tended to rely on very similar legal opinions regarding specific legal questions.

Although medieval Islamic jurists did not discuss the contribution of rulers to legal thought and writing, modern historians of Islamic law did address this issue. In the words of Joseph Schacht: 'In their function as the supreme rulers and administrators, though of course devoid of the religious authority of the Prophet, the caliphs acted to a great extent as the lawgivers of the community.'[6] After the Prophet and the early caliphs succeeded in bringing together the tribes of Arabia and creating a unified political entity and after this new political force wrested huge areas from the hands of the existing empires in the Orient, the rulers began to function as 'lawgivers' because it was essential to set down laws that would regulate the lives of their subjects. The shift from a tribal society to a global empire necessitated a wide range of adjustments in the law. For example, it was crucial to decide upon the laws of revenue collection and their distribution among the Muslims.[7] Another area in which the rulers needed to establish rules and regulations as quickly as possible was

---

[6] J. Schacht, *An Introduction to Islamic Law* (Oxford, 1982), 14; Vogel, *Islamic Law*, 185.
[7] Schacht, *An Introduction*, 23; Vogel, *Islamic Law*, 185.

their own administration. Hence, it was necessary that they address the obligations of such officials as the newly nominated governors and the local officials that they appointed such as judges and market inspectors. These were some of the central areas of Islamic law to which the caliphs contributed. In some instances they actively gave orders that were followed by their subjects, in other cases they simply followed the laws and customs of the lands that they conquered. On the whole, during the first century, Islamic rulers fashioned patterns of governance that came to be public law—even though they were not written down as such.

This gap between the rulers' central role as establishers and shapers of institutions and the marginal historiographic position that was ascribed to them has already been noted by Schacht, who wrote: 'This doctrine [which denied the ruler the position of legislator]…, effectively concealed the fact that what was actually legislation of the caliphs of Medina [the Rashidun], … entered into the fabric of Islamic law.'[8] Schacht rightly refers in this observation to an act of concealment that was performed by medieval Islamic scholars who ignored the legislative role of the early Islamic rulers. This view is corroborated by another historian of Islamic law, Frank Vogel, who writes about the relations between rulers and jurists, and points out that the '… common identification of fiqh and shariʿa in itself represents a signal ideological success for the ʿulama' [scholars]'[9] Vogel's argument is that the *shariʿa*, (the most inclusive term used to describe all matters related to Islamic law) is composed of two main bodies of law: *fiqh*, that is, the legal discourse among jurists; and *siyasa*, the legal and administrative machinations of the rulers. He notes that when Muslims think that the *shariʿa* is made up solely of *fiqh* (hence ignoring *siyasa*), they are in fact leaving their leaders' legislation out of the body of law, an act that serves the ideological agenda of the jurists.

Furthermore, not only do modern scholars depict the jurists as having removed the rulers from the historical narrative of Islamic law, they also assume that such a step promoted the interests of the jurists at the expense of the rulers. Noel Coulson, who wrote about the relations between 'government and *shariʿa* law', described several institutions that the rulers established and pointed out that despite the crucial role of these institutions in the actual governance of early Islamic empires, 'the

[8] Schacht, *An Introduction*, 53–54.
[9] Vogel, *Islamic Law*, 172.

early doctrine contained no system of constitutional law.'[10] Furthermore, Coulson places the onus for the split between legal doctrine and political administration upon the jurists. He argues that 'the scholars' self-imposed terms of reference,' is the main factor that distanced the jurists from a wide spectrum of political issues.[11] In other words, Coulson assumes that it was the jurists who determined the spheres of activity and authority of the jurists and the rulers. Vogel, much in line with Coulson, views the dynamic by which public law (*siyasa shar'iyya*) was separated from the Islamic legal discourse (*shari'a*) as the jurists' victory.[12] Schacht's position is similar to that of Coulson and Vogel in that he assumes that the authority to legislate in the first century of Islam was held by the rulers, but towards the end of the first century and the beginning of the second, it was passed on to the jurists, due to the immense respect that the rulers felt towards the jurists.[13] Even though the role that Schacht ascribes to the rulers is more active than the role that Coulson or Vogel ascribe to them, his description of the rulers is obfuscated and a little naïve. Few rulers have ever passed authority and power to their subjects simply because of their respect towards them.

This essay shares the views expressed by modern historians of Islamic law that argue that the early rulers participated in legislation and that public law was forged by them. However, the reading and analysis put forth in this study regards the relations between rulers and scholars differently. The argument put forth in this essay is that the negligible role of the rulers in the historical narrative of Islamic law, as well as the removal of public law out of the Islamic legal discourse, is the result of an interest that the rulers and the scholars shared, and not a clash between them. In other words, the study of the *mazalim* points to the mutual benefit that both sides derived from the division of roles and the exclusion of the rulers from the historical narrative of Islamic law, as it developed in the first centuries of Islam.

The omission of the rulers from the historical narrative of Islamic law is a fascinating phenomenon that merits an in-depth study that is far beyond the scope of this chapter. However, this essay will examine one case of this dynamic by looking at the *mazalim* tribunals. According

10 Coulson, *A History of Islamic Law*, 123.
11 Coulson, *A History of Islamic Law*, 123.
12 Vogel, *Islamic Law*, 172.
13 Schacht, *An Introduction*, 23–27, particularly 27.

to Mawardi, the *mazalim* tribunals were an ancient institution that was adopted by the 'Abbasids in the eighth century.[14] Its main purpose was to enable ordinary subjects to complain about the administrative elite of the empire. The *mazalim* was a means by which the rulers addressed the abuse of power perpetrated by powerful state officials. There is evidence that it was practiced in several cities throughout the 'Abbasid empire. It probably functioned at least into the Mamluk period.[15] One of its most conspicuous characteristics was that it went unmentioned in contemporary legal works.[16] The fate of the *mazalim*, I will argue, reflects the general attitude of jurists towards the rulers' activities in the field of law.

The Discourse and Ideological Context of the Mazalim *Tribunals*

Although Islamic legal literature did not elaborate a comprehensive and sustained tradition that deals with political institutions, Muslim statesmen and officials did write about good governance. These works were often called 'advice literature' or 'mirror for princes' (*nasihat*), and their approach to statecraft combined a seemingly odd pair, morality and political sophistication.[17] Much of the 'advice literature' was composed by caliphs who wrote for their heirs or *wazirs* and even jurists who wrote for their rulers. Often they were influenced by pre-Islamic imperial traditions such as the Sasanians, Indians and Greeks. Eventually 'advice literature' evolved into an important component of the ruling elite's discourse about

[14] From this point on, this essay will rely solely on Mawardi's composition, due to its centrality in primary and secondary literature. For Mawardi's historical review of the *mazalim* see 97–100; English trns. 87–90.

[15] For a statement that the *mazalim* tribunals stopped after the Mamluk period see Albrecht Fuess, '*Zulm* by *Mazalim*? The Political Implications of the Use of *Mazalim* Jurisdiction by the Mamluk Sultans', *Mamluk Studies Review* 13, no. 1 (2009), 141. I want to thank Professor Yaakov Lev for bringing this article to my attention.

[16] Just as authors of legal texts paid little attention to the institution of *mazalim*, so have the authors of biographical dictionaries paid little attention to the individuals who filled this position. This has been pointed out by Mathieu Tillier, '*Qadis* and the Political Use of the *Mazalim* Jurisdiction Under the 'Abbasids', in Christian Lange, and Maribel Fierro, eds., *Public Violence in Islamic Societies, Power, Discipline and the Construction of the Public Sphere, 7th–19th Centuries CE* (Edinburgh, 2009), 52. This article makes an important contribution by placing the *mazalim* in its historical and political context. I would like to thank Professor Yaakov Lev for bringing this article to my attention.

[17] On *nasihat* see *Encyclopedia of Islam* (second edition), '*Nasihat al-muluk*', Bosworth; the connection between *nasihat* literature and the institution of the *mazalim* has been made by Patricia Crone, *God's Rule, Government and Islam* (New York, 2004), 158–161.

the craft of governance, the responsibilities of a ruler, and the measures that can be taken in order to attain his goals.

One of the topics that come up in the 'advice literature' is the institution of *mazalim*. In addressing the *mazalim* the authors address three major issues: justice, access and information. First and foremost is justice, which the authors of 'advice literature' depict as a crucial moral value. At the same time the authors of these works are experienced men of affairs who are aware of the political dividends that justice can generate, such as social stability and economic growth. Another aspect of the institution of the *mazalim* is access to the ruler. The *mazalim* was established to enable the subjects to air their complaints before the ruler, who was expected to act upon these complaints and correct these wrongdoings. The writers of the 'advice literature' were aware that the *mazalim* can also serve the ruler as an important source of information about the administrators and officials that run the empire on a daily basis. Thus, in the 'advice literature' the institution of *mazalim* was seen as both a means for attaining and advancing the moral fibre of the empire, and at the same time, an efficient means of governance.

A widely known work of this genre is *The Book of Government* written by Nizam al-Mulk (d. 485/1092).[18] One of the central themes of this work was the corruption of the regime's officials. Thus the reader will find in the opening chapter, in which the author introduces the main themes of good governance, references to the possibility that the ruler will be served by officials that commit 'impropriety or oppression.'[19] Throughout the book, Nizam al-Mulk pays a great deal of attention to the problems that arise from the misbehaviour of officials and their tendency to take advantage of their positions of power. He advises the ruler to engage directly with these officials, and if that fails, to remove them from office. Clearly, Nizam al-Mulk identifies the administrators as both the mainstay of the regime and at the same time, a source of potential instability. Due to the dual nature of the administrators, the ruler must devise means of allowing them to do their work and at the same time he must monitor their conduct.

Nizam al-Mulk advises the ruler, over and over again, to actively pursue information about his officials. He states that it is crucial to 'see if they are fulfilling their function properly or not'.[20] He continues this line of

---

[18] Nizam al-Mulk, *The Book of Government or Rules for Kings*, trns. Darke, H., (London, 1978 (1960)).

[19] Nizam al-Mulk, *The Book of Government*, 10.

[20] Ibid., 23.

thought when he refers to judges, '[I]t is necessary for full information to be available about every single judge in the country.'[21] Perhaps the most potentially volatile position is that of the official who collects money from the subjects and transfers it to the rulers, i.e., the tax collector:

> Tax-collectors . . . must be instructed to deal honourably with their fellow creatures, and to take only the due amount of revenue, and to claim that too with civility and courtesy, and not to demand any taxes from them until the time comes for them to pay; because when they demand payment before the time, trouble comes upon the peasants . . . whereby they are driven to extremities and have to emigrate.[22]

The crucial point in this citation is the reference to the economic damage that corrupt officials can cause, mainly, that their incompetence and corruption may lead to the evacuation of peasant communities. It is quite clear from this paragraph and others that Nizam al-Mulk is acutely aware of the rulers' dependence upon the agricultural production of the peasants and that the misconduct of tax collectors can lead to the disintegration of this system.

Having stated that the officials ought to be subjected to supervision and be at risk of losing their jobs if they are corrupt, the ruler must know that the ultimate responsibility for the efficient and moral functioning of the administration lay with him. Nizam al-Mulk emphasizes that when dealing with officials, particularly those who perform such sensitive tasks as taking money from the peasants, the ruler must give them clear instructions and their conduct must be monitored. If they do not get good guidance and are not subjected to tight supervision, the ruler is to be faulted for their misconduct.[23]

Nizam al-Mulk's ideas about ways to restrain state officials are quite detailed. As was mentioned above, the first step in controlling them is to know what they are up to. Therefore, the ruler must devise a system of surveillance to spy on his officials. Nizam al-Mulk recommends that the ruler's inquiries about the affairs of the *wazir*s be conducted 'secretly';[24] that the ruler employ a group of 'upright and honest' individuals to 'supervise the collection of taxes and revenues';[25] that he set up a network of postmasters, who will inform him about 'everything that goes on, good

[21] Ibid., 42.
[22] Ibid., 22.
[23] Ibid., 63.
[24] Ibid., 23.
[25] Ibid., 63.

and bad.'[26] The key to effective rule is to have the clearest, most detailed picture of all strata of society, particularly central officials such as the *wazir* and tax collectors.

Alongside the ruler's active steps to learn about his empire and officials, Nizam al-Mulk suggests that the ruler create an institution that will enable his subjects to approach him directly. This, as was pointed out earlier, is one of the underlying concepts of the *mazalim*. In the third chapter of *The Book of Governance*, Nizam al-Mulk writes: 'It is absolutely necessary that on two days in the week the king should sit for the redress of wrongs, to extract recompense from the oppressor, to give justice and to listen to the words of his subjects with his own ears, without intermediary.'[27] Nizam al-Mulk's recommendation that the ruler meet his subjects in person and hear their complaints directly from them is in fact a way to remove these officials from his channels of direct communication with his subjects. It is essential to remove them from their mediating role so as to prevent them from presenting a distorted picture of events. Furthermore, not only must the ruler listen to his subjects directly, he must take their accusations seriously and confront his administrators if proven guilty.

Nizam al-Mulk, one of the best known and most successful administrators in Islamic history, harboured a deep suspicion towards administrators and warned the ruler about their behaviour. This need for vigilance is mentioned in several remarks and stories that appear throughout the text. In one of them Nizam al-Mulk describes how the Persian kings sat on their horses out in the open so that subjects who had grievances would be able to approach them. He explains that they did so because '... when a king sits in a place protected by doors, gates, locks, vestibules, screens and chamberlains, self-interested and oppressive persons can keep people back and not let them go before the king.'[28] In other words there is not much sense in setting up an institution that would monitor the empires' administrators and at the same time enable a handful of them, dubbed in this paragraph as 'self-interested and oppressive persons', to interfere in the rulers' communication with his subjects.

Direct contact between ruler and subjects is depicted by Nizam al-Mulk as a crucial tool of governance. When the tool is not used, i.e., 'when the king is difficult of access the affairs of the people are put into suspense,

[26] Ibid., 64.
[27] Ibid., 13.
[28] Ibid., 14.

evil-doers are encouraged, facts remain concealed, the army suffers harm and the peasants fall into trouble.'[29] Direct access to the ruler exposes the facts that would otherwise 'remain concealed.' If this access were blocked, two crucial interests of the regime would suffer: agricultural production and security. The lesson that Nizam al-Mulk is conveying to the readers of his tract is that if the ruler wishes to maintain a smoothly running empire that has at its disposal a well-functioning economy and army, he must devise efficient ways to supervise his administrators, be they overt, as in the case of the *mazalim*, or covert, such as networks of spies.

The tensions between the rulers and their administrators can be discerned in the dynasties and empires that followed the 'Abbasid empire and in empires outside of the Islamic world. Although it is possible to trace changes in this institution during the Mamluk and Ottoman empires, many of the *mazalim*'s tasks, such as supervision of officials and *qadi*s, were taken over by the Ottoman chief judges.[30] Similar situations would arise in Europe. Most European medieval societies were plagued with corrupt elites whose members abused their privileged social status. The unequal application of the law in European courts of law has been commented upon by Georges Duby as he describes the '...brutal and summary punishments inflicted upon ordinary folk and the weak enforcement of judgments against nobles.'[31] The inability or lack of motivation on the part of the courts of law to confront the nobles, the wealthy or the influential bureaucrats of their societies drove rulers who were powerful enough to establish adjudicative mechanisms that would bring to justice these powerful yet corrupt elements in society. In thirteenth-century England, where kings had 'a deep-seated concern for the behaviour of the mass of officials in royal service at all levels', the kings initiated a series of investigations into the conduct of these officials.[32] Furthermore, their subjects could petition the kings and gradually there evolved a 'court of the Chancery' that attended to the growing numbers of these appeals. The *mazalim* courts, which were established by the 'Abbasids in the eight

[29] Ibid., 118.

[30] On the *mazalim* courts in the 13th to 14th centuries see Jorgen S. Nielsen, *Secular Justice in an Islamic State: Mazalim Under the Bahri Mamluks, 662/1264–789/1387* (Leiden, 1985).

[31] G. Duby, *The Chivalrous Society* (trns. Cynthia Postan) (Berkeley and Los Angeles, 1980), 15. A similar assessment regarding the difficulties to implement the law is found in Raoul Charles van Caenegem, *Legal History, A European Perspective* (London, 1991), 147.

[32] Anthony Musson, *Medieval Law in Context, The Growth of Legal Consciousness from Magna Carta to the Peasant's Revolt* (Manchester, 2001), 160.

century, were an effort to limit upper-class and official corruption. In both cases the king or caliph confronted his officials through an institution of adjudication that was based on royal discretion and not ordinary legal procedure. In both societies, the injustice perpetrated by the powerful social classes was addressed by the supreme power of the land.

The Mazalim *Tribunals in Practice*

Before we examine how the *mazalim* tribunals actually worked, we should take a brief look at the individuals who administered them.[33] Although the advice literature warmly recommends that the ruler sit in on the sessions of the *mazalim*, this did not happen often. It seems that only a few ʿAbbasid caliphs, such as Mahdi (r. 775–785), Ma'mun (r. 813–833) and Muhtadi (r. 869–870), ever presided over the *mazalim*. However, the rest of the caliphs usually nominated other officials to run the tribunals. Most often it was the *wazir*s (chief ministers) that either sat in on the tribunal or nominated representatives to do so. In other cases the rulers nominated *qadi*s (judges) to run the tribunals. On the whole, it was the prerogative of the ruler to nominate anyone he saw fit to perform the task.

The most exceptional case of a *mazalim* administrator, which illustrates that it was the ruler's whim that determined who will run the *mazalim* tribunals, was Thumal.[34] Thumal belonged to a network of women headed by Sayyida, the mother of the caliph Muqtadir (r. 908–932). Sayyida built her power when her 13-year-old son was appointed to the position of caliph precisely because he was young and incompetent. Sayyida came to be extremely wealthy and was involved in court politics. She had a large retinue of secretaries who oversaw her economic affairs, and a circle of women that attended to her personal and political matters. The key position among these women was the *qahrmana*, a handful of women who were extremely influential in the court of Muqtadir.[35]

---

33 For an overview on the administrators of the *mazalim* tribunals see Emile Tyan, *L'organisation Judicaire*, 475–494.

34 References to her appointment to the position of *nazar al-mazalim* ʿArib b. Saʿd al-Qurtubi, *Silat ta'rikh al-Tabari* (Leiden, 1897), 71; Ibn al-Jawzi, *al-Muntazam* (Beirut, 1358 Hijri) 6: 148; Ibn al-Kathir, *al-Bidaya wa-al-Nihaya* (Beirut) 11: 129. On Thumal and her appointment to the position of *mazalim* see David Marmer, *The Political Culture of the Abbasid Court, 279–324 (A.H.)* (Ph.D. dissertation, Princeton University, 1994), 174–176.

35 For an overview of the position of women in Muqtadir's court see Marmer, *The Political Culture*, 151–181.

One of the most significant characteristics of Sayyida's circle of aides was their involvement in political appointments. The most notorious of Sayyida's aides was Umm Musa who had a network of protégés which she tried to promote in the court, including candidates to the position of *wazir*. Apparently, she paid with her life for her involvement in court intrigue and power politics. Yet these political activities by Sayyida, Umm Musa or other *qahrmana* were for the most part carried out behind the scenes. These women played the political game by pulling strings in the corridors of the court, but they rarely took upon themselves public positions. One of the main exceptions to this pattern of behaviour was the appointment of Thumal to the *mazalim*. According to one of the sources, this step, i.e., the appointment of a woman to the position in the *mazalim*, caused discomfort among the populace. However, after a while they got used to it and she continued to perform her job.[36]

The appointments that the rulers made to the post of *mazalim*, be they *wazir*s, *qadi*s or even unorthodox nominations such as a woman, illustrate that this institution was a legal and administrative tool that would often deviate from traditional norms and hierarchies of power. It is therefore hardly surprising that in some of the *mazalim* cases we come across a Jew challenging a *qadi* or an ordinary woman confronting ʿAbbasid royalty. Both in personnel and contents, the *mazalim* was a framework that obeyed the rulers' needs and decisions and as a consequence would on occasion break from the conventional power structure. A number of case studies will illustrate this practice.

In the early twelfth century, a petition was sent to the Fatimid caliph Amir (d. 1130). Its author introduced himself as 'Musa ibn Sadaqa the Jewish merchant.'[37] He complained that upon his return from a voyage to India and Yemen, the goods he brought back with him had been detained by the *qadi* for no good reason. Musa asked the caliph to see that his property be given back to him.

Although we do not know the outcome of this complaint, it is important to point out that this Jew, a member of a community that was legally inferior to Muslims, challenged one of the pivotal figures in the Islamic legal system—a *qadi*. The social and legal inequality between them is glaring. Yet despite this inferiority, Musa ibn Sadaqa felt confident enough to confront this Muslim official. Granted, Musa was probably from the

---

[36] For details see Marmer, *The Political Culture*, 174.

[37] Samuel M. Stern, 'Three Petitions of the Fatimid Period', *Oriens* 15 (1962), 179–80.

higher economic strata of society. As the petition discloses, he was a merchant engaged in international commerce and therefore probably a man of means who may have had good connections in the upper echelons of twelfth-century Egyptian society. At the same time it seems that the *qadi* considered his properties easy prey. From our perspective it is important to note that the *mazalim* enabled people who were of lower social or legal standing to confront their superiors.

The second case, mentioned by Mawardi, tells of a woman who approached the ʿAbbasid caliph Maʾmun as he was leaving a *mazalim* session.[38] This 'woman in rags', as she is described by Mawardi, recited a poem that ended with the lines: 'Once protected, her lands from her are now taken away// For family and children are no longer there to defend her.' Maʾmun answered that he will attend to her matter on Sunday. When they met he asked her who wronged her, and she answered that it was the man standing alongside of him, meaning his son ʿAbbas. Upon hearing this accusation Maʾmun turned to his judge and asked him to look into the matter, while he sat back and observed from a distance. In the final analysis Maʾmun believed the woman and ordered that her property be returned to her.

This woman who has fallen from riches to rags—from days in which she had properties and a family to a state of poverty and loneliness—cannot be considered a typical subject of the ʿAbbasid empire. At some point in her life she possessed properties which were valuable enough to attract the attention and arouse the greed of an ʿAbbasid prince. Furthermore, she probably had a good education if she could address the caliph with a line of poetry. Yet despite her cultural and economic affiliation with the upper classes of ʿAbbasid society, she was no match for a prince. Due to her social and legal inferiority, the only path she had open to remedy her grievance, was the *mazalim*.

Both of these cases illustrate the most important feature of the *mazalim*: upholding the rights of all subjects of the empire, by confronting state officials who abused their power. In these two cases the accused offenders were quintessential members of the ruling elite, a *qadi* and a prince, one by virtue of knowledge, the other by virtue of birth. The *mazalim* tribunals were established to curb the corrupt practices of these, and other, privileged groups.

---

38 Mawardi, *al-Ahkam* 106. English trns. 95.

Although combating administrative corruption was perceived and presented as a central task of the *mazalim*, the *mazalim* tribunal attended to other matters as well. The petitions that are at our disposal indicate that the *mazalim* was asked to intervene in a variety of communal crises. Some of them were internal communal matters, such as conflicts among the Jews living in Palestine over positions of leadership.[39] Others dealt with inter-communal friction, as in the case between the monks of Mt. Sinai and their Bedouin neighbours.[40] In cases of this nature the main purpose of the caliph's intervention was to promote social stability.

In one such case, which has been studied by Samuel Stern, a long-standing dispute among the Jews of Palestine moved them to write several petitions to the *mazalim*.[41] The *mazalim*'s reaction to the Jews' appeal was to nominate a respected Jew to mediate between the two sides. However, we learn from subsequent petitions that this step did not satisfy the hostile camps, and the conflict continued. Approximately two years after the nomination of the Jewish mediator, one of the groups involved in the conflict persuaded local officials of Ramla to side with them, open the synagogue that was closed for several years due to this conflict, and enable them to hold a service in it. This step outraged the other group, and they turned to the *mazalim* with a new petition.

It seems that the Jewish community was not able to settle this feud on its own so they turned to the ruler who opted to settle the matter through mediation. Yet, the mediation did not succeed and after some time the ruler's representatives, i.e., the police, were called in by one of the sides to intervene. At this point the grievances of the side that was hurt by the police intervention were exacerbated. Alongside the existing feud with a group of their own coreligionists, they now felt that they had been wronged by state officials. The new petition that they composed included a request to reverse the decisions that were made by the police.

Although this sequence of petitions ends with a complaint against the police, it is first and foremost a request to the *mazalim* to intervene in an inter-communal conflict. In this instance, as well as others, the ruler is not seen as battling injustice, but rather, as a wise and impartial mediator who can be trusted to act justly and solve the disputes of his subjects. The

---

[39] Samuel M. Stern, 'A Petition to the Fatimid Caliph al-Mustansir Concerning a Conflict within the Jewish Community', *Revue des Etudes Juives* 128 (1969), 203–222.

[40] Samuel M. Stern, 'Petitions from the Ayyubid Period', *Bulletin of the School of Oriental and African Studies* 27 (1963), 1–32.

[41] Stern, 'Conflict within the Jewish Community'.

mazalim, which is based on the assumption that the caliph is the supreme implementer of justice operated on two levels: The first, as an institution of adjudication that enables the caliph to intervene in the daily affairs of his subjects and attend to their grievances. The second, as an important element in the image-making of the caliph, in which he is perceived as the most powerful individual in the empire, an impartial advocate of justice and a wise mediator.

In one of the few remarks made about this institution in the first centuries of Islam, Sayrafi (d. 1131), a high-ranking Fatimid official who lived and wrote in the twelfth century, noted that the people who turn to the *mazalim* do so 'believing that they approach one who will help them and redress their grievances and assist them against their adversaries.'[42] According to Sayrafi, the *mazalim* is an institution that enables the caliphs to combat corruption and help their subjects in their efforts to attain their rights. Yet Sayrafi is also aware that the *mazalim* deals with perceptions, as he points out that the *mazalim* creates the belief that the caliphate can remedy injustice, either by siding with the petitioners against their opponents or by mediating between the two sides.

The notion and practice of caliphal justice are the outcome of the cooperation between the caliph and his common subjects who seemingly united against the straying members of the empire's highest echelons, who might include the above-mentioned princes and *qadi*s, as well as generals, governors, tax collectors, courtiers and other well-connected and powerful, yet dissolute, individuals.

In the first comprehensive legal discussion of the *mazalim*, which appears as a chapter in the *al-Ahkam al-Sultaniyya*, Mawardi wrote that the rulers established this institution to look 'into oppression and maltreatment of the public by government officials.'[43] Hence, this informal collaboration between caliphs and their subjects against the empires' potentially corrupt officials was widely recognized and stated explicitly. Mawardi also pointed to another potential problem in which the *mazalim* was expected to intervene, which arose when the *qadi*s were not able to implement their own sentences. As he described it, when the 'judges are too weak to enforce them due to the sentenced person's power or social standing.'[44] This remark indicates that alongside the problem of corruption,

---

[42] Stern, 'Three Petitions', 187.

[43] Mawardi, *al-Ahkam*, 101; Eng. trns. 90.

[44] Mawardi, *al-Ahkam*, 104; Engl. trns. 93. It is worth noting that alongside cases in which the *qadi*s were too weak to confront the upper echelons of society, there were instances in

there was another severe problem—the honest officials who were supposed to enforce the law were often too weak to do so. Hence, it was necessary to establish an institution that would cut down to size the overly powerful upper echelons of society and implement the courts' sentences.

It would have been very difficult to perform these tasks had the *mazalim* been obligated to abide by *shariʿa* court procedures such as the right to retract a confession or reject evidence furnished by immoral witnesses or had they been prohibited from using torture. However, this was not the case. As Mawardi remarks, the *mazalim* were allowed to follow much looser investigative procedures. They were permitted to intimidate witnesses, place suspects under surveillance, rely on circumstantial evidence and take into consideration information provided by unreliable sources.[45] In short, they were not constrained by the rules and procedures that tied the hands of the *qadi*-run *shariʿa* courts.

The contrasting approaches of *shariʿa* courts and *mazalim* tribunals stem from two different value systems and social visions. The underlying value that guided *shariʿa* courts was to do justice and therefore to defend the rights of suspects. This implies that they demand high standards of proof. Conviction of a suspect is made on the basis of solid evidence arrived at through stringent investigative procedures. These requirements protected suspects from potentially abusive courts of law. The main advantage of this approach is that it reduces the likelihood of convicting innocent individuals. Yet the price that society as a whole paid for a system that protected the rights of suspects was that its court system found it difficult to convict active criminals, and therefore, many of them roamed the streets to the detriment of the law-abiding inhabitants of the empire. The *shariʿa* court system protected the rights of innocent suspects but ran the risk of high crime rates.

The procedures of the *mazalim* tribunals and police were based on a very different social vision. Their main priority was to prevent crimes that were perpetrated by common criminals or the corruption of state officials. To facilitate these goals they needed to round up and convict as many criminals as possible. As a consequence their procedures of interrogation enabled them to utilize harsh measures of investigation, threaten suspects and resort to other acts that disregarded suspects' rights. While this

---

which the *mazalim* served the rulers as a means to limit *qadis* that have attained too much authority. See Tillier, '*Qadis* and the political use'.

[45] Mawardi, *al-Ahkam*, 101–104; Engl. trns. 90–93.

approach may well have produced more cases of personal injustice due to convictions of innocent individuals, at the same time there were probably fewer criminals roaming the streets. Hence, this approach chose the safety of the empire's subjects over the rights of potentially innocent suspects.

The moral tension between these two procedures of investigation is found in the European context as well. According to James Brundage, twelfth- and thirteenth-century canon jurists were grappling with the same set of questions regarding criminal investigation, and eventually there evolved two trends of thought on the matter. One of them emphasized the rights of defendants and insisted that they 'must be cited before the judge... informed of the charges... had the right to offer a defence'.[46] Furthermore, they argued that 'full proof of guilt' must be established before a suspect is convicted.[47] Others were not satisfied with a court system that sets a 'high standard of proof,' because it 'would allow guilty defendants to escape just punishment.'[48] Such an approach would hinder the abilities of society to repress crime. Both Middle Eastern and European medieval societies faced a similar dilemma: Will injustice be caused by the state (via a harsh procedure of investigation) or by fellow subjects (due to high crime rates)?

Ever since the earliest stages of Islamic empire-building the caliphs took it upon themselves to maintain social order. They were able to pursue this task because they took criminal law into their own hands and established institutions that monitored the conduct of state officials.[49] In order to implement criminal law they enabled their governors and police to capture the criminals, try them and punish them. The investigative procedures used by the police were much looser than those of the *shariʿa* courts, and similar to those of the *mazalim* mentioned above. Both *mazalim* and police procedures enabled quick convictions of suspects and as a result, the attainment of low crime rates. Yet despite the significant role that the caliphs played regarding law enforcement, establishing institutions of adjudication and the shaping of rules, regulations and norms, the rulers' contributions were not mentioned in the legal works composed by jurists.

46 James Brundage, *Medieval Canon Law* (London, 1995), 149.

47 Ibid., 149.

48 Ibid., 150.

49 Schacht, *An Introduction*, 15; Coulson, *A History*, 120–121; Uriel Heyd, '*Kanun* and *Shariʿa* in Old Ottoman Criminal Justice', *Proceedings of the Israel Academy of Sciences and Humanities* 3, no. 1 (Jerusalem, 1967), 1.

Mazalim *and Legal Discourse*

In the eleventh century, when Mawardi and Abu Ya'la wrote about public law, they had little literature to draw upon. While the Qur'an and *hadith*, the holy scriptures which are the foundation of Islamic law, made a few and vague statements about the topic, the vast majority of jurists in the first five centuries of Islam ignored it. Compendia of Islamic law from that period referred to a bare handful of topics that could be considered as public law. As a consequence the challenge that Mawardi and Abu Ya'la faced was to create a narrative that would address public law. They had to identify and decide what would constitute the sources for public law; what topics public law needed to address; and how a legal point of view would be constructed when it has no precedents to rely on. A close reading of Mawardi's chapter on the *mazalim* will expose some of the characteristics of his discourse on public law.

The *al-Ahkam al-Sultaniyya* is made up of twenty chapters.[50] Ten of them deal with classical legal topics such as prayer leaders, taxation and spoils of war. These are topics that have received a great deal of attention from Islamic jurists and as a consequence they constitute large chapters in the existing legal literature. In his treatment of these topics, Mawardi follows the norms of Islamic legal discourse, which means that whenever relevant he makes references to scriptural citations from the Qur'an or accounts of Muhammad (*hadith* literature), that constitute legal precedents. Often, Mawardi mentions the opinions of esteemed jurists that expressed their thoughts on these subjects. Sometimes he brings together several conflicting opinions of different jurists on the same matter. Thus, when Mawardi writes about issues that have a long-standing written tradition, he draws upon this literature and bases his exposition of the matter on the existing opinions within the milieu of jurists.

The remaining ten chapters deal with topics that have not been addressed in legal discourse. The *mazalim*, *wazir* (minister), and *muhtasib* (often compared to the Greek *agoranomos*) are some of the governmental and public roles that Mawardi addressed in legal terms for the first time. As mentioned above, due to the fact that in the past these topics generated little legal discourse and did not attract the attention of earlier jurists, Mawardi had little to draw upon. As a consequence, we rarely find in these chapters scriptural citations or the opinions of major scholars.

[50] For a more detailed analysis of the text see Hurvitz, *Competing Texts*, mainly 6–28.

Mawardi introduced into the narrative that he construed a variety of new themes. For example, the chapter on the *mazalim* starts with a description of the traits that an administrator of the *mazalim* ought to possess, which is followed by an historic overview of the institution's development, its jurisdictions, a comparison with the *qadi*-run *shari'a* court, and instructions for how the administrator ought to conduct the affairs of the tribunal. In order to appreciate Mawardi's originality, it is important to stress that these types of topics, historic overviews of institutions and comparisons between different jurisdictions, rarely appear in classical legal texts.

Yet the most distinctive feature of these chapters is their sources. Mawardi constructs a legal narrative from two unconventional sources. The first is made up of his own ideas and opinions on the *mazalim*. He does not cite or refer to authoritative sources such as Qur'an, *hadith* or previous jurists. The narrative unfolds on its own and not as a dialogue with previous legal texts, neither as a commentary nor as disagreement. For example, a comparison to the *shari'a* court or the historic survey of the *mazalim* institution offers straight-forward accounts that express Mawardi's knowledge and opinions on these matters, but are not part of any existing legal literature. The second source is his explicit reliance on historical precedents. In these parts of his account, Mawardi described how different caliphs had conducted their affairs. However, Mawardi's tendency to describe caliphal behaviour should not mislead us. Early Islamic writings do not have corpora of caliphal policies that served future rulers or jurists and guided them regarding doctrines of public law. Mawardi does not turn to written rules and policies laid down by earlier caliphs, such as the capitularies of the Carolingians, the laws of Henry II, or the *kanuns* of Süleyman the Magnificent. Rather, he was a well-informed scholar and jurist, who was very knowledgeable about Islamic history and was capable of choosing stories about the caliphs and fitting them into his legal presentation. He drew upon events that occurred during the reigns of the Rashidun, the Umayyads, and the 'Abbasids. From each of these periods he chose stories that suited his agenda. It was an act of historical interpretation, in which he inserted specific historical descriptions and placed them alongside a general statement about the policy he considered to be correct. He was not merely recording a traditional, well-known caliphal policy.

The need to create a legal discourse from scratch is a clear indication that public law did not have much of a past. It should also be noted that it did not have much of a future. Notwithstanding a handful of jurists, the topics that Mawardi was the first to cover in the *al-Ahkam al-Sultaniyya* did not receive much attention from future jurists. Mawardi's opinions are often quoted and well respected, but we do not come across legal compositions that pay systematic and comprehensive attention to public law. Whereas most areas of Islamic law attract commentaries and spark disagreements, Mawardi's and Abu Ya'la's *al-Ahkam al-Sultaniyya* did not trigger these types of responses.

Concluding Remarks and Comparison

This essay accords with the views expressed by contemporary historians of Islamic law that assert that in the first centuries of Islam there evolved a division of labour between rulers and jurists. According to this division, the rulers and political elites forged traditions of governance that are known as public law (*siyasa shar'iyya*), which enabled them to administer a variety of social and political institutions. Concurrently, Islamic jurists elaborated a body of legal doctrine, known as *fiqh*, which determined mainly civil law and religious ritual. Public law was inferior to *fiqh* in terms of its religious status. Evidence to the effect that public law was of a lower and marginal religious standing is the fact that this area of the law was not based on Qur'an and *hadith* and was not included in the early legal discourses of Islam. In fact, as discussed above, the first comprehensive legal composition about public law was composed in the eleventh century, and subsequent works did not leave a significant mark on legal literature.

In this study, the marginality of public law was examined through the case study of the *mazalim* tribunals. The scarce attention that jurists gave to the *mazalim* tribunals is indicative of the jurists' lack of involvement with administrative institutions. At the same time a close inquiry into the *mazalim* tribunals illustrates the practical significance of these institutions. For example, the *mazalim* tribunals were an important means by which the rulers addressed social issues such as the corruption of senior officials and members of the ruling elite and in so doing strengthened the stability of the society that they ruled. The case of the *mazalim* tribunals also highlights that the rulers' policies were motivated by a value system that differed greatly from that of the jurists: Whereas the jurists were principally concerned about the rights of humans that were sanctified by the Qur'an and *hadith*, the rulers' main concern was to prevent crime.

According to contemporary historians, it was the medieval jurists that determined their own spheres of authority, as well as those of the rulers. This line of reasoning asserts that the jurists determined that they would deal with civil law and religious ritual and that public law would remain outside of the legal discourse. However, I believe that we need to re-examine this narrative and explore the possibility that the rulers had their own motives for encouraging this division of labour and authority. We need to examine the possibility that the interests merged and that both sides benefited from the placement of public law outside the sphere of legal discourse. It is possible that the jurists were interested in this division because it enabled them to maintain their special status regarding the interpretation of holy texts, and in so doing to strengthen their claim for a unique legal and spiritual authority. As for the rulers, they were interested in this division of labour because it exempted them from the constraints that would arise if there evolved a legal discourse that was based on holy texts regarding public law. This approach does not view the division of authority of legislation as a result of tension and conflict between rulers and jurists, but rather as a consequence of interests that are mutually beneficial.

A detailed examination of the *mazalim* tribunals can bring to the fore the advantages that derive from their spiritual inferiority and marginality. The distinctive feature that determined the spiritual inferiority of the *mazalim* tribunals was that they were not based on Qur'an and *hadith*, whereas civil law and religious ritual were based on the holy texts of Islam. We also need to consider the option that the low status of public law, and in this specific case the status of the *mazalim* tribunals, may have served the interests of the rulers because it did not impose upon them the restrictions that derive from the rigid laws of revelation. In other words, the separation of public law from holy scripture created a situation in which the rulers were able to manoeuver outside the confines of holy law. Furthermore, due to the lay nature of patterns of governance and administration, there was no need to document public law, comment upon it or explicate it because it was merely an ephemeral regulation that administered concrete political circumstances. As a result, the rulers' policies were not constrained by any sort of legal literature, sacred or lay.

The absence of any documentation regarding public law in general, and the *mazalim* tribunals in particular, probably served the interests and agendas of both jurists and rulers. It meant that most jurists did not study or write about public law, and that the rulers were not burdened by the restrictions that sacred texts would have imposed upon them. It is worth noting that in order for the jurists to keep away from the field of public law, it was necessary for all sides to agree that public law was not based on revelation. This was an important requirement because it was the only way that the jurists would not have been compelled to intervene and interpret public law. Had public law been construed of revelation, the jurists would have had to express their learned opinions on the matter, since this was their recognized role in Islamic societies. Hence, I argue that it was convenient for both sides to place public law outside the realm of scripture and as a consequence below the spiritual standing of revelation. The decoupling between divinely inspired legal discourse and ad hoc, transitory principles of governance enabled the jurists to maintain their position as the supreme authorities regarding scripture, and for the rulers to shape their governments in accordance to their needs.

CHARLEMAGNE AND THE GOVERNMENT OF THE FRANKISH COUNTRYSIDE

Carine van Rhijn

Introduction

Charlemagne (769–814), king of the Franks crowned Emperor by the pope on Christmas Day of the year 800, was the ruler of a vast empire that covered a substantial part of modern-day Europe. The realm was a patchwork, made up of many regions with very different histories, populations and traditions. In order to govern it, Charlemagne relied on a large number of faithful counts, abbots and bishops who governed in his name over regions in which he sometimes never set foot himself.[1] These men were his advisors, his military leaders and his local ears and eyes, but also the people responsible for the execution of royal decisions within their own regions. In order to communicate his wishes and orders, Charlemagne, like his father Pippin and the Merovingian dynasty before him, used so-called *capitularia* as one of his most important tools of government: written-down lists of prescriptions, outright orders and decisions.[2] These texts have survived in different forms, ranging from very brief lists of keywords

[1] The work of Janet L. Nelson is fundamental on the subject of Carolingian royal government, see for instance her 'Kingship and empire in the Carolingian world', in Rosamond McKitterick ed., *Carolingian culture: emulation and innovation* (Cambridge, 1994), 52–87 and her 'Kingship and royal government', in Rosamond McKitterick ed., *The New Cambridge Medieval History II, ca. 700-ca.900* (Cambridge, 1999), 383–430.

[2] The literature on this subject is vast, see for instance the classic study by Frans-Louis Ganshof, *Wat waren de capitularia?* Verhandelingen van de Koninklijke Vlaamse Akademie voor Wetenschappen, Letteren en Schone Kunsten van België, Klasse der Letteren, verhandeling 22 (Brussels, 1955); Carlo De Clercq, *La législation religieuse franque de Clovis à Charlemagne. Étude sur les actes de conciles et les capitulaires, les statuts diocésains et les règles monastiques (507–814)*, Recueil de travaux publiés par les membres des conférences d'histoire et de philologie de l'Université de Louvain 38, 2 vols (Louvain, 1936); Hubert Mordek, 'Karolingische Kapitularien', in idem ed., *Überlieferung und Geltung normativer Texte des frühen und hohen Mittelalters. Vier Vorträge, gehalten auf dem 35. Deutschen Historikertag 1984 in Berlin*, Quellen und Forschungen zum Recht im Mittelalter 4 (Sigmaringen, 1986), 25–50. For discussion of the historiography and a fuller bibliography see Thomas Martin Buck, *Admonitio und Praedicatio. Zur religiös-pastoralen Dimension von Kapitularien und kapitulariennahen Texten (507–814)*, Freiburger Beiträge zur mittelalterlichen Geschichte 9 (Frankfurt am Main, 1997).

to long and elaborate texts.[3] They were Charlemagne's main instrument for instructing his leading men from a distance and for, via them, governing his kingdom.[4] Not only the capitularies' form, but also their contents are a mixed bag in modern eyes—one single text can contain prescriptions about the abduction of nuns, weights and measures, hospitality and soothsaying, for instance.[5] Not all of these prescriptions were new: the Carolingians were convinced that old law was good law, and hence we find many an instruction in Charlemagne's *capitularia* taken from earlier capitularies, the Bible (God's law) and canon law. Via the capitularies, then, 'old law' was part and parcel of Carolingian government.

The Carolingians inherited a lot of prescriptive texts from their various predecessors, which were copied and re-used enthusiastically in Charlemagne's day. Such 'old law' was also actively collected, witness for instance the *Collectio Dionysio-Hadriana*, a collection of canon law compiled in Rome and sent to Charlemagne by Pope Hadrian at the king's request.[6] This collection supplied the Carolingian court with a wealth of authoritative old law; canons of early church councils cited from the collection, such as those of Nicea (325) and Chalcedon (451), make up the first 59 chapters of the king's famous *Admonitio Generalis* of 789. This capitulary proposed moral reform to the Christian people of the Franks, for which the king deemed knowledge and implementation of these old conciliar canons indispensable.[7] According to Gerhard Ladner, the same

---

[3] The most recent and generally used edition is *Monumenta Germaniae Historia, Capitularia regum Francorum* I, Alfred Boretius, ed., (Hannover, 1883) [= MGH Cap. I hereafter]. The new edition by Mordek et al. had not yet appeared when this article was written.

[4] This view of capitularies as primarily tools for government and communication rather than law is recent, see: Christina Pössel, 'Authors and recipients of Carolingian capitularies, 779–829', in Richard Corradini, Rob Meens, Christina Pössel and Philip Shaw, eds., *Texts & identities in the early middle ages*, Forschungen zur Geschichte des Mittelalters 12 (Vienna 2006), 253–74; Matthew Innes, *Introduction to early medieval western Europe 300–900: the sword, the plough and the book* (London/New York, 2007), 429–36; Rosamond McKitterick, *Charlemagne. The formation of an European identity* (Cambridge, 2008), 233–37. Pioneering and now widely received work on the role of writing in Carolingian government: Rosamond McKitterick, *The Carolingians and the written word* (Cambridge, 1989).

[5] The examples are taken from the famous *Admonitio Generalis* of 789, MGH Cap. I, no. 22, 52–62.

[6] The *Collectio Dionysio-Hadriana*, a chronological collection of canon law and papal decrees, was compiled before 774 at the request of Pope Hadrian I. It was a highly influential collection, witness the large number of surviving manuscripts (90, excluding fragmentary survivals). See Lotte Kéry, *Canonical collections of the early middle ages (ca. 400–1140). A bibliographical guide to the manuscripts and literature* (Washington DC, 1999), 13–20.

[7] *Admonitio Generalis*, Boretius, ed., MGH Cap. I, no. 22, 54–7. In his introduction to the prescriptions, Charlemagne states that he considered them to be 'highly necessary' (*magis necessarius*) and he admonished the recipients of the text (presumably bishops, amongst others) to use them in their sermons and admonishments.

Admonitio also shows the influence of Justinian's *Corpus Iuris Civilis*, both in the wording of its introduction and in its conceptual framework, for instance in the idea that law-givers should 'restore old law' and 'correct' it where necessary.[8] This Roman inheritance is also present in the so-called 'barbarian *leges*', the written-down versions of the laws of different peoples (Bavarians, Burgundians, etc.) discussed elsewhere in this volume,[9] which, in turn, were a source of knowledge about Roman law in the Carolingian period.[10] Furthermore, in his own capitularies, Charlemagne faithfully repeated decisions taken by his father Pippin.[11] The Carolingians, then, did not lack prescriptive texts and ideas about the way a kingdom should be ruled; to what extent they could put these texts and ideas to work, however, is a different matter entirely.

This article discusses some aspects of how such an extensive kingdom could, and could not, be ruled from the royal court via prescriptive texts. It first of all sets out the context of Charlemagne's kingship and the structures of government and power, followed by a brief discussion about the problems and possibilities of written-down instructions in the Carolingian world. Finally, a case will be presented of how, notwithstanding all kinds of obstacles, the Carolingian countryside could indeed be reached by royal government. A series of intermediaries was needed to get to this local level, and the actual reception of ideas expressed in the royal capitularies was probably not very fast—but slow government is government too, and local manuscripts show how the royal court could indeed influence the lives of some local communities of Franks, the majority of whom probably never saw their king in the flesh.

Christian Kingship, Ministerium *and the Delegation of Power*

In contemporary eyes, including his own, Charlemagne ruled by the grace of God as a Christian king over his Christian people of the Franks.[12]

[8] Gerhard Ladner, 'Justinian's theory of law and the renewal ideology of the "Leges barbarorum"', *Proceedings of the American Philosophical Society* 119, no. 3 (1975), 191–200 at 199.

[9] See the chapter by P. Hoppenbrouwers below.

[10] P.G. Stein, 'Roman law', in J.H. Burns ed., *The Cambridge History of Political Thought 2, c. 350–c. 1450* (Cambridge, 1988), 37–47 at 37.

[11] For instance in the Capitulary of Herstal (779), MGH Cap. I, no. 20, 46–51.

[12] This idea of royal responsibility to God goes back to the time of the Emperor Constantine the Great, see P. Wormald, 'Kings and Kingship', in P. Fouracre ed., *New Cambridge Medieval History I, c. 500–c. 700* (Cambridge, 2005), 571–604 at 580; Janet L. Nelson,

This meant great power and great responsibility at the same time, for although God's approval and support would lead to peace and prosperity for the realm and to victory in battle, He demanded rulership and behaviour according to His rules. This was a stern, Old Testament-style God who punished when angered, and Charles was well aware that he was held responsible for the behaviour of his entire people, theoretically down to the last farmer in the smallest hamlet. Governing the Frankish kingdom therefore went beyond its defence, expansion and the keeping of internal peace. The morality of the people, their religious practices and their behaviour according to Christian principles were also daily royal concerns that needed to be steered and directed by his laws. Such 'moral government' could not work without political and military power: a king needed loyal counts and bishops throughout the kingdom who could be entrusted with the realization of royal decisions. Yet, the royal office was made up of both the moral-religious and the political-military, which were fully intertwined in Charlemagne's government: as Mayke de Jong has pointed out, 'church' (*ecclesia*) and 'empire' became increasingly synonymous in the Carolingian period.[13] These different sides to Charlemagne's kingship is what, together, constituted his royal ministry (*ministerium*). A successful king would keep God on his side, ensure justice, peace and prosperity for his people, inspire unity (*concordia*) among his leading men and win wars. All these concerns are reflected in the prescriptions and 'laws' he issued, which, in modern eyes, may therefore look like a strange mix between the religious and the secular, the very general and the unexpectedly detailed.

Learned advisors, mostly theologians, whom he gathered at his court in Aachen, advised Charlemagne on how to deal with these complicated tasks. Good kings listened to good counsel, and therefore there was a small group of learned advisors at the court on a more or less permanent basis, such as the famous Anglo-Saxon scholar Alcuin and the Visigothic theologian Theodulph. These were Charlemagne's day-to-day counselors, but his rule over the kingdom was dependent on a much wider group of people. During assemblies of leading men (secular, clerical or both),

'10. Kingship and empire', in J.H. Burns ed., *The Cambridge History of Medieval Political Thought, c.350–c.1450* (Cambridge, 1988), 211–251, at 214–15.

[13] Mayke de Jong, 'The empire as *ecclesia*: Hrabanus Maurus and bibliocal *historia* for rulers', in Yitzhak Hen and Matthew Innes eds., *The uses of the past in the early middle ages* (Cambridge, 2000), 191–226; eadem, 'Charlemagne's church', in Joanna Story, *Charlemagne. Empire and society* (Manchester, 2005), 103–35 esp. 106–11.

current affairs were discussed and collective decisions were taken on subjects religious and military, moral and political. The gathered ruling elite supported the decisions taken at assemblies (sometimes written down as a capitulary) with their consent,[14] which has led Chris Wickham to call the Carolingian empire 'an immense oligarchy'.[15] The delegation of power and responsibilities by the king to these trusted men was a vital element of Charlemagne's government. They were, after all, the same leading men who took these decisions home with them, where they were expected to implement them on behalf of the king, backed by his royal authority. Ties between these men and the royal court were often close: many young aristocrats had been trained at the court in Aachen, and powerful bishops and abbots too had often started their careers in Charlemagne's entourage.[16] Such men, the elect among the nobility, were favoured by royal patronage, and it was in their best interest to keep this favour by their loyalty to the king.[17] These leading men too were considered to have a *ministerium*, a set of duties towards God, the king and the kingdom, which derived from the royal ministry and ideally counterbalanced their local interests. By being tied to the king in various ways, then, these faithful men were the ideal agents to implement royal decisions within their own territories. The notion of shared responsibility and proximity to royal power meanwhile bound the ruling elite together at supra-regional levels and contributed, at least in Charlemagne's day, to the stability of the realm.[18] The language of the royal capitularies bears out this idea, by underlining the co-operation

---

[14] On assemblies see Timothy Reuter, 'Assembly politics in western Europe from the eighth to the twelfth century', in P. Lineham and Janet L. Nelson, eds., *The medieval world* (London, 2001), 434–450; Stuart Airlie, 'Talking heads: assemblies in early medieval Germany', in P.S. Barnwell and Marco Mostert, eds., *Political assemblies in the earlier middle ages*, Studies in the Early Middle Ages 7 (Turnhout, 2003), 29–46.

[15] Chris Wickham, *The inheritance of Rome. A history of Europe from 400 to 1000* (London, 2009), 389.

[16] Stuart Airlie, 'The court of memory: the Carolingian court as political centre', in Sarah Rees Jones, Richard Marks and A.J. Minnis, eds., *Courts and regions in medieval Europe* (York, 2000), 1–20 at 8.

[17] On the Carolingian dealings with the nobility see: Timothy Reuter ed., *The medieval nobility: studies on the ruling classes of France and Germany from the sixth to the twelfth century*, Europe in the Middle Ages 14 (Amsterdam, 1979); Stuart Airlie, 'Charlemagne and the aristocracy: captains and kings', in Joanna Story ed., *Charlemagne. Empire and society* (Manchester/New York, 2005), 90–102.

[18] After the division of the realm in the days of Charlemagne's grandsons, there were several kings and an emperor, which made things more complicated. See, for instance, Janet L. Nelson, *Charles the Bald* (Harlow, 1992), especially chapter 3: 'The context of politics', 41–74.

between ruler and ruling elite in the best interest of the ruled.[19] As a means of control and as an expression of royal justice, Charlemagne devised a system of control in the shape of royal envoys, the so-called *missi dominici*, chosen from the ranks of the high aristocracy. These *missi*, often a combination of a count and a bishop working together, travelled around in a designated area (their *missaticum*) to check whether royal instructions were being followed as expected. The *missi* also acted as general trouble-shooters and as judges on behalf of the king. They reported back to him and were able to override the judgement of local counts in case of unjust verdicts.[20] Royal capitularies, then, did not disappear into the realm without at least some means to monitor their effects.

The chain of delegated power did not stop at the level of the ruling elite, however, but continued downward and outward. When Charlemagne wrote a letter to Bishop Ghaerbald of Liège in 807, instructing fasts and litanies to avert God's anger which had caused failed harvests and famine, he instructed the bishop to copy and distribute his letter to every baptismal church in his diocese.[21] Once there, the actual execution of the instructions became the responsibility of the local priests. In this example, the priests of the churches in the countryside may be considered as the most local representatives of the Frankish Church and hence of Frankish royal power: they were in the position to pass the emperor's instructions on to the local lay population and make sure that there would be fasts and litanies.[22] As this example shows, royal commands travelled to their destination via chains of delegated power, which connected court and countryside via just a few intermediaries.[23] If everything went as prescribed, royal decisions would, indeed, reach the localities.

---

[19] See the example of the *Admonitio Generalis* below.

[20] Rosamond McKitterick, 'Charlemagne's *missi* and their books', in Stephen Baxter, Catherine E. Karkov, Janet L. Nelson, David Pelteret, eds., *Early medieval studies in memory of Patrick Wormald* (Farnham, 2009), 253–67 at 258–60.

[21] 'Karoli ad Ghaerbaldum epistola (807)', MGH Cap. I, 245–246. On the special relationship between the Franks and God see M. Garrison, 'The Franks as the New Israel? Education for an identity from Pippin to Charlemagne', in Y. Hen and M. Innes, eds., *The Uses of the Past in the Early Middle Ages* (Cambridge 2000), 114–61; Nelson, 'Kingship and empire', 214–15.

[22] See Carine van Rhijn, *Shepherds of the Lord. Priests and episcopal statutes in the Carolingian period* (Turnhout, 2007), chapter 2, 49–100.

[23] See Airlie, 'The court of memory'; Janet L. Nelson, 'Aachen as a place of power', in Mayke de Jong, Frans Theuws with Carine van Rhijn, eds., *Topographies of power in the early middle ages*, The Transformation of the Roman World vol. 6 (Leiden/Boston/Cologne, 2001), 217–42.

Capitularies and the Problem of Local Government

What may have happened with these decisions once they had reached their destination is, however, a different matter. Were they obeyed as a matter of course? Were they respectfully put in a cupboard and ignored? Although the Carolingians inherited a lot of legal and prescriptive material useful for their government of the Frankish kingdom, their laws could not be applied in the same way as had been common in, for instance, the Late Roman Empire. What Charlemagne did not inherit was a quick and straightforward way of enforcing his decisions, in the shape of, for instance, a state army or a well-oiled bureaucratic apparatus. To historians of the nineteenth and part of the twentieth century, this limitation to Charlemagne's government was problematic, for what is a royal decree, even when it has been discussed at an assembly and promulgated in writing, if it cannot be imposed? Or, put differently: how effective could Charlemagne's rule have been if he could not even impose his laws?[24] The discovery that there is virtually no evidence of the actual application of these prescriptions did not make things better in the eyes of the pessimists. As it turned out, the world of the early Middle Ages was one in which written laws or prescriptions were used as guidelines rather than as cast-iron rules that could (and should) be understood in one way only.[25] Conflicts were often settled out of court[26] so, all in all, collections of prescriptive texts were used in rather different ways than we use our modern-day laws.[27] As a result, especially the scholars linked to the influential German *Rechtsschule* were led to doubt the authority and effectiveness of the Carolingian capitularies. Were these prescriptions at all realistic, did they have any discernable effect, or did they merely reflect the ruler's ideology without any significant connection to what happened in the kingdom? Real law, so these scholars thought, goes together with

[24] See, for instance, R. van Caenegem, '9. Government, law and society', in J.H. Burns ed., *The Cambridge History of Medieval Political Thought, c.350–c.1450* (Cambridge 1988), 174–210 and the literature cited there. I cannot do justice to this long and complicated discussion here.

[25] Rio, 'Charters, law codes and *formulae*', 26; McKitterick, 'Perceptions of justice', 1093–99.

[26] The role of dispute settlement in early medieval Europe was first explored in the seminal work by Wendy Davies and Paul Fouracre, eds., *The settlement of disputes in early medieval Europe* (Cambridge 1986).

[27] Alice Rio, 'Charters, law codes and formulae: the Franks between theory and practice', in Paul Fouracre and David Ganz, eds., *Frankland. The Franks and the world of the early middle ages. Essays in honour of Dame Jinty Nelson* (Manchester, 2008), 7–27 at 21.

a real state in which real authority could be wielded—and none of these elements were sufficiently present under Charlemagne's rule to impress these researchers.[28]

A more optimistic point of view has nevertheless been gaining influence over the past decades. Hubert Mordek's monumental study of the manuscripts containing royal capitularia has shown that these texts were copied and distributed all over the realm.[29] Even though the existence of manuscripts does not automatically mean that every single prescription was actually passed on from there and eventually obeyed, it does show that these texts were at least available at the level of bishoprics, monasteries and counties. Moreover, scholars have come to realise that modern definitions of complex concepts such as 'state' and 'law' cannot be projected back onto the Carolingian period in any meaningful way, if only for the simple reason that the infrastructure within which our laws function, was not there.[30] As a result, the study of early medieval prescriptive texts such as the capitularies has changed direction. Attention has moved away from attempts to fit capitularies into the straightjacket of post-Napoleonic codified law, making room for questions that try to take the texts, their specific terminology and the (political) context in which they had a place as starting-points. How, for instance, was justice understood in the early Middle Ages, and what was the role of *consensus* in maintaining it?[31] How did kingship and royal government work? What role did capitularies and related texts play in royal government?[32] The effectiveness of Charlemagne's rule is now generally regarded more positively than it was

---

28 Good examples of this approach are R. van Caenegem, '9. Government, law and society', 174–210; Reinhard Schneider, 'Zur rechtlichen Bedeutung der Kapitularientexte', *Deutsches Archiv* 23 (1967), 273–94; Hermann Nehlsen, 'Zur Aktualität und Effektivität germanischer Rechtsaufzeichnungen', in Peter Classen ed., *Recht und Schrift im Mittelalter* (Sigmaringen, 1977), 449–502.

29 Hubert Mordek, *Bibliotheca capitularium regum Francorum manuscripta. Überlieferung und Traditionszusammenhang der fränkischen Herrschererlasse*, MGH Hilfsmittel 15 (Munich, 1995). There are hundreds of extant manuscripts containing one or more Frankish capitularies.

30 Matthew Innes, *State and society in the early middle ages. The Middle Rhine Valley 400–1000*, Cambridge Studies in Medieval Life and Thought, fourth series, vol. 47 (Cambridge, 2000), 4–12

31 Rosamond McKitterick, 'Perceptions of justice in western Europe in the ninth and tenth centuries', *Settimane di studio del centro Italiano di Studi sull'alto medioevo* XLIV (Spoleto, 1997), 1075–1102; Janet L. Nelson, 'Kings with justice, kings without justice: an early medieval paradox', *Settimane* XLIV, 797–822; Régine Le Jan, 'Justice royale et pratiques sociales dans le royaume franc au IXe siècle', *Settimane* XLIV, 47–85.

32 Pössel, 'Authors and recipients'; Buck, *Admonitio et praedicatio.*

fifty years ago, but not because he could 'enforce his laws' or live up to other ideals of the modern state. What Charlemagne did accomplish was to generate and keep active co-operation and support for his government from the high aristocracy, ecclesiastical and lay, *without* modern means to impose his will.

Yet, the question to what extent his rule reached the rural areas of the kingdom has thus far not received an equally positive re-evaluation. The countryside is often regarded as a world apart, connected to that of the king and his court in very rare cases only.[33] The effects of royal government, so it is generally thought, were very limited.[34] Local charters, the primary sources studied most often in this context, show the workings of small, closely knit societies, and usually record the interactions between small land-owners who operated within a limited area. Only on rare occasions (such as complicated disputes) do we catch glimpses of the higher social strata at a local level, such as the abbot of a local monastery or a bishop. Influence on these local charters of the kind of royal government laid out in the capitularies seems to be virtually non-existent. On this basis, then, the conclusion that Charlemagne's rule hardly reached the localities due to lack of local influence and coercive power seems justified.[35]

There are, however, other ways of approaching the local levels of the Carolingian world, using sources and manuscripts other than the charter-collections, interesting and important as these may be.[36] The material

---

[33] Two 'pioneers' studying early medieval local societies are Wendy Davies, *Small worlds. The village community in early medieval Brittany* (London, 1988) and Chris Wickham, *Early medieval Italy. Central power and local society, 400–1000* (Ann Arbor, 1981). More recently: Chris Wickham, 'Rural society in early medieval Europe', in McKitterick ed., *The New Cambridge Medieval History* II, 510–37; Warren Brown, *Unjust seizure. Conflict, interest and authority in an early medieval society* (Ithaca NY, 2001); Catherine Bullimore, 'Folcwin of Rankweil: the world of a Carolingian local official', *Early Medieval Europe* 13, no. 1 (2005), 43–77; Bernhard Zeller, 'Karolingisches Imperium und regionales Urkundenwesen am Beispiel St. Gallens', in Christoph Haidacher and Richard Schober, eds., *Bericht über den 24. Österreicher Historikertag in Innsbruck*, Veröffentlichungen des Verbandes Österreichischer Historiker und Geschichtsvereine 13 (Innsbruck, 2006), 65–72.

[34] See for instance Matthew Innes, 'Charlemagne's government', in Joanna Story ed., *Charlemagne. Empire and society* (Manchester/New York, 2005), 71–89 at 73.

[35] See D.E. Luscombe, '8. Introduction: the formation of political thought in the West', in J.H. Burns ed., *The Cambridge History of Medieval Political Thought, c.350–c.1450* (Cambridge, 1988), 157–73 at 164; Innes, 'Charlemagne's government', 78; Chris Wickham, *The inheritance of Rome. A history of Europe from 400 to 1000* (London, 2009), 415.

[36] For instance, Carl Hammer Jr., 'Country churches, clerical inventories and the Carolingian renaissance in Bavaria', *Church History* 49 (1980), 5–19.

that concerns me here consists of texts written for and gathered by local priests, who lived and worked within the local communities. They were in the ideal position to carry out instructions issued by the royal court relating to the lives and *mores* of the Frankish local laity. With diocesan bishops as intermediaries, local priests were made into the local exponents of some aspects of royal government in Charlemagne's time.[37] The tasks delegated to priests described in these texts concern first and foremost their co-operation with Charlemagne's 'moral government' and his ambitions to shape the Frankish kingdom into a society of ideal Frankish Christians. This was the main purpose of a much wider phenomenon generally called 'the Carolingian Renaissance', or, preferably, 'the Carolingian reforms'.[38] The project was devised by Charlemagne and the intellectuals at his court and first outlined in the famous capitulary called 'the General Admonition' (*Admonitio Generalis*) of 789, to which I will return shortly. This reform-programme targeted the entire population. The question whether it, in fact, achieved this purpose is directly relevant in determining the extent to which Charlemagne's plans, set out in prescriptive texts, managed to reach their ultimate destinations. Although 'the people' themselves, let alone their reactions to Charlemagne's reforms, are invisible in the historical record, we can get rather close to the local communities via their priests. This approach yields results different from those gathered via the charters and leads to more positive conclusions. It is therefore worth following the reform-programme step by step from court to countryside in some detail.

Let us, therefore, start at the royal court and look at perhaps the most important programmatic capitulary Charlemagne ever issued, the *Admonitio Generalis*.[39] It is generally accepted that this text initiated the Carolingian reforms, which aimed at the moral improvement of the entire kingdom and all its inhabitants. The text is very wide in its scope, too wide

---

[37] Van Rhijn, *Shepherds*, 64–8.

[38] There is over a century of scholarship about the Carolingian reforms, also known as the 'Carolingian Renaissance'. Important work includes R. McKitterick, *The Frankish Church and the Carolingian Reforms*, 789–895 (London 1977); G. Brown, 'Introduction: the Carolingian Renaissance', in R. McKitterick ed., *Carolingian Culture: Emulation and Innovation* (Cambridge, 1994), 1–52 with bibliography; J. Barrow, 'Ideas and Applications of Reform', in T.F.X. Noble and J.M.H. Smith, eds., *The Cambridge History of Christianity* III (Cambridge, 2008), 345–66.

[39] The term 'programmatic' is borrowed from Rosamond McKitterick, who uses it to describe capitularies that 'set out royal policy' as distinguished from 'regional' and 'administrative' capitularies. See her *Charlemagne. The formation of a European identity* (Cambridge, 2008), 234–38.

to do it full justice here. Three points will therefore be addressed: first of all, the authority on which it built. Secondly: how was the programme envisaged to reach the countryside, or, in other words, how did the system of delegated authority work in this case? Finally, it is important to see what the plans to reform 'the whole people' entailed exactly, so that we can follow these ideas later through other texts.

The Workings of a Carolingian Programmatic Capitulary: The Admonitio Generalis

The *Admonitio Generalis* was issued on March 23, 789 and is perhaps the most famous of Charlemagne's capitularies.[40] It consists of a lengthy introduction in which the king addressed his secular and especially his ecclesiastical office-holders, followed by 82 chapters: the first 59 of these were taken from a compilation of canon law, the *Collectio Dionysio-Hadriana* given to Charlemagne by Pope Hadrian; the remaining 23 chapters were new. This was an influential and widely-read text, which was copied all over the Frankish realm, and cited or excerpted in many later capitularies and collections.[41] The work of Thomas Martin Buck is important here, for he has found a way of interpreting the text that provides an excellent alternative to reading it as 'law'. If we do not try to read the text as royal commands but instead as pastoral admonitions, so Buck maintains, we get a better understanding of what Charlemagne was trying to do by phrasing his programme in this specific way.[42] Although he admonished all social segments of his kingdom instead of giving them outright commands, he did so on the basis of cleverly constructed authority.

In his introductory statement, Charles greets all ecclesiastical orders and his secular leading men as 'I Charles, king and leader of the realm of the Franks by the grace and mercifulness of God and devote defender and humble helper of the Holy Church'.[43] The text is issued by the king himself, and therefore bears his royal authority. It is not he, however, who holds the highest power, but God, who has granted him his kingship.

---

40 McKitterick, *The Frankish church*, 1; Brown, 'Introduction', 17.

41 Mordek lists over 40 extant manuscripts with a full or partial text: *Bibliotheca capitularium*, 1082.

42 Buck, *Admonitio et praedicatio*, 67–156.

43 'Admonitio Generalis', introductory statement, 53: '*Ego Karolus, gratia Dei eiusque misericordia donante rex et rector regni Francorum et devotus sanctae aeclesiae defensor humilisque adiutor*'.

Hoping that God will continue His support to his reign, Charles wishes to mobilise especially the bishops to help him lead the Franks, whom he calls *populus Dei* ('God's people'), to eternal life. In order to make the bishops' task easier, he has had 'some *capitula*' written down, and sent *missi* who can help them 'to correct what should be corrected' in his name.[44] The inspiration for his initiative, Charlemagne explains, comes directly from the Old Testament: 'For we read in the Book of Kings how the holy Josiah tried to lead his God-given realm back to the cult of the true God by travelling around, correcting and admonishing.'[45] According to Buck, this is the reason why the text admonishes rather than commands: it is a direct imitation of the famous Old Testament king Josiah, who, like Charlemagne, led God's Chosen People.[46] Both kings were concerned that their predecessors had been lax in following God's law and called for reform by correction;[47] both kings fought superstition and idolatry.[48] According to the Book of Kings, 'There was no king before him like unto him, that returned to the Lord with all his heart, and with all his soul, and with all his strength, according to all the law of Moses: neither after him did there arise any like unto him.'[49] King Josiah was a powerful role-model, and the bishops would certainly understand its allusions.[50]

The *Admonitio Generalis*, then, was not a piece of fatherly advice that anybody could afford to ignore. Not only was it issued in the name of the divinely ordained king in the best interest of God's people, it also explained that God's favour to the realm and all its inhabitants depended on the good behaviour of the selfsame people. The question whether or not the realm would flourish until the end of time, therefore, depended on the co-operation of all Christian Franks. Whereas the text was issued by the king and therefore bore royal authority, it makes clear how the king could rule only if God willed it, which lent the text divine support. The evocation of the Old Testament king Josiah, who was unsurpassed when it came to following the laws of God and tirelessly worked to correct

[44] Idem: '*Quapropter et nostros ad vos direximus missos, qui ex nostri nominis auctoritate una vobiscum corrigerent quae corrigenda essent.*'

[45] Idem: '*Nam legimus in regnorum libris, quomodo sanctus Iosias regnum sibi a Deo datum circumeundo, corrigendo, ammonendo ad cultum veri Dei studuit revocare* [...]'

[46] Buck, *Admonitio et praedicatio*, 83.

[47] Compare 2 Kings 22, 13. On ideas of reform see: Gerhard Ladner, *The idea of reform: its impact on Christian thought and action in the age of the Fathers* (Cambridge, 1959).

[48] 2 Kings 23, 24 and *Admonitio Generalis*, c. 18.

[49] 2 Kings 24, 25.

[50] See Isabelle Rosé, 'Le roi Josias dans l'ecclésiologie politique du haut Moyen Âge', *Mélanges de l'École française de Rome. Moyen Age* 115, no. 2 (2004), 683–709.

the errors of his people, strengthens this point. Such layering of authority continues in the *capitula* themselves: the first part of the text contains material from the councils of the early church and papal decretals from the same period. These *canones* dated back from the time that the church was still pure and uncorrupted; the *canones* cited were the work of the Holy Fathers. Disobedience to what the Fathers decreed, so the *Admonitio* reminds its audience, would lead to *anathema* (excommunication).[51]

The second part, that consists of new material added by Charlemagne himself, works differently and draws directly on the Law of God: it brims with biblical quotations that support the king's prescriptions. This second section is addressed to the bishops only, and asks them to admonish everybody to obey the instructions that follow. The requirement that those with the power to judge, judge justly (c. 63), for instance, cites three biblical quotations that state the same thing.[52] The prohibition of 'theft, wrong marriages and false testimony' (c. 68) is supported by the simple statement that 'God's law forbids it'.[53] Although the *Admonitio* does not 'command' but admonishes, it draws on a series of powerful sources of authority, which leaves no doubt as to its intention: this is a text that had to be taken seriously and observed by all. In this sense, the text may be considered as 'law' in a broad sense of the word: the *Admonitio* contains prescriptions, and both heavenly and earthly consequences are implied for those who disobeyed. Yet, these are not instructions of the kind that can be applied just like that. The text seems to envisage an ideal society of the future that would take some time to create, and it tries to convince the whole people that it was important to emend their lives and habits.

Now how did Charlemagne envisage this programme of reform reaching the countryside? The *Admonitio* provides a good example of the system of delegated responsibility described above, and in the next section of this article it will become clear that this was a system that might have actually worked. Only three steps separated the king from his whole people, and by writing down the *Admonitio* and having copies sent to his bishops, Charlemagne himself took the first step. Although he admonished his bishops to lead the Franks to eternal life by their good example

---

51 *Admonitio Generalis*, c. 60: *'Scit namque prudentia vestra, quam terribili anathematis censura feriuntur qui praesumptiose contra statuta universalium conciliorum venire audeant.'*

52 Zach 8, 16; Deut 16, 19 and Deut 16, 18.

53 *Admonitio Generalis*, c. 68: *'Item et furta et iniusta conubia necnon et falsa testimonia, sicut saepe rogavimus, prohibete diligenter, sicut et lex Domini prohibet.'*

and tireless pastoral advice, the *Admonitio* also shows that Charlemagne did not expect them to do all of that by themselves. The second section, which is addressed to the bishops only, opens with the prescription 'that the christian belief should be diligently read and preached to the whole people by the bishops and the priests'.[54] The bishops, as the heads of their dioceses, were also expected to supervise the local clergy, who should be well-educated.[55] The *Admonitio* stresses that bishops should make sure that their priests themselves understood what they were supposed to explain to the local laity and had the know-how to deliver decent pastoral care (c. 70). The priests, in turn, had to behave honourably and thereby set the right example for the laymen in their care (c. 72). The last and longest chapter of the *Admonitio* is entirely devoted to what priests should preach to the laity (c. 82). Here we see the third and final step in the chain that connected court to countryside: the king instructed bishops, bishops instructed the priests of their diocese, and the priests, finally, instructed the local lay communities.

Finally, given the importance of the Franks' living lives pleasing to their stern God, what would such a good lay life look like? The first section of the *Admonitio* is mostly devoted to the clergy and does not tell us much about this subject. It repeats a few canonical prescriptions 'to all' (*omnibus*), forbidding amongst other things usury (c. 5), avarice (c. 33), and re-marriage as long as the first spouse was alive (c. 43). Charlemagne's own additions in the second part are more revealing, although they, too, are very general. Chapter 62, for instances, prescribes peace and concord amongst the whole Christian people, 'be they great or humble persons', for peaceful people are the sons of God, while those who sow discord are the sons of the devil.[56] All should also be admonished not to commit perjury (c. 64), refrain from superstitious behaviour (such as saying prayers to stones and springs, c. 65), not to steal (c. 68) and to avoid working on Sundays (c. 81). Sermons were an important way of educating the laity, teaching them why, for instance, it is wrong to hate and dangerous to desire (c. 66).[57]

---

[54] *Admonitio Generalis*, c. 61: '. . . *ut fides catholica ab episcopis et presbyteris diligenter legatur et omni populo praedicetur* . . .'

[55] Brown, 'Introduction', 19–20.

[56] *Admonitio Generalis*, c. 62: '*Omnibus. Ut pax sit et concordia et unianimitas cum omni populo christiano inter* . . . *omnes ubique seu maiores seu minores personas* . . . *quia filii diaboli semper dissensiones et discordias movere satagunt: filii autem Dei semper paci et dilectioni student.*'

[57] Thomas L. Amos, 'Preaching and the sermon in the Carolingian world', in idem, Eugene A. Green and Beverly Mayne Kienzle, eds., *"De ore Domini" Preacher and Word in the middle ages*, Studies in Medieval Culture 27 (Kalamazoo, 1987), 165–80.

By means of sermons, the laity should also learn the main principles of their religion, such as the Trinity, the Resurrection, and the Last Judgement. The lay population should also be taught, so Charlemagne emphasizes, what crimes would bar them from entrance into the Kingdom of Heaven and condemn them to suffer for all eternity at the hands of the devil. Good books with correct information were essential here, for 'false writings and dubious tales' would cause error and deviation from the right path. This is an important theme that will return below: only 'canonical books and catholic tracts and sayings of the holy authors' should be read and passed on (c. 78).[58] Charlemagne's reform, then, was a matter of *correctio* (correction) and *emendatio* (improvement): it was not just Christianity, but the right kind of Christianity that mattered, the criteria for which could be found in the writings of the Fathers, the decrees of the early councils and in the Law of God, the bible.[59]

It will be evident that the prescriptions for the local laity do not exactly add up to a comprehensive and easily applicable programme. This was not due to the vagueness of Charlemagne's ideas, however: it should not be forgotten that most of the *Admonitio* is addressed to the bishops, and that the king makes it abundantly clear that the training and supervision of the priests was their task, for which they could get help from the *missi*. For the bishops, the responsibilities delegated to them meant that they had to find their own ways to put the reforms into practice within their own dioceses, with only some broad outlines as their starting-points. This is why, I think, bishops started to write texts for their priests in the years around 800.[60]

Between Court and Countryside

From the turn of the ninth century onwards, bishops began to 'rework' the decisions from royal capitularies such as the *Admonitio Generalis* into more specific regulations that were fit for local use. These so-called 'episcopal statutes' were sent or read to the local priests.[61] Like the royal

---

58 *Admonitio Generalis* c. 78: '*Omnibus. Item et pseudografia et dubiae narrationes, vel quae omnino contra fidem catholicam sunt... nec credantur nec legantur sed conburentur, ne in errorem per talia scripta populus mittatur. Sed soli canonici libri et catholici tractatus et sanctorum auctorum dicta legantur et tradantur.*'

59 Brown, 'Introduction', 17–9.

60 Van Rhijn, *Shepherds of the Lord*, 33–48.

61 There are about sixty extant episcopal statutes, edited in three volumes of *MGH Capitula episcoporum*. This material was first described and characterised by Peter Brommer,

capitularies, they usually consist of a list of chapters with or without a preface, and just like the king, the bishops built on canon law and the Bible to support their prescriptions. Like the *Admonitio Generalis*, many statutes do not order but instead admonish. Let us now look at one of these texts to see what a single bishop did with the general ideas of the royal reform-programme to make them fit for the use of local priests.

The statute written by Bishop Haito of Basle will serve as an example here. He was one of Charlemagne's most trusted men,[62] who was appointed to the see of Basle just after 800. Some years later, presumably between 806 and 813, he composed a statute for the priests of his diocese.[63] Although he never cites directly from the *Admonitio Generalis*, it is clear that he drew inspiration from it and tried to work with the programme for priests and laymen outlined there. His statute has three main themes, each of which Haito subdivided into a number of detailed prescriptions for his priests. His first and most extensive theme concerns their knowledge and ability to administer pastoral care and teach, as sketched in the *Admonitio* (c. 70). In a series of chapters, he prescribed knowledge of the sacraments of baptism and confirmation, and understanding of the Transubstantiation (c. 5). In order to deliver decent liturgy and sacraments, priests should also know a whole series of books, such as the sacramentary, lectionary, antiphonary, a penitential 'and homilies appropriate for every Sun- and feastday of the year' (c. 6).[64] They should know the right times to baptise and be properly equipped with a baptismal font to perform the rite (c. 7). The bishop went to considerable lengths to explain in fine detail what he wanted his priests to do, listing, for instance, every single feast day they ought to celebrate (c. 8). Above all, they should be able to teach the laity to adhere to the right kind of Christendom (c. 1). One important tool for such education in the basics of the Christian religion was teaching

---

'*Capitula episcoporum*. Bemerkungen zu den bischöflichen Kapitularien', *Zeitschrift für Kirchengeschichte* 91 (1980), 207–36; idem, *'Capitula episcoporum'. Die bischöflichen Kapitularien des 9. und 10. Jahrhunderts*, Typologie des Sources du Moyen Âge Occidental 43 (Turnhout, 1985).

[62] Haito undertook a diplomatic mission for Charlemagne to Byzantium, and was also a witness to the emperor's will.

[63] Haito of Basle, 'Episcopal statute', *MGH Capitula episcoporum* I, Peter Brommer, ed., (Hannover, 1984), 210–19.

[64] The list of books is long, and fits in well with Charlemagne's general conviction that education by means of 'correct' books was essential. Haito of Basle, 'Episcopal statute', c. 6: '*Sexto, quae ipsis sacerdotibus necessaria sunt ad discendum, id est sacramentarium, lectionarius, antiphonarius, baptisterium, compotus, kanon paenitentialis, psalterium, homeliae per circulum anni dominicis diebus et singulis festivitatibus aptae.* [...]'

the people the Lord's Prayer and the Creed, both in Latin and in the local language, and explaining to them what the prayers meant and how they should be understood (c. 2).[65] The need for priests to lead exemplary lives, Haito's second theme, is similarly explained in a series of chapters on the basis of just a brief admonishment in the *Admonitio*. Haito's main point here is that a priestly life-style ought to be fundamentally different from that of the laity: priests should not not live with women (c. 9), refrain from frequenting taverns (c. 10), and keep away from hunting-parties (c. 11), to mention a few forbidden pleasures only.[66] The third theme of his statute is what priests should teach the laity by their word and/or example, for instance how they should prevent incestuous marriages (i.e. marriages within the fifth degree of consanguinity, including spiritual relatives),[67] about good works (c. 22) and the duties of godparents (c. 25).

This boiled-down description of Haito's statute shows how this bishop envisaged the application of the reform-programme in practice. He took the lead of the programmatic *capitulare* issued by the king and filled in the details himself. Other bishops wrote similar texts for their own dioceses, but details and emphases are different in every text. In this way, Charlemagne's capitulary—or at least, those parts of the *Admonitio* deemed relevant by the bishops for the localities in their dioceses—travelled to the churches of his realm.

From this point onwards, research becomes more difficult, for as far as we know, priests themselves have left few traces in the historical records. They are relatively rare in charters, but even more so as the owners of manuscripts. Yet, such manuscripts do exist, albeit in moderate numbers. A book can be recognised as a 'priest's manuscript' based on its content. Apart from bishops, only priests were allowed to dispense the sacraments and say Mass, and priests were, as we have seen, those responsible for local pastoral care. A manuscript containing texts about these subjects and not going into specific episcopal duties (such as confirmation and

65 Haito of Basle, 'Episcopal statute', c. 2: '*Secundo iubendum, ut oratio dominica, in qua omnia necessaria humanae vitae comprehenduntur, et symbolum apostolorum, in quo fides catholica ex integro comprehenditur, ab omnibus discatur tam latine quam barbarice, ut, quod ore profitentur, corde credatur et intellegatur.*'

66 About the conflict of loyalties this could cause for priests see Carine van Rhijn, 'Priests and the Carolingian reforms: the bottlenecks of local *correctio*', in Richard Corradini, Rob Meens, Christina Pössel and Philip Shaw, eds., *Texts and identities in the early middle ages*, Forschungen zur Geschichte des Mittelalters 12 (Vienna, 2006), 219–37.

67 See Mayke de Jong, 'An unresolved riddle: early medieval incest legislation.', in Ian N. Wood, *Franks and Alemanni in the Merovingian period. An ethnographic perspective*, Studies in Historical Archaeoethnology 3 (Woodbridge, 1998), 107–40.

visitation) would therefore qualify as a priest's manuscript. The manuscript we shall now briefly discuss to take the final step from court to countryside contains such texts and bears clear traces of Charlemagne's reform-programme. Although the local laity has not left us its own written records, and we will therefore never know if they, in turn, were much influenced by the owner of this manuscript, its very existence shows that Charlemagne's government did, indeed, reach the local levels of his realm.

Manuscript Laon, Bibliothèque Municipale 288 dates from the first third of the ninth century and was probably compiled in eastern France. It is a modest manuscript, made up of 91 rather small *folia* and written in an irregular hand.[68] It contains 23 different texts, organised in two sections. The first 37 *folia* contain a series of commentaries and so-called *expositiones*, explanations of, amongst others, the Lord's Prayer, the Creed, prayers from the baptismal ritual and Mass. The second part is filled with eleven homilies attributed (albeit often falsely) mainly to Augustine, but also to Jerome and Isidore—only two are anonymous. It is, then, a manuscript eminently practical for a local priest in two different ways. To begin with, it contains a number of ready-made homilies by the most eminent Fathers of the Church, as well as texts helpful for explaining the meaning of fundamental elements of Christianity to the laity. Secondly, it also kept the priest's own knowledge fresh: the explanation of baptismal prayers and the Mass-exposition might have been included primarily as brief works of reference about complex subjects that had to be handled with care. These latter texts also contain information that the priest might want to share with his lay flock, such as the explanation for why he baptised laymen in the first place.

There are a few clear parallels between the contents of this manuscript and Charlemagne's reform-programme, especially when we assume that they were passed down to this priest in a more detailed version by his bishop as an episcopal statute. The entire manuscript was meant for teaching and preaching, exactly what Charlemagne wanted the priests to do. In itself, this was not a new idea, but the way in which it was filled in by the Carolingian reformers, was. The difference lies in the details: as we have seen, Charlemagne wanted everybody to use texts of undisputed

[68] According to its brief description in *Catalogue général des manuscrits des bibliothèques publiques des départements* I (Paris, 1849/1968), 171 it has 'l'écriture et l'ortographie barbares'. In her more extensive description, Keefe notes that there are some *folia* missing in its last quire: *Water and the word* II, 29 n. 19.

authority (*Admonitio Generalis*, c. 78), such as those written by the Fathers of the Church—whom we encounter as authors of the homilies in the manuscript. He also wanted priests to teach the laity the essentials of the Christian religion. Many bishops, not only Haito, emphasized the importance of the Creed and the Lord's Prayer in this context, expositions of which were included as well.[69] Teaching the laity about living good Christian lives, another task the priests were set, was often done by means of homilies—we have seen how Haito prescribes knowledge of these. The owner of the manuscript was also well-equipped for this duty: the homilies were not only written by authorities, but also addressed subjects such as the importance of charity, good and bad Christians, Judgement Day and Paradise.[70]

The influence of the ideals of reform is also present in less obvious ways. For a priest to understand and use this manuscript, for instance, he already had to have a certain level of knowledge, which meant that he had been schooled.[71] Explanation of the prayers of baptism, moreover, assumes that he owned the text of the entire ritual (the '*baptisterium*' on Haito's list) or knew it by heart. Likewise, explanations of Mass supposed ownership of a *missale* and intimate knowledge of its contents. This was not a half-literate country-priest who hardly knew what he was doing—there is hardly anything in this manuscript that cannot be ascribed to the influence of Charlemagne's *Admonitio* and a bishop's elaboration of its main points. Only one aspect is out of tune with Charlemagne's ideals: its Latin is far from impeccable.[72] Interestingly, however, not a single bishop mentions the importance of correct Latin in his episcopal statute, although it was emphasized for monks, nuns and canons[73]—could it be that the bishops considered it overly ambitious to demand that local priests master the fine points of the language?

---

[69] See Haito, 'Episcopal statute', c. 2 with n. 2.

[70] Keefe, *Water and the word* II, 27–9.

[71] Charlemagne explained the importance of schooling and learning most eloquently in his 'Epistola de litteris colendis' (780–800) to Abbot Baugulf of Fulda, MGH Cap. I, no. 29, 78–9.

[72] Keefe, who edited the explanation of the prayers of baptism [her Text 31, *Water and the word* II, 429–37] remarks at 429 that '[t]he poor orthography … make (*sic*) it difficult always to determine what is meant.'

[73] 'Epistola de litteris colendis', 78–9.

Conclusion

Although Carolingian capitularies are and remain one of the richest and most complicated sources of early medieval history, I hope to have demonstrated that there is reason to be somewhat more optimistic as to the possibility of their local effects than has generally been thought. In the case of Charlemagne's reform-efforts, outlined in his *Admonitio Generalis* of 789, there can be no doubt that his decisions did reach the Frankish countryside—probably not everywhere, certainly not everywhere in the same way, but the influence of this programmatic capitulary did certainly not stop at episcopal courts. Although priest's manuscripts that show the effects of these royal admonitions are rare, they give us an important perspective on Charlemagne's rule. As the example of Laon, Bibliothèque Municipale ms 288 has shown, there were local priests who owned manuscripts that would help them dispense pastoral care 'à la Carolingienne'.

The way in which Charlemagne's decisions reached 'the people' was indirect and slow, but at the end of the day they arrived and influenced the way in which local priests set about their tasks. This was to a large extent due to the efforts of bishops, who not only advised Charlemagne but also set to work to select and rephrase his directions in such a way that they themselves could pass them on. It took time and effort, but eventually the message arrived. In this case, the local priests stood at the far end of a chain of delegated responsibility that connected them to the court. Even though the royal instructions came via their diocesan bishops, the priests were in a certain sense agents of royal government in the field, albeit in a very modest way. It was only by means of all these local shepherds of lay souls that the king could steer his Frankish flock to eternal life, and it was only via delegated authority and responsibilities that he could govern his whole people.

THE LAW FACTOR IN OTTOMAN-CRIMEAN TATAR RELATIONS IN THE EARLY MODERN PERIOD

Natalia Królikowska

The end of the twentieth century was marked by renewed interest in empires and their political organization. Many a researcher has made an attempt to understand how the successful empires integrated and ruled over multicultural societies and controlled their vassal and buffer states. This paper endeavours to shed light on the law factor in centre-periphery relations using the example of the Ottoman influences on the Crimean Khanate's law in the sixteenth-eighteenth centuries.

In order to make some sense of the issue, my central argument must be preceded by some general characterization of Crimean-Ottoman relations in the Early Modern Period. It will be followed by a description of law enforcement in the Crimean Khanate. The elements in Crimean law, which differed from the *shariʿa* with respect to state and private law, attract our special attention. The central question is: how did the Crimean judiciary supplement or modify the *shariʿa*? Did they invoke old Mongol customs or did they apply Ottoman solutions? What role did the law play in the process of integrating the Khanate into the Ottoman world? Did Ottoman legal influences result in strengthening Ottoman political control over the Khanate?

An Overview of Crimean-Ottoman Relations

One of the major problems in the history of Crimean-Ottoman relations concerns timing, and the ways and extent to which the Crimean Khanate was dependent upon the Sublime Porte. Their mutual relations date back to the middle of the fifteenth century. In this period, the Crimean Khanate, the newly founded state claiming to be the heir of the Golden Horde, and the Ottomans, who in 1453 had conquered Constantinople, the capital of the Byzantine Empire, clashed over the control of the Genoese colonies in the Black Sea region. The Ottomans, who were far stronger than the Tatars, succeeded in conquering the Genoese cities situated on the Crimean peninsula in 1475. Only three years later the Khanate entered under the protection of the Sublime Porte. It used to be thought that the

Ottoman suzerainty over the Tatars was stipulated in a treaty concluded between Khan Mengli I Giray and Sultan Mehmed II in 1478.[1] However, the existence of this treaty was questioned by Halil Inalcık in the 1940s[2] and effectively discarded by later scholars. Alan Fisher, who points out that the degree of the Khanate's dependency on the Ottomans evolved between the late fifteenth century and the end of the eighteenth century, questions the view that the Tatars had been servile vassals of the Ottoman Empire during the entire period, arguing that they conducted a separate foreign policy, which could differ from that of the Ottomans.[3]

One illustration of this more independent policy is that in 1569, the Tatars ruled by Khan Devlet I Giray succeeded in scuttling the Ottoman project of recapturing Astrakhan from Muscovite hands. Apparently, the Ottoman presence on the northern shore of the Caspian Sea posed a threat to the Tatar claims to this territory.[4] Additionally, Carl Max Kortepeter has given us a fascinating example of an independent Crimean ruler, Gazi II Giray (1588–1596; 1597–1608). The author demonstrates that the different aims of the Ottomans and of the Crimean clans made it possible for the khan to seize enough power to control his vassals and to conduct a more independent policy towards the Ottomans.[5] Yet, the studies of Akmes Nimet Kurat on the early eighteenth century demonstrate that in this period the khans could not act independently from the Ottomans. For example, Khan Devlet II Giray (1699–1702, 1708–1713), was yet another outstanding Crimean ruler, who failed to conduct anti-Russian policy independently from the Ottomans. During the war with Russia in Moldavia in 1711, he could not convince the Ottomans to pursue their advantage over Tsar Peter I. Against the khan's advice Grand Vizier Baltacı Mehmed Paşa concluded the Prut armistice on terms proposed by

---

[1] Vasilii Smirnov, *Krymskoe khanstvo pod verkhovenstvem Otomanskoi Porty do nachala XVIII veka* [The Crimean Khanate under the Suzerainty of the Ottoman Porte] (St. Petersburg, 1887), 294.

[2] Halil İnalcık, 'Yeni Vesikalara Göre Kırım Hanlığının Osmanlı Tabiliğine Girmesi ve Ahidnamesi Meselesi' [The Problem of the Treaty and Accepting the Ottoman Sovereignty by the Crimean Khanate in light of the new documents], *Belleten* 8 (1944), 185–229.

[3] Alan Fisher elaborated on this subject in numerous articles collected in two volumes see idem, *Between Russians, Ottomans and Turks: Crimea and the Crimean Tatars* (Istanbul, 1998); idem, *A Precarious Balance: Conflict, Trade and Diplomacy on the Russian-Ottoman Frontier* (Istanbul, 1999).

[4] Smirnov, *Krymskoe khanstvo pod verkhovenstvem Otomanskoi Porty do nachala XVIII veka*, 325.

[5] Carl Max Kortepeter, *Ottoman Imperialism During the Reformation: Europe and the Caucasus* (London, 1972).

the Tsar.[6] Alan Fisher suggests that 'at some undetermined time between 1600 and 1750, the entire configuration of Ottoman-Crimean Tatar political relations changed completely.'[7] They shifted towards strengthening Ottoman patronage over the Khanate. Yet, it should not be ignored that even in the eighteenth century the khan claimed to be an independent ruler and exercised power in the areas distinguished by Hanafi jurists as symbols of sovereignty.

The Shari'a *and the Secular State Law in the Khanate*

It has long been recognized that the *shari'a* had not been the only law in numerous Islamic states. The famous 'mazalim courts'[8] could be considered a good precedent for a specific application of law. Many Muslim rulers followed their example and introduced two systems of justice: one based on the *shari'a* and entrusted to a Muslim judge (*qadi*), and the second based on customary law supplemented by the royal decrees, and enforced by non-religious officials. Such solutions had their sources in the perceived drawbacks of the *shari'a* such as its rigidity or its lack of prescriptions concerning some important areas of day-to-day life, including criminal law, land tenure and taxation.

By the sixteenth century, many Muslim rulers had adopted the administration of justice based on both the *shari'a* and customary-royal law. For example, the Ottoman sultans, as early as in the mid-fifteenth century, started to promulgate detailed regulations (*kanun*), which evolved into the codes of law (*kanunname*). Their sources were rooted in customary law. They were concerned, above all, with taxation, land tenure and criminal law. In the sixteenth-century Ottoman Empire, the disparity between sacred and secular law was clearly visible. For this reason, as Colin Imber demonstrated, scholars such as the Ottoman chief *mufti*, Ebussuud

[6] Akmes Nimet Kurat, *Isveç Kıralı Karl'ın Türkiye'de Kalışı ve Bu Sırada Osmanlı Imperatorluğu* [The Stay of the Swedish King Charles in Turkey and the Ottoman Empire in This Period] (Istanbul, 1943), 399–458; idem, *Prut Seferi ve Barışı* [The Prut Campaign and Peace] (Ankara, 1953), vol. 2, 501–502.

[7] Fisher, *Between Russians, Ottomans and Turks: Crimea and the Crimean Tatars*, 67.

[8] The '*mazalim* courts' had come into being by the early 'Abbasid times, possibly already under the Umayyads. The caliphs adopted the practice of the Sasanian rulers to preside in person over courts. The law, which was applied in the '*mazalim* courts' differed from the *shari'a* and was rooted in the ruler's decrees and local customs; see Roger M. Savory, 'Law and traditional society', in Roger M. Savory, ed., *Introduction to Islamic civilization* (Cambridge, 2000), 58.

(d. 1574), decided to redefine Ottoman law using the terms of religious law, specifically that of the Hanafi school.[9] As they managed to explain the practice of the centralized state in terms acceptable to the Muslims, they succeeded, at least partly, in eliminating the dichotomy between religious and secular jurisdictions.

To what extent, then did secular law coexist with the *shariʿa* in the Crimean Khanate? It is certainly true that Islamic law was by no means a monolith. For this reason one should start with a brief discussion about which doctrine prevailed in the Khanate and what practical consequences followed from this fact. A description of specific aspects of secular law in the Khanate will follow. Unfortunately, sources dealing with Crimean history contain only a few references to secular law. Nevertheless, even such a limited base of research should bring us closer to understanding the roots of prescriptions, which supplemented or modified Islamic law in the Khanate.

Islamic Law in the Khanate

The origin of Islamic law dates back to the seventh century, and the *shariʿa* was believed to have its roots in the Divine Revelation expressed in the Quran as well as in the recorded words and actions of Prophet Muḥammad and his Companions. By the eleventh century, it had become well formulated and widely practiced. The *shariʿa* was by no means homogenous, as it encompassed Sunni and Shiite doctrines. The former could be divided into four schools of law: the Hanafi, Shafiʿi, Hanbali and Maliki schools. They were named after the famous jurists considered as their founders: Abu Hanifa (d. 767), Ash-Shafiʿi (d. 820), Ibn Hanbal (d. 855) and Malik ibn Anas (d. 795). Their doctrines differed in regulations concerning many vital day-to-day matters. It is not always clear why a particular school became dominant in a particular area. Not every Muslim state chose one of them as an official school. For instance, the Mamluks honoured all four schools equally. Yet, the Crimean Khans decided to elevate the authority of one school. Like the Ottoman Sultans and the khans of the Golden Horde they chose the Hanafis. It does not mean that the Crimean ruler did not allow the adherents of other schools to be judged according to

[9] Colin Imber, *The Ottoman Empire, 1300–1650. The Structure of Power* (New York, 2002), 244.

their chosen doctrine. Nonetheless, the Hanafi jurists were given the most important judicial posts, if not every single one.

The fact that the Hanafi school gained an elevated status in the Khanate had certain practical implications. As noted above, numerous daily matters remained unresolved by the *shariʿa*. In such cases, when all instruments of classical law had failed, the Hanafis would recognize custom (*ʿurf*) as a source of law. Moreover, some areas omitted from the religious prescriptions were left to the ruler to decide. The Hanafi doctrine, therefore, recognized the need for practical flexibility and offered the ruler an opportunity to shape the law in certain matters.

The degree of the Khan's influence on shaping the law merits further deliberation. The Crimean Khanate had a complicated political and administrative structure based on Mongol as well as Islamic-Ottoman traditions. The influence of these two systems on various areas of the Khanate's law will be discussed below. Since the term Mongol laws (*yasa*) may be interpreted in various ways, we will explore briefly this notion in the context of the Crimean Khanate. There have been numerous attempts to define the term *yasa*. In the past, scholars believed it to be a code of law written and promulgated by Chingis Khan.[10] However, David Morgan and Denise Aigle redefined this term to denote the body of laws governing the social and legal behaviour of the Mongols and to some extent their non-Mongols subjects. Although in the Khanate it might have been believed that the *Yasa* had been promulgated by Chingis Khan, it should rather be viewed as the body of law consisting of customary and state law, which preceded this ruler and continued to evolve even after his death.[11] We propose to define the terms 'old laws' or 'chingisid laws' in the Crimean documentary sources and chronicles accordingly.

State Law in the Khanate: Mongol Influences on State Administration

According to Mongol custom, the Khan embodied the Supreme Power and his very title referred to his supreme authority. The Crimean-Tatar

---

[10] François Petis de la Croix, *The History of Genghizcan the Great* (London, 1722); George Vernadsky, 'The Scope and Contents of Chingis Khan's Yasa', *HJAS* 3 (1938), 337–360; Valentin Riazanovsky, *Fundamental Principles of Mongol Law* (Bloomington, 1965), 83–91; David Ayalon, 'The Great Yasa of Chingiz Khan: a reexamination', *Studia Islamica* 33 (1971), 97–140; 34 (1971), 151–180; 36 (1972), 112–158; 38 (1973), 107–56.

[11] David O. Morgan, 'The Great Yasa of Chingiz Khan and Mongol Law in the Ilkhanate', *BSOAS* 49 (1986), 163–176; Denise Aigle, 'Le grand *jasaq* de Gengis-khan, l'empire, la culture mongole et la shariʿa', *JESHO* 47 (2004), 31–79.

tradition provided some rules concerning the succession. Firstly, as the Khanate was a continuation of the Chingisid Empire, the Khan had to be a male member of the Giray dynasty, which traced its origins to Chingis Khan. Secondly, it was expected that the eldest man would come to the throne. Yet, the new Khan was supposed to be selected by the *kurultay*. This institutional grouping of the Crimean nobles was dominated by the *karaçı begs*, the most powerful of the Khan's vassals, and their diverging political goals as well as the personal ambitions of various members of the Giray dynasty were of utmost importance in the process of selecting a new Khan. Thus, in practice any member of the Giray dynasty could come to power as the candidate of a successful faction. After the Ottoman conquest of the southern part of the Crimean peninsula, the sultans began to play an important role in the designation of new Khans. It comes as no surprise that rival groups sought the Sublime Porte's support to turn the scales in their favour. Consequently, the conflicts allowed the Sublime Porte to intervene more and more frequently in the Crimean succession. The rival groups and the Ottomans evoked the rule of agnatic seniority only when it favoured their candidates, who were always recruited from among the members of the Giray dynasty. Up until the very end of the Khanate in 1783, it was clearly understood that only the descendants of Chingis Khan could make claims to the heritage of the Golden Horde.

The crucial political institution and dignitaries of the Khanate, such as the *kurultay*, *karaçı beg*s, and the first and second deputy of the Khan, were of Mongol origins. Although much remains unknown about the *kurultay*, it is clear that in the Crimean Khanate it was a consultative institution grouping together the Tatar nobles. It has its roots in the Mongol custom of gathering for military purposes. It could be summoned by the Khan or the most powerful *karaçı beg*. In case of conflict, the Khan and the *karaçı beg*s would seek support from the remaining members of the *kurultay*. If the rebelling nobles were successful, they would start a 'lawful rebellion' designed to change the Khan's policy or even to replace him with a new ruler. The elevated position of the heads of the most powerful noble families (*karaçı beg*s) constituted a part of the Chingisid heritage as well. The noble families who settled in the Crimea in the times of the Golden Horde owned semi-autonomous family estates (*beylik*s), which constituted the base of their economic, military and social position. Finally, the posts of the first (*kalga*) and the second deputy of the khan (*nuraddin*) had their roots in Mongol tradition. Yet, they did not exist at the time of the formation of the Crimean Khanate but were created later to serve political goals of two Khans. The post of *kalga* dates back to the reign of Mengli I Giray (1478–1515),[12] while the post of *nureddin* was created by Mehmed II Giray in 1579.[13] Only members of the Giray dynasty could hold these positions. A prince appointed to the office of *kalga* was assigned a part of the Khanate's territory with Ak Mescid (Simferopol) as its capital. Within his domain he enjoyed certain autonomy as he controlled it through his own officials, whose titles and functions were modelled on those of the Khan (which will be described in the next sections). Unfortunately, our sources offer us ambiguous data on the existence of the *nuraddin*'s domain. Although it is beyond doubt that this dignitary modelled his court on that of the Khan, it remains uncertain whether any well-defined territory was permanently assigned to him.[14] Finally, it is worth noting that the *karaçı begs*, the *kalga*, and the *nuraddin* influenced foreign and domestic policy as they had the right to participate in the Khan's council.

Ottoman Influence on State Administration

The Khan's council is only one of the administrative institutions in the Khanate, which consisted of officials of both Mongol and Ottoman origin. The reshaping of the old administration started as early as the first half of the sixteenth century and is connected with the reforms of Khan Sahib I Giray (1532–1551). He started to reshape the Crimean ruler's position on the Ottoman model in order to strengthen his own power. From this period onwards Ottoman solutions were implemented more and more frequently in organizing the Khan's household and in shaping and naming the majority of central and provincial offices. For example, many of the officials during the reign of Murad Giray (1678–1683) bore the titles known from the Ottoman court such as *vizier*, *mufti*, *qadiasker*, *defterdar*, *kethuda*, *katib* of the council, *kapıcı başı*, *mirahor* or *silahdar*.[15] Moreover, they had

---

[12] Josef Matuz, 'Qalga', *Turcica* 2 (1970), 101–129.

[13] Muzaffer Ürekli, *Kırım Hanlığının Kuruluşu ve Osmanlı Himayesinde Yükselişi* [Founding of the Crimean Khanate and Its Growth under the Ottoman Protection] (Ankara, 1989), 74–77.

[14] Nicole Kançal-Ferrari, *Kırım'da Kalan Miras. Hansaray* [A Treasure Left in the Crimea. The Palace of the Khans] (Istanbul, 2005), 52–53, 57.

[15] The Crimean judicial records, 121 volumes in all, constitute an important source of information for this study. They are preserved in the Russian National Library in St. Petersburg (Otdel Rukopisev Rossiiskoi Natsionalnoi Biblioteki, St. Petersburg [hereafter, ORRNB]), Fond 917). Before 1799, the collection was handed over to the Russian

duties similar to those of their Ottoman counterparts. Ottoman influence was also visible in provincial administration. The Crimean Khanate had two systems of territorial division. Firstly, the land was divided between the Khan, his family and clients, on one hand, and the great vassal families and their clients, on the other. Secondly, the Khans introduced court districts (*qazas*)—typical territorial units in a Muslim state. Judges (*qadi*s) performed both judicial and administrative functions. In the Crimean Khanate as in the Ottoman Empire, in addition to passing sentences and acting as public notaries they performed various administrative duties. A *qadi* was, in fact, the most important official of the ruler within a court district. Ottoman influence on the Khanate is also visible in the structure of the provincial court as in both states the *qadi* had at his disposal minor officials such as deputy judges (*naib*s), scribes (*katib*s), summon officials (*muhzır*s) and dividers (*qassam*s). Yet, it remains unclear whether the Crimean *qadi*s and their officials could perform their duties on the territories of the great vassal families. The narrative sources and the Crimean *sijill*s offer us only ambiguous answers to the question.

Taxes

Tax law is another important branch of public law. Since no tax register from the Crimean Khanate has survived to our times, research on the local taxes presents a great challenge. Our data on the subject are limited to the taxes mentioned in the Khan's orders and income entries recorded in the Crimean *sijill*s. The taxes levied in the Khanate, like other branches of law, seem to combine Islamic, Mongol and Ottoman solutions. For this reason, Crimean taxes shall be divided according to their origin into three groups: Islamic canonical taxes, Mongol taxes, and non-canonical and non-Mongol taxes, which presumably had their roots in Ottoman practice.

---

authorities by Mehmed Ağa, the last Crimean *qadiasker*. It was kept in the Archives of the Governor of Simferopol till 1905, when it was sent to the Public Library in St. Petersburg (Olga Vasileva, 'Krymsko-Tatarskie Rukopisnye Materialy v otdele rukopisii' [The Crimean-Tatar Manuscripts Preserved in the Department of Manuscripts], *Rossiiskaia National'naia Biblioteka. Vostochnyi Sbornik* 5 (1993), 37–45). The collection contains judicial records of *qadiaskers* and *qadis* of major Crimean cities (Bahçesaray, Kara Su, Gözleve) along with a few registers, whose territorial affiliation remains unidentified. Two registers of real estate left by Christians, who emigrated from the Crimean peninsula in 1778, were also included in this collection. On the officials during the reign of Murad Giray see: ORRNB, Fond 917, defter 22/22a/6; 23b/7a/2; 23b/245a/1; 23b/125b/3.

Islamic Canonical Taxes

The first group of taxes reflects the Islamic idea of division of individuals into Muslims and non-Muslims. It consisted of taxes such as:

- Tithe ('ushr) from all agricultural products. There is no data as to how the Crimean Khans proved their right to collect this tax. It is clear from the Khan's orders and from the cases recorded in the *sijill*s that the tithe was collected by the Khan and the *kalga* as well as by the great vassal families. Perhaps they adopted Ottoman principles, as expressed by the chief *mufti*, Ebussuud. His theory concerned the 'tribute' land, i.e., the land conquered as a result of a holy war and not divided among the Muslim soldiers at the time of the conquest. The real substance of this land was thus reserved for the common treasury of the Muslims, which remained at the disposal of the Muslim ruler. The ruler could lend the fields to his subjects, but in exchange they were obliged to pay to the treasury a proportional tribute (*haraçi mukaseme*) in the form of tithe ('ushr). In the Ottoman Empire, the tithe paid by peasants often formed a source of income assigned to various types of beneficiaries, for example, the *timar* holders.[16] The khans also confirmed the right of the *karaçı beg*s to collect various taxes, though admittedly the tithe was not explicitly listed. Nonetheless, the extant orders contain vague expressions such as 'the customary usage of fields along with winter and summer pastures,' which might also allude to the collection of tithe.[17]
- Poll-tax (*jizya*)—a canonical tax unconnected with the land, payable by adult non-Muslim males. The Hanafis based assessment of its individual amount on the level of income of a tax-payer. According to Islamic law, the *jizya* was to be collected on behalf of the ruler, who should spend the income on his army. Thus, also in the Khanate the poll-tax should go to the khan's treasury. The orders preserved in the *sijill*s give evidence that the khan's officials did collect this tax.[18] Judging by the contents of a letter of the *kaymakam* of Kalga Devlet Giray, dating back to 1683 and confirming the *kalga*'s right to collect poll-tax

[16] Colin Imber, *Ebu's-su'ud. Islamic Legal Tradition* (Edinburgh, 1997), 125; Suraya Faroqhi, *Crisis and change, 1599–1699*, in Halil İnalcık, Donald Quatert, eds., *An Economic and Social History of the Ottoman Empire* (Cambridge, 2000), vol. 2—*1600–1914*, 531–538.

[17] Fiodor Lashkov, 'Sbornik dokumentov po istorii krymsko-tatarskogo zemlevladeniia' [Collection of Documents on the History of the Criman-Tatar Landownership], *Izvestiia Tavricheskoi Uchenoi Arkhivnoi Komissii* [hereafter *ITUAK*] (1895), 123–128.

[18] ORRNB, Fond 917, defter 25/115a/4.

in his domain,[19] the *jizya* also constituted a part of the *kalga*'s stable income.

- Fifth (*hums*) of the spoils of war. The ruler was entitled to a fifth of all spoils taken in a holy war. The Crimean chronicles make it clear that the khan also received a share of the spoils of war.[20] Yet, it seems that the Islamic fifth was replaced by the Mongol 'savga,' which amounted to 10% only. The latter will be discussed in the next section.
- Alms (*zakat*), i.e., the voluntary offerings from all Muslims, which should be spent on the poor. A letter of Devlet I Giray to Ebussuud, invoked by Colin Imber, proves that the khan deliberated how this tax should be collected in the Khanate.[21] The Crimean ruler asked the famous *mufti* whether he should pay *zakat* from his own treasury. This suggests that in the 1570s there were still no developed procedures concerning the collection of *zakat* in the Khanate. Perhaps the tax had been introduced quite recently or was about to be introduced. As there are no other sources on the subject, it remains unclear whether *zakat* was collected at all in the Crimean Khanate, and thus whether the khans were in a position to follow Ottoman practice in this matter. In the Ottoman Empire, according to Colin Imber, *zakat* 'never existed as a reality'.[22]

Mongol Taxes

The Mongol tax regulations have been treated by a considerable number of scholars, including the classical studies of Herbert F. Schurmann,[23]

---

[19] ORRNB, Fond 917, defter 25/120a/2; the term *haraç*, used in the *kaymakam*'s letter, should be identified as *cizye*. In fact, both terms were often used interchangeably to describe the poll-tax; cf. Nenad Moačanin, *Town and Country on the Middle Danube 1526–1690* (Leiden, Boston, 2006), 199. According to the classical law, there were two forms in which the canonical tax called *haraç* could be imposed on non-Muslims: as a fixed annual tribute (*haraç-i muvazzaf*) or as a proportional tribute (*haraç-i mukaseme*). The *haraç* could not be imposed along with the tithe since the jurists made a sharp distinction between the 'tithe lands' and 'tribute lands.' Hence, if the tithe was regarded as a form of *haraç-i mukaseme*, according to Ebussuud's theory, the term *haraç* encountered in the kaymakam's letter must have referred to *jizya*.

[20] Abdulgaffar el-Kırımi, *Ümdetü't-tavarih*, N. Asim Bey, ed. (Istanbul, 1343/1927), 157; Mehmed Senai z Krymu, *Historia Chana Islama Gereja III*, Zygmunt Abrahamowicz, ed. (Warsaw, 1971), 111/30; Seyyid Muhammed Riza, *Essebü'sseyyar ili sem' planet soderzhavshchii istoriu krymskikh khanow ot Mengli Girej Khana pierwogo do Mengli Girej Khana vtorogo t. e. s 871/1466 po 1150/1737* [The Seven Planets], Mirza Kazembeg, ed., (Kazan, 1832), 167.

[21] Imber, *Ebu's-s'uud. The Islamic Legal Tradition*, 82.

[22] Idem, *Ebu's-s'uud. The Islamic Legal Tradition*, 139.

[23] Herbert F. Schurmann, 'Mongolian Tributary Practices of the 13th century', *HJAS* 19 (1956), 304–389.

I.P. Petrushevsky,[24] John M. Smith, Jr.,[25] or Ann K.S. Lambton.[26] Over forty Mongol taxes are attested in the Chingisid Empire and its successor states. In general Mongol taxes can be divided into two groups: the permanent tribute; and extraordinary levies paid occasionally to the ruler. However, the multiplicity of terms does not necessarily imply that such a wide range of taxes was actually collected. Rather it testifies that different terms applied in different times and places to the same or similar taxes. Unfortunately, most of these terms were recorded in non-Mongolian sources and in non-Mongol languages, for example in Persian, Russian, Turkic or Chinese, which has made them subject to distortions and further contributed to the present difficulty in their interpretation.

It has therefore been questioned whether there were any taxes common to all the post-Chingisid states. Did the Mongols develop their own tax system? David Morgan doubted whether 'what the Mongols did in this sphere [i.e., taxes] can be dignified with the name of "*system*"'.[27] Ann Lambton pointed out that even the most typically 'Mongol' taxes, such as *qubchur, qalan* and *tamga*, 'meant different things at different times and in different places.'[28] These theories suggest that a tax name did not suffice to determine the type of obligation it imposed. In the case of the Crimean Khanate, mentions of a number of taxes and duties, referred to with Mongol terms or described as 'ancient' or 'Chingisid,'[29] have survived to our times, but we rarely know their precise meaning and function. These taxes are listed below:

- *tamga,*[30] *tumanend, savga, buralka, koluş-kalanka.*[31] Such taxes are mentioned in the nineteenth-century Russian translations of the Khans' orders dating back to the fifteenth and sixteenth centuries. Except for

[24] I. Petrushevsky, *The Socio-Economic Condition of Iran under the Il-Khans*, in J.A. Boyle, ed., *The Cambridge History of Iran* (Cambridge, 1968), vol. 5, 494–524.

[25] John M. Smith, 'Mongol and Nomadic Taxation', *HJAS* 30 (1970), 46–87.

[26] Ann K.S. Lambton, 'Mongol Fiscal Administration in Persia', *Studia Islamica* 64 (1986), 79–99.

[27] David Morgan, *The Mongols* (Oxford, 2007), 83–87.

[28] Lambton, 'Mongol Fiscal Administration in Persia', 84.

[29] In the sources, these taxes are referred to as following the 'Chingisid law' (*kanun-i cingiziyye*) or being in accordance with the 'ancient law' (*kanun-i kadim*).

[30] Vasilii Smirnov, 'Tatarsko-krymskie iarlyki iz kollektsii Tavricheskoi Uchenoi Arkhivnoi Kommissii', *ITUAK* 54 (1918), 13; *tamga* was a tax on commercial goods, a kind of stamp duty.

[31] Fiodor Lashkov, 'Istoricheskii ocherk krymsko-tatarskogo zemlevladeniia', *ITUAK* 23 (1895), 88; Lashkov 'Sbornik dokumentov po istorii krymsko-tatarskogo zemlevladeniia', 127.

savga and *tamga*, they are not found in the extant sources from the second half of the sixteenth century on. It remains unclear whether they were still levied in the seventeenth and eighteenth centuries. Unfortunately, for the reasons discussed above, the nature of these taxes remains vague.[32] Yet, documentary and narrative sources provide some data on the *savga*. It was a tithe from the booty collected by a Mongol ruler.[33] In the Crimean Khanate, it seems to have been associated with the Islamic fifth (*hums*). The Khan's share was limited to a tenth, but the chroniclers justified his right referring to both Mongol custom and Islamic law. Thus, the collection of *savga* constitutes an interesting example of an impost prescribed by both Mongol and Islamic law. It is noteworthy that the Khan settled for a lower rate, i.e., 10% instead of collecting 20%.

- *şişlik*, a tax on sheep, apparently lower than its Ottoman counterpart named *adet-i agnam* as in 1609 Khan Ghazi II Giray prohibited the collection of sheep tax other than *şişlik*. His order was issued in response to a petition presented by his subjects, who had asked the khan to follow Mongol tradition rather than introduce Ottoman practice.[34]
- A tax due from the owners of slaves, to be paid every thirty years to the khan.[35] Information about this tax derives from the account of Evliya

[32] The term *tumanend* might refer to *tuman*, a typically Mongol military unit. The *buralka* constitutes a mystery. The *koluş-kalanka* is a generic binom expressing an unidentified tax. According to Shamil Muhamedyarov and István Vásáry, the term *koluş* derives from the verb 'kol-,' which means 'to ask for, to pray.' The scholars found it in the binom *qoluš-qoltka* in an early 16th-century yarlığ of Sahib Giray, the khan of Kazan. They argued that its 'Russian contemporary translation must have been <<zapros>> or <<zaprosy>>. These terms must have denoted several sorts of compulsory bounty given to the khan, the landlord, etc. on certain occasions;' see Shamil Muhamedyarov, István Vásáry, *Two Kazan Tatar Edicts. (Ibrahim's and Sahib Girey's Yarliks)* in Gyorgy Kara, ed., *Between the Danube and the Caucasus. Oriental Sources of the History of the People of Central and South-Eastern Europe* (Budapest, 1987), 196–197. The term *kalanka* seems to refer to the Mongol tax *qalan*. Scholars differ in opinions as to the precise meaning of 'qalan.' According to John M. Smith Jr., it was a catch-all term for pre-Mongol taxes; see John M. Smith Jr., 'Mongol and Nomadic Taxation', 59, 83. Ann Lambton, who discussed various usages of this term in Persia, proposed that the *qalan* had most probably meant a kind of labour service; see Lambton, 'Mongol Fiscal Administration in Persia', 94. David Morgan agreed in some aspects with Lambton as he stated that, although the 'qalan' tax remains obscure, it rather meant some kind of labour service than the pre-Mongol imposts; see Morgan, *The Mongols*, 89. As both terms, *koluş* and *qalan*, remain poorly understood, it is hard to determine what type of obligations a tax referred to by their conjunction imposed.

[33] Abdulgaffar el-Kırımi, *Ümdetü't-tavarih*, 157.

[34] Cf. Halil Inalcık, 'Kirim Hanlığı Sicilleri Bulundu', *Belleten* 140 (1996), 175.

[35] *Księga podróży Ewliji Czelebiego (Wybór)* [The Book of Travels of Evliya Çelebi (A Selection)], trans. Z. Abrahamowicz, A. Dubiński, S. Płaskowicka-Rymkiewicz (Warsaw, 1969), 354–355.

Çelebi, who stressed that it was collected only after the *mufti* had proclaimed it legally valid.

Other Taxes

In this section we will discuss the taxes levied in the Khanate, which seem to have had no clear Islamic or Mongol roots. These were:

- Taxes for the maintenance of musketeers (*tüfenkçi*). According to Crimean chroniclers, the tax was introduced by Gazi II Giray (1588–1596, 1597–1608). It was paid in sheep to be delivered to the Khan's kitchen.[36] Crimean *sicil*s from the Kara Su district contain an entry concerning the collection of tax for the purchase of guns (*tüfenk*).[37] It is dated to the year 1683. Each neighbourhood (*mahalle*) within the town constituted a tax-unit. The neighbourhoods were charged different rates, which might reflect their inhabitants' ability to pay. It remains unclear whether the tax was levied regularly or extraordinarily to finance the Vienna campaign.
- Extraordinary taxes for military campaigns. Before his departure to 'punish' the Circassian begs in 1707/1708, Khan Kaplan I Giray ordered a population census in the Khanate. His order stipulated that one man from every household should take part in the campaign. Country households, where there was no man, as well as town dwellers, apparently not valued as warriors, were obliged to pay a cash equivalent for the maintenance of the khan's regular troops (referred to as *kapıkulu* and *sekbans*).[38] We may assume that such taxes were levied more often during the preparations for military campaigns.
- Cask fee on wine consumption (*fiçıları haraç*).[39] A similar tax on wine consumption was levied in the Ottoman Empire and termed *resmi fuçi*.
- Fines on crimes (*jara'im [resmi]*).

[36] Seyyid Mehmed Riza, *Es-sebü'sseyyar ili sem' planet soderzhavshchii istoriu krymskikh khanow ot Mengli Girej Khana pierwogo do Mengli Girej Khana vtorogo t. e. s 871/1466 po 1150/1737*, 110; Halim Giray, *Gülbünü Hanan yahud Kırım Tarihi/Rozovyi kust khanov ili istoriia Kryma* [The Rosebush or the History of the Crimea] A. Ilmi, ed. (Simferopol, 2004), 195.

[37] ORRNB, Fond 917, defter 25/119b/4.

[38] Abdulgaffar el-Kırımi, *Ümdetü't-tavarih*, 143. This extraordinary tax was also mentioned by Seyyid Mehmed Riza, *Essebü'sseyyar ili sem' planet soderzhavshchii istoriu krymskikh khanow ot Mengli Girej Khana pierwogo do Mengli Girej Khana vtorogo t. e. s 871/1466 po 1150/1737*, 312.

[39] ORRNB, Fond 917, defter 25/18a/2.

Three of the five above-mentioned taxes were levied to support military units such as *sekbans*, which were patterned on the Ottoman Janissaries. It is known from other sources that the Crimean *sekbans* were supported by the Ottomans, who paid a stipend to the khan for this purpose. Therefore, the above-mentioned taxes might have been an additional source of finance for the military. They resemble the Ottoman extraordinary wartime tax called *avarız* which became a permanent tax in the seventeenth-century Ottoman Empire; this was initially collected in kind, and then gradually, it started to be paid in cash. In the Crimean Khanate in the second half of the sixteenth century, Gazi II Giray taxed his subjects in kind for military purposes as well, ordering the delivery of flocks of sheep for the maintenance of his *sekbans*. The tax for the purchase of guns imposed on Kara Su inhabitants in 1682 and the war-time tax requested by Khan Kaplan I Giray were already paid in cash. The individual rate of the former presumably reflected the unequal incomes of its payers as the tax-load was distributed among taxable units comprising unequal numbers of individuals. The same rule applied to the Ottoman tax-units termed *avarızhane*, whose size also reflected unequal incomes of subjects, obliged to pay the *avarız* tax. The only notable difference was that the Ottomans introduced a new tax-unit especially for the purpose of collecting this tax while the khan used as a tax-unit the already existing institution of neighbourhood (*mahalle*).

To sum up, it is highly probable that the Ottoman *avarız* constituted a model for the khans' taxes imposed for military purposes. Yet, it should not be ignored that the rulers of other post-Chingisid states used to levy extraordinary taxes to support their armies, too. Thus, Crimean extraordinary taxes might have been collected in accordance with both Ottoman and Mongol traditions.

This brings us to the next area of interest: the specified taxes from products and economic activities of which the cask fee on wine consumption is an example. The fact that it was imposed in the Khanate has two vital implications. Firstly, it might suggest direct Ottoman influence on tax policy in the Khanate. As noted above, a very similar tax was levied in the Ottoman Empire. Secondly, it indicates that the Khanate, like the Sublime Porte, introduced non-canonical taxes for specific economic and social activities.

Did the Khan also collect other taxes typical for the Ottoman Empire, such as the bride tax, the Christmas tax or the tax on pigs? The privileges for the Khan's clients, published by Lashkov, referred to several taxes, such as the bride-tax levied on non-Muslims, the fee on pasturage or the fee on crimes, which might have been similar to their Ottoman counterparts.[40] Unfortunately, our knowledge of these specified fees is based on fragmentary sources. One cannot exclude the possibility that the specified taxes levied in the Khanate had both Ottoman and Mongol origins. It should also not be ignored that the Mongols imposed a tax on various economic activities called *tamga*, which was levied in the fifteenth-century Khanate.[41]

Although research on the tax system of the Crimean Khanate is still in its infancy, our preliminary remarks offer some indications concerning the origins and development of the Crimean tax system, which seems to have combined Islamic prescriptions with Mongol and Ottoman ones. Nonetheless, it remains unclear how exactly these three different systems coexisted. Perhaps the Mongol or Ottoman practices were applied to the areas in which Islam offered few or no applicable solutions. There are some indications that, over time, Ottoman solutions replaced Mongol ones in the Khanate's tax law. Extant sources note fewer taxes bearing Mongol names in the seventeenth and eighteenth centuries than in the sixteenth century. Moreover, they inform us with rising frequency about taxes which seem to have been modelled on Ottoman solutions. Finally, the sources refer to at least one attempt at replacing a Mongol tax with an Ottoman one (the tax on sheep, discussed above). It is worth noting that in that case the tax-payers managed to successfully prevent a tax reform which increased their obligations. An equally interesting example of the *savga* demonstrates that the Tatars were well aware of certain similarities between Islamic and Mongol taxes. In such cases the khan did not impose a double tax but remained satisfied with one. In the case of *savga*, the ruler seems to have contented himself with a less profitable version.

Private Law

The data preserved in the court registers indicate that the Crimean Muslims followed the Hanafi school of Islamic law in private matters, as did the Ottoman Empire and the Golden Horde.[42] According to Evliya Çelebi,

[40] Lashkov, 'Istoricheskii ocherk krymsko-tatarskogo zemlevladeniia', 88–89.

[41] Vasilii Smirnov, 'Tatarsko-krymskie iarlyki iż kollektsii Tavricheskoi Uchenoi Archivnoi Kommissii', *ITUAK* 54 (1918), 13.

[42] Devin DeWeese, *Islamization and Native Religion in the Golden Horde. Baba Tükles and Conversion to Islam in Historical and Epic Tradition* (University Port, 1994), 132.

the other three schools enjoyed the Khan's protection as well. The famous traveller described how their *muftis*, along with the Hanafi one, were members of the khan's council.[43] However, it remains unclear how the khan's courts delivered justice to the followers of non-Hanafi schools. The entries in the *sijill*s dating back to Murad Giray's reign contain no data about the application of legal solutions typical for non-Hanafi schools. Still, it does not mean that the Khan's judges could not use their prescriptions in cases involving non-Hanafi individuals. As the verdict was not a part of the formal registration of a case, only a limited number of recorded entries in the Crimean *sijill*s end with the judges' sentences. It is hard to establish whether non-Hanafi solutions were used in Crimean practice as in most cases the verdicts are concealed under vague, standard formulae.

There are some indications that Crimean rulers integrated Ottoman legal solutions regarding private matters with the Hanafi doctrine. Let us focus on two examples, which concern a statute of limitation and religious foundations.

Classical Islamic Law did not mention a statute of limitation, let alone determine its duration in various types of cases. For this reason, in the Ottoman Empire the problem was regulated by the Sultans, who defined the length of the statute of limitations for various types of litigation. For example, suits concerning the ownership of a private piece of land should not be heard after fifteen years.[44] As the same statute of limitation was applied in the Crimean Khanate during the reign of Murad Giray,[45] it is possible that the idea might have come to the Khanate from the Ottoman Empire.

The Khanate's law seems to have adopted some of the Ottoman solutions with regard to religious foundations, too. In classical Islamic law there was no unanimity as to what kinds of property could legally endow a religious foundation. The Hanafis alone offered three different opinions on the subject. The controversy focused on the possibility of converting movable property into a trust. In the sixteenth century, after decades of judicial arguments, the Ottomans finally defined what could be lawfully donated to a religious foundation. For practical reasons, the Sultans permitted religious foundations to accept a wide range of objects, including

---

[43] *Księga podróży Ewliji Czelebiego (Wybór)*, 277.

[44] Boğaç Ergene, *Local courts, provincial society and justice in the Ottoman Empire. Legal Practice and Dispute Resolution in Çankiri and Kastamonu (1652–1744)* (Leiden, Boston, 2003), 147.

[45] ORRNB Fond 917, defter 23a/150b/1; 23a/171b/2.

animals and cash, whose donation had been banned previously.[46] The same practical approach characterized the Crimean judges, as among the entries recorded during Murad Giray's reign one encounters various kinds of movable property successfully converted into religious foundations.[47]

These two examples indicate that in the Crimean Khanate private law was supplemented or interpreted on lines similar to reforms adopted in the Ottoman Empire in the sixteenth century, and it is thus probable that the Tatars adopted them due to their close relations with the Sublime Porte. If so, the fact would bear testimony to Ottoman influence on the day-to-day legal practice in the Khanate.

Criminal Law[48]

Criminal law in the Crimean Khanate developed on the basis of the Hanafi doctrine supplemented by Ottoman legal practice.[49] There is no evidence of Mongol influence in this area with the exception of the crimes committed against the ruler (*crimen laesae maiestatis*).[50]

In contrast to the limited Mongol influence, one can cite several examples of possible Ottoman impact on Crimean proceedings in criminal cases. Firstly, it is visible in such aspects as the introduction of the administrative justice system (*siyaset*), used by the Ottomans. If a *qadi* failed to establish the truth, he could, according to the doctrine of administrative justice (*siyaset*), order the executive officials to use torture to extort a confession.[51] The eighteenth-century travelogue of Nicolas Kleemann contains the only reference to the use of torture in the Khanate to collect evidence. In the case cited by Kleemann, the official called *zabit* and his assistants personally arrested an individual accused of cheating a

46 Imber, *Ebu's-s'uud, The Islamic Legal Tradition*, 142–146.

47 For instance, a woman named Rahime donated nine *altuns* for the benefit of the pious foundation of the Great Mosque in Bahçesaray; ORRNB, Fond 917, defter 23b/83b/7.

48 According to classical textbooks, the criminal law is divided into three groups: offences against person, violation of God's claims, and acts endangering public order or state security.

49 Recep Çiğdem, 'Crimes Threatening Bodily Integrity (Assault and Battery): A Legal Analysis of Four Cases From the Judicial Registers of the Bakchisaray/Crimea Law Court', *Ankara Üniversitesi Hukuk Fakültesi Dergisi* 54, no. 1 (2005), 61–71; idem, The Judicial Registers of the Bakchisaray/Crimea law court: A Study of Murder Crimes, *Hamdard Islamicus* 28, no. 4 (2005), 41–53.

50 *Tarihi Sahib Giray Han*, Ö. Gökbilgin, ed. (Ankara, 1973), 69–70/209.

51 Baber Johansen, 'Signs as Evidence: The Doctrine of Ibn Taymiyya (1263–1328) and Ibn Qayyim al-Jawziyya (d. 1351) on Proof', *Islamic Law and Society* 9, no. 2 (2000), 168–193.

merchant. The *qadi* threatened the latter that if he did not start to speak the truth, he would be tortured.[52] While classical Islamic jurisprudence considered torture to be unreliable and an illegitimate means of establishing the truth, the Islamic states starting with the Mamluks allowed its use under certain circumstances. Most likely, the idea of using torture during court processes came to the Khanate from the Ottoman Empire. We cannot establish whether its use in both states was subject to similar rules, as Kleemann's description does not offer sufficient information on the subject.

Secondly, the statute of limitation on criminal cases introduced in the Khanate seems to have been a direct copy from Ottoman legal practice. As has already been noted, the problem whether an offence could be prosecuted indefinitely remains largely unresolved in classical Islamic law. The Hanafis defined the statute of limitation only in cases concerning the violation of God's claims. The Ottoman sultan solved the problem in 1550 by issuing an imperial decree, in which he forbade the *qadis* to hear cases if more than fifteen years had elapsed since the crime.[53] Likewise, the fifteen-year statute of limitation was applied to all types of claims in the Crimean Khanate.

Conclusions

The Khanate's political institutions were rooted in the Islamic, Mongol and Ottoman traditions. Similarly, the Khanate's tax system exemplifies how prescriptions of various origins could coexist in one state, although the reasons for the applicability of one rule of a particular origin rather than another remain unclear. Politics and the security of the ruler were important motives. In the field of public law, institutions and taxes derived from the Ottoman model were shaped by the Khans in order to strengthen their own position against the great vassals. Rebellions of the Crimean nobles as well as conflicts concerning certain taxes indicate that the Khans had to take into account the interest of their subjects and could

[52] Nicolas Ernst Kleemann, *Voyage de Vienne à Belgrade et à Kilianova, Dans le pays des Tartares Budziacs et Nogais dans la Crimée, et Kaffa à Constantinople; qu travers de la mer Noire; avec le retour à Vienne; par Trieste. Fait dans les années 1768, 1769 et 1770, par Nicolas-Ernest Kleeman. On y a joint description des choses les plus remarquables concernant la Crimée* (Neuchatel, 1780), 90–107.

[53] Rudolph Peters, *Crime and Punishment in Islamic Law. Theory and Practice from the Sixteenth to the Twenty-first Century* (Cambridge, 2005), 11.

not introduce new measures at will. The case concerning the sheep tax demonstrates that Crimean subjects could successfully prevent their ruler from changing the law to their detriment.

In the field of private and criminal law the Muslim Hanafi doctrine was followed, but it was supplemented with some Ottoman legal solutions. The data preserved in the court registers indicate that a mixture of *shari'a* and Ottoman law was applied in the whole territory of the Crimean Khanate, at least as reflected in the cases which were resolved or registered by the khan's *qadi*s. The dominance of the Hanafi school was rooted in the heritage of the Golden Horde and further strengthened by the Ottoman impact.

The Ottomans wielded continuous influence on the Khanate's law, and some of the Ottoman solutions introduced in the early modern era were applied in the Khanate as well. Although much remains unknown about their introduction, there is no evidence that the changes were part of a deliberate policy aimed at strengthening the Sultan's influence in the Crimea. It seems that the Ottomans had a very practical approach to the Khanate's law system. This attitude is well illustrated by an anecdote recounted by Jan Gniński, the Polish envoy to the Sublime Port in 1678. His report contains a description of the replacement of one Khan by another. In 1677, Selim I Giray was deposed, while Murad Giray, the former *nuraddin* sent into exile in Yanbol in 1666, was designated as the new Khan. The sultan apologised to Murad Giray that he had not appointed him as the new Khan instead of Selim I Giray during the previous change on the throne in 1671. The sultan alleged that he had been misled by the Grand Vizier as to who was the eldest member of the Giray dynasty; when he realized the truth, he restored the throne to the legal heir.[54] From other sources, however, we know that the real reason that Selim I Giray was deposed was the defeat of the Ottoman-Crimean army during the first siege of Chykhryn (1677). The story therefore demonstrates that depending on Ottoman political interests, the Sultan exploited or ignored the law of the Khanate, as he saw fit.

54 Franciszek Pułaski ed., *Źródła do poselstwa Jan Gnińskiego wojewody chełmińskiego do Turcyi w latach 1677–1678* (Warszawa, 1907), 67.

QING IMPERIAL JUSTICE? THE CASE OF LI SHIYAO

R. Kent Guy

The conflict between justice and consistency is common to many legal orders, everywhere there are instances where criminals guilty of the same crime are justly punished in inconsistent ways, and conversely where consistency in sentencing produces unjust results. In an empire where the final decisions in legal cases are made by a single monarch, the issue of justice and inconsistency becomes especially vexed. Is judicial inconsistency in such instances a product of a monarch's personal predilections or an inevitable by-product of the attempt to apply fixed laws to all-too-human contingencies? The desire for justice is surely universal, and the capacity to provide justice is one basis of imperial legitimacy. But the arguments for justice may take very different forms in different cultural contexts. How imperial legal systems worked through this problem highlighted in vivid terms the character of the legal orders they preserved and the political and cultural constraints that shaped those orders. This paper will argue that in China, justice was due to communities as well as to individuals.

In imperial China these issues arose forcefully in the case of Li Shiyao (d. 1788), governor general of Yunnan and Guizhou, who was found guilty in 1780 of extorting money from his subordinates. He was given a sentence that left open the possibility of exoneration. This sentence caused controversy, a dispute which the state took particular pains to contain and redirect. The debate over the appropriate sentence for Li was occasioned by the fact that one of Li's predecessors as governor-general of Yunnan and Guizhou, Hengwen, had been sentenced to execution for the same crime, extorting money from his subordinates. The prosecutions of both officials were quite well known in official circles, and the Qianlong Emperor (r. 1736–1796) actually encouraged the discussion and even engaged it himself before rendering his verdict.

The case presents a vivid example of late-imperial Chinese legal reasoning, highlighting the concerns of consistency and justice as they were applied in the prosecution of senior officials of the dynasty. The dispute over Li Shiyao's sentence took place at a particularly significant moment in late-imperial Chinese history, a time when a buoyant economy in many areas of China posed temptations to dynastic officials, and the legal order had not evolved adequate means to deal with the dimensions and directions of corruption. The sections below will first review the case against Li Shiyao and the debate over his punishment. Then, the case will be set in the context of the expectations of the official community, which were shaped by officials' experience with administrative punishment. Finally, the emperor's judgment will be assessed, not as an act of capriciousness but as an effort to address concerns of justice within the official community.

Li Shiyao and Privilege in Eighteenth-Century China

Chinese law was acutely, in some views fatally, sensitive to the social circumstances of the crime and the criminal, and few cases were investigated or prosecuted without a clear sense of family and communal influences. Studies of administrative discipline often ignore such circumstances, influenced by the modernist assumption that an individual became an abstract functionary when appointed to office.

But family circumstances crucially affected the Li Shiyao case. Li Shiyao, and other Chinese governors-general inhabited a stratum of Qing officialdom where families were well known and their entitlement to position and privilege well respected. Although most candidate officials entered Qing service through the examination system, climbed a bureaucratic ladder which in theory led from the lowest official post to the highest, the ten governor-general positions were the highest in the Qing territorial service and were entrusted to men whom the court knew, either through long official service, or other sorts of connections. The crimes and punishments of such men were not ordinary transgressions, although their treatment could not be extraordinary: they were visible and powerful representatives of the Son of Heaven.

Li Shiyao had a family connection with Qing rule, but it was not one of a unique sort in Qing China.[1] At the time of the Qing conquest, in the mid-seventeenth century, a political group calling themselves 'Manchus,'

[1] The foregoing is based on four brief accounts of Li Shiyao's life: an epitaph prepared by the Qing government on his death (printed in *Qing shi lie zhuan* 23.12a–23b), a brief reminiscence by a Manchu prince Zhaolian, who served at the court of the Qianlong emperor's successor (*Xiaoting Zalu*, 88), a biography prepared in the early twentieth century by the editors of the Draft History of the Qing, and a 1943 biography in *Eminent Chinese of the Ch'ing* period by Fang Chaoying. The accounts differ systematically in their

incorporating Jurchens, Mongols and Chinese, had been established as the rulers of China. Status within such a group was firmly fixed: one was enrolled hereditarily in one of the twenty-four 'banner armies' (so-called because they were named after the colours of the banners under which they marched) that composed the Manchu establishment. Eight of these banner armies were called 'Manchu banners' and were composed exclusively of Jurchens or sino-Jurchens; eight more armies were composed of Chinese soldiers of the dynasty, and eight armies were composed of its Mongol affiliates. Banner ranks were passed from father to son, and banner records were both genealogical and administrative.[2] While the influence of this social order declined over time, it was still significant in the eighteenth century, and members of the Manchu banners still constituted a significant proportion of the provincial governors and governors-general of Qing China. Li Shiyao's place in this group was well established; his great-grandfather was Li Yongfang, one of the first soldiers of the Ming Dynasty to surrender to the Qing. Yongfang was made a general and married one of the daughters of the founding emperor Nurhaci. His descendants were given hereditary rank in the Chinese Banner Army, when it was created in the 1630s, and devoted their lives to the service of the Qing state. Li Shiyao's father rose to the position of Minister of Revenue during the Qianlong Reign and was made a hereditary noble with the title 'Earl of Zhaoxin.'[3]

To family pedigree was added, in Li Shiyao's case, a certain luck of timing. Li was presented to the Qing court by his father, who employed the privilege of a senior official to place one son in office without the benefit of examinations, in 1736. This was the first year of the reign of the Qianlong Emperor, a moment when the twenty-one-year-old prince sought out companions younger than his father's senior councillors. The two young aristocrats, both great-great-great-grandsons of the founding emperor, almost certainly met and perhaps became friends. The emperor was said to have remarked on meeting Li 'This is one of the most extraordinary talents under heaven.'[4] Promotions followed steadily for Li Shiyao,

emphases: early accounts emphasize Li's accomplishments for the Qing dynasty, while the later accounts emphasize his corruption.

[2] See Mark Elliott, *The Manchu Way: The Eight Banners and Ethnic Identity in Manchu China* (Stanford, 2001), 56–63, 134–138.

[3] *Eminent Chinese of the Ch'ing Period*, 480–481.

[4] Zhaolian, *Xiaoting Zalu*, 88. The emperor was also said to have remarked that 'Li Shiyao cannot be compared to the ordinary Chinese bannerman' when court officials objected to a Chinese being given control of Manchu troops.

to adjutant, lieutenant colonel, and lieutenant general. In 1753, he was appointed commander of the military forces stationed at the imperial hunting palace at Chengde on the southern Mongolian plain. Three years later, Li was appointed as provincial commandant of Guangdong province, and the next year, he served as acting governor-general of Guangdong and Guangxi provinces. After a series of appointments in the capital, during which time his father died and Li inherited the earlship, Li was appointed in 1761 as governor-general of Guangdong and Guangxi, a post he held for eleven years. This was an extraordinarily fast rise in the Qing service, and it left Li in an extremely powerful position. Canton, where Li served, was sufficiently far from Beijing that officials there were accustomed to acting independently; at the same time, it was a posting in which large sums of money, from provincial taxes, international trade, the salt trade and customs revenue, passed through official hands. It was surely one of the most desirable postings in China, which in the eighteenth century usually went to close associates of the emperor.[5]

During this period of Li's official service, he became known for his gifts to the court. Most Qing governors presented annual gifts to the court, originally of local products, but as imperial tastes became sated, of more valuable items. Li's gifts, especially valued by the emperor, were items he acquired from Western merchants in Canton for the tea trade that was growing in importance in the late eighteenth century. Of special interest to the emperor were Western mechanical clocks, especially cuckoo clocks, which are preserved in the collection of the National Palace Museum, Beijing. When Lord MacCartney arrived thirty years later with scientific instruments from Europe, the emperor seemed uninterested, as he put it, because he had already acquired instruments through his agents in Canton.[6]

In 1771, Li Shiyao received the appointment which would nearly prove to be his downfall, as governor-general of the south-western provinces of Yunnan and Guizhou. The posting to the city today known as Kunming was not nearly as desirable as a posting in Canton, but it was in the interest of state. The Qing had made an ill-fated effort to invade Burma in 1768, which bogged down with inconclusive result in the muddy, malaria-infested headwaters of the Irrawaddy River. After this effort, the Burmese

[5] See Robert Marks, *Tigers, Rice Silk and Salt* (Cambridge, 1998), and R. Kent Guy, *Qing Governors and their Provinces: the Evolution of Territorial Administration in China, 1644–1796* (Seattle, 2010), Chapter 9.

[6] *Eminent Chinese of the Ch'ing Period*, 482.

state had suspended contact with the Qing, but in 1771, indications reached the court that the Burmese were willing to present tribute to the Qing empire and engage in trade along the border.[7] The Qianlong Emperor dispatched Li Shiyao with the following comment:

> The post of Yunnan governor-general, who must manage this affair, is a very important one. There are many honest and knowledgeable officials among the governors general who are capable of managing great affairs. But none exceeds Li Shiyao in ability. For this reason I have ordered him transferred to the post. After he reaches Yunnan, I expect that all matters will be handled appropriately. After the borders have been opened to trade, Chinese in the export business should not be allowed to cross them. The ordinary people should not go out to Burma to create disturbances. I have spelled this out in detail in my audiences [with the governor-general][8]

As in Canton, Li Shiyao was in charge of a trade regime, but in Burma he was also a diplomatic representative of the state. The Emperor must have had extraordinary confidence in Li to commit himself to the bannerman so publicly and fully. This comment is quite remarkable as appointments normally were announced by Qing emperors with the terse formula 'X is made Y,' with X and Y being the names of appointee and the post. With his appointment to Yunnan, Li Shiyao had reached a high point of his career. He was entrusted with serious responsibility, admired by the Emperor, respected, and as will be suggested, feared by his subordinates. He occupied a position to which his family background and his personal performance entitled him. It was at this moment that his extortion became known, when a former subordinate on his way to a new position in Manchuria, told friends in Beijing of his experience of governor-general Li.

The Case against Li Shiyao[9]

Accusations of corruption are surely not uncommon in complex political orders, and the Qing, like many comparable states, had formal mechanisms

---

[7] Ironically, Li's appointment may have been based on a misunderstanding of Burmese intentions, see Charles Patterson Giersch, *Asian Borderlands: the Transformation of Qing China's Yunnan Frontier* (Cambridge, 2006), and Alexander Woodside, 'The Ch'ien-lung Reign', in *The Cambridge History of China* Vol. 9 (Cambridge, 2002), 230–309.

[8] *Qing shi lie zhuan*, 23.17a.

[9] 165 extant documents on the Li Shiyao case have been collected and published by the First Historical Archives of China in Volume 1 of their four volume series *Qianlong chao cheng ban tanwu dang'an xuan bian* (A selection of documents concerning the prosecution of official corruption cases during the Qianlong reign (Beijing, 1994)), hereafter *Cheng ban tan wu*.

for handling them. From the point of view of the Qing code there were three phases to a procedure of administrative discipline: impeachment, investigation, and, if the defendant were found guilty, sentencing. Arguably there was also a fourth phase during which the terms of a sentence could be modified; this might be compared to an appellate phase in the West, though of course no Chinese subject had the right to appeal. Cases could be initiated by petition from commoners, routine or secret memorial by an official, or an imperial edict. Once an impeachment document was submitted, the emperor had the right to label the case as routine, serious or very serious.[10] Then an investigation was initiated. Often when the accused was located outside the capital a team of officials from Beijing was sent to the official's posting to look into the charges. When the investigation was complete, the investigators recommended a sentence which was sent to the Three High Courts of Judicature for review, and then to the emperor. After the sentence was announced, it might be modified in one of a variety of ways. The Qing had a system of administrative commendations and demerits, and if one had more commendations than demerits, a sentence could be reduced. Officials could also volunteer to serve in military or administrative capacities without pay, or a sentence could be converted to exile. As Joanna Waley-Cohen has shown, many members of the administration of Xinjiang in the later eighteenth century were exiled officials. Each of these phases was governed by rules, though each was ultimately dependent on the sole source of moral political and legal legitimacy in China, the emperor.[11]

The formal document impeaching Li Shiyao was an imperial edict, which was issued after a fairly lengthy and elaborate process of deliberation and investigation. The source of information for Li's impeachment was Haining, a Manchu official who had served as circuit intendant for grain and salt in Yunnan province. His role in this office was to ride his circuit, Yunnan province, making sure that relief grain supplies were adequate and the state salt monopoly was fairly administered. In the course of these travels he had occasion to visit all the local officials in Yunnan and hear their tales of interaction with the Yunnan governor general. In 1778, Haining was transferred to the post of provincial judge for Gansu, but in 1779 his father died. Under the official mourning rules, Haining gave

[10] *Da Qing Huidian*, 11.5a–6b. On the differences in modes of accusation, see R. Kent Guy, 'Rule of Man and the Rule of Law in China: Punishing Provincial Governors during the Qing', in Karen Gottschang Turner, James V. Feinerman, and R. Kent Guy, ed., *The Limits of the Rule of Law in China* (Seattle, 2000), 88–98.

[11] See Joanna Waley-Cohen, *Exile in Mid-Ch'ing China: banishment to Xinjiang, 1758–1820* (New Haven and London, 1991).

up his post and returned to the capital to honour his father.[12] After his mourning was complete, he was temporarily appointed, until a suitable position in the territorial service became available, to serve as a clerk in the Grand Council. This was the nerve centre of mid-eighteenth-century government, a body which received secret memorials from territorial officials and drafted and dispatched imperial court letters with the emperor's orders throughout the empire.[13] Haining well knew the environment, as he had been a clerk there himself in 1768, as had his father Mingshan who was a clerk in 1754, before he embarked on a territorial career that would see him governing three provinces and serving as governor-general of two jurisdictions. The pattern of service in the Grand Council followed by fairly rapid promotion in the territorial service was a fairly common one for Manchus of good family in the mid-eighteenth century. In an environment which he knew and speaking to people he likely knew, Haining shared his experiences of service in Yunnan, and stories of Li Shiyao's exactions.

It was one thing, however, for a young Manchu official to trade stories with his colleagues in the Grand Council chambers and quite another for the scion of one Manchu family to accuse the leader of one of the more prominent families in the Qing official service of an offense which could lead to expropriation and capital punishment. On two occasions, Haining was summoned to an imperial audience, and asked to repeat his charges against Li Shiyao, and on both occasions he refused.[14] Haining's reluctance to testify against the governor-general was hardly surprising in the social and political environment of the day. Even Haining's former superior, the governor of Yunnan, was so daunted by the prospect of indicting a man who had twenty years in office as a governor-general and the rank of a grand secretary that, as he put it, he was kept awake nights by anxiety, and shed tears of guilt and frustration.[15]

Accusations like Haining's were probably fairly common in the Qing bureaucracy, particularly in the latter eighteenth century when private profits from trade and investment vastly exceeded the remunerations that the state paid its own officials. But such charges had to be given legal

---

[12] All Qing officials were required to resign from office and observe a period of official mourning on the death of a parent. There were, however, two differences between Manchu and Chinese mourning. Where Chinese officials mourned for two and half years, and did so in their native places, Manchus mourned for only six months and did so in Beijing.

[13] 'Guo shi guan ben zhuan', in *Guo chao qi xian lei zheng*, 173.37b.

[14] *Cheng ban tan wu*, 986.

[15] Ibid., 966.

standing by the Emperor before they could be acted upon. It was one of the general rules of the Great Qing Code that:

> In all cases where high and low officials in the capital or outside commit offenses ... the superior official having jurisdiction will send a memorial under seal with a statement of the facts, requesting a rescript. He may not himself, without authorization, proceed with the interrogation.[16]

The purpose of such a rule was to prevent officials from initiating proceedings against each other without imperial approval: the monarch was placed firmly in control of administrative discipline. In Li Shiyao's case, the Grand Council sent a memorial to the emperor formally accusing Li Shiyao of corruption. Ultimately, the Qianlong Emperor decided that even without Haining's public testimony, there was enough evidence to launch an investigation of Li Shiyao, and secretly dispatched a two-man team to Kunming.

The historical interpretation of the case against Li would be considerably easier if the emperor had not appointed his protégé, Chief Grand Councillor Heshen to lead the investigation team to Yunnan. A Manchu poet and bodyguard, Heshen was married to one of the Qianlong Emperor's daughters, and rose rapidly in the emperor's esteem during the 1770s, finally becoming chief grand councillor in 1777.[17] In this role he earned the hatred of many of his fellow officials, and many historians since, for his extraordinary greed. At the time of his execution by the Qianlong Emperor's successor, Heshen was said to be the richest man in the world, owning real estate all over the capital city of Beijing as well as an extraordinary collection of silver, gold, jade silk and art objects. Heshen's wealth fascinated nineteenth-century historians, who published a catalogue of the objects seized when Heshen was executed; and in the twentieth century his life has been seen as an example of the sort of decadent corruption that brought the Qing empire to its knees. Although Heshen's wealth has been amply documented, the ways he acquired it have not, nor perhaps can they ever be since he was above all an actor behind the scenes. There has been a tendency to assume the hand of Heshen was beyond anything questionable happening in the later years of the eighteenth century; further, assuming that Heshen was the basic cause of the empire's downfall, few have made the attempt to determine

---

[16] William C. Jones, *The Great Qing Code* (Oxford, 1994), 40.

[17] One of the best accounts of Heshen's rise is Li Jingbing and Kang Guochang, *Qianlong, Heshen yu Liu Yong*, 1–96.

his role in various affairs. Such a task is central, however, if the legalities of his actions are to be established.

The working assumption in at least two accounts of the case has been that Heshen was behind the case, manoeuvring to unseat Li and seize his property. Writing in 1943, the Australian historian Fang Chaoying asserted that the Li Shiyao case 'smacks of collusion, for Haining, on whose testimony Li was convicted, at first declined to give evidence against Li, but laid stress on Li's ability as an administrator. Yet when subjected by imperial command to 'severe questioning' he finally testified that Li accepted gifts from his subordinates, and had sold them, 'some pearls'.[18] Although he clearly suspects some skulduggery, Fang does not indicate who was colluding with whom, and to what end. Nancy Elizabeth Park in her dissertation 'Corruption and Its Recompense: Bribes, Bureaucracy and the Law in Late Imperial China' reifies the accusation, asserting that Heshen 'instigated the former grain intendant Haining to bring charges of bribery and embezzlement against Li Shiyao.' Park's case is strengthened by the information, drawn from the account of Korean visitors to the Qing court, that Heshen had a grudge against Li Shiyao.[19] There was no direct evidence of collaboration between Heshen and Haining, and as the subsequent investigation of the case demonstrated, there was ample evidence of Li's corruption. There is no reason to approach the case as anything more than the revelation of the activities of a corrupt official, an inevitable result of the professional mobility of Chinese territorial servants like Haining, who carried stories with them from post to post.

It does seem likely that Heshen had a role in the case, and in fact in the end Heshen did personally profit from the charges against Li. However, it was likely that the role Heshen played in the beginning was the natural role of a chief grand councillor, that of bringing secret information to the emperor and assisting him in his formulation of a response. Nor was it particularly unusual that Heshen was assigned to travel to Yunnan to investigate the case. This was a fairly common assignment for grand councillors. In fact, one of Heshen's most distinguished and revered predecessors, Liu Tongxun, had made his reputation as a severe and incorruptible administrator investigating corruption cases in the provinces.[20] Heshen may himself have desired the role, not only because he stood to make

18 *Eminent Chinese of the Ch'ing Period*, 483.

19 Nancy Elizabeth Park, 'Corruption and its Recompense: Bribes, Bureaucracy, and the Law in Late Imperial China' (PhD dissertation, Harvard University, 1993), 123.

20 On Liu Tongxun's role as investigator, see Guy, *Qing Governors and Their Provinces*, chapter 4. Liu's specialty was cases involving corruption among Manchu officials.

profit in the case, but because it raised his stature in the political world to play the same investigative role as his predecessor. It was also likely that as an official traveller representing the emperor, he would be feted and gifted throughout his journey all the way across China by officials anxious to secure their place at court.

Investigation and Initial Sentencing

In the event, it was not Heshen's investigation that cracked the case, but the investigative powers of the Qing bureaucracy. The process involved a combination of secrecy and openness. When the Qianlong Emperor dispatched an investigative team to Yunnan, he decreed that the investigation be regarded as top secret, and all early communications with the investigators were by court letter, a type of edict drafted by the Grand Council, and meant only for the eyes of the recipient. These orders were issued in order to prevent Li Shiyao and his far-flung minions from learning of the charges against him and coordinating their testimony or hiding the evidence. But such orders did not mean the case was to be kept secret among Li's contemporaries whose investigative resources would be needed to establish the truth of the charges. Shortly after dispatching the investigators, the court sent a letter to Li Hu, the governor of Hunan, which lay along the most logical route from Yunnan to the capital, asking him to apprehend any messengers traveling from Beijing to Kunming, to prevent them from tipping off the governors.[21] In fairly short order, Li Hu found two such messengers, who were carrying memorials bearing imperial comments back from the capital to Yunnan. As it developed, they had left Beijing before the charges against Li Shiyao were revealed, and so had no idea that the governor-general was under indictment. They did, however, testify that on their way to Beijing they had carried significant amounts of cash and several art objects and precious stones from the governor-general's servant in Kunming to his major-domo in the capital.[22] When the court received this information, the order was given to arrest Li's major domo in the capital. But by this time word of Li's indictment had leaked.[23] Both the man and his assistant had fled, so that orders had

[21] *Cheng ban tan wu*, Vol. 1, 939.
[22] Ibid., 943.
[23] Ibid., 973. The word apparently leaked when two of Li's servants carrying memorials to the capital learned of the charges against their master while they were on the road.

to be given to the governor-general of Zhili, the area surrounding the capital, and the governor of Shandong, the nearest province, to arrest the two men. Then it developed that the precious stones and art objects had been dispatched from Beijing for sale in the wealthy lower Yangzi valley, where it was assumed they would fetch the best price.[24] The full tale of the pursuit of Li's wealth is beyond the scope of the current account, but it serves to highlight vividly the geography of corruption in mid-Qing China. Items were received, transferred, sold and distributed throughout the empire, carried by official and semi-official messengers along the dusty byways of empire, through a network of individuals so wide that it required the effort of an entire bureaucratic order to uncover. This meant that no case could be kept secret among senior officials, and every charge could be the topic of conversations in the inns and postal stations where traveling messengers and subordinate officials changed horses and spent the night on the journeys they made to carry out their superiors' orders.

The interrogation of the two representatives of Governor-general Li who were apprehended in Hunan led to the identification of one Zhang Yongshou, a Chinese bondservant, as the individual responsible for collecting and disbursing money on Li's behalf. Heshen soon received orders to arrest and interrogate Zhang, and it was this interrogation that finally provided conclusive evidence against the governor-general.[25]

Zhang reported that he had collected gifts for his superior from six subordinate officials. The intendant of the Yinan circuit in south-central Yunnan had given the governor-general 2000 *liang*, the Prefect of Dongquan Fu had given 4000 *liang*, the magistrate of the district surrounding the provincial capital, Kunming, had provided 2000 *liang*, the provincial judge had given 5000 *liang*, and a sixth official whose position was not identified had provided 3000 *liang*. The gift of the Yinan circuit intendant was specifically identified as a present made in order to secure the governor-general's support for a recommendation for appointment, and one prefect and the Kunming magistrate were in posts that could be filled only on the recommendation of provincial leaders. Once these names were revealed, the emperor ordered the territorial officials of their home districts to investigate their circumstances and property, thus spreading word of the case further among the territorial bureaucracy. Orders were also given to investigate former governors of Yunnan and Guizhou, who

[24] Ibid., 993–4.
[25] Ibid., 976.

were likely to have known of or participated in the pattern of corruption in the southwest.

Zhang Yongshou's testimony may not have revealed the full extent of Li Shiyao's corruption, but it revealed enough. Punishments for official corruption in the Qing code were based on the amount of revenue a corrupt official collected, and the 16,000 liang which officials of Yunnan acknowledged giving to the governor-general far exceeded the amount necessary to assess the most severe penalty possible in the corruption statute. Once this threshold was reached, it became possible to formally charge Li with corruption, which was done in an imperial edict on 23 March 1780.[26] In this edict, Li was formally dismissed from office and ordered to return to the capital for interrogation. Although this was the first formal announcement of the case, the emperor had earlier ordered several officials to stand by for immediate transfer to the southwest to take up Li's duties. Once these formal charges were made, it became the duty of Heshen as chief investigator to recommend punishment for the governor-general. While the Qing code had an extortion statute, Heshen felt that it would be more appropriate to charge Li under a statute devoted to official theft. Under this law, those found guilty of stealing more than 1000 liang were liable to a sentence of execution, after the autumn assizes.[27]

The crucial phrase in this sentence, which would subsequently engender so much controversy, was 'after the autumn assizes.' It was the Chinese practice to conduct executions in the autumn season, to preserve harmony with nature: the son of heaven would kill at the same time heaven was killing so the human and the natural worlds would be synchronized. Those death sentences not executed at the autumn assizes were put aside for at least a year, during which time sentences could be appealed and changed.[28] In fact, few of those ordered executed after the autumn assizes were killed at all; most had sentences reduced or were set free. The issue was not merely the time that was needed to consider a sentence thoroughly. As Li Shiyao's sentence was recommended in the spring, the Emperor and the court would have had several months to consider his guilt and the fairness of his punishment. The sentence of

[26] Ibid., 982.

[27] The document in which Heshen sentenced Li is not extant. The wording here is reconstructed from quotations in the memorials of provincial governors who reflected on the sentence. To my infinite frustration I cannot find the statute under which Li was charged, Morohashii Tetsuji, *Dai Kanwa Jiten*, Vol 1, 770 (entry 646.69) indicates that there was such a statute in the 'Granaries and Treasures' Section of the Ming code. Derk

[28] Derk Bodde and Clarence Morris, *Law in Imperial China: exemplified by 190 Ch'ing Dynasty cases* (Cambridge, 1967), 134–143.

execution after the autumn assizes was not merely a call for temporal delay, it was a different punishment. When anyone, particularly an official, was ordered killed 'after the autumn assizes' it meant in practice that they had been found guilty of a capital offense, but were unlikely to be executed. Li's initial sentence, therefore, was one which did not seem to call on him to pay the supreme price for his crime. This fact engendered comment and probably criticism from the official community, who had their own experiences of punishment, pardon and corruption

Administrative Punishment and Official Life

Administrative discipline was a constant of official life in eighteenth-century China, with nearly every official encountering it at some point in his career, and many carrying penalties with them as they went from office to office. Corporal or capital punishments were much rarer, though not unheard-of, and reserved for officials who were perceived to have grossly violated the moral order on which the Chinese empire was based. Considering the departures from office of the senior territorial officials who occupied the post of provincial governor in China provides some evidence of the statistical frequency of administrative discipline in the eighteenth century. The appointments and departures of these men were announced by imperial edicts published in the *Veritable Records of the Qing Dynasty*. In 1982, scholars at Beijing University published an index to the personnel edicts in this enormous collection, making it feasible to collect statistical information about modes of appointment and departure from office. Altogether, 532 individuals were appointed to the 14 provincial governorships during the Qianlong reign (1736–1796). Just over 21%, or 110 of these governors, left office through one of the four modes of departure linked to administrative discipline, a number nearly equal to the number who left office through promotion (113). The remaining governors left office through lateral transfer to another governorship (235, 44%) or because of illness, death, or the required period of official mourning to mark the death of a parent (74, 14%).[29]

[29] The numbers here are those from a computer-assisted count of the appointments recorded in *Qing dai zhi guan nian biao*, which I made in the summer of 1990, with grants from the National Endowment for Humanities and the Jackson School of International Studies, University of Washington.

The four modes of dismissal that were linked to administrative discipline were cashiering, demotion, relief from responsibility and summons to the capital. Cashiering represented the conclusion of a formal process in which an individual was indicted, investigated, and found guilty; during the Qianlong reign, 52 governors were cashiered. Demotion involved the same disciplinary process, but represented a less serious punishment, and only 16 individuals were demoted during the reign. Relieving an official of his responsibilities in effect deferred the investigation to a later date; moreover, the procedure allowed the court to appoint a successor for the indicted official without going through a formal process. Summons to court most often occurred during wartime, when the emperor or his counsellors wanted to consult with a field commander, or change one, without formal proceeding. Thirty-one governors were relieved of responsibility during the Qianlong reign, and eleven were summoned to the court.

For several reasons, these numbers probably understate significantly the number of officials who experienced administrative discipline. The system addressed a multitude of administrative failings and included a wide range of sanctions, only some of which involved dismissal from office. Alongside the system existed a parallel structure of commendations which allowed officials who had previously been honoured to cancel out any sanctions. Many remained in office 'carrying' their burdens of their guilt with them, though in some cases, they had committed infractions that in theory should have brought about their dismissal. The fact, for instance that many fewer people left office through demotion than cashiering did not necessarily mean that minor infractions were less frequent than major ones; it meant merely that many of those sentenced to demotion remained in office while they served their term of punishment. A second, sobering reflection on administrative discipline is that the 532 governor appointments in the Qianlong reign were held by 229 individuals, with the typical governor appointed to two or three different provinces. It is likely then that the 110 dismissals affected nearly half of the officials who were appointed.

Statistical surveys have, of course, a problematic relation to mentalities, but it seems likely that the prospect of discipline was ever on the minds of Qing officials, and that few could have reached high office without contact with it. Thomas Metzger in his analyses of the administrative discipline system of late-imperial China has seen frequent disciplinary actions as part of the late-imperial state's effort to foster a 'probationary ethic' among its officials, a sense that their efforts were constantly being measured against moral ideals. Implicitly, he compares Chinese officials to

Max Weber's tormented capitalist Protestant, who needed constantly to judge his conduct against a higher standard.[30] There is certain plausibility to this argument, particular in view of the many sanctions involved in official life and the language of personal guilt that resonates through confessions and the documents of punishments in Qing China. The argument weakens in the face of the realities of the late eighteenth century, a world in which many senior officials were enmeshed in a far-flung geography of corruption, engaging in it in spite of the ever-present possibility of punishment. Their behaviour can only be explained if, in addition to the possibility of sanction, the possibility of forgiveness, or in the Chinese phrasing of it, 'imperial grace' is considered. Indeed the uncertainty of imperial grace, or forgiveness, was probably as troubling to Chinese officials, as the uncertainly of heavenly grace was to early modern Protestants. The difference was, of course, that Chinese officials could see quite plainly who had been forgiven, and who was condemned. The question perhaps should not be who was punished, but who was forgiven, or perhaps more powerfully phrased, who was not forgiven in Qing China.

The most obvious group of officials who were not forgiven in Qing China were those who were in fact executed for their misdeeds. Among governors, this was a fairly small group whose cases were well known, the object perhaps of a terrified fascination among an officialdom who were aware of their guilt and implicitly relying on pardon. One of the most striking characteristics of the list of governors who were actually executed was that eleven of the thirteen were Manchus. This represented a disproportionate number of Manchus: Manchus constituted approximately a third of the men appointed as governor during the Qianlong reign but, because they were more likely to serve repeat terms than their Chinese counterparts, they accounted for nearly half of the appointments. The reasons for their over-representation among those executed were probably many. Manchus may have been more corrupt than their Chinese colleagues, although in the absence of quantitative information that is almost impossible to obtain, comparisons of degrees of venality are problematic. More likely, Manchus had reason to expect that because of their status they would be forgiven for their misdeeds. If so, this was a misreading of the changing attitudes in the eighteenth-century court toward Manchu legitimacy. In the decades immediately following the conquest, Manchu

---

30 Thomas A. Metzger, *The Internal Organization of Ch'ing Bureaucracy: Legal, Normative, and Communication Aspects* (Cambridge, 1973), 400–404 and *Escape From Predicament: Neo Confucianism and China's Evolving Political Culture* (New York, 1977), 170–176.

activities were less questioned by the Qing court: territorial servants and the emperor were united by their common heritage and faced a dauntingly large Chinese population of uncertain loyalty; fiscal peccadilloes were often tolerated. In the eighteenth century, as Pamela Crossley has argued, the Qing court relied more on appeals to universal values to justify its existence, values which Manchus as well as Chinese could transgress.[31] In this context, much was expected from those to whom much had been given, and the transgressions of Manchus who acted as if entitled to forgiveness needed to be treated with special severity. It was also the case that all Manchus were bound to their monarch by special ties; hereditary servants of a state defined by war and the hunt, a fact that may have made it more acceptable to ask of them the supreme sacrifice.

The Qianlong emperor's use of execution only for certain criminals or crimes resonated with the practices of late-imperial China's great lawgiving emperor, the first emperor of the Ming. In their study of China's most severe punishment, *Death by a Thousand Cuts*, Timothy Brook, Gregory Blue and Jerome Bourgon argue that Ming Taizu used the supreme punishment in very particular ways. In fact, they note that the emperor ordered individuals killed whose crime would not, according to the letter of the law, have required capital punishment. Common to the cases where the ultimate penalty was ordered, in their view, were a 'feeling of personal betrayal' on the emperor's part, and a sense that 'justice had been perverted.'[32] They note, however, that the emperor's concern seems not to have been with the perversion of justice in the abstract, but that, absent serious punishments for the cases in question, individuals could not be held accountable, and the legitimacy of the dynasty was called into question. Given such a model from the emperor who was responsible for writing the law code that served as the basis for all late-imperial codes, it is not surprising that the Qianlong emperor felt entitled to carry out the sentence of execution primarily in those cases in which his fellow Manchus had violated the law. This finding however, renders the case of Li Shiyao even more interesting, for his status in the Qing order was somewhat ambiguous. As a bannerman, he shared with the executed Manchu governors the special status that distinguished him from fellow bureaucrats. On the other hand, he was a *Chinese* bannerman, whose execution

---

[31] See Pamela Kyle Crossley, *The Translucent Mirror: History and Identity in Qing Imperial Ideology* (Berkeley, 1999), 217–280.

[32] Timothy Brook, Gregory Blue and Jérôme Bourgon, *Death by a Thousand Cuts* (Cambridge, 2008), 113–114.

would strike a family that had historically stood for loyalty to the state. Were his and his family's loyal services to the dynasty sufficient to allow him leeway to act in a rather corrupt world? Or was he to be measured by the special standard that entitlement entailed in Qing China and punished severely for his transgressions? This is the question which the Qianlong Emperor posed to his officials in an edict of May, 1780.

Controlling the Reaction

Corruption is not only a serious problem in administrative orders. It is an incendiary charge, evoking moral passions and political and social indignation. This was particularly true in the Chinese empire, where officials heard of charges at second hand but had direct and in some cases painfully personal experiences of administrative discipline and, facing the same challenges as indicted colleagues, had to make decisions daily about their own behaviour. In such an environment, the Qianlong court had not only to judge charges, but also to control their interpretation and the lessons other officials drew from indictments. Two months after the initial recommendation of sentence for Li Shiyao, the Emperor took the very unusual step of asking, indeed requiring, Li's contemporaries to comment on his sentence. There was no statutory provision for such commentary. As the emperor described the matter, his edict was occasioned by official protest at the capital against the leniency of Li's sentence; the text of the edict also made it clear that recipients were meant to reflect on corruption in their own postings.

Those who objected to the sentence likely took their cue from an edict the emperor issued the day after he had ordered Li Shiyao dismissed from office.[33] The edict was intended to be cautionary. The emperor urged all those who served in territorial positions to avoid even the suggestion of corruption and to implement an administration of genuine benefit to the population. The edict noted that officials had recently seen many of their contemporaries punished for corruption and encouraged serving officials to take such cases to heart.[34] Officials' attention was particularly called to the case of Governor-general Hengwen, one of Li Shiyao's predecessors

[33] *Cheng ban tan wu*, Vol. 1, 987.

[34] Here the emperor noted four cases: those of Liangqing (1769), Jiang Zhou (1757), Qian Du (1771) and Gao Pu (1771). Documents on these four cases are collected in Volume I of *Cheng ban tan wu*, 1–937.

as governor-general in the southwest, who had been found guilty and executed for extorting money from his subordinates, and ordering them to buy gold for him at artificially low prices.[35] The case against Li Shiyao, the emperor observed, was even more serious than that against Hengwen, and so officials needed to pay especial attention to it.

It was a cardinal principle of Chinese justice that sentences of capital punishment rendered by investigators should be reviewed in the capital by senior officials and those responsible for consistency in judicial actions. When Li's sentence was reviewed, it was challenged. The group responsible for this challenge was likely to have involved a fairly broad spectrum of senior officials. By law death sentences were to be reviewed by representatives from the Three High Courts of Judicature. These were the Board of Punishments, whose duty it was to record sentences and assure consistency, the Censorate, which monitored the activity of Chinese officials, and the Court of Judicature and Revision, a small, free-standing organization overseen by the grand secretariat.[36] The Three High Courts' opinion in Li's case was joined by a group referred to as the nine lords (*jiu qing*). In the early years of the Qing, there were in fact nine specific individuals who had the responsibility of advising the throne, but by the Qianlong reign, this term seemed to have no longer referred to specific individuals, but rather more generically to the emperor's senior counsellors.

The conclusion that capital officials drew from the emperor's edict to governors on the Li case, logical enough under the circumstances, was that if Li Shiyao's case was more serious than Hengwen's, his punishment should be no less severe. Since Hengwen had been executed, Li Shiyao should be as well, rather than being given the opportunity for pardon that a sentence of execution after the autumn assizes would afford. Court officials argued that to sentence Li under the law for theft of items over 1000 liang was 'fooling with the law (fu yu fa)', and while they did not suggest another law under which Li could be sentenced, they made it clear that the outcome should be his death.[37] It is of course possible that jealousy of Li Shiyao's rapid rise to power or resentment of his often attested arrogance influenced the protest against his sentence. But even without these

[35] On the Hengwen case, see Park, 'Corruption and its Recompense', 166–171, and *Cheng ban tan wu*, Vol. I, 1–66.

[36] See R. Kent Guy, 'The Central Court', Stanley N. Katz, *The Oxford International Encyclopedia of Legal History, Vol. 2* (Oxford, 2009), 242–243.

[37] The three high courts' response to Li's sentence is not extant. The wording here is reconstructed from quotations of the document. See note 25 above.

additional factors, the nine lords and three high courts had a point. Justice in this instance seemed to require consistency.

The emperor responded to this challenge to Li's sentence with an edict issued on the 19th of June, 1780.[38] The argument of the edict was divided into three parts. In the first, the monarch presented his view of the case against Li Shiyao, and the reasons for his eminence:

> Li Shiyao is one of the most distinguished of those who have served as governor and governor-general. For this reason, I have appointed him with the rank of grand secretary for ten years. He has received our repeated generosity. I would never have imagined him guilty of the sorts of corruption in this case: the extortion of items worth tens of thousands of *liang*, requiring officials to buy pearls from him at inflated prices and then demanding they return these items to him as tribute, or extorting a payment of 8000 *liang* to reinstate an impeached official to his post.

The sharp contrast between Li's previous privilege and his present corruption set the tone for the edict; what was at stake was as much the wisdom of the repeated appointments and honours conferred on Li as his present punishment. Instead of tipping his hand on the issue of punishment, however, the emperor pushed the argument in an unexpected direction. The charges against Li were sufficiently severe as to force the emperor to question the paradigm of trust under which all territorial officials served:

> Now, I cannot guarantee that there are not others who buy items at reduced prices, or perhaps demand them without payment. Li Shiyao's corruption and private pursuit of wealth so exceeds my imagining that it has become impossible for me to trust any governor.... Each governor and governor-general should examine himself thoroughly. Let no one say that he didn't look carefully enough or made a quick calculation of his own advantage. In brief: if there is corruption, reform it; if there is none, be diligent. Keep a sharp eye and a cautious temperament. The goodness of heaven lies in this.

In a world where politics was modelled on interpersonal relations, the emperor's claim that he could trust no governors was both remarkable and ominous. There is reason to believe it was not merely rhetorical. Very likely corruption was indeed widespread in the eighteenth century. The growth of the Chinese economy provided territorial officials with temptations and opportunities beyond previous imaginings, and surely Haining was not the only official who reported to the court that officials were on

[38] *Cheng ban tan wu*, Vol. I, 1067.

the take. Moreover, the emperor probably had fewer bonds with the governors of the 1770s than he had with earlier territorial officials. Many of the territorial officials the emperor knew well had passed from the scene in the late 1760s, and the early 1770s had seen a new generation of individuals rise to higher territorial office. There may well have been few the emperor could trust, and many whom he suspected may have been guilty, if the corruption prosecutions of the 1780s were any guide.

Governors were charged to engage in a period of self-reflection, and the outgrowth of this was to be a recommendation on Li Shiyao's sentence. In the conclusion to the edict, the emperor required all officials to comment on Li Shiyao's sentence in light of their reflections: let each weigh Heshen's recommendation that Li Shiyao be sentenced to execution following the autumn assizes, and the grand secretaries' and nine lords' recommendation that it be changed to immediate execution. 'Let each set forth his views in a memorial. There can be no equivocation'. Governors were also requested to inform the emperor how they went about purchasing items within their jurisdiction.

This edict certainly did not constitute an effort to turn Li's case over to a jury of his peers. Nor did the emperor need to secure advice of other governors on the case in the southwest. The emperor had the authority to pardon or for that matter execute Li without any concurrence whatsoever. Rather than seeking advice the purpose of the emperor's edict seems to have been to harness the discursive power of corruption and turn it toward the ends of the court. It was an attempt to turn discussion of the case, which must have been occurring in all the offices of the empire, away from the question of what Li Shiyao did to the possibility that all might be involved in a broad culture of corruption which could exist only because of imperial trust and the willingness of the emperor to forgive. Faced with such a question, few could or did argue for leniency. Of the nineteen extant replies to the edict, only one argued for the more lenient sentence.

Two Legal Arguments

Two of the responses are of particular interest, one urging severity by the Governor of Jiangsu, Wu Tan, and the sole argument for leniency written by the Governor of Anhui, Min Eyuan. Wu Tan's argument was not unique; it paralleled in form and substance the comments of most of his fellow senior territorial officials. What made Wu's brief interesting was that of all the governors in office in the 1780s he probably knew the most about law. Tan, his brothers and his father had all served on the Board of Punishments, shuffling back and forth between the capital and the provinces. Wu Tan's father had been the compiler of the Qianlong edition of the Qing code, and Wu Tan himself had written one of the most popular eighteenth-century commentaries on the code.[39] But in spite of, or perhaps in an ironic way because of, Wu's background in the law, he was inclined to approach the case in moral terms. Given his many advantages and repeated appointment to office, Wu argued, if Li had any self-respect he would have conducted himself in a proper manner. Instead he had been corrupt and so earned the hatred of his fellow officials. Comparing Heshen's sentence with that of the nine lords and three courts, Wu declared that Heshen's sentence was in accord with the law, whereas the revised sentence was in accord with circumstance.[40]

There were thus two elements in Wu's response, the argument that the law was inadequate, and the argument that circumstances, or sentiment, would provide a better basis for sentencing. One respect in which existing law was inadequate in the Li Shiyao case involved the amount of corrupt revenue that the law envisioned an official would realize. The most severe punishment for theft was for an official who received more than 1000 *liang*, but Li Shiyao had received tens of thousands of *liang*. The statute was in this respect somewhat dated, having been drafted in the reign of the first Ming emperor Zhu Yuanzhang (1368–1399), when the economy was less developed. It seems unlikely, however, that this was what Wu Tan meant in his comment about Li's sentence. As Wu Tan well knew and had written in his commentary, the Qing was able to change its statutes as needed. The statute on extortion, for instance, had been revised numerous times in the eighteenth century. Some of the most interesting revisions, in fact, involved the corruption of officials from the southwest, where Li served. In the late Ming, a sub-statute was added about corruption on military expeditions to the southwest, and during the Yongzheng reign, another sub-statute was added to prevent officials from extorting revenues from indigenous peoples as they regularized governmental forms in the region. Neither of these sub-statutes dealt with the particular kind of corruption in which Li was engaged, though they showed that the region where he

39 *Qing shi gao*, 4253. Wu's commentary is published in a recent edition, entitled *Da qing luli tong kao jiao ju* (Beijing, 1991).
40 *Cheng ban tan wu*, Vol. 1, 1074–77.

served was one where corruption was rampant.[41] Left in its Ming form, the statute made the point that any amount of revenue corruptly gained would subject an official to criminal punishment, a point which was well worth preserving, even as the amounts and modes of corruption changed.

Wu Tan's point was probably not that the text of the law was inadequate, but that the crime Li committed was so serious that it could not be judged within the formal context of law. The proper context, in his view, was that of *qing*, which is translated above, provisionally and for convenience as 'circumstance'. In fact, this word had a fairly wide range of meanings in late-imperial China from 'circumstance' to 'sentiment' or 'emotion'. The view that *qing* was important in political and social affairs was part of a growing recognition in sixteenth- and seventeenth-century China that Song Dynasty Neo-Confucianism, which divided the world into principle and psycho-physical stuff and focused the scholar's attention securely on principle, was too rigid as a basis for political and social affairs. Human sentiments, philosophers would argue, needed to be taken into consideration in judgments if they were to be correct.[42] Wu's comments also probably reflected a long-standing Chinese suspicion that written law could never fully incorporate all the contingencies that should properly be involved in legal judgments. This was not to say that law was useless; indeed Wu had devoted his life to its interpretation and preservation. But it could only provide an outline, a direction, which needed to be further modified if justice were to be achieved. In the Li Shiyao case, consideration of circumstances led Wu to recommend the more serious sentence, that of immediate execution.

Ironically, the sole governor who supported the more lenient sentence for Li, Min Eyuan, governor of Anhui, also called on circumstance rather than the law to support his argument. Like Wu, Min was a legal expert. After taking his *jinshi*, the highest civil service degree in 1745, he had served for sixteen years on the Board of Punishments. But after this service, he served for nineteen years in provincial administration as provincial judge and lieutenant governor of four provinces before being appointed as governor of Anhui.[43] He thus combined legal knowledge with fairly extensive administrative experience. From his perspective the case looked somewhat different. Acknowledging that Li had certainly violated the trust

[41] *Da qing luli tong kao jiao ju*, 905–924, see esp. 919.

[42] On 'qing' in eighteenth-century politics, see William Rowe, *Saving the World: Chen Hongmou and Elite Consciousness in Eighteenth Century China* (Stanford, 2001), 103–105.

[43] *Qing shi gao*, 4269–70.

placed in him by the emperor, Min went on to suggest that 'It may be the ritual vessels are out of order.' This was a classical allusion, referring to the possibility that a problem of administration was systemic, rather than individual. If so, Min suggested, this may have been why the emperor could not guarantee that others had not engaged in corruption. Delicately repeating the emperor's double negatives back to him, Min seemed to recognize that the emperor was not as concerned about Li's sentencing as about corruption among other governors. Min went on to argue that Li was a man of real accomplishment, much admired by his fellow officials. Then, the Anhui governor made a claim that seemed irrelevant to the arguments he was making. Weak and incompetent governors, he wrote, try to talk their way out of punishment and evade the law, whereas the strong and competent acknowledge their fault quickly and accept the consequences. There seemed to be no direct circumstance Min could have be referring here, except perhaps one. Governor Hengwen, the predecessor of Li who had been sentenced to execution, in fact claimed that he was extorting money from his subordinates in order to provide tribute gifts for the emperor, a claim that in effect linked his own corruption to the emperor's receipt of tribute gifts. Li Shiyao made no such claim, in fact there is no indication in the extant record that Li attempted to exonerate himself at all.[44]

In view of Li's many accomplishments, and the fact that he had not tried to manoeuver his way out of punishment, Min argued that Li's sentence could in fact be reduced. The third article of the Qing code, as he noted, specified eight categories of persons whose cases should be especially considered. Dating from the Wei Dynasty in the sixth century, a moment when China was governed largely by a hereditary aristocracy, who imposed their particular stamp on the form of dynastic affairs, this statute provided that the sentences of individuals in eight categories should be especially reviewed by the emperor. Among those cases deserving special consideration were cases involving relatives, old servants of the emperor, those who had great merit, the virtuous, those with great ability, those who are industrious, those with high rank, and those who are regarded as guests (i.e. foreigners, or descendants of former dynasties who have been received as guests of the nation.).[45] Urging that Li Shiyao

---

[44] *Cheng ban tan wu*, Vol. 1, 1091–1093.

[45] Jones, *The Great Qing Code*, 36–38, *Da qing luli tong k'ao jiao ju*, 206–07.

was both industrious and able, Min argued that his case should merit special consideration and be reduced.

The remarkable element common to both Wu's and Min's arguments was that in deciding on the punishment of Li Shiyao, the emperor was obligated to ignore the letter of the law. Li's status—either the fact that he had enjoyed repeated appointments from the emperor, or that having received privilege he had the audacity to violate the law, or that he was a particularly industrious and competent servant of the dynasty—entitled him to special consideration. Moreover, because of his special status, punishing Li according to the law would be, in fact, unjust. The question of whether capital punishment can ever be just or whether it is always, in the parlance of American law, cruel and unusual perhaps can never be conclusively resolved. But it must have taken special form in China, where law was carried out in the name of morality. Precisely because the Qing Empire claimed the authority to execute its subjects on moral grounds, it could not afford to carry out an execution that was deemed to be immoral. Li Shiyao's sentence could be determined only by the son of heaven, who had the ultimate responsibility for determining Heaven's will.

It all came down to the emperor, who rendered his decision in the autumn of 1780, after receiving advice through what must surely have been, for Li Shiyao, a long hot summer. Li's case was a very serious one, the emperor wrote, not to be compared with the case of an earlier governor whose servants practiced extortion at a moment when he was too old and sick to object. But it was also not to be compared to that of Hengwen, who in the emperor's view had not accumulated the record of distinguished service that Li had. Moreover, there was Li's family history of distinguished service to the dynasty to be considered, along with the fact that his ancestors had pledged their allegiance at a critical moment in the dynasty's history. Many officials had rendered honest judgment that Li Shiyao be executed immediately. But it was Min Eyuan's memorial that seemed to the emperor most correct, and the eight categories of those who received special consideration to be the most relevant statute. Li was sentenced to execution after the autumn assizes.

Conclusion

The enormous multi-ethnic, multi-confessional and multi-lingual imperial polities of the early modern world had their own political needs and dynamics. Territorial government in such enormous states depended not on the enforcement of a set of written rules, although of course there were such rules. But rules could hardly be formulated that would be universally applicable in such diverse polities. Rather, central rulers had to rely on the judgment and moral compass of those who were appointed as officials. In the worst case, the actions of incompetent or venal local officials provoked sufficient opposition that actions needed to be taken at the central level. But short of such a worst case much had to rest on trust and violations of trust, and judgments of their significance were personal. Li Shiyao's personal and family histories were probably as widely known among late-imperial Chinese officialdom as were the circumstances of his corruption. The details of his punishment would also have been known, and had enormous implications for the relationships of other officials, both the large number of investigators who followed the path of Li's ill-gotten gain through the empire, and others who learned of the case through the edicts published in the imperial gazette. From the court's point of view, the impact of Li's case on this community was at least as important as the implications for Li himself. It was more important to use the case to force officials to reflect on their own corruption than it was to execute Li.

Was the emperor's judgment just? The testimony of eighteen of the nineteen people who responded to the emperor's edict was that it was not. However, they were not responding as a jury to evidence, but answering to an implicit imperative to reflect on the issue of corruption in the Qing state. Li Shiyao had been put in a position of great authority, and on the whole he had fulfilled the court's expectations. Moreover his family's history entitled him to some special consideration; just as Chinese were liable to collective punishment under the Qing code so the members of a collectivity were allowed to benefit from their relatives' accomplishments. Corruption most certainly had to be condemned, but the corrupt official could be pardoned, particularly when his pardon might serve some purpose for the state. From the imperial point of view, a live but chastened Li Shiyao represented a more just outcome than the repudiation of nearly forty years of honours.

In fact, the case may well have been meant to serve as a signal to the community, which was left reflecting, uncomfortably perhaps, on the pervasiveness of corruption rather than celebrating the execution of a scapegoat. If the outcome in the case was meant to be a signal, it was one easily misread. Within five years, three of the nineteen governors who argued for Li Shiyao's immediate execution were themselves executed on corruption charges, and the Qing state embarked on one of the most massive corruption cases in its history, the investigation of the sale of offices in Gansu. After a brief time in prison and several years of service in the military in Xinjiang, Li was returned to his original rank and was involved in the Gansu prosecution, in which ironically enough Min Eyuan's son was found guilty of corruption and cashiered. Other than Li, perhaps the only beneficiary of the Li Shiyao case was Heshen, who was given Li's 143-room house in Beijing for his pains.

PART THREE

LEGAL PLURALISM IN EMPIRES: ENCOUNTERS AND RESPONSES

THINKING THROUGH LEGAL PLURALISM: 'FORUM SHOPPING' IN THE LATER ROMAN EMPIRE

Caroline Humfress*

Introduction: Legal Pluralism and the Later Roman Empire

> Of the entire area that is subject to the Romans, some is ruled by kings, some they rule under the designation 'provincial' territory, appointing governors and tax collectors to the inhabitants. There are also free cities, some of which attached themselves to the Romans as friends from the outset, while to others the Romans themselves granted freedom as a mark of honour. Some dynasts, tribal chieftains and religious rulers are also subject to the Romans; these people regulate their lives in accordance with certain ancestral laws.[1]

According to Strabo's *Geography*, written at Rome early in the first century CE, Rome's command over her subject territories encompassed many different types of political and economic relationships, including both direct and indirect forms of imperial rule. For Dionysius of Halicarnassus, also writing at Rome during the Augustan era, the imperial city possessed a 'universal hegemony'—as P.A. Brunt has noted, Dionysius probably chose the term hegemony with care in order '...to indicate that Rome's Empire was not composed entirely of provinces under her direct administration'.[2] By the late third century CE, however, the situation had changed: Roman governance now appears to be characterized almost entirely by direct rule from an Imperial centre. Historians of the later Empire accordingly tend to equate Roman law with Imperial law / law-giving *per se*, and there are good reasons for this. For example, Classical jurisprudence under the early Empire had been developed primarily

* I would like to express my gratitude to the Trustees of the Philip Leverhulme Prize for enabling the period of research leave during which this article was written. My sincere thanks also to Jill Harries for reading and commenting on earlier drafts.

[1] Strabo, *Geography* 17.3.24 quoted from David Mattingly, *Imperialism, Power, and Identity. Experiencing the Roman Empire* (Princeton, 2011), 76, with revision. For further discussion of this passage see Eckhard Meyer-Zwiffelhoffer, *Politikos Archein: Zum Regierungsstil der senatorischen Statthalter in den kaiserzeitlichen griechischen Provinzen* (Stuttgart, 2002), 9.

[2] Peter A. Brunt, 'Roman Imperial Illusions', in Peter A. Brunt, *Roman Imperial Themes* (Oxford, 1990), 434. Compare Philo, *Legatio ad Gaium* 153 on Augustus and his care to maintain 'native customs'.

by individual jurists, known to us by name and of provincial as well as Roman origin, whereas postclassical legal development was underpinned by the centralised Imperial authority of the dominate itself (often seen as culminating in the codification projects of the emperors Theodosius II and Justinian I). To move from early to late Empire is thus to shift—in the broadest terms—from a Roman hegemony in which complex interactions between multiple legalities are taken as fact, to a late Roman hegemony in which emperors and centralised bureaucrats laid down the law for their provincial subjects.[3] However, as we shall see, and contrary to the conventional 'centralised' model for late Roman law-related activity, multiple legalities were also a feature of later Roman law and legal practice. In sections II and III below, therefore, I shall argue, using 'forum shopping' as a case study, that numerous litigants went to great lengths in their attempts to place their cases strategically in specific legal venues.

To consider first, then, the top-down model. Late Roman imperial legal texts refer explicitly to the emperors' duty to legislate for the common advantage of all their subjects; for example, the opening sentence of a 440 CE constitution, promulgated by Theodosius II at Constantinople, states: 'We always provide for each and all by provisions of that majesty by which the Roman State has gradually advanced to empire over the whole world.'[4] The capacity to 'provide for each and all' through the promulgation of legal decisions was a fundamental part of late Roman imperial ideology. Nonetheless, as the anthropologist Clifford Geertz has argued, it is all too easy for us to become blinded by command-theories of law, so that 'impressed with command, we see little else'.[5] To what extent, for example, would the provincial inhabitants of the later Roman Empire have thought of the *ius Romanum* as the law of Roman Emperors; or the Roman legal system as a top-down 'Imperial' structure, rather than something that they could attempt to negotiate their own way around?

---

[3] For recent perspectives on the early Roman Empire see Julien Fournier, *Entre tutelle romaine et autonomie civique. L'administration judiciaire dans les provinces hellénophones de l'Empire romain (129 av. J.-C.–235 apr. J.-C.)* (Athens, 2010) and Georgy Kantor, *Roman Law and Local Law in Asia Minor* (unpub. Oxford DPhil., 2009), esp. 256–9 on choice of forum and grants of Roman citizenship. On the third century CE see Peter Eich, *Zur Metamorphose des politischen Systems in der römischen Kaiserzeit* (Berlin, 2005).

[4] Theodosius II, *Novel* 7.3pr (addressed to Cyrus, Praetorian Prefect).

[5] Clifford Geertz, *Negara: The Theatre State in Nineteenth Century Bali* (Princeton, 1982), 121. See also the comments of Simon Roberts, 'After Government? On Representing Law Without the State', *The Modern Law Review* 68, no. 1 (2005), 1–24 at fn. 37.

When, for example, Augustine bishop of Hippo, addressed the following words to a North African audience c. 406–407 CE, he had a specific motivation in arguing that the Emperors were the source of all property rights, as well as the source of *ius* itself (in the general sense of *droit, diritto, Recht* etc.):

> Do you want us to read the laws of the emperors and have us act according to them concerning the rural villas? If you wish to possess by human right (*ius*), let us read aloud the laws (*leges*) of the emperors. Let's see if they wish anything to be possessed by heretics. 'But what has the emperor to do with me?' Well, it's by his right (*ius*) that you own the land. Remove the rights [given by] the emperors and will you still dare to say 'That's my villa, or that is my slave, or that's my house?...'[6]

Augustine goes on to explain that possessing a title to land by human *ius* (right) was equal to possessing a title to land by Imperial *ius*: 'Because God has granted these human rights to humankind through the kings and emperors of the world'.[7] Moreover, Augustine states, if the emperors' authority created rights to property then it could also, by legal right, take them away—as in the case of ('Donatist') schismatics and heretics. We may be tempted to read Augustine's argument that the laws of the emperors were the source of all property rights as a simple, Christianized, statement of Roman legal fact, but it was in reality a highly specific claim: the immediate context for Augustine's preaching was a concrete court case, probably pleaded using anti-heretical Imperial legislation passed in 405 CE, in which Augustine had sought the transfer of property rights from Faustinus the 'Donatist' bishop of Hippo to himself (although Augustine is also at pains to point out that the property was not thereby actually owned by him, but by his/ 'the' Catholic Church). In this sermon, then, Augustine sought to justify his own recent actions—in the course of doing so he also articulated a particular Christian ideology of imperial legal power. Framing his words as a homily on the *Gospel of John* I:32–33, Augustine attempted to convince a volatile North African audience that the Christian emperors' legal authority had been given directly from the Christian God—hence Imperial laws would guarantee the rights of only 'Catholic' Christians to their property. The long *nachleben* of this kind of ideological argument in Western political theory should not obscure the

---

[6] Augustine, *In Evangelium Iohannis Tractatus* VI.25 (CCL 36: 66). Translation quoted from Brent Shaw, *Sacred Violence* (Cambridge, 2011), 516 (modified).

[7] Augustine, *In Evangelium Iohannis Tractatus* VI.25 (CCL 36: 66). See also the Pauline text of *Romans 13*.

fact that other individuals in late Roman North Africa precisely *were* asking the question 'But what has the Emperor to do with me?'[8]

More generally, Augustine—a bishop within the institutionalized 'Catholic' church—was seeking to represent a claim to power in terms of law, as central authorities very widely tend to do, according to the anthropologist Simon Roberts.[9] As Roberts himself argues, however, the endurance of ideological productions is not dependent on their propositional content: a late Roman (Christian) ideology of imperial power exercised according to rule-of-law values does not provide us with a picture of the world as it actually was. Would all late Roman North Africans have agreed that their title to property was dependent on Imperial *ius* and *leges* and ultimately on the Christian God himself? Would individuals across the later Roman Empire have wholly identified 'Roman' private law institutions, inheritance structures, property rights, etc. with imperial legislation? What of normative titles to property that were seen to rest on localized Roman legal traditions, on customary practice, or on (archived) documentary records?[10] To take one third-century example, in Dura-Europos (Syria)—a Roman town from 165 CE and the site of a Roman Garrison by the early third century—the Seleucid 'inheritance law of the registry office' was still being copied in the later third century CE.[11] In terms of the life of property in Dura-Europos, the Seleucid rules remained relevant under direct Roman administration. Moreover, as recent 'critical property research' within contemporary legal studies has demonstrated: 'Property laws are rarely formed in capital cities, disseminated and then accepted uniformly—they are negotiated along historically specific contexts amongst various actors, agencies, and contesting parties.'[12] In fact the official fifth- and sixth-century Imperial *Codes* of the emperors Theodosius II and Justinian point outwards towards exactly these kinds of complex scenarios. Thinking about law-in-empires thus clearly demands more than just exploring '... the possibilities, limitations and restrictions

[8] This observation seems valid even when we acknowledge the rhetorical force of Augustine's phrasing here, which is a variant on the famous riposte made by Donatus himself to the Imperial legates Paul and Macarius in 347 CE (Optatus of Milevis, 3.3, *CSEL* 26.73).

[9] Roberts, 'After Government', 15 For Justinianic statements of this principle see Justinian, *Novel* 105.2.4 (536 CE) and *Codex Iustinianus* 1.14.12, 3–5 (529 AD).

[10] Michael G. Donovan, *At the Doors of Legality: Planners, Favelados, and the Titling of Urban Brazil* (unpub. UC Berkeley PhD, 2007), 39.

[11] *P.Dura*, 12, noted by Kantor, *Roman Law and Local Law*, 220.

[12] For this kind of anthropological approach see Timothy Jenkins, *The Life of Property* (New York, 2010). See also Section III below.

surrounding the exercise of power through bureaucratic or administrative means'; it also demands, as we shall see via the case study of 'forum shopping' in sections II and III below, thinking about the socially constructed nature of late Roman institutions and the situated behaviour of late Roman legal actors.[13]

Histories of law are, of course, bound up with histories of state formation, rulership and governance—so much so that law itself is often understood to be *the* traditional language of the state.[14] There are dangers, however, in buying into a state-centric concept of law and then structuring our analyses solely according to law's perceived relationship with (monarchic, imperial or indeed national) sovereignty.[15]

Over the last forty years or so, some historians of law, social scientists and anthropologists have been more open to the fact that *multiple* forms of state and non-state laws can be identified within (Western) societies, both past and present; alongside multiple legal fora—these scholarly analyses of multiple legal orderings and polycentricities have tended to merge under a broad category of 'legal pluralism'.[16] As Brian Tamanaha commented in a 2008 essay: 'Understanding Legal Pluralism: Past to Present, Local to Global', legal pluralism is now to be found everywhere: multiple local orders are identified 'from the lowest local level to the most expansive global level', whilst the concept of legal pluralism itself appears across a remarkable range of scholarly disciplines.[17] Once we begin to look for them, multiple legal orderings and inter-legalities can be found

---

[13] Quotation from Christopher M. Kelly, 'Later Roman bureaucracy: going through the files', in Alan Bowman and Greg Woolf, *Literacy and Power in the Ancient World* (Cambridge, 1997), 161–76 at 166.

[14] For further discussion see Christopher Tomlins, 'Framing the Field of Law's Disciplinary Encounters: A Historical Narrative', *Law & Society Review* 34, no. 4 (2000), 911–972.

[15] Megan Wachspress, 'Rethinking sovereignty with reference to history and anthropology', *International Journal of Law in Context* 5, no. 3 (2009), 315–330 at 317.

[16] On 'polycentricity' see Hanne Peterson and Henrik Zahle, eds., *Legal Polycentricity: Consequences of Pluralism in Law* (London, 1995) and also Franz von Benda-Beckmann, 'Who's Afraid of Legal Pluralism?', *Journal of Legal Pluralism and Unofficial Law* 47 (2002), 37–82 at 73–4. On 'legal pluralism': John Griffiths, 'What is legal pluralism?', *Journal of Legal Pluralism and Unofficial Law* 24 (1986), 1–55; Gordon R. Woodman, 'Ideological Combat and Social Observation. Recent Debate about Legal Pluralism', *Journal of Legal Pluralism and Unofficial Law* 42 (1998), 21–59, esp. at 34–36 and Carol J. Greenhouse, 'Legal pluralism and cultural difference, What is the difference?', *Journal of Legal Pluralism and Unofficial Law* 42 (1998), 61–72 at 64. More systematic attempts to conceptualize legal pluralism can be found in the scholarship of Masaji Chiba, Boaventura De Sousa Santos, Warwick Tie and Patrick Glenn amongst others.

[17] Brian Z. Tamanaha, 'Understanding Legal Pluralism: Past to Present, Local to Global', *Sydney Law Review* 30 (2008), 375–411.

everywhere within the later Roman Empire too—but the concept of legal pluralism itself needs a certain amount of unpacking before we can begin to develop this observation in any systematic way.[18]

With respect to law in the later Roman Empire, legal pluralist approaches pose two fundamental theoretical problems, while offering a series of important insights into the *social* working of legal rules and institutionalized practices. I will turn to a detailed analysis of these insights in Sections II: 'Forum' and Section III: 'Shopping' below, but will briefly address the two more general theoretical problems raised by legal pluralist approaches now.

Our first theoretical problem was carefully (re-)stated by Simon Roberts in a 2005 essay: 'After Government? On Representing Law Without the State'. Roberts makes the important point that if we 'represent law as present beyond the state, even as having nothing to do with governing' and if we attach the 'identity "law" to a disparate range of normative orders', then we are ultimately left with 'a diminishing sense of what law "is" '.[19] Legal pluralist approaches, according to Roberts, need to take the self-proclaimed identity of [Western] state law *as* law seriously, not least because both historical and ethnographical arguments support the 'old', 'unfashionable' view that 'law is a concomitant of centralising processes'.[20] As such, according to Roberts, state law has a peculiar 'capacity to bring into being a jural world': a world ordered according to distinctively legal—rather than social—relations.[21] Roberts is careful not to attribute the functioning of this jural world entirely to centralised authority, noting that: 'Even the smallest centralised polities in their nature provide more or less extensive arenas within which qualified local autonomy—locally negotiated order—is permitted, encouraged (sometimes required) to operate.'[22] Roberts thus agrees with a fundamental tenet of legal pluralism that we should not neglect local-level orderings, but he rightly contends that: 'The question is *how* we should understand and talk about them'.[23] A legal order is not just '...something "out there" apart from the

[18] I owe this point to discussions with Peter Fitzpatrick, Paul Dresch and Judith Scheele.

[19] Roberts, 'After Government', 3 and 12.

[20] Roberts, 'After Government', 13. For a similar critique, from the very different perspective of neo-systems theory, see Gunther Teubner, 'The Two Faces of Janus: Rethinking Legal Pluralism', *Cardozo Law Review* 13 (1992), 1443–1462.

[21] Roberts, 'After Government', 15.

[22] Roberts, 'After Government', 16.

[23] Roberts, 'After Government', 3. See also Section III below.

agents who created it'.[24] But how locally negotiated is any particular local-level ordering within a given centralised polity? More specifically, what might it mean to talk about local law and individual agency in relation to 'state' law and legal institutions under the later Roman Empire?

Our second theoretical problem relates to the issue of state law's autonomy, as well as to questions concerning its (self-asserted) dominance within law-and-society contexts. Once we acknowledge the existence of multiple 'official' and 'unofficial' legal fields, we also have to ask how each relates to the other; can we draw distinct boundaries? The broad concept of legal pluralism seems to imply a jumble of multiple inter-legalities, but how 'plural' is legal pluralism in reality? Peter Fitzpatrick has highlighted the importance of this question with respect to modern law, via his concept of 'integral plurality'. Fitzpatrick argues that state law appears as a plural phenomenon because it depends 'integrally' on other social forms, yet it should not be understood as just one social form amongst many because '...in the constitution and maintenance of its identity, state law stands in opposition to and in asserted domination over social forms that support it. There exists a contradictory process of mutual support and opposition.'[25] In other words, state law appears *as* a social form (convergence) but is, at the same time, dominant *over* other social forms (opposition). Fitzpatrick's concept of 'integral plurality' thus helps to reveal the indeterminacy and multiplicity of state law, whilst at the same time acknowledging its self-proclaimed capacity to communicate and impose centralised commands. This leads to a paradoxical situation in which, as Carol Greenhouse puts it: 'Law is controlling without ordinarily being determinative, variant but not necessarily in ways that are homologous with cultural variation.'[26] We shall return to this point in Section III below.

Under the Roman Empire, the involvement of the state in the administration of justice was formally structured via a centralised system of delegated and territorial power. In this sense, we can speak of the Roman Empire as being governed through a unitary rule-of-law principle in

---

24 Quotations from Gavin W. Anderson, *Constitutional Rights after Globalization* (Oxford, 2005), 39. The classic early attempt at a sociological systematizing of law is usually taken to be Eugen Ehrlich, *Grundlegung der Soziologie des Rechts* (Munich and Leipzig, 1913) but 'pluralist' critiques had been proposed earlier by Otto von Gierke, Frederic William Maitland, Max Weber, John Neville Figgis and others.

25 Peter Fitzpatrick, 'Law and Societies', *Osgoode Hall Law Journal* 22 (1984), 115–122 at 116.

26 Greenhouse, 'Legal Pluralism', 66.

which Fitzpatrick's concept of 'integral plurality'—developed with reference to modern technologies of law and governance—also has relevance. The Roman *ius civile* certainly stood in 'asserted domination' over other social forms. According to the discussions of late Classical Roman jurists, *iurisdictio*, from *ius dicere*—the power to speak *ius*, to administer justice—was a capacity defined by law and held only by magistrates with *imperium*. *Imperium* (from the Latin *imperare*, to command) was the central concept in Roman public law and was ranked by degrees: '...so that a consul had greater *imperium* than a praetor, and the emperor [in Latin, *imperator*] had *imperium* greater than that of any magistrate'.[27] In Roman jurisprudence, *iurisdictio*—the power to administer justice—was understood to be conceptually subordinate to *imperium*; there could be no *iurisdictio* without some degree of *imperium* (but both, subject to certain limitations, could be delegated).[28] Any given magistrate's *imperium* and hence their *iurisdictio* could also be subject to specific financial and territorial restrictions: the *imperium* of a provincial governor, for example, could be exercised only within their given province, hence their *iurisdictio* could extend only over those persons who had the appropriate domicile (a question that the governor himself was expected to decide upon). We should also note, however, that individuals who were not subject to a magistrate's *iurisdictio* could seek to co-opt it for themselves.[29] By the later Empire, the involvement of state officials in the administration of (Roman) justice could take place in numerous different settings: from the summary hearings of military officers, financial officials and other kinds of imperial bureaucrats to the various audiences and tribunals presided over by imperial magistrates and their delegates. Some of these jurisdictions, such as that of the urban prefect at Rome or the late Roman *defensor civitatis* have been the subject of detailed modern studies—as have the various rules and institutionalized procedures that came to define 'the' late Roman imperial system. The multiple, diverse and localised settings in which this formal system operated have, however, tended to receive less scholarly attention; as has the extent to which certain individuals and

[27] David Johnston, 'The General Influence of Roman Institutions of State and Public Law', in David L. Carey Miller and Reinhard Zimmermann, eds., *The Civilian Tradition and Scots Law* (Berlin, 1997), 87–101 at 92–93.

[28] Johnston, 'The General Influence of Roman Institutions', 98.

[29] Johnston, 'The General Influence of Roman Institutions', 93 and also the discussion below on *Digest* 5.1.1 (Ulpian, *Edict* book 2) and *Digest* 5.1.2pr. (Ulpian, *Edict* book 3)

groups were able to manoeuvre within, across and beyond the imperial justice system.[30]

Fitzpatrick's concept of 'integral plurality' can help us to understand how Roman law framed itself *as* state law, but we also need to think about 'convergence' between Roman law and other normative orders: how, when and why did legal actors (litigants, imperial officials and others) appeal to Roman law as a 'dominant' social form and when did they treat it as one social form amongst others? One way of addressing this complex question is through a focus on Roman legal institutions *as social constructions.* The potential of an institutional approach to legal pluralism, and to the phenomenon of forum shopping in particular, has already been demonstrated by Ido Shahar through a series of case studies on the interrelations between *sharīʿa* courts and other tribunals in Mamluk, Ottoman and present-day Jerusalem.[31] A similar focus on local 'institutionalised' contexts and on the point of view of litigants may also open up new perspectives on multiple legal orderings and institutions under the later Roman Empire.[32] Even within universalising legal systems the work of courts, for example, is revealed to be 'locally shaped and culturally entwined in place and setting.'[33]

This essay thus seeks to explore the socially constructed nature of Roman legal institutions through a case study of 'forum shopping'. Approaching legal procedures as situated practices—such as 'forum shopping'—rather than as a set of (static) regulative rules, should also help to reveal the importance of local knowledge and local reasoning in institutional

---

[30] On the idea of place being important in the formal administration of late Roman justice see Francesco de Angelis, ed., *Spaces of Justice in the Roman World* (Leiden, 2010). See also the essay by Jill Harries, 'Creating Legal Space: Settling Disputes in the Roman Empire', in Catherine Hezser, ed., *Rabbinic Law in its Roman and Near Eastern Context* (Tübingen, 2003), 63–81.

[31] Ido Shahar, 'State, Society and the Relations between Them: Implications for the Study of Legal Pluralism', *Theoretical Inquiries in Law* 9, no. 2 (2008), 417–441 and Ido Shahar, *Practicing Islamic Law in a Legal-Pluralistic Environment: The Changing Face of a Muslim Court in Present Day Jerusalem* (unpub. Ph.D. Dissertation, Ben Gurion University, 2006).

[32] The classic ethnographic study on forum shopping is Keebet von Benda-Beckmann, 'Forum Shopping and Shopping Forums: Dispute Processing in a Minangkabau Village in West Sumatra', *Journal of Legal Pluralism and Unofficial Law* 19 (1981), 117–153.

[33] Carroll Seron and Susan S. Silbey, 'Profession, Science, and Culture: An Emergent Canon of Law and Society Research', in Austin Sarat, ed., *The Blackwell Companion to Law and Society* (Malden and Oxford, 2004). Note that this approach is distinct from focusing on 'corruption' within any given legal system.

contexts. Our concern here, then, is not so much with 'law in action', but rather with social actions that involve law.[34]

'Forum'

> When you believe . . . that power in law resides in fields of practice, it is important to speak of places and people as well as ideas.[35]

The Roman administration of justice was based on the principle that an individual with a 'right' (*ius*) should have a remedy i.e., the ability to pursue that claim through some kind of formalised process. In the Later Roman Empire and through into the Byzantine period, there were a number of different institutionalised fora in which Roman justice could be sought from Roman officials: from cases heard by the Emperors themselves and those who judged *vice sacra*, to hearings conducted before the Senates of Rome and Constantinople and before the higher-ranking imperial bureaucrats, through to the provincial-level governors' hearings and the various jurisdictions associated with (new) Imperial officials established in the municipalities. There were also 'special jurisdictions', including those relating to the army; specific administrative bureaus within the Imperial bureaucracy; and fiscal matters (including taxation and inheritance).[36] In addition, as we shall see, late Roman Imperial officials also—in different ways and within certain limits—acknowledged legal hearings conducted before various municipal-level officials; heads of guild societies; Christian clerics; rabbis and others within Jewish communities, etc.[37] In terms of an institutional approach to legal pluralism, then, late Roman and Byzantine legal officials were familiar with the concept of the competent court, and they also acknowledged the reality of concurrent jurisdictions.[38] In any given dispute, in any given locality, there could be a number of different

---

[34] For the striking idea that different situations, in specific contexts, can involve 'more' or 'less' law see Donald Black, *The Behaviour of Law* (New York, 1976).

[35] John Brigham, 'The Constitution of Interests', quoted from Tomlins, 'Framing the Field', 911.

[36] For detailed discussion see Arnold Hugh Martin Jones, *The Later Roman Empire* (Oxford, 1964), 479–494.

[37] On Jewish courts under the Roman Empire see Natalie B. Dohrmann, 'The boundaries of the law and problem of *jurisdictio* in an early Palestinian Midrash', in Catherine Hezser, ed, *Rabbinic Law in its Roman and Near Eastern Context* (Tübingen, 2003), 83–104.

[38] On the later Byzantine Empire see Ruth Macrides, 'The Competent Court', in Angeliki Laiou-Thomadakis and Dieter Simon, eds., *Law and Society in Byzantium, Ninth-Twelfth Centuries* (Washington D.C., 1994), 117–129.

fora, before which, in theory at least, the hearing of a legal dispute could take place.

Those late Roman litigants who appeared before magistrates with imperial jurisdiction were subject to certain institutionalised rules regarding where their case should be heard. It was a well-established principle of Roman law that a prosecutor or plaintiff would usually proceed in the forum which had jurisdiction over the accused or defendant: in ordinary cases this could mean a bureaucratic court within whose area the defendant was domiciled, but there were numerous exceptions, including criminal cases in which a prosecutor could proceed in a court within whose jurisdiction the alleged crime had been committed.[39] Plaintiffs did not have a right to choose the jurisdiction in which to file suit—nonetheless, both legal and extra-legal sources reveal various procedural customs and practices that could be exploited by litigants in order to place or bar hearings before a particular bureaucratic forum, or to move a case between fora. One way of 'placing' a (civil) case, according to classical jurisprudence was for litigants to agree to appear before a particular official with competent *iurisdictio*—thus effectively bypassing the rule that a 'plaintiff should follow the forum of the defendant'.[40] Litigants also had the legal capacity to agree between themselves on a competent bureaucratic forum under the later Roman Empire—this practice should be understood as operating in addition to the various 'private' arbitration procedures, governed by formal agreement and/or sanction.[41] But what if the parties did not agree on a competent court?

There were a number of legitimate ways in which cases could be placed before a specific forum and manoeuvred between different Imperial courts and other kinds of institutionalised jurisdictions. At the most basic level, the way in which a case was framed could determine the forum in which it was heard: for example, *Theodosian Code* 2.1.8, given at Milan

---

39 See *Codex Iustinianus*, 3.13.2 (Diocletian to Alexander, Aug. 27, 293); *Codex Theodosianus* 9.1.10 (Valentinian, Valens and Gratian to Count Florianus, given at Marcianopolis, Nov. 13, 373 / Nov. 9 368) and *Codex Theodosianus* 9.1.16, March 30 386. For further discussion see Jones, *Later Roman Empire*, 484–5.

40 *Digest* 5.1.1 (Ulpian *Edict* bk 2) and *Digest* 5.1.2 (Ulpian *Edict* bk 3); the latter specifies that 'people are considered to have agreed if they know that they are not subject to [the magistrate's] *iurisdictio* and agree upon him'. The Byzantine text of the *Basilica* 7.3.39 thus correctly states that a non-competent *magistrate* becomes competent by the consent of the parties.

41 Paolo Garbarino, 'La "praescriptio fori" nei secoli V e VI: Aspetti procedurali', in *Legislazione, cultura giuridica, prassi dell'impero d'Oriente in età giustinianea tra passato e futuro*. Atti del Convegno di Modena, 21–22 maggio 1998 (Milan, 2000), 1–41 at 30–1.

in 395, refers to persons deliberately framing a suit 'under the guise of a criminal action' in order to lodge it before a certain named Imperial magistrate. As Keebet von Benda-Beckmann has argued with reference to contemporary disputes in Western Sumatra: '...since most disputes have several aspects, the definition of the dispute is a means to establish jurisdiction and thus a means of forum shopping, both for parties and functionaries.'[42] Late Romans could also seek the benefit of an Imperial rescript—enabling them to prosecute or defend a civil or criminal case before a specific forum that would otherwise have been barred to them.[43] As numerous cases involving Christian bishops and clerics in the fourth and fifth centuries demonstrate, a litigant might petition the emperors for the right to pursue their case in a specific forum prior to lodging a case in a formal jurisdiction; or whilst a case was in the process of being heard (according to repeated Imperial constitutions such petitions ought to be refused); or even after a magistrate's sentence on a case had been delivered. In fact the Imperial chancellery frequently had to explain that seeking a rescript authorising a new trial, in a new forum, after a magistrate's sentence had been given, amounted to an appeal of the existing sentence and was thus subject to certain (complex and constantly revised) institutional rules and procedures.[44] In each of these examples we see litigants seeking out formal Roman institutions and attempting to make them work to their advantage; we also see the imperial administration, in turn, responding to the practices of those litigants case-by-case. The establishment of what we would term procedural rules should thus be understood as a non-linear process, grounded in practical patterns of action and institutional response.

According to late Roman rhetorical treatises, forensic advocates were expected to know a set repertoire of rhetorical techniques for getting a case lodged before a specific forum in their client's favour, as well as knowing how to formally prevent a case from being heard in any given venue. The latter procedure was referred to in Latin as *praescriptio fori*: one of several different types of procedural *praescriptiones* (prescriptions) which could be pleaded in order to effectively bar or restrict a suit

---

[42] Benda-Beckmann, 'Forum shopping and shopping forums', 118.

[43] See, for example, *Codex Iustinianus* 3.13.5 (Honorius to Vincentius PP of Gaul, given at Milan, Dec. 18, 397). According to Classical Roman law, petitioning against someone was not the same as summoning him to litigate (*in ius vocatus*)—the provisions of the praetorian edict applied only to the latter (*Digest* 2.4.15, Paul *Questions* 1).

[44] On appeals see Federico Pergami, *L'appello nella legislazione del tardo impero* (Milan, 1996).

from being heard in a particular place or by a specific official.[45] If summoned before a magistrate or other administrative official an individual had to answer the summons and *then* set up a defence that the forum in question had no jurisdiction.[46] An early fifth-century rhetorical treatise describes this process as a kind of pre-trial hearing, in the context of a highly technical discussion concerning rhetorical *stasis* theory (how to classify questions or issues 'according to the underlying structure of the dispute that each involves').[47] For our fifth-century author, the question of whether something should be brought to trial is an 'especially necessary' type of question and is 'often resorted to in public matters':

> For I recognise that nothing is of more interest to those threatened with a trial than to avoid a trial, furthermore, that the avoidance of a trial has some semblance of a trial. For if a legal matter were handled in this way that whenever anyone who did not wish his case to be tried, this would be within his power, there would be no investigation; at the present time, however, since those always arise who would prevent a trial, that contention itself in which one party demands a hearing and the other makes an objection against it, constitutes an 'issue' [a 'rational' question, as defined by *stasis* theory]...[48]

The first-century BCE rhetor Hermagoras of Temnos, the fifth-century text continues, called this issue *metalepsis* (transference); Latin authors, however, refer to it as both *reprehensio* and *translatio*:

> Those who have called it *reprehensio* did so obviously because at the very moment when the case is brought into court, it is laid hold of again and, so to speak, pulled back; those who have called it *translatio* did so because the defendant does not preclude court action altogether but, in order to free himself from the present conditions of the action, he transfers the trial to another kind of court, either now in session or to be convened in the future.[49]

---

45 *Digest* 2.5.2 (Paul, *Edict*, book 1).

46 *Digest* 2.5.2 (Paul, *Edict*, book 1): if, however, an individual who exhibited *rusticitas* (ignorance, inexperience, in the sense of a 'rustic peasant') failed to turn up, he/she was to be exempt from the resulting court fine. For further exceptions see *Digest* 2.4.2–24.

47 Malcolm Heath, 'The substructure of stasis-theory from Hermagoras to Hermogenes', *Classical Quarterly* 44 (1994), 114–29.

48 PseudoAugustine, *De rhetorica* 10, Karl Halm, ed., *Rhetores latini minores* (Leipzig, 1863), 143. Translation by Otto A.L. Dieter and William C. Kurth, 'The *de rhetorica* of Aurelius Augustine', *Speech Monographs* 35, no. 1 (1968), 90–108 at 101.

49 Loc. cit.

Institutionalised procedures for transferring (some) cases between different legal fora thus existed in the later Roman Empire—but it was up to litigants, or their rhetorically-trained advocates, to make these technical arguments work in their favour. In this sense, we can thus begin to think of such institutionalised 'procedures' as potential resources to be exploited by litigants, rather than simply as bureaucratic rules to be followed (or not).

The fact that individuals did, in practice, plead prescriptions against specific fora is clearly demonstrated by a number of late Roman Imperial constitutions that attempt to regulate the practice. For example, one issue that caused confusion during the fourth century was whether an appeal could be taken from a judge's (technically pre-trial) decision on a litigant's plea of *praescriptio fori*. Ordinarily, appeals were permitted only after a case had been tried and a definitive sentence given, but no appeals could be made from an interlocutory decision (i.e., a temporary decision that often referred to a single aspect of a case).[50] An Imperial constitution given by Constantine at Trier in 313 CE implies that an appeal arising from a judgment concerning prescription is allowed—because a judge's decision on a 'peremptory prescription' can terminate the whole case, even before the case has formally begun.[51] A 378 CE constitution, also given at Trier, repeats the sense of the earlier Imperial text but further specifies that since there are so many kinds of prescriptions available to litigants, they must all be dealt with at the same time during the hearing so that only one appeal arising from all of them can be made—the emperors want to stop the practice of referring a case 'many times to us'.[52] In 415 CE, the emperors legislated again in order to state a clear distinction between appealing from a judgement concerning a prescription and appealing from an 'interlocutory decision': a plea of *praescriptio fori* must be brought forward by litigants at the beginning of a suit and (again) there are to be no appeals from interlocutory decisions. It seems reasonable to assume that litigants were doing the opposite in practice, as part of their

[50] For a concrete example relating to the courts of the provincial governor of Apulia and the urban prefect at Rome see Symmachus, *Relatio* 38, with Bettina Hecht, *Störungen der Rechtslage in den Relationen des Symmachus* (Berlin, 2006), 295–305.

[51] *Codex Theodosianus* 11.30.2 = *Codex Iustinianus* 7.62.12 (addressed to Catullinus, possibly *praeses Byzacenae*, given at Trier, 313 CE).

[52] *Codex Theodosianus* 11.30.37 (addressed to Thalassius, proconsul Africae, given at Trier, 378 CE); probably to be joined with the texts at *Codex Theodosianus* 11.36.23–25.

attempts to make the institutionalised practices of the imperial bureaucracy work for them.[53]

The reasons for attempting to plead *praescriptio fori* could be multiple and the ability to do so would have depended on status, wealth and in some cases, patronage networks. Those rich in connections, time and cash would have '...found it convenient to have claims and charges against themselves heard in a court which was naturally sympathetic to their side and tended to uphold their interests'; just as the officials of the courts concerned would have welcomed the increased revenue from legal fees and 'tips'.[54] Litigants also pleaded *praescriptio fori* in order to cause inconvenience and expense to their adversary; to shorten or lengthen the duration of the proceedings; or in attempts to seek the application of 'special' rules (see below). As William Twining states: 'Within a legal order some users may have power to manage, to exploit, to manipulate, avoid, or evade the existing order for their own ends; for others law is a manifestation of other people's power that confronts them; and, of course, there are many gradations in between.'[55] It is thus important to ask which late Roman litigants, or groups of individuals—acting where and under what circumstances—expected to be able to influence the outcome of disputes by determining the fora in which they were heard.

The concept of *privilegium fori* (choice between different courts) was established under the early Empire: an Edict of Vespasian from 74 CE, for example, grants doctors and teachers the privilege of suing against any breaches of its provisions in whatsoever court they choose.[56] From the early fourth century, however, an increasingly complex mosaic of jurisdictional rules developed whereby groups of individuals, including certain kinds of military and bureaucratic officials; members of city guilds in Rome and Constantinople; members of the senatorial order (Roman or Constantinopolitan); tenants of Imperial lands; Christian bishops and some clerics could appeal to specific 'privileged' jurisdictions, under certain circumstances (again variously defined by Imperial legislation).[57]

---

[53] *Codex Theodosianus* 11.30.65, = *Codex Iustinianus* 8.35.13 (addressed to Symmachus, Proconsul Africa, given at Ravenna, 415).

[54] Jones, *Later Roman Empire*, 487.

[55] William Twining, 'A Post-Westphalian Conception of Law. Review Essay: Brian Tamanaha, *A General Jurisprudence of Law and Society* (New York: Oxford University Press, 2001)', *Law and Society Review* 37, no. 1 (2003), 199–258 at 247–8.

[56] AE 1936 no.128 = FIRA I 73, noted by Kantor, *Roman Law and Local Law*, 259.

[57] See Jones, *Later Roman Empire*, 484–494.

Imperial constitutions issued in 355, 365 and 397 CE specify that military commanders, for example, should hear criminal cases in which soldiers (under their command) have been accused.[58] A soldier accused of a crime before a civilian forum, such as a provincial governor's court, could thus plead *praescriptio fori* and have the case transferred to military jurisdiction. The same three imperial constitutions also specify that all civil actions, including those involving soldiers, should be heard in the court of the civil governor. An edict issued by the *praefectus Aegypti* Tatianus between 367–370 CE nonetheless permits civilians to petition the commanders of local military garrisons (i.e., the *praepositi*) whenever they have a complaint against a soldier: '... if any civilian has a difference with a soldier and relies on the vengeance of the *praepositus* and is confident of receiving assistance from him, let him petition; for he cannot obtain requisite assistance on the spot from anyone else.'[59] Here Tatianus seems to be making an exception for inhabitants of the *chora*: those who lived in close proximity to (established) military forts and may have interacted with soldiers on a daily basis, perhaps as suppliers of goods and services. The main point of Tatianus's edict, however, is to underscore the fact that disputes between civilians cannot be heard by a military commander—a situation which, Tatianus has heard, occurs across every city and its territory: 'That this is forbidden by law is clear. For the *praepositus* has authority over soldiers, but not over civilians; it is enjoined on the governors of the provinces to [judge?] them and to receive their petitions'. Tatianus's edict goes on to specify different penalties against those of 'common rank' (*humiliores*) and those of the curial order (*curiales*). The fact that civilians continued to petition military commanders is demonstrated by subsequent Imperial legislation: *CTh* 2.1.9, 397 CE, states that individuals were ignoring the authority of provincial governors and taking their cases before military fora (without the benefit of an imperial rescript).[60]

As Tatianus's edict highlights, military fora held out the hope of local, on-the-spot justice, but they were also *institutional realities* for individuals

[58] *Codex Theodosianus* 2.1.2 (July 25 355); *Codex Theodosianus* 9.2.2 (365); and *Codex Theodosianus* 2.1.9 (397). For further discussion see Bernhard Palme, 'Römische Militärgerichtsbarkeit in den Papyri', in Hans-Albert Rupprecht, ed., *Symposion 2003. Vorträge zur griechischen und hellenistischen Rechtsgeschichte* (Vienna, 2003), 375–408.

[59] *P. Oxy* VIII 1101 (Oxyrhynchus, AD 367–370).

[60] *Codex Theodosianus* 2.1.9 (addressed to Archelaus, Augustal Prefect and given at Constantinople, November 397).

on the ground.[61] For example, the fourteen petitions preserved in the mid-fourth-century archive of Abinnaeus, *praefectus* of the military fortress at Dionysias, a village in the Egyptian Fayum, record both soldiers and civilians from numerous surrounding cities and villages repeatedly seeking the judicial assistance of military officials in assaults, burglaries, financial disputes etc. (sometimes with Abinnaeus acting as an intermediary for the *dux* of Egypt).[62] A judicial decision from a military commander may also have held out the hope of instant enforcement—unlike most judicial decisions given by civil imperial magistrates. Thus regardless of what formal *iurisdictio* a military commander did or did not have in any particular case, his legal decisions were 'real' in their localised context.

As noted above, *privilegium fori* was granted piecemeal to Christian bishops and, under certain circumstances, to other clerics.[63] The argument that bishops should have jurisdiction over other bishops had been implicitly acknowledged by the late third-century Emperor Aurelian with reference to the case of Paul of Samosata, but it was explicitly confirmed and then variously limited and re-interpreted both in later Roman Imperial constitutions and in canons agreed at local, regional and universal Church councils.[64] In fact from the fourth century onwards we find numerous examples of bishops (and other ecclesiastics) manoeuvring their disputes across a range of different institutionalised fora: at hearings conducted before local, regional and universal Church councils; before delegated episcopal judges; before local municipal officials; provincial governors and other Imperial officials; and before emperors themselves. To take one concrete example: in 369 the Gallic ex-bishop (*ex-antistite*) Chronopius was deposed by a synod of seventy bishops, but chose to contest his deposition before the court of the Proconsul of Africa.[65] It is

---

61 See further John E.G. Whitehorne, 'Petitions to the Centurion', *Bulletin of the American Society of Papyrologists* 41 (2004), 161–9 and Michael Peachin, 'Petition to a Centurion from the NYU Papyrus Collection', in Boudewijn Sirks and Klaas Worp, eds., *Papyri in Memory of P. J. Sijpesteijn* (*P. Sijp.*) (Oakville CT, 2007), 79–97.

62 *P.Abinn.* 44–57 (most dating from between 346 and 351 CE, when Abinnaeus was *praepositus alae* at Dionysias).

63 See Antonio Banfi, *Habent Illi Iudices Suos: Studi sull'esclusività della giurisdizione ecclesiastica e sulle origini del privilegium fori in diritto romano e bizantino* (Milan, 2005).

64 On Paul of Samosata see Fergus Millar, 'Paul of Samosata, Zenobia and Aurelian: The Church, Local Culture and Political Allegiance in Third-Century Syria', *Journal of Roman Studies* 61 (1971), 1–17.

65 *Codex Thedodosianus* 11.36.20 (addressed to Claudius, Proconsul of Africa, given July 9 369). Jill Harries kindly noted a further 'forum-shopping' comparison here with the case

unclear whether Chronopius then appealed to Valentinian I against the Proconsul's judgment or whether the Proconsul himself sent a *relatio* to the emperor requesting advice on Chronopius's appeal from the synodal judgment—whichever scenario is correct, the decision of the seventy bishops was upheld by Valentinian I.[66] The important point to note here is that whilst some bishops were pleading *praescriptio fori* on the basis that their cases should be heard only by other bishops, individuals such as Chronopius were appealing to imperial fora in order to undo judgments made by their episcopal peers. A similar dialectic can be seen in imperial constitutions from the mid-sixth century: early in his reign the emperor Justinian confirmed *privilegium fori* for Christian clerics as an enforceable *ius* (right), but certain clerics were also apparently swearing by written agreement that they would *not* claim *privilegium fori* on account of their 'sacerdotal prerogative'. We then find Justinian, in turn, legislating to confirm the binding nature of the clerics' agreements, in line with the 'ancient rule' that anyone could renounce a privilege introduced for their benefit.[67]

A 405 Imperial constitution, given at Ravenna, complains more generally about bishops petitioning emperors after having been deposed by church councils and thereby fraudulently obtaining 'responses and furtive rescripts'. The text also condemns deposed bishops who remain in their cities, claiming that they are innocent after they have been judged guilty, collecting 'riotous mobs' and being saluted about town as if they were still bishops—an important reminder that institutionalised authority is based as much on localised power and social relations, as on formal titles granted or revoked from above.[68] A late fourth-century constitution given at Constantinople also highlights this fundamental point, albeit from a different angle: members of an (un-named) Jewish community have complained to the emperor because Jews whom they themselves had cast out, 'by their own decision and will', had been readmitted to their community

of Priscillian of Avila, on which see Henry Chadwick, *Priscillian of Avila. The Occult and the Charismatic in the Early Church* (Oxford, 1978), 12–20 and 132–48.

[66] Compare Eusebius, *Life of Constantine* IV.27.2, on Constantine 'putting his seal' on the decrees of bishops made at synods so that they could not be annulled by provincial governors.

[67] *Codex Iustinianus* 2.3.29 (Justinian to Johannes PP, given at Constantinople September 531), also mentioning those who agree not to claim *privilegium fori* on account of their official status or rank.

[68] *Sirmondian Constitution* 2 (given at Ravenna, February 405) = *Codex Theodosianus* 16.2.35. Compare *Sirmondian Constitution* 3 (Thedosius I, addressed to Optatus, Augustal prefect and given at Constantinople, February ?384), referring specifically to Egypt.

by the authority of imperial magistrates.[69] In other words, the expelled (ex-)members had resorted to the Imperial courts to gain re-admittance and had won their case, despite the protests—we are told—of the Jewish community's leaders. In this instance the emperors ordered that the decisions of the imperial magistrates were not to be upheld.

We should note, finally, that individuals did not necessarily have to have any direct contact with institutionalised legal fora in order for those fora to have an impact on their actions. Institutionalised fora—whether presided over by civil or military Imperial officials, Christian bishops, Jewish rabbis etc.—provided late Roman individuals and groups with what legal sociologists term 'bargaining endowments': sets of 'counters' that can be used in 'extra-legal' negotiations.[70] Formal legal rules are one part of this endowment, in the sense that they enable some degree of predictability or at least calculability in determining the outcome of pursuing a dispute in a given context: 'In seeking legal services, what a person is often buying is a sophisticated prediction by a professional concerning how judges in a local jurisdiction will probably apply vague legal standards to the circumstances of the particular case.'[71] Mnookin and Kornhauser were commenting on the behaviour of American disputants in the late twentieth century, but consulting a *nomikos* or *iurisperitus* who was 'skilled in the laws of the Romans' would have had a similar effect, in this respect at least. In addition to formal rules, any given institutional forum's 'bargaining endowment' also includes knowledge about the relative costs, delays, uncertainties, stigmas, etc. of using that specific forum, which can then be deployed when making a *threat* to invoke a particular official or jurisdiction. The value of this 'bargaining endowment' is variable and 'depends on the characteristics of the disputants'.[72] As Marc Galanter concludes: 'The principal contribution of courts to dispute resolution is providing a *background of norms and procedures* against which negotiations and regulation in both private and governmental settings take place [my italics]'.[73] In order to understand the significance of institutionalised legal fora, in any given time and place, we thus need to situate them within a much broader field of social action.

---

[69] *Codex Theodosianus* 16.8.8 (addressed to Tatianus PP of the East, April 392).

[70] See Marc Galanter, 'Justice in many rooms: Courts, private orderings and indigenous law', *Journal of Legal Pluralism* 19, no. 1 (1981), 1–48, esp. 5–8.

[71] Mnookin and Kornhauser quoted from Galanter, 'Justice in many rooms', 5 at fn. 5.

[72] Galanter, 'Justice in many rooms', 8.

[73] Galanter, 'Justice in many rooms', 6.

My intention in exploring late Roman fora for justice in this section—deliberately casting the net wide and moving away from the idea of an imperial legal system that was simply imposed from above—has been to draw attention to the realities of institutional pluralism in late Roman dispute processes. I am also interested, however, in how repeated patterns of individual and collective action can shape a given institutional legal system on the ground and how, in turn, much broader socio-legal structures shape that individual and collective behaviour. To what extent is the regularity that we perceive in late Roman 'procedural law' due to repeated institutional responses to the pragmatic actions of litigants? And what, exactly, might the term 'pragmatic' mean in late Roman socio-legal contexts?

'Shopping'?

> Certain persons are hastening to adapt prescriptions of forum, by a harmful interpretation of the law, to their own claims....[74]

Institutional *fora* and institutionalised practices provide the structure within which litigants act, but those litigants have their own agency—as individuals and also potentially as members of specific groups. For example, in late 438 or early 439 CE the Praetorian Prefect of the Eastern Roman empire, Florentius, wrote to the Emperor Theodosius II to complain about certain practices in the provinces concerning *praescriptio fori*. Theodosius II's *Novel* 7.1, issued at Constantinople on January 20, 439, was the Imperial response. From this text we learn that some individuals, having first secured nominal ('sinecure') positions within the Imperial service, were attempting to use their titular imperial status in order to plead exemption from the jurisdiction of provincial governors. Pleading *praescriptio fori* before the courts of provincial governors was apparently particularly useful to *conductores*: individuals who had leased land from great estates (whether owned by the emperor himself or 'powerful men')—they could thus evade lawsuits forcing them to undertake their 'public obligations', including, presumably, municipal duties and payment of public taxes to the governors themselves. Hence 'private' individuals, as *Novel* 7.1 terms them, were pleading a privilege that had been intended to benefit those who 'rightfully' performed the duties of 'public' (i.e. imperial) service; such

[74] Theodosius II, *Novel* 7.2, pr.

pleas were not, strictly speaking, illegal and presumably provincial governors were allowing them in practice, hence the need for Florentius's report to the Emperor. In order to close the legal loophole, Theodosius II's *Novel* 7.1 specified that no prescriptions of forum could be pleaded by imperial officials before provincial governors in cases concerning the performance of public obligations; the emperors also ruled that, henceforth, *all* lessees of land from great estates, as well as imperial officials who were conducting private business in the provinces without an official leave of absence '... shall answer their adversaries when they bring suit, in order that under the pretext of imperial service the due private or public obligations may not be abandoned'.[75] As far as the drafters of Theodosius' *Novel* 7.1 were concerned, the legal privileges bestowed upon imperial officials were not to be used to further pragmatic, self-interested motives.[76]

Less than two years later another Theodosian constitution reveals that the problems highlighted by *Novel* 7.1 were endemic within the Eastern Empire. Responding once again to a report from the Praetorian Prefect of the East, now a certain Cyrus, the preamble to Theodosius' *Novel* 7.2 explains that: 'Certain persons are hastening to adapt prescriptions of forum, by a harmful interpretation of the law to their own claims, since they think that by the prerogative of their "belt" of office they can elude judicial trials.'[77] In other words, some Imperial officials were attempting to forum-shop and thereby '... answer to charges only before their own judges'.[78] According to *Novel* 7.2, previous laws (*veteres leges*) had already blocked pleas of prescription of forum in a number of cases, including all criminal suits and those concerning contracts—yet, states the preamble, these litigants do not know this. Section 1 of the same *Novel* explains further that, according to Cyrus's own report, individuals summoned before the Praetorian Prefect himself were claiming prescriptions of forum 'under the pretext of imperial office', in order to avoid service on municipal councils and gubernatorial office staffs; to sidestep the payment of public debts; and to escape criminal accusations for overzealous tax collection and extortion. The emperors rule that no such 'cunning' prescriptions of forum can be pleaded before provincial governors and no prescriptions

[75] Theodosius II, *Novel* 7.1, section 2 (compare *CI* 3.25.1). See also Jones, *Later Roman Empire*, 490.

[76] Compare *Codex Iustinianus* 3.13.7 (Anastasius to Constantinus PP, given at Constantinople on February 15, 502).

[77] Theodosius II, *Novel* 7.2, pr. See also Jones, *Later Roman Empire*, 339–40.

[78] Theodosius II, *Novel* 7.2, section 2.

of forum whatsoever are to be used before the Praetorian Prefect—even when the individual litigant concerned could produce an Imperial letter to the opposite effect. As we shall see, however, Theodosius's *Novel* 7.2 itself quickly became the subject of yet more 'cunning' interpretations by individual litigants.

The preamble to Theodosius's *Novel* 7.3, addressed to the same Praetorian Prefect as *Novel* 7.2 and issued just over three months later (in December 440), explains that the Roman Empire rose to greatness through making provisions for 'each and all': 'But sometimes certain persons attempt to distort by a wrong interpretation laws that have been most beneficially promulgated'. The emperors have learnt that some individuals are claiming (wrongfully) that the recent restrictions on pleas of *praescriptio fori*—as detailed in Theodosius's *Novel* 7.2—are valid against all members of the imperial militia, including armed soldiers and 'tribunes who are in command of the service units'.[79] Reading between the lines of the text, something like the following scenario perhaps lies behind the promulgation of Theodosius's *Novel* 7.2: a Roman soldier on active duty within an Eastern frontier zone has been cited as a defendant in a case before a provincial governor or a praetorian prefect, thus potentially requiring him to leave active service and travel to the provincial capital for a lengthy period of time; the soldier has claimed *praescriptio fori* on the basis of earlier imperial rulings, but his opponent has countered with the provisions of Theodosius's *Novel* 7.2; a member of the office staff of the presiding Imperial magistrate, or perhaps someone acting on the soldier's behalf, has in turn objected to this use of Theodosius's *Novel* 7.2 with the question being forwarded for decision to the imperial chancellery—hence the promulgation of Theodosius's *Novel* 7.3. In fact, Theodosius's *Novel* 7.4, issued about two months later, gives us yet further refinements on *Novel* 7.3, this time in response to a report from a certain Ariobindus, Master of Soldiers: apparently members of his office staff also wanted to forum shop, free from the restrictions of Theodosius's *Novel* 7.2.[80]

When understood in relation to each other, Theodosius's *Novels* 7.1–7.4 provide us with a classic example of how individual litigants act both *within* and *upon* legal systems. For instance, they attempt to forum shop. Their strategic behaviour thus *reproduces* existing institutional

[79] Theodosius II, *Novel* 7.3, section 1.
[80] Theodosius II, *Novel* 7.4 addressed to Ariobindus, Magister Militum, given at Constantinople, March 6, 441.

structures: litigants seek out specific institutional fora and behave according to their understandings of 'institutionalized' conventions, whilst also, at the same time, contributing to the production of new structures—for example, prompting the development of new formal rules as in the case of Theodosius's *Novels* 7.2 and 7.3. Although Giddens developed his celebrated theories of agency and structure with reference to modern liberal democracies, his observation that: '... institutions do not just work "behind the backs" of the social actors who produce and reproduce them' seems equally valid in Roman institutional contexts.[81] According to the centralized, imperial rhetoric of our Theodosian *Novels* 7.1 and 7.2, litigants who attempted to 'manipulate' Imperial laws were motivated purely by self-interest to act against the 'common advantage of all'. What then can we, as historians of empire, hope to understand by focusing upon 'the litigant's perspective'?

As we have begun to see already, adopting the litigant's perspective might seem—initially at least—to reveal the potential for individual choice-making and strategising between multiple legal *fora* and across different types of legal processes. To take a sixth-century example: the emperor Justinian's *Novel* 93 (538 CE) tells of a certain Hesychius—possibly of high, illustrious rank—who lost his case before a delegated judge, appealed to the praetorian prefect at Constantinople against the verdict, then abandoned this appeal in favour of arbitration by formal written agreement; two years later, with the arbitration procedure also having been abandoned, Hesychius sought to reopen the original appeal—which the emperor Justinian allowed him to do.[82] To our modern eyes, Hesychius and his adversaries may thus seem like toga-clad consumers of legal services: rational choice actors, choosing between different fora and processes, weighing means and ends, costs and benefits, to their personal (elite) advantage. Yet no social actor—no matter how wealthy, elite or connected to the centre—is simply free to behave in any way he or she chooses.[83] Our concern in the following discussion, then, is not so much with 'shopping' for legal *fora* in an individualistic, 'consumerist' sense, but

[81] Anthony Giddens, *Central Problems in Social Theory. Action, Structure and Contradiction in Social Analysis* (Berkeley and Los Angeles, 1971).

[82] Justinian, *Novel* 93 (addressed to John PP and given at Constantinople, October 538). This Hesychius could possibly be identified with 'Hesychius 15' listed by John R. Martindale, *Prosopography of the Later Roman Empire* II (Cambridge, 1980), 555.

[83] See Michel De Certeau, *The Practice of Everyday Life* (Berkeley, Los Angeles and London, 1984), xi on rejecting modern Western models of 'social atomism'.

rather with concrete historical experiences of agency and restraint, choice and compulsion.

Choice-making—including actions by wealthy elite individuals such as Hesychius—depends upon 'situated agency': an agency that is situated in past cultural practices and historical traditions, as well as in present conditions.[84] Situated agency is also dependent on local contexts: Hesychius' forum shopping in sixth-century Constantinople—the capital city of the Eastern Empire and the centre of Imperial power—would have demanded local knowledge. 'Local knowledge' that was, as Clifford Geertz puts it: 'local not just as to place, time, class and variety of issue, but as to accent—vernacular characterizations of what happens connected to vernacular imaginings of what can'.[85] Roman rules of inheritance, for instance, may have been (written down) exactly the same in sixth-century Constantinople as they were in Alexandria or Aphrodisias, but each city would have had its own specific cultural practices and historical traditions; it was these local cultural practices and historical traditions which influenced how and when 'Roman' rules were invoked by (potential) litigants and used in concrete situations. Law can thus be thought of in terms of both centralised principle and 'local knowledge'; we will take each in turn.

The fact that Roman laws and institutions were understood by litigants to be 'Roman', not Constantinopolitan, or Alexandrian or Aphrodisian, is fundamentally important: 'Roman' rules and institutions offered the possibility of escaping 'local' contexts. As Sally Engle Merry explains with reference to modern European colonialism:

> One of the intriguing patterns of European, and particularly British, colonialism was the rush to use the new courts the imperial powers created. In many cases relatively powerless individuals such as women or people of low social status led this enthusiasm. Many saw in the new institutions opportunities to escape the bonds of kinship or unfree status. It was common in colonial situations for less powerful individuals to seek out the colonial courts as an opportunity to escape other forms of subordination.[86]

The fact that the Roman Governor of Egypt received over 1,809 petitions during his visit to the city of Arsinoe, during a three-day stay c. 209 AD,

---

[84] Mark Bevir and Rod A.W. Rhodes, *The State as Cultural Practice* (Oxford, 2010).

[85] Clifford Geertz, 'Local knowledge: Fact and Law in Comparative Perspective', in Clifford Geertz, *Local Knowledge* (London, 1983) 167–234 at 215.

[86] Sally Engle Merry, 'Colonial Law and its Uncertainties', *Law and History Review* 28, no. 4 (2010), 1067–1071 at 1068.

suggests a similar pattern.[87] Seeking justice amongst 'outsiders' is also an acknowledged phenomenon in terms of Christians appealing to non-ecclesiastical *fora* under early Islam; as well as Jewish subjects under the Ottoman empire preferring to use *shari'a* courts, rather than rabbinical courts.[88] It is not even essential that individual or group actors understood the workings of the formal institutions or rules that they invoked: as David Nelken suggests, 'official law' can function as a resource even when its details are not known or understood.[89]

Our second—related—point in terms of the relationship between situated agency and legal strategising is developed from the anthropologist Tim Jenkins's research into family, property and inheritance structures in the region of Béarn, southwest France. Jenkins explains that legal rules—in the sense of written legislative statutes—are understood by the inhabitants of Béarn to come from somewhere beyond the local (i.e., from Paris, from Parlément, from Brussels, etc.). These legal rules are part of a 'complex of possibilities' available to the Béarnaise, but: '... the form that this complex of possibilities persists in is embodied in a series of *local* practices and institutions ... [my italics]'.[90] Hence in discussing the impact of new state legislation on inheritance strategies in Béarn, Jenkins concludes that: '... the laws are not, in the local instance, primary; they are, rather, secondary features that come into play in the expression of the life of property.'[91] Thinking through Jenkins's argument in relation to law and empire suggests that 'Imperial' law—issued from and identified with the centre—may have a value 'beyond the local', but it is nonetheless embedded within 'local practices and institutions'. Similarly, Galanter argues that instead of thinking in terms of individuals who 'bargain in

[87] *P. Yale* 61. See also in this context Caroline Humfress, 'Laws' Empire: Roman Universalism and Legal Practice', in Paul du Plessis, ed., *New Frontiers: Law and Society in the Roman World* (Edinburgh, 2013), 73–101, on the archive of Babatha from second-century Judaea.

[88] See Uriel Simonsohn, 'Seeking Justice among the 'Outsiders': Christian Recourse to Non-Ecclesiastical Judicial Systems under Early Islam', *Church History and Religious Culture* 89, no. 1–3 (2009), 191–216 and Amnon Cohen, ed., *Jews in the Muslim Religious Court: Society, Economy and Communal Organization in the Sixteenth Century. Documents from Ottoman Jerusalem* (Jerusalem, 1996–2003).

[89] David Nelken, *Comparing Legal Cultures* (New York, 1997), 461.

[90] Timothy Jenkins, "Thinking through the relationship between anthropology and history: forms of law and social forms in Béarn, south-west France", unpublished seminar paper (Cambridge, October 2011).

[91] Jenkins, *The life of Property*, 116.

the shadow of the law', we should instead think of 'law in the shadow of indigenous ordering'.[92]

Both Jenkins's and Galanter's arguments highlight the inadequacy of any kind of simple evolutionary view in which '... lesser, dispersed and informal regulatory elements are displaced or transformed by the growth and elaboration of the centralized bureaucratic system.'[93] Individual agency and choice-making depend upon local indigenous ordering, as well as Imperial institutionalised practices and *fora* that reach beyond the local. Imperial law and legal institutions never simply replace or displace local situated behaviours and practices. As the institutional legal-pluralist perspectives discussed above demonstrate, it is not only sovereign powers that determine the functioning of legal systems within empires. Law is never simply the product of an Imperial will.

[92] Galanter, 'Justice in many rooms', 23.
[93] Galanter, 'Justice in many rooms', 21 at fn. 31.

LEGES NATIONUM AND ETHNIC PERSONALITY OF LAW IN CHARLEMAGNE'S EMPIRE

Peter Hoppenbrouwers

It would be an exaggeration to say that Charlemagne's Empire was governed by the rule of law, but laws and law-giving certainly did constitute an important aspect of both royal representation and performance, as well as of legal practice. In this essay I intend to concentrate on one aspect of this well-explored field of study, the constitution of so-called 'national law codes' and the deployment of the legal principle of ethnic 'personality of law' as important instruments of Carolingian government control. Because undoubtedly there was a strong ideological motive behind the princely duty to legislate, I shall also discuss the difference between legislative ideal and legal practice.

Carolingian Ideals of Government and Legislation

Charlemagne and his successors liked to present themselves as rulers over many peoples.[1] Their empire was a multigentile as well as—in certain respects—confederative state, a union of many 'kingdoms' and peoples (*regna et gentes*). How many exactly would always remain unclear. In Carolingian documents (esp. annals, capitularies) *regnum* has various meanings that were easily contaminated, while its connection to *gens* (people) was rather vague. *Regnum* could refer to a former kingdom that had been incorporated into the Frankish empire: for example, Frisia, Thuringia, Italy and Aquitaine (the former kingdom of the Visigoths in Gaul). It could also refer to a territory that had never been ruled by a king, but still was supposed to be inhabited by one identifiable people. The best example is Saxony. In Carolingian political practice territories designated as *regna* (in both meanings) were drawn on to provide sons of a ruler with their own kingdoms, which remained, however, subordinated

[1] E.g. Rosamond McKitterick, 'Political ideology in Carolingian historiography', in Y. Hen, M. Innes, eds., *The uses of the past in the early middle ages* (Cambridge, 2000), 162–174; Janet L. Nelson, 'Kingship and royal government', in Rosamond McKitterick, ed., *The new Cambridge Medieval History* Vol. 2 (Cambridge etc., 1995), 383–430.

to their father's superior power. There was a clear preference to use certain *regna* rather than others for this purpose. Aquitaine, Italy, but also Burgundy and Alemania, frequently had the status of sub-kingdom. Other *regna*, such as Frisia, Saxony, Thuringia, and Bavaria, never had such status, probably for political reasons—these were areas with restive native aristocracies vulnerable to the risk of separatism. Regna that were not 'in use' as kingdoms, were as a rule called *ducatus* (duchy) and put under the authority of a duke.[2]

Expressing the ideal of multi-ethnicity was not the same as declaring that all 'peoples' in the empire were considered to be equal. In a revealing passage of Ermold the Black's panegyric on Charlemagne's son, Louis the Pious, the author states that all those different peoples that had been subjected to the Frankish king should 'rejoice at being so favoured that they deserved to be called by the name "servants of the Franks".'[3] This strongly suggests that the ideal of multi-ethnicity was subordinate to two other, and even more important, ideological concerns of Carolingian imperial rule, both of which stressed Frankish superiority. One was the ideal of assimilation. No matter how many peoples made up the Carolingian empire, in the end they all should become one, that is to say, integrated into the Christian Frankish people.[4] Ironically, this invitation to become Frankish was expressed most urgently with respect to the Saxons, who had been bullied into submission with more violence than any other 'people' conquered by the Franks. After their subjection, so Charlemagne's biographer, Einhard, tells us, the Saxons, just 'had to abandon the cult of

---

[2] Indicative for the confusion of what *regna* were, is the only serious attempt undertaken by the ageing Charlemagne to divide his empire by testament between his three legitimate sons then alive: Louis, Pippin, and Charles Jr. This document is known as the *Divisio regnorum*, but from the text it does not clearly appear which of the many territories mentioned were considered to be regna. *Regna* that we know from other sources are not called *regna* in this document; moreover they are mixed up with other types of administrative districts such as *marcae* (marcher counties/duchies, e.g. Wasconia, Hispania [the marcher counties straddling the western and eastern Pyrenees, respectively] and the Bavarian Nortgau), *ducatus* (e.g. the ducatus Curiensis), *pagi* and *civitates*. In one passage both the whole (Francia) and its constitutive parts (Austr[as]ia and Neustria) are mentioned separately. And from other territories the status remains unclear, such as Provence (Provincia) and 'Septimania vel Gothia' (present-day Languedoc). *Capitularia Regum Francorum. T. 1*, A. Boretius, ed. (Hannover, 1883)(Monumenta Germaniae Historica, Leges) (further: CRF1), nr 45, 126- 130; for a recent summary: Rosamond McKitterick, *Charlemagne: the formation of a European identity* (Cambridge etc., 2008), 96–9.

[3] *Charlemagne and Louis the Pious. The Lives by Einhard, Notker, Ermoldus, Thegan, and the Astronomer*, Thomas F.X. Noble (Eng. trl.) (State College PA, 2009), 67.

[4] E.g. McKitterick, *Charlemagne*, 271.

demons and let go of their ancestral rites, receive the sacraments of the Christian faith and religion, and unite themselves to the Franks so that they might become one people with them (*et Francis adunati unus cum eis populus efficerentur*).'[5] The other concern was related to the strong conviction that the Franks were God's newly chosen people—*vivat qui Francos diligit Christus* ('Long live Christ, who loves the Franks').[6] The Franks saw themselves as the vanguard of the *unus populus christianus* that, from an eschatological perspective, was soon going to extend over all the inhabited parts of the earth. An important task of their king was to keep them on the road to Salvation. By implication, there was no separation of State and Church in Charlemagne's empire; both were led by the emperor—not the pope!—and legislative activity could as easily be directed at improving morals and condemning sin, as at secular matters.

The ambiguous ideal of Carolingian government—to maintain a multigentile confederacy and to establish imperial unity dominated by the Franks—generated two different strategies of legislation. One was aimed at issuing laws that were valid for all. It was realized by a flood of capitularies—decrees and legal precepts many of which were general in scope. The other, with which we are going to deal, was to provide each regnum—and each people living in it—with its own written law code, the text of which had to be issued by the ruler after it had been established and approved by legal experts. Carolingians thought *lex* (written law that was issued) by definition to be superior to unwritten customs, witness, for instance, the following provision in one of Charlemagne's eldest son Pippin, king of Italy's capitularies: *Placuit nobis inserere: ubi lex est, praecellat consuetudinem, et nulla consuetudo superponatur legi.*[7] The high-profile presence of such legal maxims tempted nineteenth-century historians of law to invent a new umbrella term to indicate early-medieval law codes: *leges barbarorum*. By doing so they closed their eyes to the fact that these codes at close reading contain both *lex*, law imposed from above (*Satzung* in modern German) and *consuetudo*, local/regional customary law that until then had been orally transmitted (*Weistum* in modern German).[8] One could even say that, by having popular law issued from above, rulers

---

5 *Charlemagne*, Noble, 28–29. Further, also with quotation of the Latin text: Matthias Becher, *Rex, Dux und Gens. Untersuchungen zur Entstehung des sächsischen Herzogtums im 9. und 10. Jahrhundert* (Husum, 1996), 41.

6 Nelson, 'Kingship', 424. The Latin quote is from the [proemium] to the *Lex Salica*.

7 CRF1, nr. 95, article 10, at 201.

8 Cf. Gabriele von Olberg, *Die Bezeichnungen für soziale Stände, Schichten und Gruppen in den Leges Barbarorum* (Berlin/New York, 1991), 23–5.

displayed an ostentatious deference to the laws generated in the bosom of their subjects, while at the same expressing in no uncertain terms that these popular law codes always were subordinate to royal legislation from above.[9] Even so, we have to realize that the written law codes (*leges*) as we know them have never been complete, systematic, surveys of the living law that was applied in courts at the time; often they refer to unwritten customs that would remain unwritten for a long time to come.[10]

Charlemagne and the 'National' Law Codes

What was Charlemagne's role in this Carolingian legislative enterprise? What activities did he undertake to provide the peoples under his rule with their own 'national' law codes? During the first decades of his reign, the years of the great wars against the Lombards, the Muslims of Al-Andalus, the Saxons, the Avars and the Danes, his interventions were limited to incidental 'precepts' aimed at controling newly won territories and the people living in them. But soon after 800 this changed. A new policy of peace and territorial consolidation was accompanied by purposeful legislative activity, famously summarized in chapter 29 of Einhard's biography of Charlemagne:

> After he [Charlemagne] received the imperial name, he realized that his people's (*populi sui*) laws were deficient in many ways, for the Franks had two sets of laws, which differed sharply in many respects. He resolved to supply whatever was lacking, to reconcile the differences, and to correct whatever was badly or even falsely promulgated. But of this plan nothing else was done by him except that he added a few chapters to the laws, and these were incomplete. Still, he did command that the unwritten laws of all the peoples under his authority (*omnium nationum quae sub eius dominatu erant*) be written down.[11]

McKitterick saw this as 'the royal recognition [of] what was appropriate' for each and every people in the king's realm, and, from that perspective,

---

[9] Patrick Wormald, 'The *Leges Barbarorum*: law and ethnicity in the post-Roman West', in H.-W. Goetz, J. Jarnut, W. Pohl, eds., *Regna et gentes. The relationship between Late Antique and early medieval peoples and kingdoms in the transformation of the Roman world* (Leiden/Boston, 2003), 21–53, at 45.

[10] Rosamond McKitterick, *The Carolingians and the written word* (Cambridge, 1989), 37.

[11] *Charlemagne*, Noble, 44. For the Latin text: *Einhardi Vita Karoli Magni*, O. Holder-Egger, ed., (Hannover; Leipzig 1911). (MGH, Scriptores Rerum Germanicarum in usum scholarum 25), 33.

more 'as a unifying rather than divisive measure'.[12] Note, for a start, that Einhard made a difference between 'his people', who were the Franks, and all the 'nations' over which Charlemagne ruled. The measures that Charlemagne undertook are somewhat belittled by Einhard, and with good reason. Charlemagne certainly did not originate the practice of committing national laws to writing. By 800 many 'peoples', the Franks to start with, already had written law codes. So, what did Charlemagne's undertaking really imply? We can get a glimpse of the emperor's role at a large meeting, held at Aachen in the autumn of 802 and extensively discussed in the Lorsch version of the royal annals, where legislation featured on the agenda:

> And while this synod was being held the emperor also assembled the dukes, counts, and the rest of the Christian people together with men skilled in the laws and had all the laws in his realm read out and each man's law read out to him and emended wherever necessary and the emended law written down. And he declared that the *iudices* should judge in accordance with what was written and not accept gifts and that all men poor or rich should enjoy justice in his realm.[13]

Although neither of these narrative texts is precise as to which laws were 'emended and written down', other sources are more helpful. These also warn us that the information in Einhard and the Lorsch annals, even if not incorrect, may have been condensed (as was often the case), or else that the Aachen meeting was only the climax of a production process that in reality took several stages. This is suggested by the fact that in the same year 802 an assembly was held in the 'public palace' at Erfurt in Thüringen, at which 'the Lex Thuringiorum was drawn up by royal agents'.[14] However, on the outline of what happened, there is general agreement. There were activities of three kinds.

First, the two Frankish law codes, *Lex Salica* and *Lex Ribuaria*, were emended and 'published' in a final Caroline version. Einhard indicated, not very subtly, that there were very few last-minute modifications. Indeed, in the recent past there had been repeated restoration work on these law codes. The *Lex Salica*, for instance, had been amended both by Charlemagne and his father, Pippin the Short, in the second half of the

[12] McKitterick, *Charlemagne*, 275–276. Charlemagne's initiative of amending 'national' laws was repeated at the beginning of Louis the Pious' reign. Ibidem, 277.

[13] Quote in McKitterick, *Charlemagne*, 276.

[14] In the words of Matthew Innes, *State and society in the early Middle Ages: the Middle Rhine valley, 400–1000* (Cambridge, 2000), 115.

eighth century, but the strange thing is that, when Charlemagne wanted to establish the definitive text in 802—that would become the *Lex Salica Karolina*—he fell back on a much earlier, Merovingian, text version.[15] Besides, the text of the *Lex Salica Karolina* proved to be less permanent than Charlemagne and his legal advisors may have imagined at the time, because soon his successors issued official additions.[16]

The second activity was the revision and updating of those law codes of other 'nations' in the empire of which written versions already existed. This was the case for the Burgundian and Aleman laws.[17] No such work was done on Bavarian law, but with respect to Lombard law in Carolingian Italy there is a robust tradition of promulgating legislation in the form of capitularia, which was set in motion immediately after Charlemagne's take-over of the Lombard crown.[18] These capitularies not only provided for a Frankish administrative organization, centred on the count and his placitum, but many involved legal precepts that in one way or another interfered with Lombard law. One of the earliest Italian capitularies, issued by Charlemagne's eldest son and king of Italy, Pippin, provided for the coordinated operation of Frankish and Langobard courts under Frankish and Langobard counts. In several provisions of the important *Capitulare Italicum* of 801 'Roman law' and 'Lombard law' are compared with 'Frankish law'.[19]

The third, and last, activity consisted in the provision of a written law to peoples within the empire who did not yet have one. To this activity we can ascribe the *leges* of the Thuringians, the Saxons, and the Frisians, as well as a shorter code known under two names, the *Lex Francorum Chamavorum* and, more correctly, the *Ewa quae se ad Amorem habet*. None of these law codes are unproblematic. The *Lex Saxonum* had been preceded by two harsh, legal precepts for the Saxons that were issued while the Saxon wars were in full swing. The Lex itself was cast into 'a form greatly affected by [similar] Frankish codes'.[20] The existing text of

[15] McKitterick, *The Carolingians and the written word*, 40–41.

[16] The earliest examples are CRF1, nrs. 134 and 135 (Capitula legi addita), both issued by Louis the Pious in 816.

[17] Cf. McKitterick, *Charlemagne*, 276. See for a later addition to Burgundian law the Thusey capitulary of 865. *Capitularia Regum Francorum. T.* 2, A. Boretius, V. Krause, eds. (Hannover, 1897) (Monumenta Germaniae Historica, Leges) (further: CRF2), nr 274 (329 sqq).

[18] See CRF1, section V: *Karoli Magni et Pippini filii capitularia Italica.*

[19] CRF1, nrs. 91 and 98, respectively.

[20] McKitterick, *Charlemagne*, 253–54.

the *Lex Thuringorum*, although clearly influenced by the Frankish *Lex Ribuaria*,[21] has at least two unique features that raise the suspicion that beneath the *lex scripta* that was issued shortly after 800 were much older textual layers. One is the recognition of *adelingi* as a most privileged social group, protected by a wergeld three times higher than the wergeld of an ordinary freeman. Although obviously etymologically related to the old-German/old-English word 'æthel' (modern German 'edel'), *adalingus* should not be interpreted primarily as 'belonging to the nobility', but more as something like 'a freeborn heir to the family estate of a native Thuringian family' that had been rooted in Thüringen for many generations.[22] Another atavism is the identification of the Thuringians with the Warni and the Angles. The former was altogether common and understandable, but the latter remains rather mysterious. It might refer to remnants of one of the ethnic groups living in the Thüringen area in Late Antiquity that had lost its name and ethnic identity because of the migration of many Angles to Britannia. Or it might refer to groups of Angles that had resettled from England in the Thüringen area around 540.[23] In both cases these were events that had happened many centuries before Charlemagne's reign, going back to a period when *Thuringi*[*a*] was an ethnographic umbrella term of the sort well known from the migration period, with 'Franks' as an important example. The *Lex Frisionum* is fraught with other difficulties of interpretation, not the least of which is that no manuscript of it has been preserved—the oldest material witness is an editio princeps of 1557. Compared to other *leges nationum* from the Carolingian empire, another unique feature is its enormously detailed so-called 'wound list', which very much looks like the tariff list of a modern health insurance company (what can you expect to receive as a compensation [now: reimbursement] for damage [now: medical treatment] suffered for this or that 'wound' [now: illness or injury] that had been inflicted on you?).[24]

---

21 Heike Grahn-Hoek, 'Das Recht der Thüringer und die Frage ihrer ethnischen Identität. Mit einer Bemerkung zur Entstehung von Begriff und Institution "Adel"', in Helmut Castritius, Dieter Geuenich, Matthias Werner, eds., *Die Frühzeit der Thüringer* (Berlin, 2009), 415–456, at 432–33.

22 Grahn-Hoek, 'Das Recht', 421–429.

23 On this event: Mathias Kälble, 'Ethnogenese und Herzogtum Thüringen im Frankenreich (6.–9. Jahrhundert)', in Castritius, Geuenich, and Werner, *Die Frühzeit*, 329–413, at 337–41 and 349.

24 Cf. Han Nijdam, *Lichaam, eer en recht in middeleeuws Friesland. Een studie naar de Oudfriese boeteregisters*. 2 Vols. (Hilversum, 2008), 67–69. On the editor, Johannes Basilius Herold, and the quality of his work, see Harald Siems, *Studien zur Lex Frisionum* (Ebelsbach

The Ewa ad Amorem *as a Special Case*

The *Ewa* is a maverick altogether—not a 'national law code' in the usual sense, but a set of laws applied in a specific pagus or administrative district. Its title in modern editions, *Lex Francorum Chamavorum* ('Law of the Chamavi Franks'), is a misnomer, created by scholars in the nineteenth century and not justified by anything in the text itself. The idea that the Ewa would have been the law code of the Chamavi has originated from linking the geographical term *ad Amorem* ('at the Amer [river]') from the original (?) law code's heading to the name of a *pagus* (a district led by a count), which appears in sources of the ninth century: *Hama[r]land.* Both the identification of this Hama[r]land with the Amor of the Ewa and the etymological interpretation of Hama[r]land as 'Land of the Chamavi', one of the many Germanic tribes living north of the Lower Rhine mentioned by classical authors such as Tacitus and Ammianus Marcellinus, have been disputed.[25] The Ewa is not a 'national law code' for yet another, formal, reason, which is quite revealing about the extent of Charlemagne's legislative activities. The text starts with what must be seen as answers to a questionnaire that was made up on behalf of *missi dominici* (royal envoys) who came on inspection. That is why in the opening provisions a distinction is made between '[what] *we* have [as a law]' and what '[the] other Franks' (*alii Franci*) 'have'. The latter phrasing has been explained in the sense that the Ewa must have been some sort of extension to the Frankish national law codes, and in particular to the *Lex Ribuaria.* If that were the case, its implication would be that the Amor territory was outside the old Frankish kingdoms, Neustria and Austrasia. At the same time the text gives ample proof that the Amor land had already been fully organized as a standard administrative district within the Frankish empire at the moment when the Ewa was written: Amor appears to be the name of a gau or pagus; the king's 'ban' (sovereign power) and the king's peace (*fredus dominicus*),

---

am Main, 1980), ch. 3. The annexe of Siems' book contains a photographic facsimile of Herold's edition.

[25] The name of the Chamavi also appears on the late-Roman road map known as the Tabula Peutingeriana. The first scholar to argue that the Ewa would have been the Lex Chamavorum was Ernst Theodor Gaupp in 1855. 'Lex Francorum Chamavorum', Rudolph Sohm, ed., in *Leges in folio*, V (MGH, Leges), 113–123, at 114–15. For a survey of modern debate on the significance of the Ewa: E.J. Harenberg, 'De homines franci uit de *Codex Laureshamensis*', in a.a.v.v. *Ad fontes. Opstellen aangeboden aan prof.dr. C. van de Kieft ter gelegenheid van zijn afscheid als hoogleraar in de middeleeuwse geschiedenis aan de Universiteit van Amsterdam* (Amsterdam, 1984), 39–60.

both sanctioned by a penalty to be paid to the king, were asserted; the territory had a count (or several counts?), who held *placita* (law suits) and on the local level there were *centenarii* ('hundredmen'; leaders of centenae); it was visited by *missi dominici* on inspection tour.

There is no doubt that this Amor land was situated somewhere north of the Lower Meuse in the present-day Dutch provinces of Gelderland and Overijssel. Articles 28 and 29 mention *Fresiones* and *Saxones*, respectively, as the only non-Frankish perpetrators of crimes the informants could think of, and from article 27 we can infer that the Pagus Amor was adjacent to the Meuse gau (*Mashau*). As to the Ewa's dating, it is safe to say that the text as we know it would have been drawn up somewhere in the early ninth century, when the missaticum system, to which it refers in clause 8, was fully operative. However, because the opening provisions of the Ewa serve to confirm the existence of an already functioning law code rather than to create one ex nihilo, it is likely that most provisions reflect an earlier situation, when the disputed lands between the territories of Frisians and Saxons north of the Meuse were still in turmoil, that is to say, between the Frankish conquest of the Frisian coastal area in the 730's and the scaling-up of the Saxon wars at the end of the 770's. There are two important indications that support this view. One is that the two clauses of the Ewa that refer to misdemeanors of Frisians and Saxons obviously think of them as foreign enemies who are to be subjected to a crude 'an eye for an eye' rule, instead of being treated in accordance with their own law, as the personality principle (see below) would have required. This suggests that at the time of the first formulation of many provisions of the Ewa, the Frisians and the Saxons had not yet been definitely incorporated into the empire and had not yet received their own law codes (*Lex Frisionum* and *Lex Saxonum*), which would have provided a formal basis for the application of the personality of law principle. The second indication is that, according to the Ewa, the lives of four kinds of persons were protected by a wergeld that was thrice the standard amount of 200 solidi that had to be paid for killing an ordinary free man: counts, *missi dominici*, *wargengi* (foreigners—often mercenaries—who stood under the special protection of the king), and so-called *homines Franci*, who get by far the most attention. All four had a special relation to the king himself and could always count on his special protection, so why stress this extra protection by raising their lives' value in law?

In trying to answer this question, it is revealing to take a closer look at the position of these *homines Franci*. Not only did these people have a raised wergeld of 600 solidi, they were also protected by high fines against being tied up, grabbed by the hair or wounded; fines were also levied on those who broke into their houses or infringed on the boundaries of their farmsteads or estates (*curtes*). Finally, the Ewa laid down some basic inheritance rules that were specifically applicable to *homines Franci*. Why was there a need for these special measures? In my opinion this was the case because of the strained situation in the area, in which Frankish power still must have been shaky and not yet firmly established. In other words, although it is impossible to get a more precise idea of the type of (para)military obligations such men would have had or of the rewards (in land?) on which they could count in addition to extra legal protection, these were militarized Frankish colonists of substantial social status who had settled in a semi-warzone or in recently conquered territory.[26] The real existence (and not just in law) of such a special category of people at the northern frontier of the Carolingian empire is confirmed by more or less contemporaneous lists of possessions of the abbeys of Prüm in the German Eiffel, and of those of Saint-Bavo and Saint-Peter at Ghent—all bearing on the years around 800—which all mention *Franci homines* as substantial landholders in areas just south of the Lower Meuse delta.[27]

This proliferation of *Franci homines* as a form of expansionist outpost of Frankish imperialist power raises the question whether people with the same status and function existed in other border areas as well. The

[26] The clause on inheritance (clause 42) does not hint at any possession of specific types of land, such as (royal) beneficia. Neither does the Ewa disclose anything about the (para)military obligations that may have been demanded from the F/franci homines in exchange for their legal protection. The seven clauses that specify the public duties of a free man in Frankish society—military and paramilitary service (clauses 34–39), and the attendance of public court sessions (clause 40)—are neutral in their indication of which categories of men living in the Ewa land were expected to participate in them. These clauses all start with *si quis* (...) ('if somebody (...)').

[27] *Oorkondenboek van Noord-Brabant tot 1312. I. De meierij van 's-Hertogenbosch (met de heerlijkheid Gemert)*. H.P.H. Camps, ed., 2 Vols. ('s-Gravenhage, 1979), I.1., nr. 17. Adriaan Verhulst, 'Das Besitzverzeichnis der Genter Sankt-Bavo-Abtei von ca. 800 (Clm 6333). Ein Beitrag zur Geschichte und Kritik der karolingischen Urbarialaufzeichnungen', *Frühmittelalterliche Studien. Jahrbuch des Instituts für Frühmittelalterforschung der Universität Münster* 5 (1971), 193–234; for his dating of the list: 219; for the text fragment on the homines Franci: 234. *Diplomata Belgica ante annum millesimum centesimum scripta. I. Teksten*. M. Gysseling, A.C.F. Koch, eds. (Ghent, 1950), nr. 49. Recent articles on these source texts are Harenberg, 'De homines franci', who remains convinced that not only were these homines so-called franci *Königsfreien*, they also would have been royal vassals. The latter opinion is also held by P.A. Henderikx, 'Walcheren van de 6e tot de 12e eeuw: nederzettingsgeschiedenis in fragmenten', *Archief van het Koninklijk Zeeuwsch Genootschap der Wetenschappen* (1993), 113–156, there 123–124 and note 42. Georges Declercq, Adriaan Verhulst (†), 'Villa et mansus dans le *Liber Traditionum* du Xe siècle de l'abbaye de Saint-Pierre-au-Mont-Blandin de Gand', *Revue Belge de Philologie et d'Histoire* 81 (2003), 1015–1022.

most obvious place to look would be Franconia, whose original name, *Francia orientalis/australis*, was given to a duchy that covered the southern part of the former kingdom of Thuringia, which had been annihilated by the Franks as early as 531.[28] Not only does this reference to the name of the Franks suggest that, after this event, Frankish infiltration into the region must have been substantial, but also that Franks who settled outside the Frankish heartlands somehow remained recognizable as 'Franks', not unlikely because they maintained their own law. Regrettably, the process of Frankicisation (*Verfrankung* in German) in this area is not easy to follow. The extant sources show how first missionaries and Frankish royal dignitaries took up their places, then how Frankish organisational structures—duchy, counties, dioceses, (royal) monasteries, royal palaces and estates—were grafted upon the area. But none of the sources related to the early history of Franconia mention *Franci homines* as people with a special legal status. The closest hint we have is in a precious territorial circumscription of the Franconian diocese of Würzburg from around 780 which states that in the diocese there are three special categories of landed possessions: estates of the bishop, royal estates, and *friero Franchono erbi* ('lands of free Franks'—which is not the same as 'of Frankish men').[29] Equally sparse and ambiguous are mentions of *Franci homines* from other border areas. One is a relatively late reference in the Annals of St-Bertin to 'some *Franci homines*' who in 874 were involved in the killing of the Breton chief, Salomon, 'to whom Salomon had been extremely oppressive.'[30] Clearly, the perpetrators of this crime were men of some social weight from the Breton march, who had played a role in representing Frankish interests in Britanny.

Apart from the shortage of data, the major problem with tracking down the *Franci homines* as a special category of military colonists under royal

---

[28] According to Notker the Stammerer, Franconia consisted of two parts which he named *Francia Antiqua* and *Francia Nova*, respectively. Modern historians have identified these with Rheinfranken and Ost- or Mainfranken, respectively. The most important place in Mainfranken was, and still is, Frankfurt—*Franconofurd* in the Annales regni Francorum. *Charlemagne*, Noble, 76 and 78. *Notker Balbulus, Gesta Karoli Magni Imperatoris*, Hans F. Haefele, ed., (Berlin, 1959) (MGH, Scriptores Rerum Germanicarum; nova series 12), 27, note 5.

[29] Wilhelm Störmer, *Franken von der Völkerwanderungszeit bis 1268* (Munich, 1999), 42–66. The document is at 191, nr. 37.

[30] *The Annals of St-Bertin*, Janet L. Nelson (trl.) (Manchester/New York 1991), 186. Nelson, in footnote 5, qualifies them as 'the local squirearchy of western Neustria', being descendants of 'free tenants owing special military service' who had been 'settled in the Breton March by Carolingian rulers.'

protection remains that we also encounter them in sources related to the possession of land rights in the Frankish heartlands, in which case the 'francus' probably must be interpreted as '[of] free [birth]'. This suggests that *homines F/franci* could mean two different things at more or less the same time: in documents related to the Frankish heartlands they were first of all 'free [Frankish] men',[31] whereas in documents related to territories outside Francia they were first of all '[able-bodied] Frankish [free] men'. The term francus/Francus could have both these social and ethnic connotations, and it may not be too far-fetched to assume that the Franks liked this ambiguity—a real Frank is a free man who is willing to carry arms[32]—but it drives modern text editors crazy. Should they print 'francus' or 'Francus'? By doing the former they would (over?)stress the social connotation, by doing the latter the ethnic connotation. To make things even more complicated, one could point out that in Charlemagne's time the ethnic meaning of the term 'Franci' was clearly receding in favour of a more territorialized meaning. In Carolingian legal and administrative documents, 'Franks' first of all means the inhabitants of *Francia*, that is to say, the original Frankish kingdoms, Neustria and Austrasia, which roughly comprised the area between the rivers Loire and Rhine.[33] Not much later, the Astronomer, in his Life of Louis the Pious, written shortly after 840, was the first to make the distinction between 'Franks' and 'Germans', although for a long time the opposition West-Franks against East-Franks was preferred.[34]

'National' Law in the Carolingian Empire: A Survey

With the final redaction and writing down of the law codes of the Thuringians, Saxons and Frisians during the first decade of the ninth century, all of Charlemagne's empire's vast territory could now be said to be 'covered' by written law, as asserted by Einhard and the royal annals. The Frankish heartlands were ruled by the laws of the Salian and Ripuarian Franks,

---

[31] As in CRF1, nr. 15 (anno 757), at 38, item 7 ('Si Francus homo (..). Similiter et femina ingenua'), and nr. 142 (anno 819), at 292, item 3.

[32] Cf. Wormald, 'Leges barbarorum', 28–33.

[33] That is why Charlemagne's biographer, Notker the Stammerer, did not think of himself as living in *Francia*: he was a monk in the Aleman monastery of St-Gall. *Charlemagne*, Noble, 89.

[34] *Charlemagne*, Noble, 269 and 276. In earlier, Merovingian, texts Francia could also include the old kingdom of Burgundy. Rosamond McKitterick, *The Frankish kingdoms under the Carolingians, 751–987* (London/New York, 1983), 17–19.

the regnum of Burgundy, including parts of Provence(?) by the corpus of Burgundian law, which was heavily influenced by Roman law, North- and Central Italy by (Romanized) Lombard law, the upper Rhine region and the lower part of modern Switzerland by Aleman law, and Bavaria and the Ostmark (present-day Austria) by Bavarian law. This is just a sketch in broad outlines, if only because we do not know the exact borders of all *regna*, nor to what extent *regna* really coincided with 'national laws'. In particular the areas in which some form of vulgate Roman law remained in use are difficult to reconstruct. The chance survival of a private law book from around the middle of the ninth century—probably once in possession of a judge or a notary—reveals that at that time Visigothic Roman law was still in use in Raetia, that is to say, in the eastern Swiss Alps.[35] Furthermore we have to reckon with the existence of specific legal provisions—usually called *praecepta*—that were made for frontier regions/pagi or groups of subjects that had settled there. The *Ewa ad Amorem* is one good example as are the successive statutory provisions made for the so-called *Goti* or *Hispani*, meaning refugees from the former Visigothic Kingdom of Spain, that was now under Muslim rule. After the first Carolingian conquests in the direction of the Ebro river these Hispani were settled on deserted lands or *aprisiones* in the Spanish march, which covered the territory between about Béziers in the north and Barcelona in the south.[36] From the start, these refugee-settlers had a legal status-aparte, which carried with it the obligation to perform military and paramilitary service (such as reconnoitring and keeping watch along the border) just as other Franks or free men.[37] In recompense, however, they would be free of the payment of any other *census, tributum aut obsequium* to the count of their district or to any of his subordinates. They also acquired limited jurisdictional autonomy, i.e. they could try minor cases (*causae minores*) among themselves and *more suo* i.e. according to their own Spanish-Visigothic law; only the trial of *causae majores* (serious crimes) should be left to the count. Further, they were free to settle more

---

[35] On this *Lex Romana Raetica Curiensis*, e.g. McKitterick, *The Carolingians and the written word*, 109–110.

[36] On the *aprisio* in earlier, Visigothic law: Jean-Pierre Devroey, *Économie rurale et société dans l'Europe franque (VIe–IXe siècles). Tome 1. Fondements matériels, échanges et lien social* (Paris, 2003), 74–75.

[37] Significantly, one of the two constitutive documents in which the legal status of the Hispani/Goti was defined, issued in 844, has *sicut caeteri Franci hominess*, while the other, issued in 815 has *sicut caeteri liberi hominess*. CRF2, nr. 256, at 259, and CRF1, nr. 132, at 261, respectively.

people (from anywhere) on their *portiones* (the land assigned to them) and to become vassals of the count and receive a *beneficium* (or a fief) from him.

This legal construction, explicitly called *ius aprisionis* in a royal charter of 844, but whose outline and workings can be traced back to several previous capitularies and charters, the oldest one from around 795,[38] leads one to suspect that the Carolingian kings and their prefects in the Spanish march made arrangements with aristocratic refugees, who then acted as leaders of groups of colonists and organizers of land reclamation on estates in deserted frontier areas. Modern authors who studied the case of these *aprisiones* have pointed out different possible motives behind their constitution: military defense against Muslim threats, repopulation of deserted areas, reinforcement of secular Frankish presence in conjunction with the simultaneous increase of the number of monasteries in the area, and reinforcement of the 'royal power base' in border regions at the cost of counts. The last of these points, stressed by Cullen Chandler, is the most intriguing because it says a lot about the balance of power between various aristocratic interest groups and their mutual struggles exactly in border regions far away from the Carolingian heartlands.[39] In this case, the tensions between the Hispani, the counts of the districts in which they lived, and other, native, landowners there surfaced in 812, when a delegation of 40 'Goths' traveled to the imperial court at Aachen to complain about their harassers. The whole procedure firmly suggests that the Hispani stood under the special protection of the emperor himself,[40] even if this protected position was not nearly the same as a grant of immunity, which monasteries under royal protection often received.[41]

38 I do not see why the capitulary in favour of the Hispani, presumably issued by Charlemagne around 780, printed in *Catalunya Carolingia. Vol. 2. Els diplomes carolingis a Catalunya*, R. d'Abadal i de Vinyals, ed., 2 vols. (Barcelona, 1926–1952), I, 412–414, should ever have really existed. The editor reconstructed almost the entire text from the two constitutive *praecepta pro Hispanis* from 815 and 844. However, only recently, Cullen Chandler still took it for genuine, despite earlier, and sensible, caution by Dupont who concluded that the 'constitution' of the special legal status of the Hispani was established somewhere between 780 and 800. Cf. Cullen J. Chandler, 'Between court and counts: Carolingian Catalonia and the *aprisio* grant, 778–897', *Early Medieval Europe* 11 (2002), 19–44, at 25–27, and A. Dupont, 'L'aprision et le régime aprisionaire dans le Midi de la France (fin du VIIIe–début du Xe siècle)', *Le Moyen Âge* 71 (1965), 179–213 and 375–399, at 183 and 188–189.

39 Chandler, 'Between court and counts', 32, 36.

40 Dupont, 'L'aprision', 190–193.

41 As was suggested by Chandler, 'Between court and counts', 25–26. Immunity would have freed the Hispani completely from any interference by counts, but neither of the

National Law Codes and Legal Practice

Whether these law codes, general/national or special, were in fact used in court, is heavily discussed by modern specialists. Some, like the late Patrick Wormald, have stressed 'the predominantly symbolic function and primarily ideological character of the written laws [of the early Middle Ages]'.[42] German scholars who shared this view underlined the function of written law as 'Ausdruck fränkischer Herrschaftspotenz', as 'Program und Integrationssymbol des fränkischen Grossreiches', or as 'Prestige- und Demonstrationsobjekte' that had to prove that the Frankish leaders were on equal footing with the Roman emperors of the past.[43] Others, however, led by Rosamond McKitterick, have argued, mainly on the basis of (substantial) numbers of manuscripts and traces of intensive use in them, that Carolingian laws, and especially the so-called 'national laws' must indeed have been widely applied in legal practice and public administration (for instance by *missi dominici*).[44] The latter point has led to new discussion. On the one hand, there are those who think that the practice of putting together legal collections (*Sammelcodices* in German) of 'national laws' served the interests of ecclesiastical large landowners (monasteries, bishops) which often owned estates in different parts of the empire.[45] On the other hand there are those who believe that this well-attested practice proves the application of personality of law in courts of law where litigants were of various ethnic/national background.[46]

Ethnic Personality of Law in the Carolingian World

This brings us to the second major aspect of Carolingian legislation that we distinguished at the beginning: the application of the legal principle of ethnic or 'national' personality of law. This principle holds that different ethnic groups or nations in a multigentile state not only live according to

capitularies that regulated their legal position, nor such documents as the Aachen charter of 812 suggest that this was the case.

42 Quoted by McKitterick, *The Carolingians and the written word*, 38.

43 Quotes by W. Sellert, 'Aufzeichnung des Rechts und Gesetz', in idem, ed., *Das Gesetz in Spätantike und frühem Mittelalter* (Göttingen, 1992), 67–102, at 72.

44 McKitterick, *The Carolingians and the written word*, esp. chapter 2. Also: McKitterick, *Charlemagne*, resp. 249 and 265–266, 277–278.

45 Clausdieter Schott, 'Der Stand der Leges-Forschung', *Frühmittelalterliche Studien* 13 (1979), 29–55, at 49.

46 E.g. Sellert, 'Aufzeichnung', 84–87 and 90, note 135.

their own law, but also that each individual who is implicated in a trial or a legal dispute can claim his or her own 'national' law, regardless of where the trial or lawsuit takes place.[47] The application of this principle was certainly no Carolingian novelty. It existed in the Roman Empire as well as in the barbarian successor kingdoms of the early-medieval West, but in both cases one should speak of strictly dualistic systems, which recognized only two legal groups: in the Roman Empire Roman citizens versus (free) foreigners living in the empire, in the early-medieval kingdoms the native Romanized population versus the foreign barbarian ruling elite. In the latter the ethnic personality principle was gradually undermined by two tendencies: one towards the contamination of ethnicity with socio-professional status (the ethnic names Goti and Romani in Ostrogothic Italy came to indicate, respectively, military men and civilians), the other towards the territorialization of ethnic names (in early-medieval Burgundy the meaning of the name Burgundio would have changed from 'a member of the people of the Burgundians' into 'a person living in the kingdom of the Burgundians').[48] As we saw, this last tendency—in fact a move away from a racial conception of ethnicity to a territorial one—could also be observed at the constitution of 'national' law codes in the Carolingian empire, which in reality were not so much law codes of ethnic groups as laws of all the people who lived in a certain territory. The difference is more than a detail. Not coincidentally several of the law codes that have been discussed contain very precise territorial demarcations. Most elaborate is the Lex Frisionum, whose validity extended from the river Weser in the north to the Sincfall estuary (near Bruges) in the south, but this territory had three parts, separated from one another by the Flie and the Lauwers estuaries, which sometimes had deviating laws. Also narrowly circumscribed was the Carolingian duchy of Thüringen which was

[47] The principle is often called 'the principle of [the] personality of law' outright, also in the title of the standard work on ethnic personality of law in the earlier Middle Ages: Simeon L. Guterman, *The principle of the personality of law in the Germanic kingdoms of Western Europe from the fifth to the eleventh century* (New York etc., 1990). In fact, personality of law had various other applications in the European Middle Ages (think of the special legal status for clergy or for unfree persons), which Guterman duly recognized, after which he concluded that 'it might be more correct to speak of nationality or ethnicity of law than of the personality of law' (34).

[48] I follow the line of the directional article by Patrick Amory, 'The meaning and purpose of ethnic terminology in the Burgundian laws', *Early Medieval Europe* 2, no. 1 (1993), 1–28.

enclosed by clear, natural borders: the Harz mountains, the Thüringer Wald, and the rivers Werra and Saale.[49]

So when the Carolingian rulers allowed the principle of ethnic personality of law in connection with territorial law codes, what they actually did was create a system of 'mobile territorial law within a multinational empire' according to the felicitous expression of Patrick Amory, that has been adopted by major specialists in the field such as McKitterick.[50] In practice this meant that people could claim the law of their place of birth, or were tried in accordance with it, wherever they were (in the empire). For example, the Ewa ad Amorem stipulates that he who kills a count or a *missus* shall pay three times the normal wergeld [i.e. of a free man] *sicut sua nativitas est* ('in accordance with his place of birth')—although it remains obscure whether the place of birth of the perpetrator or the victim is meant.

In Charlemagne's time, this principle was anything but new. The earliest traces of it in Frankish law go back to the *Lex Ribuaria* and the so-called *Formulae* of Marculf, both from the seventh century. In particular, article 35 of the *Lex Ribuaria* ('De homine ingenuo repraesentando') is revealing. Subsection 3 of this clause states, in the form of a new regulation:

> We lay down (*constituimus*) that when within the Ribuarian district (*infra pago Ribuario*) a Frank, a Burgundian, an Alaman, or whoever is there from another nation is questioned in a court of law (*in iudicio interpellatus*), that he shall answer in accordance with the law of the place where he is born (*sicut lex loci ubi natus fuerit*).[51]

The next subsection states that whoever is convicted to pay a fine, will do so in accordance with his own law (*secundum legem propriam*), not with Ribuarian law. According to Simeon Guterman, the author of the only monograph ever published on the subject of personality of law in medieval Europe, these two rulings epitomize two crucial elements of the personality principle: in a lawsuit between parties with different nationalities, 'the law of the defendant is applied', while this law of the defendant is

49 Kälble, 'Ethnogenese und Herzogtum', 337 and especially 371–73.

50 Amory, 'Meaning and purpose', 22. McKitterick, *Charlemagne*, 244–45.

51 MGH, *Leges Nationum Germanicarum. Tomi III pars II. Lex Ribuaria.* Franz Beyerle, Rudolf Buchner, eds. (Hannover, 1954), at 87. The subject in the first part of the sentence is in fact in the plural; I have turned that into a singular, because the second part of the sentence is in the singular.

specified as 'the law of the place of origin' of the defendant.[52] I would add as a third element that defendants who are fined or punished(?), receive their fine or punishment(?) in accordance with their own law, not that of the place where the offense or the crime(?) was committed or of the place where the offender is tried.[53] The question marks are there because there is some doubt regarding whether the personality principle was applicable only to private law, or also to the trial of crimes subject to corporal punishment. At first consideration, Guterman's work lacks consistency on this point. On the one hand, by constantly using the term 'system of private international law', it suggests that the personality principle applied only to private law. On the other hand, it sometimes explicitly refers to the application of the personal law principle in the trial of criminal cases.[54] The problem is that in the Middle Ages the dividing line between private law and criminal justice differed from that in modern legal systems, particularly in cases of homicide and grave injury which, if not dealt with by immediate physical revenge, were resolved by a formal reconciliation between the families of perpetrator and victim after the payment of a substantial compensation (wergeld). In Guterman's view, and I cannot but agree, such reconcilable acts of violence were seen as 'private offences due to individuals', and therefore submitted to the personal law system. Crimes that were deemed irreconcilable, however, were seen as 'violations involving the public interest', and therefore dealt with by or on behalf of the king himself, without regard to the personality principle.[55]

There is indeed no doubt that the personality principle extended to wergeld payments. This also appears most clearly from the Lex Ribuaria, from the intriguing article 40, whose text Guterman condemned to a footnote:

> If some Ribuarian kills a Frankish foreigner (*advenam Francum*), let him be condemned to the payment of 200 solidi, if found guilty.
>
> If some Ribuarian kills a Burgundian foreigner, let him be fined to twice 80 solidi.

[52] Guterman, *The principle*, 105. Guterman still used the older MGH edition by Rudolph Sohm from the 1880s (which has a different numeration).

[53] This was not necessarily the case. Sometimes the crime scene (the *locus delicti commissi*) determined the law at the trial. Guterman, *The principle*, 163–166, is not quite precise enough in distinguishing crimes from offenses (in accordance with criteria that were in force at the time).

[54] Most clearly: Guterman, *The principle*, 164–166.

[55] Guterman, *The principle*, 186.

> If some Ribuarian kills an Aquitanian foreigner (*advenam Romanum*), let him be fined to twice 50 solidi.
>
> If some Ribuarian kills a Aleman foreigner, or a Frisian, or a Bavarian, or a Saxon, let him pay twice 80 solidi, if found guilty.[56]

This provision is revealing for three reasons. First, since the older redactions of the Lex Ribuaria go back to the (early) seventh century, one could expect all the peoples mentioned in this clause to be called foreigners or, better still, foreign immigrants (*advenae*). Their homelands may at times have groaned under Frankish pressure and agression, but none of them were at that time definitely incorporated into the Frankish kingdoms, except, of course, that of 'the Franks'. 'Franci' in this context—and the same goes for the Franci of clause 35—means 'Salian Franks', that is to say, Franks from the Neustrian kingdom, who lived under the Lex Salica, as opposed to the Austrasian kingdom, whose Frankish subjects lived under the Lex Ribuaria. During most of the seventh and early eighth centuries these kingdoms had their own kings, although almost always from the Merovingian dynasty. Obviously, that sufficed to qualify the Neustrian Franks as foreigners. But at the same time they were the most valuable foreigners, and that is the second revelation: not all foreigners were valued equally. The Aquitanians, the people living south from the Loire river, were valued least, while the Frankish brothers from Neustria were valued highest—they had the same wergeld as a Ribuarian free man. The third reason to wonder is that the Lex Ribuaria gives proof of the existence of a truly inter-ethnic system of international law, which would change into a pseudo-international system once all the 'peoples' mentioned in clauses 35 and 40 of the Lex Ribuaria had been taken under the protective wings of the Carolingian empire.

Ethnic Personal Law in Practice

Even if the new situation would have made it easier to really apply the (ethnic) personality principle in courts of law, the question remains whether Charlemagne's 'ramshackle empire' was capable of setting up a judicial system sophisticated enough to make the principle of ethnic personality of law work.[57] Guterman was sceptical. Right at the beginning

---

[56] MGH, *Lex Ribuaria,* at 92.

[57] 'Ramshackle empire' is a qualification by Julia M.H. Smith, *Province and empire: Brittany and the Carolingians* (Cambridge etc., 1992), 9.

of a number of chapters on the personality principle in legal practice, he pointed to the fact that there 'was no legislation or clearly defined procedure whereby a person was forced to continue to live by his own law.' This sounds a bit like the complaint of a modern bureaucrat, as does the lament that often in 'medieval political life' legislation was not accompanied by rules for implementation or by sanctions. Apart from that, it is easy to see that in legal practice all kinds of complications arise from the interference of personal ethnic/national law with other legal customs. Whose law prevailed when a woman was married to a man from a different nation? Which 'national' law had to be followed by freedmen (manumitted slaves)? Could members of the clergy still invoke their personal ethnic/national law or were they always treated under Roman law because the Roman Church fell under Roman law?[58]

I tend to be more optimistic. There are many and diverse signs that personal ethnic law worked in practice. An early example is provided by the Thüringian rebellion against Charlemagne of 785–786, the immediate cause of which was the bethrothal of a Thüringian woman to a Frankish man *secundum legem Francorum* ('according to Frankish law').[59] Another one is in the so-called *capitula Italica*, a series of extracts from capitularies—many of which have been lost—issued by Charlemagne and his eldest son Pippin as kings of the Langobards that have been collected in a Lombard lawbook. One of the items states that if a legal dispute arose between a *Langobardus* and a *Romanus* the ethnic personality principle would be applied to cases of inheritance (*successio*), alienation (*conscriptiones*), the taking of oaths, and dealings with wergeld compensations. In all other cases a common law was applied (*communi lege vivamus*), and that common law could be found in Charlemagne's edict—which then followed.[60] In this particular context, Langobardus probably means anybody who lived according to Lombard law (i.e. people from North- and Central Italy), while Romanus stood for all living according to Roman law (i.e. people from the Papal State or southern Gaul?). Furthermore, Guterman collected extensive evidence from lawsuits on disputed marriage

---

[58] All these issues are treated in Guterman, *The principle*, ch. 5–8. The quotes are from page 135.

[59] Kälble, 'Ethnogenese und Herzogtum', 386–87.

[60] CRF1, nr. 105, item 14, at 218–19. That this general rule was indeed followed, may appear from clause 16 of the instruction given by the Emperor Lothar to his counts in Italy in 822–823, which states that a 'Roman woman', or a woman of any other nation (*natio*), married to a 'Langobard man' may return to her own law (*ad suam legem revertatur*) after her husband died. CRF1, nr. 158, at 319.

gifts, donations or sales of landed property, acts of emancipation, etcetera, from the ninth to eleventh centuries (mostly based on Hübner's list of records of judicial proceedings [*Gerichtsurkunden*]), which proves that the principle of national personal law was indeed put into practice. It is true that most of the law suits summarized by Hübner bear on civil actions in *placita* held in (present-day) southern France between a party that wants to stick to 'Roman' law and a party that wants to have 'Salic' law applied.[61] Since 'Roman' in such cases stands for Aquitanian/Languedocian/Provencal and 'Salic' for northern French, this means that for a long time, and doubtlessly despite frequent intermarrying, migrants from the north must have kept their northern '[national] identity' while living in the south. In the southwest it sometimes happened that a party in a lawsuit appealed to a third law code, the 'Gothic' or Spanish one. This could turn a lawsuit into an extremely complicated business, as appears from a case about the rightful possession of an estate that was pleaded in 918 in the public court (*mallus publicus*) of Alzonne near Toulouse. For some reason—the extant document does not say what this was—the trial required the presence of 17 judges, five *Romani* (experts in Roman law), four *Goti* (men versed in Spanish law), and eight *Salici* (experts in North-French-Salic law).[62]

One does not have to be a trained jurist to see that such tedious (and expensive) procedures would always have been something that only the rich and the powerful could afford or, more in general, that systems of personal law have predictable disadvantages in legal practice. The chaos that could arise when people living under different laws met in court and needed their own judges was already denounced ca. 830 in a famous quip of bishop Agobard of Lyons (himself a Spaniard, where territorial 'Gothic' law had existed since the seventh century) who particularly loathed the frequent appeal to old Burgundian law in his diocese. Fortunately there was one law of Jesus Christ but before that would be accepted by everyone this horrible Burgundian law, issued long ago by King Gundobad, 'a great enemy of the Catholics' because he had been 'an adherent of the Arian heresy' was better 'transferred' to Frankish law! And why stop with Burgundian law? Would it not please God 'that under a single devout king

[61] That is to say, in the first part of Hübner's list; the second, even larger, part is entirely on Italy.

[62] Rudolf Hübner, 'Gerichtsurkunden der Fränkischen Zeit. Erste Abteilung. Die Gerichtsurkunden aus Deutschland und Frankreich bis zum Jahre 1000', *Zeitschrift der Savigny-Stiftung für Rechtsgeschichte, Germanistische Abteilung* 12 (1891), 1–118, at 90–91 (nr. 487). For the complete text of the verdict: Marcel Thévenin, *Textes relatifs aux institutions privées et publiques aux époques Merovingienne et Carolingienne* (Paris, 1887), nr. 123.

a single law may direct all the nations of this empire'?[63] Agobard's call to legal unification would prove to be centuries ahead of its time. In Agobard's days the first ones to flout the bishop's good advice were the Carolingian rulers themselves, who just like anyone else invoked their personal law, which was the 'lex Salica aut Ribuaria'.[64]

Ethnic Personal Law and Frankish Migration

One could argue that problems caused by the application of ethnic personal law in the form of mobile territorial law would always have been very limited because, compared to modern standards, most people in the earlier Middle Ages were not mobile at all. This is true, but, on the other hand, the central Middle Ages were a period of relatively rapid population growth, which led to extensive internal and external colonization. Besides, Frankish military and political expansion must have gone along with a substantial emigration of people from the Frankish heartlands into newly conquered territories. Consequently, in Charlemagne's empire the personality principle clearly supported Frankish territorial conquest and occupation, and Franks must have profited far more from mobile law than non-Franks did. This already appears from one of the earliest legal provisions regarding the application of ethnic personal law from the Carolingian period: the capitulary issued for the kingdom of Aquitaine by Charlemagne's father, Pippin, in 768.[65] Clause 10 states that 'all men should have their own law, both Romans [that is to say, natives from Aquitaine] but also Salians [that is to say, Frankish immigrants from the north]'. With respect to Carolingian Italy, Paolo Delogu remarked that 'the promulgation of special laws for the kingdom of Italy' indeed reduced 'the prominence of [long existing] Lombard law' in favour of people of other origins—read: Franks—who came to live in Italy and could appeal there to their own 'national law'.[66] The same can be said for the papal territories. By ordering everybody who lived in the city of Rome—the cradle of Roman law!—to

[63] *Agobardi Lugdunensis Opera omnia*, L. van Acker, ed. (Turnhout 1981) (Corpus Christianorum. Continuatio Mediaevalis; 52), 19–28. For the background of the case: Guterman, *The principle*, ch. 10, who also gives an English translation of the relevant parts of the text (241–246).

[64] Guterman, *The principle*, 136, note 11.

[65] CRF1, nr. 18, at 43.

[66] Paolo Delogu, 'Lombard and Carolingian Italy', in Rosamond McKitterick, ed., *The new Cambridge Medieval History* Vol. 2 (Cambridge etc., 1995), 290–319, at 306.

profess *qua lege vult vivere* ('according to which law he wants to live'), clause 5 of the *Constitutio Romana* of 824, issued by Louis the Pious' son, Lothar, King of Italy, who had restored order in Rome after a revolt against the Frankish party in the city, was clearly intended to protect the local interests of the Franks.[67]

Epilogue

At the time of the *Constitutio Romana* the Carolingian empire had reached its apogee. Not long afterwards the empire—as an empire—would start to desintegrate, and in its wake the ideals of both 'national' and universal law-giving were lost. The principle of ethnic/national personality of law soon followed. Simeon Guterman, in his standard work, mused about several other possible reasons for its demise besides the decline of central power.[68] An interesting one is that, outside Italy, Roman law, by far the most sophisticated legal system available in medieval Europe, somehow failed to (re)gain attraction and win ground for the time being. The crucial factor, however, was the proliferation of strong local lordships whose owners exercised full rights of jurisdiction without accounting for their actions to higher powers. One of the additional effects was the 'localizing' of law: law became locally formulated, mostly unwritten, customary law. Under these circumstances not much remained of the national law codes that had been so prominent in the Carolingian world. What happened in the kingdom of France, for example, was that north of the Loire river—the *pays de droit coutumier*—Salic law was completely watered down, to be replaced by local customary law, while Roman law gradually became subsidiary law for cases for which local customs did not provide. South of the Loire—the *pays de droit écrit*—Roman law remained prevalent, but in far more local varieties than before and, despite the region's name, often 'through the medium of unwritten custom.'[69]

One of the paradoxes this new situation raised was that ethnic personality of law seemed to regain for a while its original 'racial' rather than later territorial character. Now that the Neustrian kingdom no longer existed,

---

[67] Thus Guterman, *Principle*, 143. On the backgrounds of the revolt: Astronomer, par. 37 and 38 (*Charlemagne*, Noble, 265–267). The text of the Constitutio: CRF1, nr. 161, esp. at 323.

[68] Guterman, *The principle*, chapters 9, 11, and 12.

[69] Guterman, *The principle*, 270.

nobody could invoke Salic law on the grounds that he or she was born in Neustria. Consequently, people who wanted to invoke Salic law started to do so with the arguments that they were born from Salic parents. But why would anyone want to invoke Salic law, whose contents were hardly known anymore? Just because this was fashionable! Bizarrely, everything 'Salic' became hot among the high aristocracy of the eleventh and twelfth centuries, probably because it created a bond with the revered French royal dynasty. It reached a point at which Salic law was seen as the law of the nobility. If that is correct, this would mark a curious transition 'from national law' (a law code for an ethnie) to 'class law' (a law code for a social class).[70] Charter evidence proves that this Salic whim also reached the German empire, especially the duchies of Brabant and Lower Lorraine. Most remarkable are the various so-called *professiones nationis* ('statements of nationality') by the famous Mathilda, marchioness of Tuscany (1046–1115), who was born to a powerful Lombard family and married to the Duke of Lower Lorraine, Godfred the Hunchback. In order to be empowered to settle Godfred's (Italian) inheritance after his death, Mathilda repeatedly had to profess that because of her late husband she lived in accordance with Salic law, although by birth (*ex natione*) she was Langobard.[71] But the Salic law that the lady Mathilda invoked in 1079 had little to do with the Lex Salica Karolina issued by Charlemagne almost three hundred years before. If law is a living thing, this one was as good as dead.

[70] The words are Guterman's: *The principle*, 138.

[71] Guterman, *The principle*, 140, wrongly, turns this around. See for a clear example: *Die Urkunden und Briefe der Markgräfin Mathilde von Tuszien*, Elke Goez and Werner Goez, eds. (MGH, Laienfürsten- und Dynasten-Urkunden der Kaiserzeit) (Hannover, 1998), nr. 28 (anno 1079), at 105–106.

NON-MUSLIMS AND OTTOMAN JUSTICE(S?)

Antonis Anastasopoulos

Introduction: Non-Muslim Legal Status

The aim of this chapter is to discuss the interaction between the Ottoman state, an early modern empire which was characterised by a clear Islamic ideology but ruled over a religiously mixed population, and its non-Muslim subjects in the field of justice, understood as legal practice and dispute-resolution mechanism. This is a topic which has attracted a fair amount of scholarly attention,[1] and one issue which has been stressed by the relevant literature is the opportunity that the non-Muslims of the Ottoman Empire had to practice 'forum shopping' among various judicial authorities. Even though I do not discard the concept of 'legal pluralism', which theorizes this opportunity to choose different forms of adjudicators and courts,[2] I will not place any particular emphasis on it in my treatment of the subject, as I share the doubts that have been voiced about its actual contribution in substantially changing the way in which we study judicial practice, either in individual case studies or comparatively.

The chapter is divided into three parts. In the first, I discuss how official Muslim judicial institutions treated non-Muslims. Then, I turn my attention to the latter and explore their options and practices concerning the handling of their judicial affairs, as well as non-Muslim judicial institutions. In this part of the chapter I focus almost exclusively on the Greek-speaking communities of the Ottoman Empire on the basis of the relevant literature, so my points and conclusions should not be taken

---

[1] For a recent treatment of this subject, see Eugenia Kermeli, 'The Right to Choice: Ottoman Justice vis-à-vis Ecclesiastical and Communal Justice in the Balkans, Seventeenth-Nineteenth Centuries', in Andreas Christmann and Robert Gleave, eds., *Studies in Islamic Law: A Festschrift for Colin Imber* (Oxford, 2007), 165–210. Several issues discussed here are treated in more detail by Kermeli, but our emphases and conclusions do not always coincide. See also Fatma Müge Göçek, 'The Legal Recourse of Minorities in History: Eighteenth-Century Appeals to the Islamic Court of Galata', in Molly Greene, ed., *Minorities in the Ottoman Empire* (Princeton, 2005), 47–69; Fariba Zarinebaf, *Crime and Punishment in Istanbul, 1700–1800* (Berkeley, Los Angeles, and London, 2010), *passim*, esp. 146–148.

[2] See, for instance, Ido Shahar, 'Legal Pluralism and the Study of Shari'a Courts', *Islamic Law and Society* 15 (2008), 112–141.

to apply necessarily to other non-Muslim communities. In the last part, I conclude by treating the subject of non-Muslims and justice in the Ottoman Empire as a topic which can contribute towards understanding the involvement of the imperial state in society and the interaction between the two.

A brief overview of the status of non-Muslims in the Ottoman Empire is, I think, necessary before embarking on the main subject of the chapter. This status was in principle prescribed by the relevant precepts of the holy law of Islam, the *shariʿa*. The non-Muslim subjects of the sultan, defined as '*dhimmi*',[3] enjoyed the right to live, hold property and practice their religions in the lands under Islamic rule as long as they accepted the authority of their Muslim sovereign and paid a special poll-tax. In the context of this arrangement, the non-Muslims had the right to have recourse to the same judicial authorities as the Muslims did, first and foremost the *qadi* courts. Furthermore, non-Muslims shared with Muslims the right to settle their lawsuits out of court through mediators.[4]

However, non-Muslims were legally inferior to the Muslims and were, in principle, expected to be constantly reminded of their inferiority to the dominant community through restrictions and markers which affected their daily lives, such as the obligation to wear different clothing from Muslims and the prohibitions against bearing arms, building new houses of worship or extending them, or living in houses higher than those of the Muslims. Even though in actual practice these (and many other) rules were not stringently applied at all times, they never ceased to be in effect, as many decrees demanding respect for sartorial regulations[5] and the

[3] 'Dhimmi' comes from 'dhimma', meaning 'engagement, responsibility', as formally the Muslim ruler is supposed to conclude a treaty of surrender with the non-Muslims by which he guarantees their rights; Joseph Schacht, *An Introduction to Islamic Law* (Oxford, 1964), 130. 'Dhimmi' is a derivative of 'ahl al-dhimma', meaning 'people of the pact'; Benjamin Braude and Bernard Lewis, 'Introduction', in Benjamin Braude and Bernard Lewis, eds., *Christians and Jews in the Ottoman Empire: The Functioning of a Plural Society*, Vol. 1 (New York and London, 1982), 5.

[4] On settlements, see Abdülmecid Mutaf, 'Amicable Settlement in Ottoman Law: *Sulh* System', *Turcica* 36 (2004), 125–140; Işık Tamdoğan, '*Sulh* and the 18th Century Ottoman Courts of Üsküdar and Adana', *Islamic Law and Society* 15 (2008), 55–83; cf. Eyal Ginio, 'The Administration of Criminal Justice in Ottoman Selânik (Salonica) during the Eighteenth Century', *Turcica* 30 (1998), 204–208. For a rare reference to the background of an out-of-court settlement, see Paolo Odorico et al., *Conseils et mémoires de Synadinos, prêtre de Serrès en Macédoine (XVIIe siècle)* ([n.p.], 1996), 119–120 (§ 28).

[5] See, for instance, Madeline C. Zilfi, 'Goods in the *Mahalle*: Distributional Encounters in Eighteenth-Century Istanbul', in Donald Quataert, ed., *Consumption Studies and the History of the Ottoman Empire, 1550–1922: An Introduction* (Albany, 2000), 297–308; Donald

demolition of unauthorized additions to churches suggest.[6] It is admittedly very difficult to draw a balanced and nuanced picture of the life of the non-Muslims in the Ottoman Empire, all the more so because conditions were not uniform, neither in space nor in time. It is advisable not to overemphasize either the suffering or the ease of *dhimmi* life, and also to keep in mind that this is a topic with clear, even if implicit, ideological and political overtones, even for modern scholars.[7] But if we stick to the letter of the law, what is I think safe to note is that, generally speaking, the legal framework of Islamic law on *dhimmi*s meant that, in principle, non-Muslims were or should be prevented from any action which might scandalize Muslim ethics, imply that the Muslims encouraged false religious beliefs, or suggest that non-Muslims were on an equal footing with or superior to Muslims.[8] Non-Muslim inferiority in the legal field meant that in several issues a non-Muslim had half the legal capacity of a Muslim and that the testimony of non-Muslims against Muslims was not admissible in the courts of law.[9]

The administration of state justice in the Ottoman Empire rested on three legal sources: the *shariʿa*, sultanic law (*kanun*), and customary law; its principal vehicle was the *qadi* court.[10] Based on the idea of the contrast between the *kanun* as secular/human and the *shariʿa* as religious/'divine' law, there has been a long scholarly debate over which of the two prevailed

---

Quataert, 'Clothing Laws, State, and Society in the Ottoman Empire, 1720–1829', *International Journal of Middle East Studies* 29 (1997), 403–425, esp. 410, 413–414.

6 For churches, see Rossitsa Gradeva, 'Ottoman Policy Towards Christian Church Buildings', *Etudes Balkaniques* 4 (1994), 25–26; cf. Ioannis K. Vasdravellis, ed., *Historika archeia Makedonias. B'. Archeion Veroias-Naouses, 1598–1886* [Historical archives of Macedonia. II. Archive of Veroia—Naoussa, 1598–1886] (Salonica, 1954), 217 (No. 227—H. 1195 / CE 1781).

7 Cf. Antonis Anastasopoulos, 'Hoi christianoi sten Tourkokratia kai hoi othomanikes peges: he periptose tes Veroias, p. 1760–1770' [The Christians in the period of Turkish rule and the Ottoman sources: the case of Veroia, c. 1760–1770], *Ariadne* 9 (2003), 76–78.

8 Cf. Odorico et al., *Conseils*, 106 (§ 22).

9 For the legal status of and legal restrictions suffered by *dhimmi*s according to Islamic law, see Schacht, *An Introduction*, 130–133, and Braude and Lewis, 'Introduction', 5–6; for objections as to the applicability of the *dhimma* as an explicatory model for the status of non-Muslims in the Ottoman Empire, see Eleni Gara, 'Christianoi kai mousoulmanoi sten Othomanike Autokratoria ton proimon neoteron chronon: historiographikes proseggiseis' [Christians and Muslims in the Ottoman Empire in the early modern period: historiographical approaches], in Molly Greene, *Krete: henas koinos kosmos. Christianoi kai mousoulmanoi ste Mesogeio ton proimon neoteron chronon* [A shared world: Christians and Muslims in the early modern Mediterranean], trans. Eleni Gara-Themis Gekou (Athens, 2005), 25–28.

10 See, for instance, Halil İnalcık, *The Ottoman Empire: The Classical Age, 1300–1600* (London, 1994), 70–75; Haim Gerber, *Economy and Society in an Ottoman City: Bursa, 1600–1700* (Jerusalem, 1988), 187–211.

in the practice of law in the Ottoman Empire and during which periods. What is a fact is that, at least as far as the official rhetoric and ideology were concerned,[11] the *shari'a*-based *qadi* courts which followed the Hanafite school of law were the official, state-sanctioned and controlled network of courts of law in the Ottoman Empire. Even though these courts also applied the laws of the sultan and took into consideration customary legal arrangements of the societies within which they functioned (see N. Królikowska's paper in this volume), their identity and legitimacy were primarily Islamic, and, thus, it seems that in the long run they tried to stick to the application of the Islamic holy law as much as possible, at least as far as appearances were concerned; this is a possible explanation, at least in some cases, for the absence of reasoning or even of the court decisions themselves in some entries of the *qadi* registers—so as not to make it too obvious that the holy law was not applied.[12]

On the other hand, it would be inaccurate to portray Ottoman justice as being conditioned only by Islam. Apart from the fact that, as noted above, the *qadi* courts also applied sultanic law and local custom, which at times were at odds with the principles of the *shari'a*, justice as an ideal of paramount importance in official state ideology and a primal expression of sultanic paternalism was, as Halil İnalcık and others have argued, determined by other—Turkish, Persian, and ancient-Near-Eastern—traditions as well.[13] This ideal did not discriminate between Muslims and non-Muslims, and imperial justice was available to all. In practical terms, the sultans' concern for justice was expressed primarily through the right of their subjects to appeal to the sovereign and, in fact, the imperial council, consisting of high-ranking civil, religious and military officials, for the redress of wrongs that they had suffered.[14]

---

[11] Uriel Heyd, *Studies in Old Ottoman Criminal Law*, Victor L. Ménage, ed. (Oxford, 1973), 180; see also his discussion of conflict between *kanun* and *shari'a*, and of the attitude of Ottoman *şeyhülislams* towards *kanun* (ibid., 180–192).

[12] Antonis Anastasopoulos and Eleni Gara, 'Othomanikes antilepseis peri egklematos kai timorias' [Ottoman views about crime and punishment], *Mnemon* 21 (1999), 44. But see Gerber, *Economy and Society*, 197–198.

[13] Halil İnalcık is an ardent proponent of this view; İnalcık, *The Ottoman Empire*, 65–69. Cf. Olga Todorova, 'The Ottoman State and Its Orthodox Christian Subjects: The Legitimistic Discourse in the Seventeenth-Century "Chronicle of Serres" in a New Perspective', *Turkish Historical Review* 1 (2010), 101–106.

[14] Suraiya Faroqhi, 'Political Activity among Ottoman Taxpayers and the Problem of Sultanic Legitimation (1570–1650)', *Journal of the Economic and Social History of the Orient* 35 (1992), 1–39; Halil İnalcık, 'Şikâyet Hakkı: *'Arz-i Hâl* ve *'Arz-i Mahzar'*lar' [The right to complain: *'arz-i hâls* and *'arz-i mahzars*], *Osmanlı Araştırmaları* 7–8 (1988), 33–54;

If indeed, as has been argued, justice in the context of the 'circle of justice'[15]—a theory of state which makes justice one of the inter-dependent factors on which the stability of the state rests—meant protection of the subjects from the fiscal and other abuses of state officials and the powerful,[16] then from the state's perspective the notion of justice had a particular meaning, and served specific practical purposes, namely order, stability, and the proper and uninterrupted functioning of the fiscal mechanism. Thus, justice was a medium rather than a goal and represented a relative rather than an absolute value, which may explain why sometimes the Ottoman state was willing to condone arrangements not fully in accordance with the law as long as they secured its tax income (unless, of course, we theorize too much, and, in fact, this attitude stemmed from the pragmatic realization of the limits of the ability of the state to intervene in every case of complaint that it received from throughout its vast territory about its officials or the tax-collectors). On the other hand, this restrictive, so to speak, perception of justice did not prevent the Ottoman population from appealing to the imperial council for all sorts of complaints and disputes (or the council from admitting them and responding to them).

The official Ottoman sultano-centric notion of justice finds its echo, internalisation (unless there is some hidden ulterior motive here), and reproduction in the—extensively studied,[17] but still rather unique in its richness of information—memoir of a wealthy Christian priest who lived in the southern Balkans in the first half of the seventeenth century and viewed the Sultan as an ideal, virtuous, and just monarch whose task was to discipline his unjust subordinates, that is, the officials who entered into daily contact with the people and oppressed them. The priest from Serres (Ott. Siroz), named Synadinos, laments the death of Murad IV (1623–1640), a sultan known for restoring order in the Empire through a policy of

---

Linda T. Darling, *Revenue-Raising and Legitimacy: Tax Collection and Finance Administration in the Ottoman Empire, 1560–1660* (Leiden, New York, and Cologne, 1996), 246–306.

15 Cornell Fleischer, 'Royal Authority, Dynastic Cyclism, and "Ibn Khaldûnism" in Sixteenth-Century Ottoman Letters', *Journal of Asian and African Studies* 18 (1983), 198–220; Darling, *Revenue-Raising*, 283–299.

16 İnalcık, *The Ottoman Empire*, 66.

17 See, for instance, Odorico et al., *Conseils*; Johann Strauss, 'Ottoman Rule Experienced and Remembered: Remarks on Some Local Greek Chronicles of the Tourkokratia', in Fikret Adanır and Suraiya Faroqhi, eds., *The Ottomans and the Balkans: A Discussion of Historiography* (Leiden, New York, and Cologne, 2002), 195–208; Todorova, 'The Ottoman State', 86–110.

violence and intimidation.[18] Synadinos remarks that such a praiseworthy sultan would never appear again, having first explained that

> He also decapitated all those who were tyrannical, be they viziers, *pashas*, *muftis*, *qadi'askers*, *qadis beys*, *aghas*, janissary officers (*gianitzaragai kai otapasedes*) or rebel leaders (*zorpapasedes*); not a single day went by without him killing someone ... he walked around in disguise every day and collected information about everything, and he dealt personally with all the affairs of the kingdom, and this is how injustices were eclipsed; and in his days you could see the sheep walk next to the wolf.[19]

Likewise, Synadinos praises Kenan Pasha, former governor-general (*beylerbeyi*) of Rumelia,[20] who, as an agent of Sultan Murad, arrived in Serres in 1625/1626, held sessions to hear the complaints of the population of the town and the villages ('they found great justice', as Synadinos notes), and had various Muslim notables executed. As a result, 'the Turks ceased to commit injustices'.[21]

At the same time, the priest records on other pages of his memoir various cases of gross injustices that his fellow Christians suffered at the hands of local Muslim officials and notables, the *qadi* court, and the mob.[22] One of these incidents is the story of a rich Christian who initiated the process of submitting a group protest against a local Muslim notable to the imperial council in Istanbul; the notable had the Christian hanged without trial on the false accusation (if we are to believe Synadinos) that he had insulted Islam and that he had broken the law by selling wheat to European Christians (*Phraggoi*). That same evening the Muslim notable brought his false witnesses before the *qadi*, whom he bribed, and thus obtained a written sentence against his victim.[23]

Non-Muslim Adjudicators and Courts

Thus, as far as the official, state-controlled judicial institutions were concerned, non-Muslims in the Ottoman Empire were given equal access with

---

[18] On his reign, see Caroline Finkel, *Osman's Dream: The Story of the Ottoman Empire, 1300–1923* (New York, 2005), 204–222.

[19] Odorico et al., *Conseils*, 92–94 (§ 16); cf. ibid., 130 (§ 29).

[20] Odorico et al., *Conseils*, 366, where Kenan is cited as the *beylerbeyi* of Rumelia in 1622.

[21] Odorico et al., *Conseils*, 94–96 (§ 17).

[22] Odorico et al., *Conseils*, 68 (§ 1), 70–72 (§ 4), 76–78 (§ 9), 106 (§ 22), 112 (§ 24), 176 (§ 36); cf. ibid., 296–298 (§ 7–8). For a decision of the *qadi* court in favour of his father against the creditors of his village, see ibid., 120 (§ 29); see also ibid., 124–126 (§ 29).

[23] Odorico et al., *Conseils*, 92 (§ 15).

Muslims to the imperial council and the *qadi* court, but in the latter they suffered certain restrictions prescribed by the *shari'a*. But this was not all: in addition to the above-mentioned institutions, non-Muslims were given the right to resort to their own religious authorities in certain legal areas, primarily those pertaining to family law; in addition, patriarchs and metropolitans were granted authority to discipline the priests who were subordinate to them.[24] Furthermore, it should be kept in mind that, as noted above, non-Muslims had the option of settling their disputes out of court without interference from the *qadi* in such settlements, which were only sometimes ratified in his court. It seems that with time the Orthodox Christian ecclesiastical and lay authorities took advantage of these principles, namely, their right to dispense justice within the context of the episcopal court of law[25] (which in many cases also included members of the lay elite) and the non-Muslims' right to settle their disputes 'informally' outside the *qadi* court, and thus expanded their jurisdiction well beyond family law and crimes of, or accusations against, members of the clergy, into the whole of civil law, and, possibly, even into cases of penal law, when circumstances allowed them to do so.[26]

It is not always clear if this extension of their jurisdiction was formal or informal. It is reasonable to think that in an Islamic state this process would have been informal, but there are indications which suggest that

24 For a brief description of the jurisdiction of the Christian Orthodox prelates according to their patents (*berat*), see Rossitsa Gradeva, 'Orthodox Christians in the Kadı Courts: The Practice of the Sofia Sheriat Court, Seventeenth Century', *Islamic Law and Society* 4 (1997), 41; for a detailed analysis of the patriarchal *berat*s, see Paraskevas Konortas, *Othomanikes theoreseis gia to Oikoumeniko Patriarcheio: veratia gia tous prokathemenous tes Megales Ekklesias (17os-arches 20^{ou} aiona)* [Ottoman views about the Ecumenical Patriarchate: *berat*s for the heads of the Great Church (seventeenth-beginning of the twentieth centuries)] (Athens, 1998). Nikolaos J. Pantazopoulos, *Church and Law in the Balkan Peninsula during the Ottoman Rule* (Salonica, 1967), 24, maintains that the jurisdiction of the Greek Orthodox patriarch in Istanbul extended 'over all the personal differences of the Christians related to religion; that is, marriages, adoptions, divorces, wills, etc.', and that over time it expanded in the whole area of private/civil law (ibid., 43–47, 91–112). On the issue of the jurisdiction of the Church in inheritance-related matters, see Kermeli, 'The Right to Choice', 174–175. In Synadinos' account, those with authority in matters of law, justice, and order were not only the *qadi*, the *voyvoda*, the *sipahi*, the *zâbit*, and an unspecified *nazır* (for a comment on this office, see Odorico et al., *Conseils*, 454–455), but also the metropolitan; Odorico et al., *Conseils*, 102 (§ 21), 140–142 (§ 31), 182 (§ 36).

25 For Synadinos' experience in the episcopal court, see Odorico et al., *Conseils*, 110 (§ 23), 130 (§ 30), 140–150 (§ 31). This first trial was about accusations against Synadinos that he had instigated his brothers-in-law not to pay their tax(?) contribution to the community; it is possible then that it can be treated as a case beyond the official jurisdiction of the high clergy.

26 Gradeva, 'Orthodox Christians', 45 (she observes this tendency from as early as the seventeenth century); Pantazopoulos, *Church and Law*, 44–45.

over time the Ottoman state took a somewhat more liberal view, at least in the course of the eighteenth century. It is reported, for instance, that in 1764 the Sultan allowed the Greek Orthodox and the Armenian patriarchs to inflict punishment on troublemakers from their own communities, instead of referring these cases to the Ottoman authorities.[27]

The formulation of a late-eighteenth-century collection of canon law (the *Nomikon* by Theophilos, Bishop of Campania, 1788) suggests that the sultans sanctioned the expansion of the jurisdiction of ecclesiastical courts beyond religious and family matters, and forbade the interference of Ottoman officials in cases which had been decided by Christian prelates.[28] Ottomanist research has indeed brought to light sultanic decrees which forbade *qadi*s from handling or interfering in affairs which fell under the jurisdiction of the Christian metropolitans, but these refer to matters of family law.[29] Therefore, Theophilos might be inaccurate in extending the scope of a principle which in fact applied only to family law, to include all the fields of law; an obvious goal would have been to establish that the extension of the judicial authority of the bishops was legal by claiming that it had been approved by the sovereign.[30] Additional evidence against Theophilos's suggestion comes from the most detailed patriarchal patent (*berat*) in Ottoman history, that of 1835: apart from citing the obligation of all the Orthodox Christians to be obedient to their religious authorities, it still explicitly recognized the patriarch's 'judicial' authority in only two fields: marriages and the disciplining of the clergy. On the other hand, we should note that from roughly the early eighteenth century a clause was added in the *berat*s of the patriarch and the metropolitans which guaranteed their right to act as mediators in disputes between Christians and to impose an oath or inflict excommunication on Christians when they deemed it necessary.[31]

---

27 Halil İnalcık, 'Ottoman Archival Materials on *Millets*', in Braude and Lewis, eds., *Christians and Jews*, Vol. 1, 440.

28 Demetrios S. Ghinis, ed., *Nomikon poiethen kai syntachthen eis haplen phrasen hypo tou panierotatou ellogimotatou episkopou Kampanias kyriou kyriou Theophilou tou ex Ioanninon (1788)* [A legal code prepared and composed in the simple language by the most reverend and learned Bishop of Campania, Theophilos of Ioannina (1788)] (Salonica, 1960), 237 (§ 1–2).

29 Gradeva, 'Orthodox Christians', 58 n. 69 (*ferman* of 1802).

30 Compare Kermeli, 'The Right to Choice', 181–182.

31 Konortas, *Othomanikes theoreseis*, 73–104; for the last-named clause, see ibid., 79–80 (No. 20), and 387, and Kermeli, 'The Right to Choice', 175–176. For the *berat*s granted to the metropolitans, see Konortas, *Othomanikes theoreseis*, 104–112.

Thus, it seems that, up until the end of the pre-Tanzimat era (1839), the Ottoman authorities granted the patriarchs and the bishops authority to deal with matters of family law, as prescribed by the *shariʿa*, and furthermore with matters concerning their subordinate clergy as heads of the 'guild' of priests, monks, and nuns. However, the right to out-of-court settlements and the obligation of the Christians to obey their religious leadership allowed the prelates some space to formally or informally expand their jurisdiction without interference from the Ottoman authorities. In other words, it may be argued that, in areas other than family law (where the jurisdiction of the Church was unquestionable), court sessions and judicial decisions which were formal procedures and formal verdicts or penalties, respectively, for the Christian community, were, in the view of the Ottoman state and the *qadi* courts, instances of out-of-court settlements among Christians performed by the clergy, and thus acceptable.

The existence of structured judicial sessions is proven by the admittedly few church registers which survive from the Greek-speaking world.[32] Presumably the low level of literacy—and possibly a culture of orality—was a major factor that accounts for this lack of consistent record keeping,[33] which in any case suggests that episcopal justice was not as systematic or universal as, for instance, Greek scholarly literature sometimes represents it as being—although we must allow for the possibility, albeit a remote one, that a large number of pre-nineteenth-century ecclesiastical registers may survive in church archives, which have not yet surfaced.[34] Other explanations are also possible. Eugenia Kermeli has drawn our attention

32 See, for instance, Nikolaos I. Pantazopoulos with Despoina Tsourka-Papastathi, *Kodix Metropoleos Sisaniou kai Siatistes, iz'-ith' ai.* [Codex of the diocese of Sisanion and Siatista, seventeenth-nineteenth centuries] (Salonica, 1974); Nikos K. Giannoulis, *Kodikas Trikkes* [Codex of Trikki] (Athens, 1980). For a longer list, see Kermeli, 'The Right to Choice', 167–168 n. 15.

33 Even though it cannot be dismissed, the Church's support of educational institutions was not systematic: see, for instance, *Historia tou hellenikou ethnous* [History of the Greek nation] (Athens, 1974–1975), Vol. 10, 366–377; Vol. 11, 129–130, 306–310. On the interaction between orality and the written word in the Ottoman administrative and judicial contexts, see the articles in *Revue du monde musulman et de la Méditerranée*, 75–76 (1995) [thematic issue: Nicolas Vatin, ed., *Oral et écrit dans le monde turco-ottoman*], especially those by Gilles Veinstein, Nicolas Vatin, and Işık Tamdoğan-Abel (133–165); Boğaç A. Ergene, 'Evidence in Ottoman Courts: Oral and Written Documentation in Early-Modern Courts of Islamic Law', *Journal of the American Oriental Society* 124 (2004), 471–491; Marc Aymes, 'The Voice-Over of Administration: Reading Ottoman Archives at the Risk of Ill-literacy', *European Journal of Turkish Studies* 6 (2007) [Thematic Issue N°6: *Ill-literate Knowledge*, URL: http://ejts.revues.org/1333].

34 Cf. Najwa Al-Qattan, '*Dhimmīs* in the Muslim Court: Legal Autonomy and Religious Discrimination', *International Journal of Middle East Studies* 31 (1999), 430, 439.

to the possibility that high registration fees may have discouraged many Christians from having their cases entered in the church registers.[35] And there is one further possible reason for the reluctance to produce or systematically preserve written evidence of the procedures that took place within the Christian community: this is the psycho-social, so to speak, insecurity and fear of exposure to the authorities which accrued from the non-Muslims' inferior status. But this argument of fear, well-known in traditional Greek scholarly circles, and not necessarily as far-fetched as it may sound, is a hypothesis which needs further research and substantiation.

In light of the above, what is noticeable in the church registers that have been published to date is that the metropolitans were generally careful to record in them cases almost exclusively within their formal jurisdictional area, family law, which was nevertheless broadly defined. These cases include pre-marital gifts, dowries, divorces, adoptions, the guardianship and property of orphans, wills, and the division of estates (contested or non-contested). Cases outside this sphere are mostly (but not exclusively) non-contested, such as donations, regulations of guilds, registration of out-of-court settlements, loans, and transactions. When they are contested, often—but not always—a church, a monastery, or a member of the clergy is involved; in Siatista, in southwestern Macedonia, the episcopal court examined various contested cases of debts and division of profits from business partnerships, but usually one of the two parties was involved in these cases through the right of inheritance (either of the money due to them or of the debt of the deceased). On the other hand, ample evidence about the extensive use by the Church of excommunication as a penalty in a wide range of disputes between Christians, and occasionally even between non-Christians and Christians, suggests again that the Orthodox Church had found ways to extend its jurisdiction well beyond its formally prescribed bounds. Once again, this extension was made cautiously, through the use of a moral penalty supposedly imposed for the disciplining of sinners and not for the punishment of civil or penal wrongdoers.[36]

According to the dominant paradigm accepted by traditional Greek historiography, non-Muslim judicial institutions in the Ottoman period

[35] Kermeli, 'The Right to Choice', 177–178.

[36] For excommunication in the Ottoman period, see Panagiotis D. Michailaris, *Aphorismos: he prosarmoge mias poines stis anagkaiotetes tes Tourkokratias* [Excommunication: the adjustment of a penalty to the necessities of Turkish rule] (Athens, 1997); see, in particular, 97–110, 167–189 (esp. 176), 192–204.

included not only episcopal, but also communal lay courts composed of elders appointed by the local people or their leadership. This approach rests on two (often implicit) premises: first, that the Greek-speaking local communities also constituted more or less fully functional political communities; second, that the elite of these communities included the lay leadership and the clergy as two distinct groups in contest in the context of the evolutionary paradigm of church domination v. secularization.[37]

However, almost all the known cases of well-structured communal courts with systematic record-keeping procedures in Greek-speaking communities come from small Aegean islands with little Muslim presence. This suggests that on the whole these courts seem to have been quite rare and, thus, a rather marginal phenomenon (bar the unlikely option that there are archives that have suffered massive destruction or sunk into universal oblivion).[38] Furthermore, the sultanic decrees (*ahdname*) presented until recently as guaranteeing the right of the island communities concerned to dispense justice, in fact record the right of the islanders to seek out-of-court settlements without the *qadi*s being allowed to intervene or annul them.[39] Nevertheless, it is interesting to note that here again the Christian islanders' formal judicial institutions must have been seen as informal mechanisms of out-of-court settlements from the official viewpoint of the Ottoman state.

---

[37] What seems certain is that, in quite a few places, by the beginning of the nineteenth century the lay notables had managed to take control of communal affairs and restrict the authority of the metropolitans in public life; Kostas Kostis, 'Koinotetes, Ekklesia kai millet stis "hellenikes" perioches tes Othomanikes Autokratorias kata ten periodo ton Metarrythmiseon' [Communities, Church and *millet* in the "Greek" districts of the Ottoman Empire during the period of the Reforms], *Mnemon* 13 (1991), 65–69; cf. Michailaris, *Aphorismos*, 444–446.

[38] See, for instance, Dimitris Th. Siatras, *Hellenika koinotika dikasteria kata ten Tourkokratia* [Greek communal courts of law during the period of Turkish rule] (Volos, 1997), 36–38. See also Andreas Th. Drakakis, *He Syros epi Tourkokratias* [Syros under Turkish rule]. Vol. II: *He dikaiosyne kai to dikaio* [Justice and law] (Athens, 1967); Menelaos A. Tourtoglou, 'He nomologia ton kriterion tes Mykonou (17ος–19ος ai.)' [The case law of the courts of Mykonos (seventeenth-nineteenth centuries)], *Epeteris tou Kentrou Ereunes tes Historias tou Hellenikou Dikaiou* 27–28 (1980–1981), 1–257 (esp. 9–10); Eleni E. Koukkou, *Hoi koinotikoi thesmoi stis Kyklades kata ten Tourkokratian* [The communal institutions of the Cyclades in the period of Turkish rule] (Athens, 1980).

[39] Tourtoglou, 'He nomologia', 1; Elias Kolovos, *He nesiotike koinonia tes Androu sto othomaniko plaisio* [The insular society of Andros in the Ottoman context] (Andros, 2006), 57–58; Siatras, *Hellenika koinotika dikasteria*, 28–34. To my knowledge, it is the only surviving Greek translation of one of these decrees (Siatras, *Hellenika koinotika dikasteria*, 31) that refers explicitly to 'trials' with 'priests' as judges. None of the decrees about the Cyclades survives in the original. Kolovos argues that the so-called *ahdname*s are in fact *berats*; Kolovos, *He nesiotike koinonia*, 56 n. 119.

Non-Muslims and Qadi *Justice*

The fact that the non-Muslims regularly brought their contested and non-contested cases before the *qadi* suggests that, much as this court represented a different culture, it was not alien to them.[40] The knowledge that they could win their cases against Muslims certainly encouraged them to use the Islamic court of law.[41] Indications that the court could be more flexible towards non-Muslims than one would in principle have expected also helped; for instance, there are a few cases where the non-Muslims' testimony against Muslims was admitted in breach of the principles of the *shariʿa*.[42] In addition, the presence of non-Muslim interpreters,[43] or the much rarer presence of non-Muslims who served the court in other capacities, such as expert witnesses, inspectors, bailiffs, or procedural witnesses (*shuhud al-hal*),[44] must have also made the *qadi* court look a more familiar place. On the other hand, one cannot but wonder how the non-Muslims felt towards a court in whose records derogatory terms were systematically used against them, their religions and cultural values.[45]

---

[40] Various scholars have calculated what percentage of the *qadi* court cases that they have studied included non-Muslim litigants: Gradeva, 'Orthodox Christians', 41–42, 43; Fatma Müge Göçek and Marc David Baer, 'Social Boundaries of Ottoman Women's Experience in Eighteenth-Century Galata Court Records', in Madeline C. Zilfi, ed., *Women in the Ottoman Empire: Middle Eastern Women in the Early Modern Era* (Leiden, New York, and Cologne, 1997), 58; Ronald C. Jennings, *Christians and Muslims in Ottoman Cyprus and the Mediterranean World, 1571–1640* (New York and London, 1993), 133, 163–164, 166.

[41] Many such cases can be found throughout the literature that deals with non-Muslims in the *qadi* courts, including the works that are cited in this chapter, as well as in published and unpublished series of *qadi* court archival registers (*sijill*). For a characteristic case, see Nikolaos S. Stavrinidis, *Metaphraseis tourkikon historikon eggraphon aphoronton eis ten historian tes Kretes* [Translations of Turkish historical documents relating to the history of Crete], Vol. 5 (Heraklion, 1985), 10–12 (Nos 2506b–2507—H. 1166 / CE 1752).

[42] Al-Qattan, '*Dhimmī*s in the Muslim Court', 437; Gradeva, 'Orthodox Christians', 67–68.

[43] See, for instance, Kemal Çiçek, 'Interpreters of the Court in the Ottoman Empire as Seen from the Sharia Court Records of Cyprus', *Islamic Law and Society* 9 (2002), 1–15.

[44] Gradeva, 'Orthodox Christians', 67–68; Kermeli, 'The Right to Choice', 200.

[45] See, for instance, Anastasopoulos, 'Hoi christianoi sten Tourkokratia', 79; Boğaç Ergene, 'Legal History "From the Bottom Up": Empirical and Methodological Challenges for Ottomanists', in Antonis Anastasopoulos, ed., *Political Initiatives 'From the Bottom Up' in the Ottoman Empire. Halcyon Days in Crete VII: A Symposium Held in Rethymno, 9–11 January 2009* (Rethymno, 2012), 381–398; cf. Göçek, 'Legal Recourse', 56–58. However, Najwa Al-Qattan has argued against viewing the *qadi* court as a place of institutionalized *dhimmi* inferiority; Al-Qattan, '*Dhimmī*s in the Muslim Court', 430, 436, 438–440, and 'Inside the Ottoman Courthouse: Territorial Law at the Intersection of State and Religion', in Virginia H. Aksan and Daniel Goffman, eds., *The Early Modern Ottomans: Remapping the Empire* (Cambridge, 2007), 209–211.

Obviously, as has been pointed out, it is impossible to calculate what proportion of all the disputes among non-Muslims ended up in the *qadi* courts (that is, if one excludes their disputes with Muslims, since one assumes that they had no choice but to refer these to this court[46]). Likewise, in most cases it is impossible to know why these non-Muslim litigants who opted for the *qadi* court did so. Apparently, a factor that played an important part in their decision must have been the fact that this was the official court, and thus in principle the chances that its decisions would be carried out were higher than they were for the decisions of any non-Muslim court, whose authority often was, as noted above, unofficial.[47] Another practical reason for people to go to the *qadi* court might simply be the absence of alternative dispute-resolution mechanisms in their region.

In this respect, it would be interesting to know what percentage of the cases brought by non-Muslims to a given *qadi* court were contested versus non-contested (transactions, loans, appointment of proxies, etc.). A high percentage of non-contested cases should suggest that the non-Muslims used the *qadi* court mostly when they had no other—or at least no better—option, for example when they wished to secure the validity of their contracts,[48] and thus safeguard their property. Rossitsa Gradeva has noted that the purpose of registration of intra-familial property transactions might be to prevent contestation by the Ottoman authorities of the inheritance rights of the family members after the death of the original property owner.[49]

'Legal pluralism', that is, the availability (at least in some places) of various judicial alternatives meant that the non-Muslims could manipulate, so to speak, the judicial institutions. Thus, they could decide to use one or the other court of law depending on where they felt or knew that it was easier or more likely that they would win their cases or serve their interests.[50] For instance, the register of the *qadi* court of the imperial camp that had been set up outside Candia in Crete, during the long siege

---

[46] Gradeva, 'Orthodox Christians', 41.

[47] Gradeva, 'Orthodox Christians', 68–69.

[48] Gradeva, 'Orthodox Christians', 46–47, has noted that real estate transactions were often brought to court months or years after they had been concluded, and that such cases revolved around the issue of payment of the agreed price for the piece of property that had been sold.

[49] Gradeva, 'Orthodox Christians', 48.

[50] Al-Qattan, '*Dhimmīs* in the Muslim Court', 433–435; Gradeva, 'Orthodox Christians', 41, 62–63; but see Göçek and Baer, 'Social Boundaries', 58–59.

of this town by the Ottomans in the mid-seventeenth century, relates the case of a married Christian woman who converted to Islam. Her Christian husband refused to do the same, which meant that, according to the precepts of the Islamic holy law, the couple could no longer remain married, as Muslim women are not allowed to be the spouses of non-Muslim men. Thus, the woman gained the right to divorce her husband, and marry a Muslim, in all probability himself also a convert, as his patronymic suggests ('the son of Abdullah', i.e., 'the son of God's servant', a fabricated name which does not expose the convert's non-Muslim descent).[51]

Furthermore, non-Muslims could put pressure on their religious authorities to relax their rules on issues for which the *qadi* court provided a more convenient solution or a less demanding procedure.[52] The best-known example on the Orthodox Christian side is the issue of divorces: recourse of the Christians to the *qadi* court for their divorces forced the Church to start to accord divorces on grounds, such as mutual consent of the spouses, for which in earlier times it was impossible to obtain a divorce.[53] An eighteenth-century canon law collection warns bishops to be mild and fair or else run the risk of estranging their flocks, and handing them over to the Muslim unbelievers.[54]

The religious and lay leaderships of the various non-Muslim groups were generally vehemently opposed to the recourse of non-Muslims to the Islamic courts of law,[55] but this disapproval of the 'infidel' judicial

---

[51] Stavrinidis, *Metaphraseis*, Vol. 1 (Heraklion, 1975), 139 (No. 194—H. 1074 / CE 1663).

[52] Gradeva, 'Orthodox Christians', 58–59. Cf. Pantazopoulos, *Church and Law*, 102–107, and Giannoulis, *Kodikas*, 50–51, 54–55.

[53] Sophia Laiou, 'Christian Women in an Ottoman World: Interpersonal and Family Cases Brought Before the *Shari'a* Courts during the Seventeenth and Eighteenth Centuries (Cases Involving the Greek Community)', in Amila Buturović and İrvin Cemil Schick, eds., *Women in the Ottoman Balkans: Gender, Culture and History* (London and New York, 2007), 246–247.

[54] Charalambos K. Papastathis, 'Nomokanon Georgiou Trapezountiou. He eis ten neohelleniken metaglottisis ton "Diatagon ton Hagion Apostolon" kata to Ms. GR. 696 (297) tes Roumanikes Akademias' [The collection of canon law by Georgios Trapezountios: the translation into modern Greek of the 'Orders of the Holy Apostles' according to Ms. GR. 696 (297) of the Romanian Academy], *Epeteris tou Kentrou Ereunes tes Historias tou Hellenikou Dikaiou* 27–28 (1980–1981), 414–416. The original was most likely compiled in the late fourth or late fifth century in Syria (ibid., 370–371).

[55] For the Christian side, see Phokion Kotzageorgis, 'Christian (Ecclesiastical) and Muslim (Ottoman) Juridical Procedure for Settlement of Litigations according to Athonite Documents (15th c.–ca. 1820)', in *XIV. Türk Tarih Kongresi. Ankara: 9–13 Eylül 2002. Kongreye Sunulan Bildiriler* [14th Turkish History Congress: Ankara, 9–13 September 2002. Papers read at the congress], Vol. 2, Part 1 (Ankara, 2005), 854; Gradeva, 'Orthodox Christians', 44. For eighteenth-century canon law codes condemning the recourse of Christians to Ottoman justice, see Papastathis, 'Nomokanon Georgiou Trapezountiou', 440–441; Ghinis, ed.,

system should be treated as an opposition whose rationale lay more in pragmatism rather than in ideology and faith. The religious functionaries condemned the use of the *qadi* court by non-Muslims on theological and ethical grounds, but in fact political considerations must have been a more important factor in their opposition, as they despised the involvement of 'outsiders', in particular Ottoman officials, in the affairs and power balance of their communities, and were aware of the blow to their prestige, authority, and income that was caused by their flock's preference for the *qadi* court. This is demonstrated by the fact that the non-Muslim religious and lay leaders, or the monasteries, usually had no reservations themselves about appealing to the *qadi* or even to the sultan when they felt that their authority, power, property, or income was challenged from within their communities.[56]

Conclusion: Justice, the Imperial State, and Plural Society

In summary, we observe a situation in which the non-Muslims were inferior by law, but, as this law guaranteed respect of their religious practices, it gave them at the same time the opportunity to create a niche of judicial separateness—or even autonomy (a term which has to be used cautiously)—at the institutional level, and the chance to perform 'forum shopping' among 'internal' ecclesiastical (or other) and 'external', that is, Muslim, judicial bodies (*ekklesiastikos kai exoterikos*, in Greek-language sources)[57] at the individual or group level. In my view, the right of litigants to amicably settle their affairs out of court was a crucial concept which allowed the non-Muslim authorities to expand their jurisdiction, and the Ottoman authorities to condone or accept this expansion.

Nomikon, 246 (§ 72). But for the acceptance of the legitimacy of Muslim justice in the statutes of Christian guilds, see Giannoulis, *Kodikas*, 45, 77; Spyros I. Asdrachas et al., *Hellenike oikonomike historia. IE'-ITH' aionas* [Greek economic history, fifteenth-nineteenth centuries], Vol. 2: *Tekmeria* [Evidence], Eutychia D. Liata, ed. (Athens, 2003), 289–290.

56 There are many cases of clerics and notables who brought lawsuits against fellow non-Muslims to the *qadi* court or the imperial council; see, for instance, Gradeva, 'Orthodox Christians', 46, and Ioannis K. Vasdravellis, ed., *Historika archeia Makedonias. A'. Archeion Thessalonikes, 1695–1912* [Historical archives of Macedonia. I. Archive of Salonica, 1695–1912] (Salonica, 1952), 203–204 (No. 157—H. 1146 / CE 1734); cf. ibid., 166–167 (No. 128—H. 1134 / CE 1722). See also Konortas, *Othomanikes theoreseis*, 328–334, and Kotzageorgis, 'Christian (Ecclesiastical) and Muslim (Ottoman) Juridical Procedure', 849–855.

57 See, for instance, Giannoulis, *Kodikas*, 45, 51, 77; Pantazopoulos, *Church and Law*, 103 and n. 44. Cf. Odorico et al., *Conseils*, 298 (§ 8).

Ottoman society has been famously described as 'plural'. Benjamin Braude and Bernard Lewis used this term to define multi-ethnic, multi-religious and multi-cultural societies where different religious and/or ethnic groups co-exist without living together, in the Ottoman case under a regime of institutional inequality. As Eleni Gara notes, the principal characteristic of 'plural' societies is 'tolerance, which expresses itself not necessarily in the absence of discriminations, but in the fact that the minority ethnic or religious groups do not suffer persecution'.[58] This much is certainly true, as far as society itself is concerned; but what if we put our stress on the attitude of the state, and the effect that governing a 'plural society' had on it? 'Tolerance' is a notion with positive connotations: Braude and Lewis define it as 'the willingness of a dominant religion to coexist with others'.[59] But the equation does not include only 'a dominant' and 'other' religions, as the political context, and thus the state within which this relationship develops, is one of the important factors that determine what kind of tolerance will exist. When viewed from the perspective of the state towards society, 'tolerance' can emanate from an ideological base of 'contemptuous' protection, if, for instance, it is the result of a long religio-political tradition and, possibly, detachment from a part of the subject population (for instance, the 'infidels'). As many students of the Ottoman state have remarked, the latter often appeared unwilling to interfere in the internal workings of society as long as order and tax collection were not disrupted. In this respect, even though the Ottoman Empire undoubtedly provided its non-Muslim population with an environment where their religious and cultural traditions and practices could be observed and even flourish (particularly in comparison with the attitude of its contemporaneous Christian European states towards their minority groups), one should not overlook manifestations of reciprocal distrust and scorn between Muslims and non-Muslims, but also between different non-Muslim groups;[60] these phenomena do not alter the overall

[58] Braude and Lewis, 'Introduction', 1; Gara, 'Christianoi', 28–33 (the quotation is from p. 29; the translation is mine). Cf. Gradeva's comment on the issue of tolerance in her 'Orthodox Christians', 69.

[59] Braude and Lewis, 'Introduction', 3.

[60] For cases of Jewish-Christian antagonism, see Maria Efthymiou, *Evraioi kai christianoi sta tourkokratoumena nesia tou N.A. Aigaiou: hoi dyskoles pleures mias gonimes synyparxes* [Jews and Christians in the islands of the south-eastern Aegean under Turkish rule: the difficult sides of a fruitful coexistence] (Athens, 1992); Eyal Ginio, 'Coping with Decline: The Political Responses of the Jewish Community to the Eighteenth-Century Crisis in Salonica', in Anastasopoulos, ed., *Political Initiatives*, 69–90; Odorico et al., *Conseils*, 82–84 (§ 13); Vasdravellis, ed., *Historika archeia Makedonias. A'*, 380–381 (No. 265—H. 1216 / CE 1802).

picture but add an important nuance to it. Non-Muslims were generally allowed—in the wider spirit of the *dhimma* cultural tradition—to operate their institutions and settle their affairs 'internally', but only up to the point where the dominant Muslim community and the state did not feel scandalized, annoyed, or menaced. The non-Muslims, on their part, reciprocated by likewise generally treating the Muslims as 'abominable infidels', even if they did not have the institutional means to express this attitude; according to Synadinos, Christians and Muslims in Serres did live together, but also exchanged derogatory names such as 'dogs' (*skylous*) and 'infidels' (*apistous*).[61] The end result of this situation is that society and, by extension, the state were lacking in cohesion, and the latter could not count on the support of a significant segment of its population. This, of course, was not a situation that applied exclusively to the Ottoman Empire, but may be seen as one characteristic of empires.

As it was bound by its respect for the *dhimma*, the central state itself forbade, through sultanic orders, the *qadi*s, that is, its formal judicial network, from handling or interfering in the affairs which fell under the jurisdiction of the Christian metropolitans.[62] From a modern point of view, the principles that underpinned the traditional 'plural' society in the long run worked against the interests of the central state. When, in the course of the Tanzimat reforms of the mid-nineteenth century, the Ottoman central authorities sought to impose a more centralized control over the Empire and promote a common Ottoman identity and legal equality for all their subjects, the non-Muslims re-invented—with the support of the European powers—the so-called 'privileges' (such as adjudicating on family law matters) of their leadership as communal, and claimed that they should have the right to maintain them in the new circumstances; in reality, though, these 'privileges' had in most cases been accorded through patents, *berat*s, to religious and lay leaders as individual office-holders[63] and not to local communities or other groups.[64] Thus, the non-Muslim

---

[61] Odorico et al., *Conseils*, 72 (§ 4). Cf. ibid., 88 (§ 14), 90 (§ 15). Cf. Kermeli, 'The Right to Choice', 171.

[62] See, for instance, Pantazopoulos, *Church and Law*, 93; Gradeva, 'Orthodox Christians', 58 n. 69. Cf. İnalcık, 'Ottoman Archival Materials', 440; Konortas, *Othomanikes theoreseis*, 83–84, 89.

[63] The patents issued to some Aegean islands are an exception to this.

[64] Sia Anagnostopoulou, *Mikra Asia, 19os ai.–1919, hoi hellenorthodoxes koinotetes: apo to Millet ton Romion sto Helleniko Ethnos* [Asia Minor, nineteenth century–1919, the Greek-Orthodox communities: from the *Rum milleti* to the Hellenic nation], 2nd edition (Athens, 1998), 23–24, 276ff.

communities benefited from the declaration of legal equality between the Muslims and the non-Muslims, but furthermore were able to legally obtain a degree of autonomy from the Ottoman state. In an age of strong nationalistic and irredentist feelings, and with European imperialism on the ascent, the Ottomans found it impossible to avoid estrangement from a significant part of their population, especially in the Balkans, Istanbul and Anatolia, and centralization remained incomplete. It is interesting to note that judicial autonomy—a concession which at first sight did not seem to pose a political danger—was one of the 'privileges' that the non-Muslim communities claimed for themselves, and were able to partly maintain up to the beginning of the twentieth century, that is up to the time when the Empire met its downfall.[65]

[65] For the tension that was created when the Ottoman state attempted to centralize control of and unify the judicial and educational systems of its Muslim and non-Muslim subjects, see Konortas, *Othomanikes theoreseis*, 102–103; Anagnostopoulou, *Mikra Asia*, 285–287. Cf. Braude and Lewis, 'Introduction', 32–33.

ROYAL GRACE, ROYAL PUNISHMENT: CEREMONIAL ENTRIES AND THE PARDONING OF CRIMINALS IN FRANCE, C. 1440–1560

Neil Murphy

In July 1550 a street fight broke out in the city of Lyon between rival groups of young men. Although such disturbances were common for the period, on this occasion the violence escalated out of control and one of the participants was killed.[1] The perpetrator of the crime was an apprentice dyer named Claude Cleppoing, who fled into self-imposed exile in fear of the consequences of this killing, which included execution. It is what Claude did next, however, that is most interesting. He made a journey of over 600 kilometres north to the town of Fécamp in Normandy, where he immediately handed himself over to the municipal authorities to be imprisoned. This was a shrewd move by Claude, as in the summer of 1550 Henry II was making the customary post-coronation ceremonial entries into northern towns that he had postponed until his return from campaign in Italy.[2] Royal entries, such as that at Fécamp, were occasions when townspeople staged elaborate festivities and ceremonies to welcome their king, part of which included the pardoning of prisoners held within civic prisons. As Claude's crime was not pre-meditated, he successfully obtained a letter of pardon from the king which permitted him to return to his home at Lyon without threat of punishment from the judicial authorities in the city.[3]

Along with the ability to cure scrofula by touch, the right to pardon formed a key element of the *religion royale* of the French monarchy.[4]

---

[1] For youth violence during this period see: N.Z. Davis, 'The Reasons of Misrule', in *Society and Culture in Early Modern France* (London, 1975), 97–123.

[2] Two years before he entered Fécamp, Henry II had made a lavish entry into Lyon in 1548 on his way to campaign in Italy. It is possible that Claude would have witnessed and perhaps even participated in this entry. For Henry's reception at Lyon see: Maurice Scève, *The Entry of Henri II into Lyon: September 1548*, Richard Cooper, ed. (Tempe, 1997); *Entrées royales et fêtes populaires à Lyon du XV*e *au XVIII*e *siècle* (Lyon, 1970), 70–74; *Relation des entrées solemnelles dans la ville de Lyon, de nos rois, reines, princes, princesses, cardinaux, légats, & autres grands personnages, depuis Charles VI, jusques à présent* (Lyon, 1752), 80–88.

[3] Cited in N.Z. Davis, *Fiction in the Archives: Pardon Tales and their Tellers in Sixteenth-Century France* (Cambridge, 1987), 161.

[4] For the ceremony of touching for the king's evil see: Marc Bloch, *The Royal Touch: Sacred Monarchy and Scrofula in England and France*, (trans.), J.E. Anderson (London, 1973).

The issuing of pardons was a feature of important royal festivities, such as the birth of a royal child, though it was used most extensively during inaugural ceremonial entries.[5] While the pardoning of prisoners is apparent from the post-coronation entry of Louis VIII into Paris in 1223, it was during the long progresses made by his son, Louis IX, that pardoning became a regular part of royal entries into towns across the kingdom.[6] On his return from captivity in Egypt, Louis made several progresses of his kingdom, as part of his desire to bring peace to the kingdom and reform the judicial system.[7] He extended the reach of royal authority across the kingdom and sought to allow all his subjects access to the monarch in matters of the law. As part of his civic entries, Louis pardoned prisoners held in the municipal prisons and returned the banished to urban society. When he entered Tournai in 1257, for example, the civic registers tell us that he 'fit rendre l'habitation de la ville à ceux qui en avaient été bannis, sauf pour les grands crimes'.[8] Following his death and canonization, Louis's reign was looked back on as a Golden Age. In particular, Louis was praised for his judicial reforms and for his clemency. In imitation of their saintly ancestor, later Capetian and Valois monarchs incorporated the pardoning of criminals into their civic receptions.[9] By the reign of Charles VI (1380–1422) it was expected that a French king would issue

Charles VIII, Francis I and Henry II all made occasional displays of touching for the sick as part of a royal entry: Elie Konigson, 'La cité et le prince: premières entrées de Charles VIII (1484–1486)', in Jean Jacquot and Elie Konigson ed., *Les Fetes de la Renaissance, tome III. Quinzième colloque international d'études humanistes, 10–22 juillet 1972* (Paris, 1975), 59; *La Magnificence de la superbe et triumphante entree de la noble et antique Cité de Lyon faicte au Treschrestien Roy de France Henry deuxiesme de ce Nom*, Georges Guigue, ed. (Lyon, 1927), 79; Bloch, *Royal Touch*, 162–63; *Entrées royales françaises de 1328 à 1515*, Bernard Guenée and Françoise Lehoux, ed. (Paris, 1968), 23.

[5] Bernard de La Roche-Flavin, *Treze livres des parlemens de France* (Bordeaux, 1619), 53. The poet François Villon received grace at both a royal birth and a royal entry. In January 1456 he was granted a royal pardon following the birth of Charles VII's daughter, Marie. Five years later he was in the prisons of the bishop of Orléans at Meung-sur-Loire, where he received a further pardon at Louis XI's inaugural entry into the town in 1461: Ernest Sermet, *Le doit de grâce: son histoire—son fonctionnement actuel—son avenir* (Toulouse, 1902), 82; François Villon, *Poésies*, Jean Dufournet, ed. (Paris, 1992), 86. For his imprisonment at Meung see: Jean Favier, *François Villon* (Paris, 1982), 430–31.

[6] Marc Bloch, *Rois et serfs: un chapitre d'histoire capétienne* (Paris, 1920), 48–49; Charles Petit-Dutaillis, *Étude sur la vie et le règne de Louis VIII (1187–1226)* (Paris, 1894), 222.

[7] W.C. Jordan, *Louis IX and the Challenge of Crusade: A Study in Rulership* (Princeton, 1979), 141–52; Jean Richard, *Saint Louis* (Cambridge, 1993), 170–77.

[8] A. de La Grange, 'Les entrées des souverains à Tournai', *Memoires de la société historique et archéologique de Tournai* xix (1885), 12.

[9] M. Cecilia Gaposchkin, *The Making of Saint Louis: Kingship, Sanctity, and Crusade in the Later Middle Ages* (London, 2008), 106–7.

pardons as part of a ceremonial entry. Indeed, Henry VI, who claimed to be king of France, was criticised by one eyewitness of his coronation entry into Paris in December 1431 for failing to make the customary pardons.[10] By the end of the fifteenth century there was a long-established tradition of making grace at inaugural entries, and Charles VIII could claim with some confidence that the right to issue pardons at his entries was one of the 'droits royaux prérogatives dont nos prédécesseurs et progéniteurs Rois ont accoutumé d'ancienneté user à leur joyeux avènement et nouvelle entrée en chascune ville de notre royaume.'[11]

Although the issuing of pardons was a regular feature of a royal entry in later medieval and Renaissance France, this aspect of the ceremony has received little attention from historians, who have tended to use festival books as their principal documentary source in their studies of the development of the ceremony.[12] While useful for tracing the development of the symbolic programme of the French entry, festival books say little about the pardoning of criminals.[13] Once we turn to the administrative records of the urban and royal administrations, however, we find a range of information on this important element of the entry ceremony. These sources reveal that the provision of royal grace was a complex process and involved the participation of a range of groups and individuals. Criminals took the initiative to petition the king for pardon, while municipal councils sought to control the procedure by which grace was made at a

[10] He wrote that as Henry failed to act in the customary manner at a royal entry that 'Not a soul, at home or abroad, was heard to speak a good word in his praise': *A Parisian Journal, 1405–1449*, Janet Shirley, ed. (Oxford, 1968), 273; *Journal d'un bourgeois de Paris de 1405 à 1449*, Colette Beaune, ed. (Paris, 1990), 311.

[11] From M. Gaillard, 'Notice d'un registre du trésor des chartes', *Mémoires de littérature de l'académie royale des inscriptions et belles lettres* 43 (Paris, 1776–79), 682. Also cited in Lawrence Bryant, *The King and the City in the Parisian Royal Entry Ceremony: Politics, Ritual, and Art in the Renaissance* (Geneva, 1986), 26.

[12] Gordon Kipling mentions Richard II's pardoning of a criminal at his entry into London in 1392 but does not comment on the granting of pardons at French royal entries. Lawrence Bryant briefly discusses this aspect of the ceremony in his study of the Parisian entry ceremony, while the pardoning of prisoners is mentioned only in a footnote in Michael Wintroub's recent study of the Renaissance French entry: Gordon Kipling, *Enter the King: Theater, Liturgy, and Ritual in the Medieval Civic Triumph* (Oxford, 1998), 28; Bryant, *King and the City*, 24–26; Michael Wintroub, *A Savage Mirror: Power, Identity, and Knowledge in Early Modern France* (Stanford, 2006), 247, fn. 78.

[13] Although they are largely silent on the pardoning of criminals, festival books do record instances where actors dressed as captives were included in the festivities. When Henry II entered Rouen in 1550, for example, the town included actors dressed as captives in the extramural procession in celebration of the return of Boulogne-sur-Mer to French rule: *L'Entrée de Henri II à Rouen 1550*, Margaret McGowan, ed. (Amsterdam, 1979), 19.

royal entry. Interaction between the royal administration and local officials was crucial for this aspect of the ceremony, and urban elites negotiated with royal officials regarding the extent of the pardons to be issued by the king. Those criminals who successfully petitioned the king for a pardon at an entry received a letter of pardon, copies of which were registered at the *Chancellerie*.[14] These letters provide us with the name of the supplicants and give details of the crimes for which they were pardoned. The wording of the letters of remission was broad in order to cover the wide range of crimes pardoned at a royal entry, and they tended to follow a general formula. In order to understand the process that lay behind the act of pardoning, the most valuable sources are the registers of municipal deliberations. Although the presence of the king was the catalyst for the issuing of pardons, the form of the pardoning (and the entry ceremony in general) was largely controlled by the townspeople, who worked out the details of the pardoning in conjunction with royal officials in advance of an entry. In addition to these administrative records, eyewitness accounts of the ceremony, edicts and treatises on kingship provide important information on the issuing of pardons at an entry. Using these sources, this essay will examine the process by which criminals were pardoned during a ceremonial entry and seek to understand what this tells us about both the nature of royal justice and the interaction between the French crown and its municipal elites during this period.

Justice and Mercy in the Royal Entry Ceremony

Between the mid-fifteenth and mid-sixteenth centuries the French royal entry ceremony underwent a period of intense development, with the entries made by Henry II and Charles IX amongst the most magnificent ever staged in France. One of the key innovations of this period was the regular inclusion of dramatic performances along the processional route. While such performances are found in Paris from the late fourteenth century, during the second half of the fifteenth century towns across the kingdom began to include plays in their royal entries.[15] French writers developed a conception of kingship during the fifteenth century that placed a strong emphasis on justice, and this was reflected in the themes

---

[14] Davis, *Fiction in the Archives*, 8.

[15] Pageantry was first included in a French royal entry for Charles VI's post-coronation entry into Paris in 1380: Kipling, *Enter the King*, 6.

of the performances staged for the king along the processional route.[16] Royal entries were an audio-visual representation of the contemporary literary genre of *mirrors of princes* and the dramatic entertainments provided by the municipal elite highlighted the importance of royal justice in their conception of ideal kingship. At Charles VIII's inaugural entries into Paris (1484) and Rouen (1485) the king was shown pageants which highlighted the central position of justice to kingship and stressed the importance of mercy.[17] While the reign of Francis I saw a shift in the symbolism of the royal entry from one based on biblical allegory to the adoption of classical imagery, the emphasis on royal justice and mercy remained. Indeed, as royal entries became increasing elaborate during the course of the sixteenth century, the civic elites who designed the spectacles had further opportunities to include representations of justice in their entry. When Charles IX entered Valence in 1564, the town council included a representation of the king accompanied by the goddess Minerva encouraging him to both punish the guilty and display mercy, while the triumphal arches erected along the processional route carried the same message.[18]

There were two sides to royal justice: the power of life and the power of death. A king was to inspire fear as well as love, and imitate Christ in the dispensation of both pardon and punishment. Although justice was expected to be tough on those who had committed serious crimes, the potential of receiving pardon and absolution was an essential requirement of good rulership during the period. Should a king be too harsh, he ran the risk of being seen as a tyrant; but be too lenient and he could be seen as weak. We find such a concern to enact both sides of royal justice during a royal visit. As well as issuing pardons during his post-coronation entry into Paris in 1549, Henry II also had a number of Protestants publicly burned on the Place de Grève in the following days, with the king himself asking them to repent as they stood on the pyre.[19] By means of this act, Henry could claim to be fulfilling the coronation oath to drive heresy from the kingdom, which he had taken as part of his *sacre* at Reims in

[16] Jacques Krynen, *Idéal du prince et pouvoir royal en France à la fin du Moyen Age (1380–1440): Etude de la littératue politique du temps* (Paris, 1981), 186–204.

[17] Konigson, 'Cité et le prince', 62–3.

[18] *Les entrées solennelles pendant le règne de Charles IX*, Pierre-Louis Vaillancourt and Martin Desrosiers, ed. (Toronto, 2010), 154.

[19] *Registres des délibérations du Bureau de la ville de Paris. Tome troisième, 1539–1552*, P. Guérin, ed. (Paris, 1886), 184.

July 1547.[20] Outside of the capital, tours of the provinces allowed French monarchs to make a demonstration of royal justice to their subjects across the kingdom. Following his entry into Sens in 1517, Francis I had a Swiss mercenary captain, then imprisoned in the town, executed on the main square.[21] The king had recently returned from a successful campaign in Italy, where he had won a crushing victory over an army of Swiss mercenaries at the battle of Marignano. Following this victory, Francis had signed a treaty with the Swiss at Fribourg on 29 November 1516, whereby the Swiss cantons swore not to serve against him in either Italy or France.[22] By having the mercenary captain executed at Sens, Francis could recall his victory at Marignano, make an example of an oath-breaker, and give a demonstration to the townspeople that he was providing for the security of both town and kingdom.

The issuing of pardons at an entry acted as a counterbalance to the use of executions and allowed the king to show that both sides of royal justice were in balance. Executions were often performed at locations close to buildings invested with municipal power, such as the town hall, prison, or gates. The most common location for the pardoning of criminals was directly outside the gate of entry. Gates were symbolically significant in the fifteenth and sixteenth centuries and were representative of municipal liberties, one of which was the right to perform high justice. The principal gates of a town were the location where bodies, or parts of the bodies of criminals, such as amputated arms or legs, were displayed both as a mark of urban authority and as an example to others. Bodies were left hanging in gibbets, with any rotting parts that had fallen being reattached, and they remained on display during a royal entry.[23] The king expected urban elites to maintain order and stability on his behalf, and by having body parts on display the ruling elite could show the king that they were upholding his laws in the town. Municipal councils directed their sergeants to move prisoners seeking pardon to the place of justice at the gate of entry and

[20] For the text of the coronation oath see: Nicholas Menin, *Traité historique et chronologique du sacre et couronnement des rois et des reines de France* (Paris, 1772), 254–57.

[21] *Cronique du roy Françoys premier de ce nom*, Georges Guiffrey, ed. (Paris, 1860), 267.

[22] R.J. Knecht, *Renaissance Warrior and Patron: The Reign of Francis I* (Cambridge, 1994), 77–79.

[23] See: Amiens A[rchives] M[unicipales] BB 11, fol. 158. Some towns also took measures to prevent animals running off with any limbs that had dropped down from the gibbets: Pieter Spierenburg, *The Spectacle of Suffering: Executions and the Evolution of Repression* (Cambridge, 1984), 57–58.

issued the criminals with penitential clothing, which included white sackcloth, a halter to be worn around the neck, and a branch to be carried in the hand.[24] By placing those seeking pardon at this location and compelling them to appear in such a manner, officials could display both sides of royal justice to those who gathered to watch the entry. It formed a *tableau* of the Day of Judgement, with the king placed in a Christ-like role, as he prepared to enter the town which had been transformed into a New Jerusalem for the occasion.[25] There were close links between punishment and mercy, and royal entries often followed the exact same processional route as that used for executions and punishments.[26] Prior to an execution or banishment, criminals were led along a set processional route ending at the town gate, where their punishment, death or expulsion, was enacted. This route was enacted in reverse during a royal entry when, rather than being expelled from the town, they were returned to society by a Christ-like king.

The Issuing of Pardons

By the mid-fifteenth century, a set process regarding the way in which royal grace was issued at ceremonial entries had been established.[27] There were two ways to obtain pardon at an entry. In the first instance, as the king approached the town he was met by large numbers of the banished who came seeking pardon. The second element of pardoning involved those who found themselves in prison at the time of an entry. The pardoning of the banished posed the most potentially dangerous and disruptive element in the provision of grace. In preparation for an entry, the banished

---

24 See, for example, the instructions issued by Tournai's municipal council at the entry of Louis XI in 1463: La Grange, 'Entrées des souverains', 42.

25 For the symbolism of the New Jerusalem at an entry see especially: Kipling, *Enter the King*, especially chapters 1 and 2; Ernst H. Kantorowicz, 'The "King's Advent" and the Enigmatic Panels in the Doors of Santa Sabina', in Ernst H. Kantorowicz, *Selected Studies* (New York, 1965), 37–75. Although there was a shift to the use of classical imagery from the reign of Francis I, the theme of the New Jerusalem remained prevalent in royal entries throughout the sixteenth century: Wintroub, *A Savage Mirror*, 109.

26 Esther Cohen, 'Symbols of Culpability and the Universal Language of Justice: The Ritual of Public Executions in Late Medieval Europe', *History of European Ideas* 11 (1989), 410; Patricia Turning, 'The Right to Punish: Jurisdictional Disputes between Royal and Municipal Officials in Medieval Toulouse', *French History* 24, no. 1 (March, 2010), 3.

27 At Tournai, the procedure for pardoning prisoners was set by the entry of Charles VI in 1383 and remained largely unchanged throughout the sixteenth century: La Grange, 'Entrées des souverains', 35.

waited for the monarch at the edge of the town's jurisdiction and petitioned him for a pardon, which would permit them to rejoin urban society. Municipal jurisdiction did not extend beyond the *banlieue*, though any of the banished who crossed over into the town's territory without certainty of receiving the king's grace would be arrested, imprisoned and punished by the town council.[28] Criminals were banished for a set period of years, the length of which depended on the severity of their crime. Those guilty of the most serious crimes could be mutilated or marked by branding, the cutting off of ears, or the amputation of a limb, before being banished from the town. This worked as a visual sign of the nature of their crime, and there was little chance of them receiving pardon at an entry. Although municipal councils exerted considerable authority over prisoners held in civic jails, they had very little control over the banished. In an attempt to lessen the threat posed to urban society by this element of the ceremony, additional restrictions were placed on the banished who came seeking pardon outside the town. The municipal liberties of Tournai limited the number of banished that French princes of the blood could return during an entry to eighteen. Seventeen of these had to have been banished for no longer than a year, and thus guilty of only very minor offences. One person who had been banished for up to seven years could be returned, though this still excluded those guilty of the most serious crimes.[29] Geographical limits were placed on those people who came to the edge of the *banlieue* seeking pardon. The banished who obtained a letter of pardon at an entry had three days in which to present it to the municipal authorities of the town which they sought to re-enter.[30] After the three days were over, the pardon was void. In practice, this meant that the pardons issued to the banished at an entry were confined to the immediate vicinity of the town of entry. Given these restrictions, it was often only the most desperate who appealed for grace this way at an entry, such as Jacquiot Cressent and Pierre de Chaumont, who, having being declined pardon amongst the banished at Louis XI's entry into Arras in 1464, attempted to grab on to the king's horse as he crossed into the town. When Louis was on the point of entry, he turned to them and said that he could not grant them pardon as

---

[28] For a discussion of the *banlieue* see: Caroline Bourlet, 'Paris et ses banlieues: limites et définitions d'un espace médiéval', in Marie-José Michael and Jacques Verger ed., *A l'ombre de Paris. Les échanges entre Paris et ses périphéries (XIVe–XVIIe siècle)* (Paris, 2002), 9–29.

[29] La Grange, 'Entrées des souverains', 38–9.

[30] Ibid., 77.

it was not the custom of the town. The town council made written records of the king's verbal pronouncements and kept the updated documents in the civic archives as a further record of their liberties regarding the return of the banished.[31]

Although those people waiting outside the town who had been banished for more serious crimes had little chance of receiving the king's grace, inmates who found themselves in prison could be pardoned for the same crimes. Royal clemency was at its most accessible during ceremonial entries, and we find numerous cases of people bailing themselves into prison in preparation for a royal entry. The routes of royal progresses were well-known, and wealthier criminals could send a servant ahead of them in order to confirm that an entry was going to take place.[32] Kings were accompanied by large entourages and moved slowly, giving those seeking pardon the opportunity to arrive at a town in advance of the royal party. The populations of urban prisons swelled in advance of an entry, with municipal councils having to pay for extra officials to deal with the influx of criminals. Royal entries afforded more favourable access to the king than was otherwise the case. Under normal circumstances, a royal pardon would have to be obtained through the courts. This was frequently a long and expensive process, with many people preferring to wait until a royal entry to obtain their pardon. Indeed, we find people applying for pardons at royal entries for crimes a decade old, with especially high numbers in regions seldom visited by the court.[33]

Unlike the banished, who had to register their pardon at the town from which they were exiled, the imprisoned were presented with a letter of abolition or pardon at an entry which they had to register at the *Chancellerie* in Paris within six months, where it was then confirmed with a seal of green wax.[34] Although this normally required the payment of a fee, royal officials instructed the courts not to receive any payments for pardons issued at a royal entry.[35] This gave criminals from across the kingdom

---

[31] Municipal deliberations, cited in E. Lecesne, *Histoire d'Arras depuis les temps plus recules jusqu'en 1789*, 2 vols (Arras, 1880), i, 398–99.

[32] M. Nassiet, 'Brittany and the French Monarchy in the Sixteenth Century: The Evidence of the Letters of Remission', *French History* 17, no. 4 (December, 2003), 435.

[33] Jean Boutier, Alain Dewerpe, Daniel Nordman, *Un tour de France royal. Le voyage de Charles IX (1564–1566)* (Paris, 1984), 204–8; Nassiet, 'Brittany and the French Monarchy', 426–27.

[34] Jules Legoux, *Du droit de grâce en France* (Paris, 1865), 131; Ernest Sermet, *Le droit de grâce* (Toulouse, 1901), 83. In some cases it could be taken to one of the regional *parlements* instead.

[35] Sermet, *Droit de grâce*, 89. See also: Davis, *Fiction in the Archives*, 10.

the opportunity to travel and receive a royal pardon, and prisoners who had received a pardon were eligible to receive money from the crown to cover the costs of the journey. Those people who were unsuccessful in their appeal for pardon were released from the prisons following the entry.[36] Such measures helped to encourage criminals to hand themselves into prison voluntarily and thus allow the king to give a demonstration of the extent of his authority at an entry. The more prisoners there were to pardon, the greater the display of the king's power.

Prisoners who appeared at a royal entry seeking pardon could have a good hope of success. Indeed, Amiens's disgruntled gaoler, Galois du Wes, petitioned the town council to be reimbursed for the loss of income that had resulted from the emptying of prisons at the dauphin's entry in 1443.[37] Details of who was eligible to receive a pardon were worked out in advance of an entry. A panel composed of royal and municipal officials met to decide which of the imprisoned would be permitted to seek pardon at an entry. As urban elites possessed local knowledge and knew exactly who was held in their jails and for what crimes, it was generally in the best interests of both town and crown that the municipality's advice be heeded in this matter. In the days before Louis XI's entry into Tournai in 1464, the town council sent representatives to the king bearing the registers containing the names of the imprisoned and banished. The mayor and *échevins* had a list of people whom they did not want pardoned, and the civic deputies highlighted the dangers of re-admitting these people back into urban society. They appealed to past custom and precedent and told Louis that his ancestors had listened to the advice of the town when making grace at their entries. Kings took municipal advice seriously, and on this occasion Louis and his councillors worked with the municipal council and went through the list of names together.[38] It was also accepted by the crown that prisoners guilty of very serious crimes could be moved out of the town in advance of any entry.[39] Urban elites took advantage of this measure, and prior to Henry II's entry into Rouen in 1550 the municipal

[36] This was the case from 1532 at least, when the practice was confirmed by a ruling from the Parlement of Paris: Richard Jackson, *Vive le Roi! A History of the French Coronation from Charles V to Charles X* (Chapel Hill, 1984), 110; Jean Papon, *Secrets du troisieme et dernier notaire de Jean Papon, Conseiller du Roy, & Lieutenant general au Bailliage de Forests* (Lyon, 1578), 1392–93. Town councils publicised the provision of safe conduct in advance of an entry: La Grange, 'Entrées des souverains', 86.

[37] AM Amiens BB 5, fol. 228v.

[38] La Grange, 'Entrées des souverains', 42.

[39] Papon, *Secrets du troisieme et dernier notaire*, 747.

council transferred those criminals whom they did not want pardoned out of the town before the arrival of the king.[40] This measure helped to avoid any potential confrontations between town and crown that could arise over the pardoning of criminals.

The Extent of the Pardons Granted

At their entries French kings claimed the right: 'delivrer & mettre hors, s'il luy plaist, tous prisonniers, clercs, & lays, de toutes prisons, où ils sont detenus, & soyent les occasions de leur detention ciuiles, ou criminelles & à iceux remettre, quitter & pardonner à plein & à tousiours les crimes & toutes amendes & peines corporelles, criminelles & ciuiles'.[41] This right extended to all prisons in a town, including those of the town council, the *bailli* and the bishop, and the letters of pardon granted during an entry give the impression of unlimited royal power. However, while no crime was unpardonable, not all criminals could expect to receive a pardon. Although it was accepted that the king would issue pardons at his entry, it was expected that they did not go too far and they were constrained by municipal rights and liberties from exercising clemency during entries. Criminals banished or imprisoned for crimes such as rape, pre-meditated murder, banditry or sedition were normally not eligible to receive a pardon. These exemptions were enshrined in the urban privileges that the king confirmed during his entry. Should the monarch then decide to pardon serious crimes, he would have been breaking the very municipal liberties that he had just granted. The pardoning of criminals was principally a feature of inaugural ceremonial entries, when the king was working to establish good relations with the municipal elites, and it was not in his interests to provoke a confrontation over this issue.

Pardons were revoked if it was found that they had been issued in contravention of municipal liberties. When Henry VIII entered Tournai as king of France in September 1513 he pardoned all who came seeking grace, without making the usual exemptions.[42] It is likely that Henry was

---

40 Nicétas Periaux, *Histoire sommaire et chronologique de la ville de Rouen* (Rouen, 1874), 263.

41 Papon, *Secrets du troisieme et dernier notaire*, 747–78. See also: Claude Gauvard, *De Grace Especial: Crime, Etat et Société en France à la fin du Moyen Age* 2 vols (Paris, 1991), ii, 922.

42 La Grange, 'Entrées des souverains', 65–66. For an analysis of this entry see: N. Murphy, 'Henry VIII's French crown: his entry into Tournai revisited', *Historical Research* 85 (2012), 617–631.

unfamiliar with this aspect of the French royal entry ceremony, which differed from the pardoning custom in England.[43] Immediately following the entry, Tournai's municipal council went to Henry to protest that he had been too generous with his pardons, which had resulted in many dangerous criminals being readmitted to urban society. The *échevins* informed Henry of the customary exemptions to receiving pardon at entries which had been 'long temps accoustumée et observée en ladicte ville'. As a result of these protests, Henry issued a letter of patent which stated that, at the request of the town council, the murderers, traitors, rapists, and arsonists who had been readmitted into the town on the day of his entry were to be exempt from receiving pardon.[44]

Foreign Princes, French Dukes and the Provision of Pardon

Although Henry VIII claimed the right to pardon prisoners as king of France, the privilege could also be granted by the French monarch to foreign royals progressing through his kingdom. When Philip the Fair and Joanna of Castile travelled through France in 1501, Louis XII granted them the right to issue pardons in his name during their entries.[45] The progresses of foreign royals through France provided the best opportunity for criminals to obtain pardon, as fewer restrictions were placed on those who came seeking pardon at these entries. For example, as Margaret of Austria passed through France in 1501 on her way to marry the duke of Savoy, she travelled from Brussels and was met at Guise, just across the border into France, by a delegation on behalf of the king. Margaret was informed that Louis XII had granted her permission to pardon all criminals at her entries except for 'bruleurs d'eglise, violeurs de femmes et aguaiteurs

---

[43] For the practice at English entries see: K.J. Kesselring, *Mercy and Authority in the Tudor State* (Cambridge, 2003), 140–41; Kipling, *Enter the King*, 28.

[44] La Grange, 'Entrées des souverains', 75; *Letters and Papers, Foreign and Domestic, Henry VIII*, J.S. Brewer, ed., 22 vols (London, 1864–1932), i, no. 2331; C.G. Cruickshank, *The English Occupation of Tournai, 1513–19* (Oxford, 1971), 14.

[45] Jean d'Auton, *Chroniques de Louis XII*, R. de Maulde de la Clavière, ed., 4 vols (Paris, 1889–1895), ii, 211. For this progress see: B[ibliothéque] n[ationale] de F[rance] Collection Français 23934, fols. 190–225. There were also a number of restrictions placed on the entries made by members of the Habsburg family into French towns. They were not to be given a canopy, enter with an unsheathed sword carried before them or to be presented with the keys to the city: Michael Sherman, '"Pomp and Circumstances": Pageantry, Politics, and Propaganda in France during the Reign of Louis XII, 1498–1515', *Sixteenth Century Journal* 9, no. 4 (Winter, 1978), 18–19.

de chemin'.[46] This was more extensive than the pardons issued by French kings at their entries, where urban liberties excluded those guilty of a wide range of serious crimes from receiving pardon at an entry. Perhaps the most extensive display of pardoning came for Emperor Charles V's progress through France from Spain to the Low Countries in 1539.[47] Entering France at Bayonne, Francis I instructed towns lying on the route of Charles's progress to stage a ceremonial entry for the emperor. As part of these welcomes Francis granted Charles, his great rival, the right to pardon all those who came seeking grace, with the only exception being those guilty of *lèse-majesté*.[48] The 1539 progress was a carefully managed display of French royal propaganda, with the French king himself taking a major role in the design of the entry.[49] As the pardons granted by the emperor at his entries were seen as an extension of the French king's authority and issued in his name, Francis was able to give a demonstration to Charles of the extent of the power of the French monarch. Charles was en route to Flanders, where towns possessed considerable rights regarding the pardoning of criminals at entries. Indeed, in 1487 the town council of Ypres compelled Maximilian, Charles's grandfather, to annul a pardon that he had granted to a female tavern owner at his entry into the town.[50] In contrast to the French monarchy, which was in the process of consolidating the power to issue pardons into its hands, Charles did not possess the monopoly over grace in his imperial territories.[51] One contemporary commentator noted that 'plusieurs criminelz chargez de grans et énormes crimes furent délivrez' during the course of this progress.[52] In spite of the pardoning of such dangerous criminals, there were no protests from town councils over the issue of municipal liberties. Urban elites were more concerned to work with the king in devising a show of propaganda

[46] *Chroniques de Jean Molinet*, Georges Doutrepont and Omer Jodogne, ed., 3 vols (Brussels, 1935), i, 489.

[47] For this progress see: R.J. Knecht, 'Charles V's Journey through France, 1539–40', in J.R. Mulryne and Elizabeth Goldring ed., *Court Festivals of the European Renaissance: Art, Politics and Performance* (Aldershot, 2002), 153–70.

[48] For the letters of pardon issued by Charles V during his entries see: BnF Collection Français 23934, fols. 190–225; Jacques Soyer, 'Lettres de rémission accordées par l'Empereur Charles-Quint lors de son passage à Orléans (20 décembre 1539)', *Revue de la Renaissance* 11 (1910), 135–44.

[49] See his role in preparing Charles V's entry into Paris: *Registres des délibérations, Paris, 1539–1552*, Guérin, 2–10.

[50] I.L.A. Diegerick, *Inventaire analytique et chronologique des chartes et documents appartenant aux archives de la ville d'Ypres*, 7 vols (Bruges, 1853–1868), iv, 131.

[51] Legoux, *Droit de grace*, 11.

[52] *Cronique du roy Françoys premier*, Guiffrey, 317.

against France's greatest enemy than they were in safeguarding municipal rights over the pardoning of criminals.

Town councils also acted in tandem with the king to restrict the rights of French princes to issue pardons at their entries. French kings were only one of a number of political authorities who issued pardons during the early and central Middle Ages. Moves by John II in the mid-fourteenth century to make the right to pardon exclusively a royal one were reversed in the political crises of the late fourteenth and early fifteenth centuries, when civil war, foreign invasion and the insanity of Charles VI brought the French monarchy to its nadir. During this period French princes, such as the dukes of Brittany and Burgundy, stood as rivals to the king for power and sought to exploit the weakness of the French crown by asserting their right to issue pardons. With the revival of French royal power under Charles VII, urban elites entered into a period of good relations with the crown and became increasingly hostile to attempts by French princes to issue pardons at their entries.[53] When Charles, duke of Orléans, entered Dijon in 1450 he claimed the royal right to pardon prisoners held in jails across the kingdom. Rather than acceding to the duke's wishes, the town council moved all the prisoners held in the municipal jails out of Dijon in advance of the entry, leaving none for him to pardon.[54] Moves by the crown to limit the right of authorities other than the king to issue pardons were revived by Charles VII in 1449, and by the 1470s the duke of Angôuleme had to obtain the express permission of the king, Louis XI, when he wished to pardon prisoners at entries into towns in his own domains.[55] Royal dominance over rival princely authorities was largely completed during the reign of Louis XII, who issued an ordinance in March 1499 which ruled that the right to issue pardons was 'reservez en signe de souveraineté'.[56] The former rights of other judicial authorities to issue pardons were annulled, and only the king and his successors were declared to possess this privilege.[57]

[53] For this development see: Bernard Chevalier, *Les bonnes villes de France du XIVe au XVIe siècle* (Paris, 1982), 101–5; David Rivaud, *Les villes et le roi. Les municipalités de Bourges, Poitiers et Tours et l'émergence de l'Etat moderne (v. 1440–v. 1560)* (Rennes, 2007), *passim*.

[54] M. de Gouvenain, *Ville de Dijon. Inventaire sommaire des archives communales antérieures à 1790*, 5 vols (Paris, 1867–1910), i, 37. Bryant, *King and the City*, 25.

[55] *Ordonnances des roys de France de la troisième race*, M. de Laurière et al., ed., 21 vols (Paris, 1967–68), xviii, 303–4. Legoux, *Droit de grâce*, 9.

[56] *Recueil général des anciennes lois françaises depuis l'an 420 jusqu'à la révolution de 1789*, François André Isambet, ed., 29 vols (Paris, 1822–33), xi, 353. *Ordonnances des rois de France*, xxi, 228–31.

[57] This was confirmed in a longer reforming edict issued in 1507: Isambert, *Recueil général des anciennes lois françaises*, xi, 514.

Some French bishops had issued pardons at their inaugural entries since the early Middle Ages. The rights of the bishop of Orléans to deliver prisoners at his entry was believed to extend back to the appeals made by St. Aignan to the Roman governor of Orléans to free prisoners at his entry into the town.[58] This tradition persisted right through the Middle Ages, and by the fifteenth and sixteenth centuries criminals flocked to hand themselves in to the episcopal prisons at Orléans in advance of the bishop's inaugural entry.[59] The process behind the issuing of pardons at bishops' entries operated a similar way to those of the king. In advance of an entry, a commission visited the inmates and declared if they were eligible to receive a pardon. Lacking the resources to organise the full administration of the pardons, bishops were reliant on the cooperation of the municipal council in order to ensure that this part of the ceremony proceeded in good order. In advance of Charles Hémard de Denonville's inaugural entry as bishop into Amiens in 1538, the canons of the cathedral chapter and the bishop's officials approached the town council and asked them to provide sergeants to control the large numbers of the banished flocking to seek grace at this entry.[60]

By the sixteenth century pardons issued at episcopal entries were not deemed sufficient in themselves in order to guarantee the remission of a crime. Criminals who had obtained pardon at a bishop's entry appealed for letters patent to have the pardon confirmed by the king.[61] Unlike the pardons granted by the king at his entries, those issued by the clergy could be overruled by judges.[62] The downgrading of the value attached to the pardons issued at bishops' entries was a part of a wider move to strengthen the position of the crown. In 1497 Charles VIII supplanted the Church in issuing pardons on Good Friday in honour of the Passion, and in 1512 Louis XII issued a declaration curtailing the church's right to grant pardons on feast days.[63] While Louis XII moved toward limiting the clergy's ability to pardon, successive French monarchs in the sixteenth century, including Francis I, Henry II, Charles IX and Henry III, acted to confirm the rights of the clergy to pardon.[64] The drive to remove clerical

[58] Sermet, *Droit de grâce*, 114.

[59] Jean Bodin, *On Sovereignty: Four Chapters from the Six Books of the Commonwealth*, Julian H. Franklin, ed. and trans. (Cambridge, 1992), 76; Jacques Foviaux, *La remission des peines et des condemnations. Droit monarchique et droit moderne* (Paris, 1970), 55.

[60] AM Amiens BB 23, fol. 86.

[61] Foviaux, *Remission des peines*, 35.

[62] Sermet, *Droit de grâce*, 91.

[63] Foviaux, *Remission des peines*, 49.

[64] Sermet, *Droit de grâce*, 112–13.

pardons and strengthen royal privileges was led by the *parlementaires*. One of the most notorious uses of clerical pardon in the sixteenth century was the right held by the cathedral chapter of Notre Dame in Rouen to release criminals on Ascension Day.[65] This was done in honour of St. Romain, who was believed to have saved Rouen from a dragon in the sixth century with the help of a criminal. Jean Bodin lamented that the chapter of Rouen pardoned 'only the most abominable crimes that they can, crimes that the king customarily did not pardon.'[66] This was a way of asserting the superiority of clerical pardons, and French jurists in the sixteenth century sought to abolish this privilege in their drive to augment royal power. The Parlement of Rouen, in an effort to enforce royal authority, refused to recognize pardons issued on St. Romain's day and proceeded with the execution of a criminal who had been granted a pardon by the cathedral chapter.[67] The Parlement of Paris also moved to secure the rights of the French king by curtailing the issuing of pardons at the entries of visiting papal legates. In the struggle with the king over control of the French church, the pope asserted his authority in France by having his legates issue pardons in his name, rather than that of the king. Although the visiting papal legate, Jean Salviat, made grace in the name of the pope when he entered Paris in 1526, when the cardinal of Plaisance, also a papal legate, issued pardons at his entry into Paris in 1548, the Parlement of Paris ruled that these pardons were void and that all who had received them were to be brought to trial.[68]

Women and Pardoning

The Parlement of Paris was concerned to protect what it saw as an important mark of kingship, and they also moved to restrict female members of the French royal family from issuing pardons at their entries. With the resurgence of the power of French monarchy from the mid-fifteenth century, the frequency with which female members of the royal family were

[65] For the history of this privilege see: A. Floquet, *Histoire du privilege du Saint Romain*, 2 vols (Rouen, 1833).

[66] Bodin, *On Sovereignty*, 76.

[67] Ibid., 76.

[68] *Livre de raison de Me Nicolas Versoris avocat au Parlement de Paris 1519–1530*, G. Fagniez, ed. (Paris, 1885), 95; *Le journal d'un bourgeois de Paris* (1515–1536), V.-L. Bourrilly, ed. (Paris, 1910), 247–48; Legoux, *Doit de grâce*, 11.

able to make pardon increased.[69] The ability of royal women to issue pardons was not seen as an intrinsic right of their royal status. Rather, it was seen as an extension of their husband or father's position as king, from whom they derived their authority.[70] When Mary Tudor came to France in 1514 to marry Louis XII, the king granted her the right to pardon prisoners in his name at the towns she entered.[71] Although pardons issued by royal women in the name of the king were accepted as legitimate, problems arose when they attempted to issue pardons in their own name. In 1483 the Parlement of Paris acted to curtail the right of Anne of Beaujeu, then acting as regent of France for her son Charles VIII, to issue pardons.[72] The issue of a woman's right to issue pardons was raised again in 1515. Before leaving for campaign in Italy, Francis I granted his mother, Louise of Savoy, the regency, including the right to:

> delivrer hors des prisons desdits lieux tous prisonniers criminelz detenus èsdictes prisons, pour quelque cas de crime qu'ilz aient commis, et à iceulx bailler et faire expedier les graces, remissions, pardons et abolicions desdicts cas, crimes et delictz qu'ilz confesseront, lesquelles graces, remissions et pardons nous avons dès maintenant pour lors auctorisez et auctorisons et voulons estre de tel effect que si par nous ilz estoient donnez.[73]

Citing the precedent set in 1483, regarding the rights of Anne of Beaujeu as regent, the Parlement of Paris moved to obstruct the king's granting of the authority to pardon to his mother. Receiving word that the Parlement was about to send letters of remonstration to the king over this issue, Louise took the initiative and renounced her right to grant pardon before the matter could be brought to Francis and provoke a confrontation between king and Parlement. As David Potter has noted, the magistrates of the Parlement of Paris were 'profoundly shaped by the idea of the king as first and foremost a dispenser of justice' and they 'wanted to retain their role at the centre of the judicial system'.[74] The protests raised over Louise's right

---

69 See, for example, the pardons issued by Yolanda, daughter of Charles VII, at her entry into Dijon in 1461: BnF Collection de Bourgogne 45, fol. 18.

70 Karen Pratt, 'The Image of the Queen in Old French Literature', in Anne J. Duggan ed., *Queens and Queenship in Medieval Europe* (Boydell, 1997), 235–59.

71 The continuator of Monstrelet in *The chronicles of Enguerrand de Monstrelet*, T. Johnes, ed., 12 vols (London, 1810), xii, 166.

72 Elizabeth McCartney, 'The King's Mother and Royal Prerogative in Early-Sixteenth-Century France', John Carmi Parsons ed., *Medieval Queenship* (Stroud, 1993), 126.

73 *Ordonnances des rois de France. Règne de Francçois Ier*, 8 vols (Paris, 1902), i, 71.

74 David Potter, *A History of France, 1460–1560: The Emergence of a Nation-State* (London, 1995), 36. For the disputes between the Parlement of Paris and the crown during

to pardon were part of these conflicts. During the sixteenth century, the Parlement of Paris acted to conserve the rights and powers of the French monarch against rivals, even when this went against the personal wishes of the king, in order to preserve the office and dignity of the monarch.

* * *

Significant developments were made in the provision of royal mercy between the mid-fifteenth and mid-sixteenth centuries. This was also a period that saw a marked upturn in the frequency of ceremonial entries, which offered increased opportunities for criminals to seek and obtain royal pardon and for kings to display their power in pardoning them. Entries had the advantage over other royal ceremonies, such as coronations, in that they tended to reach a wider and more diverse audience. This permitted the ruler to make a demonstration of his power at places in which the court was not ordinarily resident. The changing attitudes in the issuing of pardons also reflected the changing nature of town-crown relations during the period. From the reign of Charles VII until the Wars of Religion, French towns entered into what Bernard Chevalier describes as an *entente cordiale* with the crown.[75] Rather than imposing ideas on royal justice from above, from the mid-fifteenth century French kings tended to listen to municipal delegates and respect urban privileges regarding the provision of mercy. In order for the state to function effectively during the fifteenth and sixteenth centuries, the crown had to work with local elites, not against them, in order to ensure that its laws were enforced across the kingdom. In return, the townspeople assisted the crown in its construction of royal power by denying rival political authorities, such as dukes and bishops, the right to pardon criminals during their entries.

During the second half of the fifteenth century the right to pardon at entries was increasingly understood to be a right pertaining to the king alone. Royal women were prevented from issuing pardons in their own name, while French princes had to seek the permission of the king first. Pardons issued by papal legates were declared void, and those granted by French bishops at their inaugural entries required further confirmation by the king. Although others could and did make pardons, it was only after receiving the king's permission to do so, and it was understood to be an extension of the king's power and authority. While this power

---

the sixteenth century see: J.L. Bourgeon, 'La Fronde parlementaire à la vielle de la Saint-Bartélemy', *Bibliothèque de l'Ecole des Chartes* 148 (1990), 17–89.

[75] Chevalier, *Bonnes villes*, 101.

and authority was to reach its apogee by the mid-sixteenth century, the very basis of the legitimacy on which the French king claimed the right to be the sole issuer of pardons was vigorously challenged again during the Wars of Religion. These destructive civil wars brought the Valois monarchy to the point of collapse, and the act of pardon itself came to be contested once more.[76]

[76] For example, Charles, duke of Mayenne, the head of the Catholic League, granted pardons during the reign of Henry III. They were issued in the name of 'Charles, duc de Mayenne, par et lieutenant général de l'Etat et Royaume de France': Legoux, *Droit de grâce*, 250.

DIVINE VIOLENCE TO UPHOLD MORAL VALUES: THE CASEBOOK OF AN EMPEROR GUAN TEMPLE IN HUNAN PROVINCE IN 1851–1852

Barend J. ter Haar

Introduction

Laws that are promulgated from the centre (or legitimate authority) are only a fraction of the rules that help a society reproduce itself. Paradoxically, the breaking of official laws or rules may also conform to a system of rules, consistent with an alternative value system. On the other hand, other types of rules and conventions may coincide with the goals of laws, wholly or in part. In fact, these other rules, written or unwritten, may be more efficacious than the written laws for two reasons: Most people would not be aware of the precise contents of these laws even in highly literate societies, and unwritten or unofficial rules are observed because those affected choose to do so. When we consider the case at hand, of late-imperial China, it is not difficult to ascertain that laws were important, but only if and when the local community bothered to go before the lone magistrate who ruled almost singlehandedly over tens or even hundreds of thousands of inhabitants, or in those instances that the magistrate was forced to take an interest in a given case by circumstances. Despite the increasing importance of the legal process from the early seventeenth century onwards,[1] much rule-making, -breaking and -enforcing still took place outside the bounds of the state.[2]

In this paper I investigate one specific body of evidence on the making of rules, their breaking and their enforcement on a local level. This evidence is quite unique because it derives from the 'casebook' of the spirit-writing medium(s) of the two assistants of Emperor Guan in one county

---

[1] Of course, this is difficult to measure, but it is my impression that there was a professionalization of legal practice from the late Ming onwards. See for instance Melissa Macauley, *Social Power and Legal Culture: Litigation Masters in Late Imperial China* (Stanford, 1998) and Matthew Sommer, *Sex, Law, and Society in Late Imperial China* (Stanford, 2000), among a number of recent studies.

[2] The strong state orientation of most China scholarship has largely prevented us from seeing this important fact more clearly. For some examples, see my *Telling Stories: Witchcraft and Scapegoating in Chinese History* (Leiden, 2006), *passim*.

in Hunan province in the years 1849–1851, on the eve of the devastating rebellion of the Heavenly Kingdom of Great Peace. The uniqueness of this material is in its unity of time and place, but not in the religious context as I will set out in more detail below. Other forms of rule-making and enforcing have been seriously understudied in the Chinese case because of the early presence of elaborate laws and the modern assumption—undoubtedly incorrect—that once there are laws these become the main instrument of rule enforcement. The present study was largely conceived and written before the publication of Paul Katz's wonderful study, *Divine Justice*.[3] I refer to his work for the larger context of this practice in China and similar practices in other cultures.[4]

Each tale in the casebook of the assistants of Emperor Guan concerns a moral issue involving concrete and plausible human actors, who are punished during their present lives by divine forces, usually in very visible and violent ways. This retribution forces many of them to repent and confess their evil deeds. Various details indicate that these accounts had a broad audience. It is clear that they, in ways very similar to penal sanctions, were only partly successful in enforcing norms and values. On the other hand, they indicate what some local people (minimally the community of these spirit mediums as seen by the record-keepers) thought were important norms and values. When we consider that Hunan was relatively stable at this time and would in fact give rise to the armies that would eventually defeat the massive rebellion of the Heavenly Kingdom, we can speculate that these local rules might have contributed to this stability. The use of the term casebook deserves some explanation. A more common approach would have been to refer to these accounts or stories as miracles, since they tell of divine intervention, whether punishment or reward, at the

[3] An exception is the work by the early sociologist, folklorist and historian Wolfram Eberhard, *Guilt and Sin*, who also inspired Paul R. Katz to write his *Divine Justice: Religion and the Development of Chinese Legal Culture* (London, 2009) (personal comment, December 2008). I did consult earlier work by Katz, such as 'Divine Justice in Late Imperial China: A Preliminary Study of Indictment Rituals', in John Lagerwey, ed., *Religion and Chinese Society: Volume II Taoism and Local Religion in Modern China* (Shatin, 2004) 869–901; 'Indictment Rituals and the Judicial Continuum in Late Imperial China', in Robert E. Hegel and Katherine Carlitz, eds., *Writing and Law in Late Imperial China* (Seattle, 2007), 161–185; Kang Bao, 'Hanren shehui de shenpan yishi chutan', *Bulletin of the Institute of Ethnology, Academica Sinica* 88 (2000), 173–202. These articles have been largely incorporated in his book. My own interest stems from earlier work on the Chinese Triads and research-in-progress on the deity Guan Yu.

[4] For just one example, see John Gager, *Curse Tablets and Binding Spells in the Ancient World* (Oxford, 1992).

request of a human person. However, the format of any miracle account in traditional China would always be a statement of concrete historical facts of events that took place on a concrete date to a specific person in a definite place. Furthermore, this particular type of miracle account treats the adjudication of divine justice, and several elements of a legal process can be seen in the material. To bring out the factual and legal nature of this material, I have chosen to use the term case to refer to these miracles. I suspect, but cannot prove, that the material ultimately also goes back to some form of record-keeping by the mediums of the above-mentioned spirit-writing cult, or rather their literate assistants.

A Concrete Example

The following account from the casebook is representative in its structure, but much more detailed than most of the accounts.[5] It also gives a good sense of the underlying religious cult. I will provide a complete translation with some comments on key passages. Like all accounts it starts with a brief description of the protagonist, usually the transgressor.

> Butcher Zhang So-and-so from Middle Xiang[tan] had a brutal and violent character. Selling meat was his profession. He would buy one or three creatures with paws or pigs, of which some would say that they were not suitable for killing. Zhang would cruelly ignore this and invite someone named Zhong to help him with the butchering. When Zhong ordered him to bury the paws, he would place them in the temple room for three days. At the time the weather was damp and hot, and the stench became unbearable. He loved to drink alcoholic beverages, often sitting in front of the stove to drink until he was inebriated. Thereupon he undressed himself stark naked and began to laugh and scold, without any inhibitions. Soon after his breathing started to hurt and due to swellings he could hardly move; he could not even bend his hands and feet. After some time the disease became still worse.

Zhang So-and-so committed two crimes directly against the deities, showing his total disrespect, something that must also have worried the surrounding community. He insulted the deities of the temple itself, namely Emperor Guan and his two Generals. But he also insulted the Lord of the Stove, since it is expressly forbidden by old taboos to undress in front of the stove. Since he would probably have heated his beverages on the stove,

[5] *Guandi quanshu* (reprinted in 魯愚 and others eds., *Guan di wenxian huibian* 關帝文獻彙編, Beijing, 1995), 40: 42a–43a. When no title is given, the reference is to the casebook discussed in this paper.

it is not strange that he ended up there. Since he was probably alone, it is easily imaginable that the subsequent turn of events was really caused by him falling against the stove as well in drunken stupor. The deity would use the occasion to utter a detailed warning, which reads almost like an ethical program.

> His father asked the Immortal to show a method and implored the Lord of the Stove for Command Tea. The Overseer of Life (i.e. the Lord of the Stove himself) descended and pronounced [the following partly rhymed message]:
>
> You, father and son, regularly rely on your force to oppress the weak,
> You rely on the strength of your bodies to insult the deities.
> You butcher oxen and kill dogs, butcher pigs and cut open frogs.
> You are busy the whole day
> And kill much life.
> You must try to think to yourself on a clear night,
> If there is one thing that you might ask yourself deep at heart?
> If there is one thought that you could utter to Heaven?
> I (i.e. the deity) only wish to clean up these evil creatures,
> To vent some hatred on behalf of all people.
> [You lot] wait until the disasters finally hit home,
> And only then you have feelings of regret for your faults!
> Although this is the case, when an evil man regrets his faults,
> It is superior to a good man who constantly practices.
> Once this thought [of doing good] arises,
> Heaven should inspect it and Heaven should pity it.
> But I will not rescue you,
> You have decidedly insulted the deity that he is not effective,
> So if I should rescue you,
> You will fall again in your old ways and what can we do about it.
> Zhang kowtowed and asked for mercy. He swore an oath to stop killing.

Before we continue with our translation a few comments are in order. In the imperial period the cult of the Lord of the Stove usually employed a planchette (usually a wooden instrument with which the deity who had descended into the 'pencil' could write in sand), much like those of the two Generals who assisted Emperor Guan and the supreme deity himself. It was customary for spirit-writing deities to be addressed as immortals, since they were usually literate and therefore of a higher order than ordinary deities (who would have feudal titles, ranging from Marquis to General or even Emperor). The language used by the deity either rhymes or is reminiscent of the canonical texts, such as the *Book of Documents* or the *Book of Odes*, to indicate his high status. Although we need not deduce from this that the record-keeper(s) were of the highest status, it does indicate that he/they (a she is highly unlikely in this particular cult) would have studied for the civil service examinations. In spirit-writing cults literate people always play a central role, because of the importance of written communication. We will discuss the social background of the cult, and the moral values represented therein later. Upon Zhang's entreaties, the deity hands out another message.

> He gave another instruction.
> Your respect for me
> Is not located in burning incense, lighting oil lamps,
> Or paying obeisance day and night.
> You must start your effort (*gongfu* 功夫) from your heart,
> Next come following my Classic
> And energetically bring it into practice.
>
> Thereupon [Mr. Zhang] laid down his butcher knife and respectfully maintained the fast of the [Lord of the] Stove. His illness was healed, but the itch of his craft was hard to control. After a year or so he broke his vow and his old illness broke out again. It was even worse than previously.

The Lord of the Stove, like Emperor Guan, is a well-known, late-imperial, divine rule-maker, to whom numerous moralistic tracts are ascribed. The 'Classic' undoubtedly refers to one of these texts.[6]

> Crawling he went to pay court to the temple of the General and in tears he entreated him to be rescued. The General dispensed a planchette instruction:
> Your book of evil is completely full.
> You have not turned around and cultivated or reflected,
> But you have suddenly broken your previous oath.
> Although I now have a clear instruction, it is not fitting to give you the responsibility.
> Although I have a wonderful recipe, it is not fitting to hand it over to you.
>
> Zhang cried and prayed, he swore not to transgress again. Thereupon [the General] ordered the True Man (in a later case it turns out that this is a certain True Man Hua)[7] to transmit a recipe to him. [Zhang] returned home and told his wife: 'My household relies on butchering to make a living, so although I temporarily stop this profession, it is hard to guarantee that I will not break the vow until my death.' That night he had just gone to sleep,

---

[6] Robert Chard, 'Master of the Family: History and Development of the Chinese Cult to the Stove' (Ph.D. dissertation, U.C. Berkeley, 1990); Robert Chard, 'Rituals and Scriptures of the Stove Cult', in David Johnson, ed., *Ritual and Scripture in Chinese Popular Religion: Five Studies* (Berkeley, 1995), 3–54.

[7] 40: 46a.

> when five or six men with sharp knives stabbed his body, each stab hurting, and without ever stopping a bit. Zhang only cried in secret, when he heard a big laugh saying: 'You also know bitterness now.' They only let him go until the third cry of the neighbouring rooster. He woke up while crying unwittingly. He was sweating with fright. He hurriedly kowtowed and thanked, and only then did he obtain release [from punishment].

Not everyone got away with his life, but cases such as this would have contributed to the spread of the cult and have put some fear in people. This particular instance is treated in far more detail than most accounts in this casebook, but they all correspond to the same basic structure of a transgression, punishment, confession, more punishment, and in many cases remorse. Interestingly, the temple is mentioned only in an offhand way, perhaps because the author or transmitter presumed that his audience already knew the location, but it could also be to give the material a more general impact.

The Cult of Emperor Guan

Easily one of the most widespread and most popular cults in late-traditional China was that of Emperor Guan. Among a bewildering variety of local gods, immortals, demons and the like, his was one of the cults that could be found in most Chinese cities and in northern China also in the countryside. Worship of him had started as a local cult in Dangyang County in Hubei province (somewhat to the north of the Yangzi), where a prominent Buddhist monastery was founded in the Sui-dynasty, which would play a central role in two major religious Buddhist traditions: Tiantai and Chan. He was first recognized by the state in the eleventh century, accepted as a major exorcist general by Daoist ritual specialists at least as early as the twelfth century, and became a divine emperor in the early seventeenth century. With the rising of his rank, he actually—and somewhat surprisingly—did not lose in accessibility, which is not to say that there were no changes in the nature of his cult, both regional and nationwide. Since Emperor Guan was officially recognized by the imperial state and enjoyed the highest possible sacrifices for a local cult since the early seventeenth century, anything that could be somehow connected to this cult almost automatically gained in respectability. Still, even in the late-imperial period and thereafter this cult never became the exclusive property of the Chinese elite. Individual temples might become dominated by the state, but there would also always remain public temples or even shrines. Emperor Guan was worshipped by the Hong Kong police and the Triads as much as by literati, merchants or local communities.[8]

Emperor Guan always had his lieutenants, although they did change somewhat over time. By the late-imperial period he was assisted by two figures, of whom General Zhou was the best known. They featured prominently in his iconography, represented next to him in statues and other types of visual depictions, but also in stories that were told of the efficacy of the cult. They were summoned as a group in Daoist rituals, usually to drive some demon away. Finally, there were extensive narrative traditions, such as folkloric tales (especially in the Yangzi region and northern China, much less further to the south), theatrical traditions and a major novel. People would have been as familiar with these two generals as with Emperor Guan himself.

Literati and officials would address Emperor Guan through spirit-writing cults, in which the deity descended in the wooden stylus or a pencil and wrote down poems that could then be interpreted by the participants in the cult. Such cults, however, did not allow for much interaction and could never address very concrete problems. The same was true of other means of communication, such as throwing moon blocks, drawing sticks that referred to yet other cryptic poems, or even dreams. The best way of communicating with the deities was always through a spirit medium. He or she could become the vessel of a deity, and the audience or the specialized attendant of the medium could then ask questions and engage the deity in a much more flexible dialogue. As far as we know, Emperor Guan was usually the focus of spirit-writing cults in the late-imperial period, rather than ordinary spirit mediums, and this is confirmed by the casebook. On the other hand, the lack of flexibility in the communication by means of spirit-writing was compensated by the fact that the pronouncements would possess the highest possible religious and moral status by virtue of their association with the cult of Emperor Guan.

Hagiographical Collections of Emperor Guan

The first hagiographical collection on Emperor Guan was published in the thirteenth century when the deity was still only enfeoffed as a King. Numerous collections would follow until the nineteenth century, each

[8] Statement based on my own ongoing research in this cult.

including much of the older material, reworking it and adding new material of their own. The editorial process was usually directed at upgrading the public image of the cult in line with the newest elite views of proper worship. Usually an editor would have a personal connection to the cult or its location, much in the same way as temple-building or restoration projects, donations, and the grants of imperial titles were usually grounded in an individual experience.

One such hagiographical collection was compiled after the great rebellions of the mid-nineteenth century. The work is so huge that it is unlikely that many people would ever have read it through from cover to cover. It is first and foremost a sacrifice of love and labour by an educated man, for whom an offering of meat and alcohol, or the donation of a restoration to his local temple was not enough. Curiously enough, the compiler of the hagiographical collection does not state explicitly why he undertook this huge and expensive project, but implicitly it becomes clear that he was inspired by the heroic service of the deity to the nation during the troubles of the mid-nineteenth century, both against the Nian rebels in the north, and the Triads and other groups who had laid siege to various towns in Guangdong province in the south. Furthermore, appended at the end of the collection is a remarkable set of cases involving the two assistants of Emperor Guan, and these will serve as our source base. The casebook is called *Record of Miraculous Responses by the Generals* (*jiangjun lingyanji* 將軍靈驗記).[9] Clearly the editor of the casebook felt that this body of cases was significant and true, but also wanted to demonstrate that the cult of this morally impeccable Emperor Guan possessed the ability to regenerate a region that had been severely hit by the rebellion of the Heavenly Kingdom of Great Peace and its suppression.

The record consists of 118 cases divided into two sections, based on interactive spirit sessions with two deities referred to as the General, usually General Zhou. All of them take place in the surroundings of a temple in the thirteenth *du* 都 (a sub-county administrative subdivision) of Xiangtan County, an important trading centre in Hunan province in the early nineteenth century. A small minority of the cases involves rewards for good deeds, but the large majority involve a transgression followed by punishment. Each case contains some contextual information. The preface specifies that the material stems from spirit-writing sessions with one

[9] Last *juan* of the *Guandi quanshu* (prefaces to the miracle collection from 1858 and 1888).

of the two generals in the years 1849 and 1850, which is largely confirmed by the cases themselves, with some additions from 1851. The postscript from 1888 provides a few additional cases from the other general. The compiler is most likely also the compiler of the overall hagiographical collection, but because he has not signed his preface, we cannot be certain.

The compiler of the casebook specifies that he has collected and published the material as a warning. He has taken care to anonymize the wicked people to some extent, dropping their personal names, but not their family names. From the evidence it becomes clear that the cult which yielded most of the cases was devoted to General Zhou, an assistant of emperor Guan, who descends in the stylus of the planchette to write his messages. We never learn who was interpreting the messages, although research on a slightly later period suggests these were usually literate persons, possibly on the level of a Student (the lowest grade of the examination system).[10] At any rate, they were capable of writing the traditional written language, which means they had been indoctrinated in elite norms and values for many years. This particular cult was located somewhere north of the county capital, and the cases contain some further information on its daily activities. Here I will refrain from further description of the cult and let the cases take central place.

The Cases

The Casebook as a Whole

Xiangtan is not well-known in the Western secondary literature, with the exception of one study of local rice riots in 1819.[11] Nonetheless, the county capital was actually one of the largest cities in the country in the first half of the nineteenth century, thanks to the interregional rice trade controlled by the merchants from neighbouring Jiangxi province and its central position in the transport network. Only after the advent of steamboat traffic on the Yangzi River did Changsha take over from Xiangtan, which could

[10] A systematic study of this practice is still lacking. David K. Jordan. and Daniel L. Overmyer, *The Flying Phoenix: Aspects of Chinese Sectarianism in Taiwan* (Princeton, 1986) provide excellent ethnographical information. Also see the much older study by Xu Dishan, *Fuji mixin de yanjiu* (1947; Shanghai, 1988), which is mostly a presentation of historical evidence. Otherwise my comments are based on ongoing research of my own.

[11] Peter C. Perdue, 'Insiders and Outsiders: The Xiangtan Riot of 1819 and Collective Action in Hunan Insiders and Outsiders: The Xiangtan Riot of 1819 and Collective Action in Hunan', *Modern China*, Vol. 12: 2 (1986), 166–201.

not be reached by steamboats. Curiously, the feel of the cases is not at all urban or metropolitan, but quite rural as if all of this trade had passed the countryside by. Thus, we have here a source that is far removed from our usual sources, which focus on the small but productive, literate, male elite and which are usually very remote from the large majority of the farming population. Without further research we will remain unable to judge the representativeness of the material, featuring as it does the lives of ordinary people from poor farmers to beastly butchers, slovenly housewives to shopkeepers.

The values that are furthered are general Chinese values, which have been claimed by all religious traditions, Confucian, Buddhist and Daoist. It is no coincidence that the deities, assistants to Emperor Guan, are 'conscious' of these values, for the Emperor himself is deemed to be a great advocate of proper morals, and numerous ethical treatises have been written 'by him' in spirit-writing sessions. These treatises are also included in our hagiographical collection. The large role played in the cases by violent punishment by the deities is striking.

The material is topically organized with only a little overlap between the different categories, although no separate headings are provided. This indicates the hand of the editor, since it is not likely that the miracles happened in neat groups. Otherwise, there is sufficient inconsistency, for instance, in references to the deities or the way in which the miracles unfold to suggest that material from different oral sources was collected, but not exhaustively edited. The material reflects reality as it was lived by local people in Xiangtan county on the eve of the rebellion of the Heavenly Kingdom of Great Peace, mediated by literate people at the level of the spirit-writing cult (i.e. the record-keeper) and the editor of the collection. Below we have given names to each category:

1. Filial and unfilial behaviour (22 cases; 40: 1a–8b)
2. Purity and impurity, mostly of a sexual nature (10 cases; 40: 8b–11b)
3. Good and bad wealth, i.e. at the cost of others (25 cases; 40: 11b–23a)
4. Abuse of words (ranging from disrespect to written texts to slander and legal abuse) (17 cases; 40: 23a–29b)
5. Abuse of power (17 cases; 40: 29b–36b)
6. Theft and robbery (4 cases; 40: 36b–38b)
7. Maltreatment of girls and women (2 cases; 40: 38b–39b)
8. Maltreatment of animals (10 cases; 40: 39b–45a)
9. Divine healing (11 cases; 40: 45a–51a; also mentioned in two additional cases, 9a–b; 42a–43a)

10. Prayer for rain in 1852, blaming the drought on similar egocentric transgressions as the rest of the collection (1 case, 51a–52a).

Typically, the transgressions are egocentric, with the interest of the individual taking priority over the interests and rights of other people or animals. This individual is then punished. Most transgressions are social in nature, with only a few instances involving a taboo, such as the eating of bovine meat or the maltreatment of texts (sic!). In the following small subsections I discuss each type with one or two examples. When a fragment was coherent enough for the purpose of this paper I translated it, otherwise I provide a paraphrase, which allows me to be a bit more selective in leaving out less relevant details in description or plot. Hopefully, the translations also provide the reader with some flavour of the events. I will skip my category ten since it deals with prayers for rain.

1. Filial Piety

One common value that is supported by the deity is filial piety (*xiao* 孝). Filial piety is often claimed as a Confucian value, but is better understood as a general Chinese value with different connotations in different periods, regions and socio-educational groups. Filial piety is central to many Buddhist and Daoist practices, maybe even more so than in the Confucian tradition, which is itself, after all, largely an elite epiphenomenon. Cases revolving around this value form the second largest group of material with 22 cases, second only to cases dealing with good and bad wealth.

A typical example is that of a wife who serves her mother-in-law without the appropriate decorum and controls her husband like a slave.[12] In other words, she is the classical henpecking woman, the fear of all patriarchal societies. She once scolded her mother-in-law so much that the latter returned far more cotton than she had originally borrowed.

> At that point the mother-in-law added the following imprecation: 'The efficacy of the General-Divinity is far-reaching. When you carry out this kind of cheating with such bravura, there will certainly be retribution.'
>
> And indeed,
>
> After a few days, dark clouds gather and the bright day turns dark, a sudden rain breaks out and lightning hits [the wife's] head. The woman fell

12 40: 7a–b.

> unconscious outside the gate. She was dumb and speechless, gasping for breath and about to die. Only halfway during the night did she come to again. When the mother-in-law waved her with a fan, thunder again broke out loudly. The woman cried that her belly hurt without stopping. Fresh blood gushed from her mouth.

The family organized a Daoist ritual to do penance, and the wife was spared. It is not noted in this particular account whether she also confessed to her crimes, but most accounts in this category do include a confession.

The use of lightning to punish unfilial behaviour is centuries old, and everybody who heard about this account would have made the link between the type of punishment and the nature of the offense. The value of filial piety is a mainstay of Chinese society, not only to maintain family hierarchy, but also as source of inspiration to join monastic communities (for sons to pay for the debt they owed to their birthmother) and practice a variety of rituals (such as Feeding Hungry Demons or the Blood Pond ritual, the latter to atone for the loss of blood during birth and menstruation by mothers).

2. Impurity

Not all accounts about impurity as a danger deal with sexual offenses. Thus the group starts with a story of the General's protection of a virtuous and chaste woman whose household is threatened by bandits. He wears armour and wields a large halberd or sword, and roars like thunder, to drive the bandits away.[13] In another account a widow is rewarded for her loyal service to her only son and her parents-in-law by the 'Command Tea of the General', a tea which heals the son of a disease that no other medicine or religious healers have been able to cure.[14] Very likely the ashes of an amulet containing a protective command by the divinity had been put in the tea.

Most accounts in this category, however, tell of real or intended rape, such as the following example.[15]

> A woman who is alone at home is pressurized by a nephew who wants to rape her. Alone at home, she feels she can no longer resist and cries 'General, help me quickly'.

---

[13] 40: 8b–9a.
[14] 40: 9a–b.
[15] 40: 9a.

> Immediately, [the nephew] falls down to the ground out of fear and can only utter a groaning sound. He comes to his sense again as if he wakes up. He says with his mouth: 'I know my crime, I know my crime.' But he is ashamed and afraid, without a proper way to behave himself. With hanging head he leaves and after two months he has died.

Rape is one of those crimes in traditional China, where the burden of proof was on the woman, for she had to prove convincingly that she had resisted the attacks. In this account the nephew does not use direct force, but forces her into a corner. Had she been raped, she would have had a hard time 'proving' it. Many women chose suicide as the only visible, honourable way out.[16]

3. Abusive Wealth

Another type of account deals with the problem of ill-gotten wealth, clearly a substantial concern in a fragile market economy.[17] Not surprisingly, this is the largest category in the collection, with as many as 25 cases. Whereas filial piety is always claimed by ideological and religious traditions as their own, the value of dealing honestly is no less important, but not so central in these mainstream traditions. In late-imperial society where family networks were no longer the only or even the main way of connecting people, the fear of betrayal must have been very real. For instance, two men, Mr. A and Mr. B, ran a shop together.[18] Mr. B works very hard, but Mr. A siphons all the money into his own pockets. The shop has to close. Mr. B now puts a formal plaint (the terminology is borrowed from a legal context, *judie aisong* 具牒哀訴) before the General. Soon afterwards Mr. A suffers a bout of madness and says while in a trance: 'I've cheated money from Mr. B. Today the General has given the case over to the City God to pursue further.'

The account continues by detailing Mr. A's subsequent fate. He receives some 70–80 beatings with a stick, of which the onlookers can see only the red swellings and scars on his thighs, but not the actual hitting. After this he receives an equal number of slaps on his mouth, of which the onlookers could again see only the blue-green swellings and the blood on

16 Paola Paderni, 'Le rachat de l'honneur perdu: La suicide des femmes dans la Chine du XVIIIe siècle', *Études chinoises* X: 1–2 (1991), 135–160; Paul S. Ropp, 'Passionate Women: Female Suicide in Late Imperial China—Introduction', *Nan Nü* 3: 1 (2001), 3–21.

17 Richard von Glahn, *The Sinister Way: The Divine Way and the Demonic in Chinese Religious Culture* (Berkeley, 2004).

18 40: 20b–21a.

his lips. A few days later the event repeated itself, and now he confessed each of the items which he had embezzled and returned them to Mr. B. Mr. A was lucky, for after he had visited the General's temple and publicly acknowledged his crime, he was released from his suffering.

4. Abuse of Words

A very common social practice in late-imperial China is the lawsuit, a custom that was heavily criticized by elite authors, but continued to be practised nonetheless.[19] The following example is quite typical, although here the practitioner receives a horrible punishment.[20] Someone who is explicitly described as stemming from a *nouveau riche* household loved to start lawsuits and was content only when he had caused his victims to lose their lives and ruin their families. When the spirit-writing cult of the General was active locally, many people put their complaints before him. Hereupon the man's oldest two sons died of an evil disease, followed by two healthy grandchildren who both died at a young age within a few days of one another. His third son suffered from an eye disease for more than a year. Now, from a medical perspective it is much more likely that the deaths were the result of an epidemic, but for local people they were a well-deserved retribution. In this case, there is no mention of the recognition of guilt or a confession by the *nouveau riche* in question. Instead, this account tells us of subsequent events which provided at least some satisfaction to the local community, which seems to have been powerless against the lawsuits themselves. By telling, retelling and eventually writing down this account, people regained the moral high-ground at least on the level of local discourse.

5. Abuse of Power

In a society where legal redress was limited, much depended on neighbourly relationships and communal agreements. The following account illustrates how things could go wrong, but at the same time also how disagreements could be settled mutually.[21] The ox of a local farmer, Mr. Tan, who lived off a rented plot, ate about two bushels of the rice of his neighbour, Mr. Yi. Mr. Yi agreed that Mr. Tan could pay an indemnity later, and they parted in friendship. The ox, incidentally, was undoubtedly a water

19 Macauley, *Social Power and Legal Culture* (1998).
20 40: 27a.
21 40: 29b–30a.

buffalo, used to draw a plough or a cart, and a sign of at least some moderate wealth. Mr. Tan was not necessarily a poor farmer, just because he did not own land (anymore).

> Locally someone who pretended to be a 'wise elder' perceived [Yi's] weakness and considered that he could use it to steal some money. He ordered Yi to gather the local braves and then entered the scene in order to mediate a solution. He cheated Tan out of 5000 cash in coins and split it evenly [with Yi]. Tan was furious about being cheated, and prepared a memorial and silently put forth his complaint (*judie mosong* 具牒默訟) before the General. After two months Yi became mad and said: 'Someone had pretended to be a gentleman and really was a petty man full of danger. The affair of the cow eating grain had already been put aside by me and was no longer an issue. I was then enticed by that evil man causing Tan to spend much money. Now General Zhou wishes to kill me, and set an example to you of [what happens to] someone who falsely extorts. Can you see me die without attempting to rescue me?' His household invited shamans to exorcise and he became even madder. [Tan] went straight to the temple and personally submitted a memorial of regret. Then it stopped.

Clearly, like real life magistrates, deities are only as good as the information that they are given. Curiously, we learn nothing about the fate of the pseudo-gentleman. The bout of madness suffered by Mr. Yi is the standard moment in which the guilty party confesses his or her crimes. The brief comment—which probably reflects days if not weeks of suffering—that they visited other healers and religious specialists is significant, because it implies that shamans and perhaps other sources of religious authority were less powerful than General Zhou. The religious dimension in these accounts is not just a funny ornament, but the essential mechanism that makes justice work.

6. Theft and Robbery

It could be argued that in the previous example the pseudo-gentleman was little more than a thief, but the way in which he got his money was through abuse of his position as a local mediator. The distinction between the different categories is not always clear-cut. The following example, however, is a very clear example of ordinary theft.

> A certain Mr. Yu and his family were extremely poor. The husband worked elsewhere as a hired hand, whereas his wife and son(s) had to resort to begging.
>
> Because they had no clothes, they bought four pounds of cotton flower through relatives, and agreed that once they had made cloth out of it they would return the price. One day... the wife had finished eating breakfast

> and taken her son to a mountain near the house to collect firewood. Towards noon they returned and looked for the cotton flower in the chest. It had been stolen by thieves. She cried and wept and did not know where it had been placed. The husband returned and blamed his wife that she had been careless. She was angry and sad, and before Heaven she complained in tears (*kusu* 哭訴) to the General. She asked that he manifest a response very quickly, or else her life would be hard to guarantee/preserve.
>
> The following day the son of another woman who lived in the same house was visited by the General who scolded him severely. He confessed in fear that he had stolen the cotton flower at the command of his mother. They had sold half of it and the money was hidden somewhere. The woman herself suddenly shouted loudly that 'I will kill this evil woman without proper behaviour', clearly being possessed by the General as well! She fell to the floor while bleeding out of her mouth and nose. Thanks to this turn of events, the life of the wife of Mr. Yu was spared.

7. Maltreatment of Girls and Women

One common source of misery for younger women was their problematic relationship with their husband's mother, which lasted as long as the latter was still alive. This problem was mitigated both by the fact that parents-in-law often died early on in a woman's marriage, and by common rules that expressed the need to treat one's daughter-in-law in a harmonious way. Her husband usually was not a big help, since the duty of filial piety was much stronger than the need or duty to protect his wife. The following account illustrates some of the problems.[22]

> A local woman, Ms. Zhao was cruel and inhumane. She had one son and a daughter in law, Ms. So-and-so. She was extremely dumb, but did her household chores diligently. Ms. Zhao treated her horribly, scolded her constantly and even whipped her. At one point she instructed her son to live elsewhere and even pressed the daughter-in-law to remarry, but the latter 'swore not to leave.' After this continued for some time, suddenly in the midst of the severe winter Ms. Zhao threw herself into a pond. She called loudly for help and said: 'The General is angry at my mistreating of my daughter-in-law. I deserve to receive this punishment.' When they dredged her out, she was stiff as wood. Ms. So-and-so tearfully offered prayers of thanks to (*daoxie* 禱謝) the General.

Her mother-in-law came to life again, but could no longer speak, which can be interpreted as the punishment for her incessant scolding of the daughter-in-law. Only after her relatives visited the temple to pray for

22 40: 38b.

forgiveness, could she speak again, but she now completely altered her behaviour.

The legal elements in this account are not very explicit, but we have the egocentric behaviour, followed by an oath by the daughter-in-law (who 'swore not to leave'), the intervention of the deity through punishment, the confession, a ritual intercession with the deity, and remorse as expressed through behaviour. The precise contents of the oath are not specified. It may well have included both a statement of the daughter-in-law's suffering, since later on she prays to the General to thank him for his intercession, which implies that she originally asked him for his help.

A second account in this category of maltreatment of children and women should be mentioned briefly, since it illustrates another common social problem.

> A Ms. Tan was pregnant and considered that she would drown her child if it were a girl. She then received a dream from the General that 'male and female are one, she should certainly not drown it.' She did give birth to a girl and did not dare to kill it. However, So-and-so forced her and made her kill it on the ground (*mou cu zhi, sui zhi zhi si di* 某促之。遂致之死地).
>
> After a while the woman started bleeding and became dizzy. The entire household was afraid and her mother exhaustively blamed So-and-so, scolding him to stand before Heaven and take a vow. Since a person So-and-so from the neighbourhood collected money to rescue [female children] from drowning, he vowed himself to join this club. Together they accomplished this undertaking in order to make amends for the crime. After a certain period, the woman woke up again and said: 'The General permitted me to come alive again because you knew remorse.'

The account may seem like a simple ploy to further elite values, but we should not automatically assume that everybody agreed with the lower value of daughters that is at the root of the custom of drowning daughters. There is plenty of evidence that parents could love their daughters just as much as their sons, sometimes spoiling them considerably. On the other hand, the financial burden of daughters was considerable given that they would leave the household. In the example given here, we may surmise that the mother used the generally shared belief in the general in order not to have to kill a possible daughter. She succumbed under the pressure of an anonymous person, probably her husband. Apparently, the child was then dropped on the ground and died. At least partly, the mother won after all, due to an intervention of the General, and of course thanks to the fact that the belief in the General was widely shared locally and therefore led to successful social pressure.

8. Maltreatment of Animals

The maltreatment of animals is a general issue in Chinese society, although adoption of a vegetarian lifestyle is never based on this consideration but follows from Buddhist leanings and means self-exclusion from local social networks. Nonetheless, ill-treatment of animals was noted and criticized. Two animals in particular stand out in this context: dogs and oxen.[23] Both animals had important social functions, as guards and companions (dogs) and as draught animals (oxen). As Vincent Goossaert has recently demonstrated, from the Song onwards eating the meat of an ox became the subject of an elite taboo that was eventually spread through various types of propaganda, especially from the late Ming onwards.[24] The cultural history of dogs in traditional China is as yet unwritten.

In the accounts of the killing and eating of dogs, there is always also the issue of maltreatment and never the mere transgression of a taboo on eating dogs.

> Thus Wen So-and-so has a bitch which has given birth to several puppies.[25] After a month he lets a hired labourer drown them, but the labourer is unable to do it, because the bitch is so evidently fond of the puppies. Wen then asks a cruel neighbour to drown them, which he does, eating them afterwards. The bitch seems to think that it was the hired labourer, but he tells her that it was so-and-so. The dog dies of sadness soon afterwards. A bit later during a spirit-writing session in the temple, the following message is written:
>
> I am Student Chen of this county. I was wronged and grievously killed. I came especially to the General to ask for an instruction, when I chanced upon a dog which had kneeled in front of the stairs. He submitted a plaint that Wen So-and-so was brutal and cruel. He completely killed her puppies, causing her to spit up blood and die. In tears he requested that this injustice would be avenged. I am afraid that Wen So-and-so will not be able to escape.
>
> When Mr. Wen heard this he was very afraid. In his turn he submitted a memorial regretting his mistake. Hereupon he remained without harm.

---

[23] Oxen 5x (40: 39b–40a; 40a–b; 41b; 43b; 44a); dogs 4x (40: 40ab–41a; 41a–41b; 41b; 44b); other animals 4x (40: 40b; 42a; 42a–43a; 45a). In the 1888 event, the butchering of an ox during the prayers against a drought made the entire ritual ineffective (40: 51a–52a).

[24] Vincent Goossaert, *L'interdit du boeuf en Chine: agriculture, éthique et sacrifice* (Paris, 2005).

[25] 40: 44b–45a.

9. Divine Healing

We have already encountered a botched attempt at divine healing in the account of Butcher Zhang at the outset of this article, and again in the conflict between Mr. Tan and Mr. Yi. Apparently, this cult involved a type of healing tea, which was called Command Tea (*chicha* 勅茶). Probably, this was tea in which the ashes of an amulet were mixed. Such an amulet standardly consists of a command (sometimes including the same term *chi* 'to command') in special calligraphy to divine generals to carry out a certain assignment, which could be protection or driving away demonic beings. The custom of consuming water in which the ashes of an amulet are mixed (*fushui* 符水) is an old form of faith-healing.

The following case is an example of faith-healing and also illustrates the way in which different methods competed with each other.[26]

> Tan So-and-so suffers a disease and all recipes have remained unsuccessful. He is about to invite shamans to exorcise it, but before the ritual has taken place the disease becomes even worse and they respectfully request 'Command Tea of the General.' After administering it, there is an immediate effect and after another few 'medicine tallies' even the severest pain is gone.
>
> His family thinks that now that his disease is cured, they should repay the former vow. One night they invite shamans to the household. After they have finished completely setting up the altar and ritual implements, the ritual itself is carried out. They spurred So-and-so on to come out and pay his ritual respect. After he had kneeled, he fell over to the ground. The family is totally surprised and sprinkles hot water over him. Only after a while does he wake up again, and says: 'You have almost killed me. I came across the General who said that my disease was not caused by a monster causing demonic appearances, so why do you contravene my teachings and stop believing in the orthodox way, but falsely use shamanic evil?' In tears I beseeched him several times, before I was finally forgiven and I could leave. Quickly give me Command Tea to revive me.
>
> When he came to again, he dismissed the shamans. That night he received a proper medicine from the General in his dreams.

Everything indicates that the shamans most likely were ritual specialists of a vernacular Daoist tradition or even classical Daoist priests. This comment, together with similar earlier comments, indicates that the leaders of the spirit-writing cult saw their practice as distinct from Daoist ritual culture (and probably also from many other local temples), with their cult for Emperor Guan and his acolytes as more prestigious—possibly because

---

26 40: 47b–48a.

they thought that their cult was more in line with the norms and values of the educated elite.

A Standard Scenario

When we analyse all cases as a group, we find that they correspond quite closely to a standard scenario, which I have summarized in a diagram below.

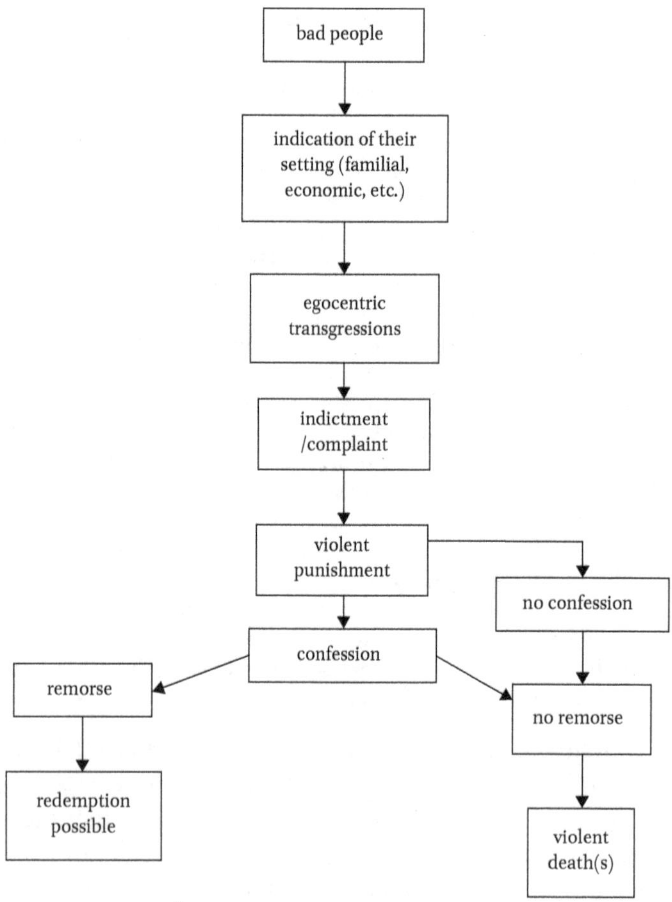

All in all, the structure of these cases is not that different from a lawsuit, including the formal indictment, punishment (playing a role similar to torture in conventional lawsuits, which is also conventionally intended to produce a confession), confession and remorse (or not). Without remorse the punishment is generally much heavier than with remorse. The role of the medium/deity is to communicate what is happening and the punitive violence appears to come directly from an anonymous heaven. Most accounts contain a confession by the perpetrator, who has tried to deny any misdoings but is now forced by his or her punishment to spit it out. If he or she does so there may be some form of redemption, although even then it is often too late. As a whole, this was a form of legal redress that was much closer to the people than the law applied by a magistrate and also more open to their own interpretations. This does not mean that the underlying moral values were fundamentally different, but that would be the topic of further investigation.

The Crucial Role of Violence

The role of violence in these accounts is dominant and was apparently considered essential to the maintenance of moral values. To the actors and audience of these accounts the violence was most certainly very real and highly visible.[27] They would be familiar with violence in order to enforce morality from secular legal practice, but also from stories and rituals surrounding the underworld in which justice was also spoken. Furthermore, there was a direct parallel with the widespread practice of swearing in front of Heaven and Earth or another publicly recognized divine force that one was speaking the truth, much like the Western oath on the Bible. Heaven was believed to oversee the oath and to punish any transgressor with impartial violence. In these stories Emperor Guan and his generals played the role of a representative of Heaven in supervising divine justice and redress. Although this particular temple in Xiangtan County in Hunan was not necessarily supported by the highest educated elites, given their relative absence from the cases, it must have mattered that it was devoted

---

[27] I deal elsewhere with the role of violence in Chinese culture and in Chinese religious culture in particular, respectively in 'Rethinking 'violence' in Chinese culture', in Göran Aijmer and Jos Abbink, eds., *Meanings of Violence: a Cross Cultural Perspective* (Oxford, 2000), 123–140 and 'Violence in Chinese Religious Culture', in A.R. Murphy, ed., *The Blackwell Companion to Religion and Violence* (Malden/Oxford/Chichester, 2011), 249–262.

to the cult of Emperor Guan. This cult had already been supported by the imperial state—in other words, the Son of Heaven or the emperor—at the highest level for many centuries, which would have contributed considerably to the deity's relevance as a guarantor of this type of public oath. Although accounts of bribing divine beings in other contexts are quite common, this was never the case in the context of this particular type of divine justice. Some divine forces could not be bribed, such as the Lord of Thunder (*lei*[*gong*], despite of the fact that it was obviously lightning which did the real killing or hurting), Heaven and Earth, the City God or Emperor Guan.

A crucial element of the oath-taking ritual was the breaking of a bowl and/or the killing of a cockerel, after which some blood of the animal would be mixed into an alcoholic beverage and consumed. Hereupon the oath would be pronounced, since the blood would have made the mouth a sacred vessel. The oath would be accompanied by self-imprecations of a highly violent nature, such as the promise that Heaven could punish the oath-breaker, for instance with 'ten thousand swords', the Five Thunders, or bleeding from his seven apertures. This type of oath has a very old tradition, going back many centuries before the Christian era and was still being practiced as late as the twentieth century.[28] In many of the cases an oath is explicitly mentioned. The crucial point of this type of ritual for our analysis is that it was deemed objective and could be practiced by everybody. It was a public event, with the eyewitnesses and record-keepers always quite explicit about the fact that the rituals eventually served to bring out in the open what had until then remained hidden. Transgressors are described as in horrible pain and sometimes even die—at least according to the extant testimony! The details of the oath are not specified in our cases, but the ensuing violent punishment is identical to that in public oath-taking rituals.

The violence in our narratives is often denoted as *bao* 暴. This term is always used for extreme violence and still used with this meaning today. The choice of words is appropriate, for we have seen that the victims in our narratives undergo concrete and harsh violence. They receive highly visible wounds or illnesses that often cause a painful, slow death.

[28] See my own *The Ritual and Mythology of the Chinese Triads: Creating an Identity* (Leiden, 1998), 162–167, 187–189 and *passim*. Niida Noboru was the first serious scholar to discuss this practice, pointing out its use in Qing courts. In my book I also adduce additional references on the presence of this type of oath-taking in secular legal cases.

The participants in and audience(s) of our narratives definitely saw the events as real, just as real as being manhandled in court at the command of a magistrate or beaten up by the rent collectors and their gangs. This was not symbolic violence.

We do not need to assume that the presumed evil-doers in these cases were always aware of their roles in actual life. Often it is explicitly recorded that they confessed their deeds and offered remorse, but in a few cases the supernatural punishment is projected on the case by local people and does not involve an actual deed of confession or remorse by the evil-doer. The example summarized above of the member of the *nouveau riche* household who loved lawsuits is a case in point. His household is severely hit by misfortune, which local people interpret as divine justice, but he himself does not explicitly confess or offer remorse.

Whose Values Are These?

As with any source, we need to ask ourselves who is talking and whose values are being furthered. Clearly, this particular spirit-writing cult saw itself as part of a larger repertoire of methods of supernatural recourse in which not everything was possible, since several anecdotes summarized above specifically state that 'the deity' disapproved of people worshipping competing deities or ritual traditions. The existence of a repertoire from which people choose is well-attested for most of the imperial period and need not concern us here any further. Once people came to this cult for help and were actually helped, a degree of value-enforcement would have taken place. The deity who was summoned through spirit writing was not General Guan himself, but one of his generals. Nonetheless, the association with his prestigious cult must have been crucial in supporting the judgments pronounced by his generals, who were speaking on his behalf.

When deities speak through the stylus, the divine writing of a wooden stick writing in sand or possibly a large pencil writing on paper is usually illegible to ordinary people and requires an interpreter. This interpreter is also common in human-medium cults. He or she is usually an older person who knows the community well. As such he or she would know of all tensions and conflicts between the members of the community, as well as their personalities and professions. This would enable the interpreter to translate (subconsciously and perhaps in part consciously) the issue with which people approached the cult and a potential solution into religious terms. In a sense, the interpreter is the real arbiter of the system of divine justice, but enjoying the supernatural support of the cult, he or she can speak with far more authority than a mere human figure would be able to. Similarly, local people could use the cult and the possibility of divine intercession as a resource to translate their worries, fears and conflicts into terms that promised some kind of solution. Directly addressing these problems would often have been hopeless. As we have seen above, most of the times the solution is supported by a harsh punishment, with or without a confession and with or without remorse. In other instances, the solution is more concrete, and something that has been lost returns or a bad human relationship is improved. So all in all, the deity is not just a divine figure, but also the projection screen of the hopes and expectations, and fears, of various groups of local people. These cases are the result of collective action, and the individual contributions are no longer visible.

The crucial role of the interpreter and his or her command of the written language mean that spirit-writing cults tend to be imbued with the values of written culture.[29] However, this does not mean that the values are not also shared by the audience of the cult. They might go to different religious specialists and cults with different value systems, but at least for the duration of the successful intervention they would share in the values of that particular specialist or cult. In the cases analysed in this paper, the legal framework of punishment does not necessitate any kind of conversion. The similarities with the oath-taking ceremony suggest that we are dealing with a ritual format. Nonetheless, the social values that are supported fit the canonical values of the literate elite, such as their dislike of legal specialists or the taboo on eating beef—although these values could easily be supported by many local people as well. As a single source, the casebook entitled *Record of Miraculous Responses by the Generals* (*jiangjun lingyanji*) cannot provide much information on the social background of certain moral values, since this would require comparison with values as represented in different types of religious practice and different kinds of sources, but it does provide good information on the kind of concerns that people had. Although here, too, more sources and perspectives need to be included, we can say that these concerns make good sense in the light of what we know about late-imperial local society.

---

[29] Overmyer and Jordan, *The Flying Phoenix* (1986); Philip Clart, 'Confucius and the Mediums: Is There a 'Popular Confucianism'?', *T'oung Pao* 89, 1–3 (2003), 1–38.

Concluding Thoughts

The belief in divine justice is part of a system for enforcing norms and values, of which the ritual of the sworn oath was also an important part. It was believed to function independently of human intervention and to be objective, although one of our examples also illustrates that the deities depended on correct information from the plaintiffs. Like a Chinese magistrate *cum* judge, the deity depended on the evidence that he was given and did not carry out many investigations of his own. The violent punishment before the confessions and, when needed, after them as well was more severe than the punishments in the secular legal system, which did not involve conscious mutilation. On the other hand, once someone had been beaten up—whether rightly or wrongly—during some kind of legal proceedings, he or she might well have been maimed for life as well. Other punishments, such as wearing the cangue or the period in prison (or the transport from the countryside to the prison) awaiting trial would all have weakened people considerably. The death penalty, beheading more often than strangulation, was also a cruel and lengthy process. The heads would be publicly exhibited in cages next to the city gate, until they were completely eaten by birds and bugs. In terms of measurable effects, the secular legal system was also a violent and bloody affair. The system of divine justice could be more violent, since before the advent of modern surgery and painkilling, diseases and wounds were much more visibly painful and bloody, and there was a good chance that an 'evil-doer' would meet such a fate eventually, which could then be explained as an act of divine justice. As we have seen, not all divine punishment followed immediately upon the crime, not because the deities waited so long, but because people had to wait for a suitable event to explain as punishment.

Although the cult of Emperor Guan and his Generals was closely connected to state expectations of divine propriety, it was not just an elite cult. The deities were worshipped by all layers of society. The recognition of the state meant that different socio-educational groups could each project their own views onto the same, shared deities. The example of the evil butcher also suggests that this cult wanted to be a bit more civilized than other cults, which is confirmed by the importance of civilizing tendencies such as the taboos on beef and dogs (although by the late-imperial period these were widely shared across all levels of society). Only a full-scale investigation of norms and values for this particular region and its varying social groups, and then the methods adopted for their imposition and enforcement, can provide a definitive answer to the issue of representativeness. What is certain is that this is not simply a popular cult, but that most of the values supported were in line with official values as well.

A final question would be whether we should understand the system of divine justice described above as an independent system or as supplementary to the secular legal system. From a modern perspective we would probably need to stress its supplementary nature, since the ideal of modern societies is an independent secular judiciary. It is plausible (although it cannot be proved) that people may have resorted to this form of divine justice (including the additional phenomenon of the underworld court) more often than to the secular court, and interacted with divine justice during their lives more frequently than with the local magistrate. Moreover, in organizational terms, divine justice was not entirely independent of the secular court, or vice versa: local magistrates might have had recourse to it during particularly baffling cases and many of the values were shared, even if the way in which justice was administered differed. One way of understanding the agreed nature of this form of justice, is by pointing out the striking similarities to the 'speaking bitterness' sessions during the Land Reforms of the 1950s and to Chinese legal practice in general, in both of which the explicit confession (often elicited by violence) and remorse play a central role without which no sentence can be pronounced.

INDEX

www.ingramcontent.com/pod-product-compliance
Lightning Source LLC
LaVergne TN
LVHW102103300926
849161LV00001B/9